NEW RELIGIOUS MOVEMENTS: A PERSPECTIVE FOR UNDERSTANDING SOCIETY

NEW RELIGIOUS MOVEMENTS:
A PERSPECTIVE FOR UNDERSTANDING
SOCIETY

EILEEN BARKER, editor

STUDIES IN RELIGION AND SOCIETY
VOLUME 3

THE EDWIN MELLEN PRESS
NEW YORK AND TORONTO

Library of Congress Cataloging in Publication Data
Main entry under title:

New Religious Movements.

(Studies in Religion and Society; v.3)
Bibliography: p.
1. Cults -- Addresses, essays, lectures.   2.   Sects
-- Addresses, essays, lectures.   3. Religions --
Addresses, essays, lectures.   4. Religion and
sociology -- Addresses, essays, lectures.   I. Barker,
Eileen.   II. Series: Studies in Religion and
Society   (New York, N.Y.); v.3.
BL85.N48   1982   291.9'09'04   82-8263
ISBN   0-88946-864-8

Studies in Religion and Society, Vol.3   ISBN 0-88946-863-X

All rights reserved. For information contact:

The Edwin Mellen Press
P.O. Box 450
Lewiston, New York   14092

Printed in the United States of America

For

Judith and Rachel

With love

CONTENTS

NEW RELIGIOUS MOVEMENTS:
A PERSPECTIVE FOR UNDERSTANDING SOCIETY

Eileen Barker

During the last decade or so the growth of interest in new religious movements has been almost as vigorous as the growth of the movements themselves. This interest has tended to manifest itself in two opposite directions. In scholarly journals there are ethnographic reports carefully describing one particular movement in detail but drawing out few, if any, of the wider implications from the study; and, mainly in the popular media, there are grandiose polemical statements telling us what the rise of these new religious movements "really means". The rhetoric with which these statements are delivered is frequently devoid of any factual basis -- at best a scanty acquaintance with a movement is invoked to explain The Movement. In other words one can find neat but limited monographs which are only of interest to those who wish to find out about that particular movement, or one can find sweeping generalisations which, in the unlikely event of their being at all testable, would collapse upon exposure to comparative evidence.

There are, of course, exceptions. There have been some genuinely interesting and valuable attempts to go beyond the mere parochial while yet remaining grounded in empirical study. But little has been done in the way of systematically comparing or assessing the various hypotheses, many of which would seem, at least on the face of it, to contradict each other quite seriously.

The aim of this book is to bring together the ideas of some of those who have a professional knowledge of new religious movements and who believe such knowledge can lead to the instigation or the examination of hypotheses which have a relevance beyond the confines of the movements themselves. The contributors were asked to consider how the study of new religious movements might contribute to our understanding of man as a social animal, what such a study might tell us about social processes, and what it might reveal about the societies within which the movements emerge, struggle for survival, flourish or disappear. Each contributor has been allowed to decide for him or herself what the rubric of "new religious movement" entails. It is acknowledged that all religions have been new at some time and that not all of those which are today called new are, in fact, new. Some of the movements to which we shall be referring are frequently denied a genuinely religious status. We make no existential claims through the use of the term "new religious movement". It is merely

a convenient way of indicating the general subject matter from
which our interests stem.   No apology is offered for the fact
that the Unification Church might seem to receive more than
its fair share of attention.   Not only is this a movement which
has, during the past decade, been the focus of considerable
public attention from the societies in which it is to be found,
it has also been the subject of more   serious academic research in more societies than any other contemporary movement.

As this book has been prepared as a basis for discussion
about the ways in which the study of new religious movements
could illuminate our knowledge of particular societies and social processes in general, it could be helpful to provide a
summary of several of the main points raised by the contributors.   The intention is that this will alert and remind the
reader of some of the differences and the similarities between
the various viewpoints expressed and, incidentally but importantly, show up some of the gaps in our knowledge.

Only a Procrustean bed could hope to arrange the papers
in this volume into unambiguously neat taxonomic bundles.
The ordering of the contributions is necessarily arbitrary as
they cover the topic in a variety of ways.   It is thus hoped
that the reader will accept that to place a particular paper
in a particular section is to offer merely a preliminary orientation to one of its central themes.   Although, for example,
Christine King's essay fits section three perfectly neatly, it
is also very relevant to section five. Bryan Wilson's contribution would certainly not be out of place in section four, but
it should also be clear why it is an excellent paper with
which to introduce several of the debates to be found in other
contributions.

I   NEW RELIGIOUS MOVEMENTS: THE WIDER COMPARATIVE PERSPECTIVE

With Werblowsky and Wuthnow, Wilson approaches the subject from a broad, comparative perspective.   He starts from
the position that the very idea of new religious movements suggests that they are offering a "surer, shorter, swifter, or
clearer way to salvation" than are the traditional religions.
But there are differences to be found in the various social experiences which give rise to the sorts of suffering from which
men seek salvation.   The movements can be seen, at least in
part, as adaptations to changing human circumstances and to
the changed expression of spiritual needs.   The fact that so
many and such diverse movements should occur around the same
time suggests not only the inadequacy of traditional religion,
but also   "latent discontents prevailing within advanced societies".   But different advanced societies have different problems.   In Japan   the new religious movements appear to act

as loci between society and the individual, the older, intermediate agencies of the social structure having broken down;
in the west they are more likely to cater to the needs of an
individuated public.

If, Wilson argues, a new religion is to become a movement (rather than a passing fashion), then it has to deal with
the problem of routinization. Some kind of control of the members' behaviour is necessary. But the type of control (whether
internal self control or external rules and sanctions), and the
extent to which it is deemed necessary to distinguish the
movement from the wider society, may reflect the particular
cultural milieu. The general cultural milieu of modern societies may also be reflected in characteristics (such as techniques of rational organization) which traditional religions are
less likely to have espoused. The paper ends with a discussion of the "technically de-moralized" society. Wilson argues
that the very existence of the new religious movements is "of
utmost sociological significance" in that they can provide a
focus for identity, commitment and loyalty in an age in which
a civil religion is a dubious alternative focus for the value consensus, traditionally supplied by religion, upon which social
integration can depend. Not that the new religions will necessarily -- or even probably -- fulfill this function for any but
a small minority. The movements would seem more capable
of pointing to needs, desires, and problems than of providing
any easy solutions.

As his subtitle indicates, Werblowsky is offering us a
fragment of an agenda for the further study of new religious
movements and their relationship to the societies in which they
arise and develop -- or fade away. The generalizations
with which Werblowsky deals turn into suggestive problems
as he drops tiny, illustrative titbits . of information about
the strange assortment of movements to which mankind has giv-
en birth. One fact that his paper makes absolutely clear is
that the sort of questions which puzzle people about the new
religions will frequently depend on the sort of assumptions
(the sort of social background) from which they are looking
at the movements. While contemporary American students of
religion may find new movements' turning to politics a
worrying phenomenon, historians of religion are more likely
to be puzzled by the separation of church and state. Those
brought up in the Christian tradition are likely to treat claims
to divinity from founders of new movements with the utmost
suspicion; in the East, however, "Gods there are galore. . .
divinity is cheap". Werblowsky ends his paper with a brief
consideration of the hostility engendered by the new movements.
One provocative suggestion with which he leaves us is that
the "really unforgivable sin of the Rev. Moon may have been

to have let the cat out of the bag and to have said the things which the average (American) liberal would like to say but will not, cannot, must not, dare not. . ."

Again very much from the vantage point of the comparative perspective, Robert Wuthnow warns us against accepting too readily the kinds of generalizations that are frequently offered about the periods which give rise to new religious movements -- generalizations which, he says, are usually so ignorant of historical conditions that they can take almost any conceivable form. Instead of assuming that the explanation for an increase in religious activity is to be found by looking merely within a society, one should, Wuthnow argues, look at what is happening between societies. It is when there is an upset or adjustment in the balance of interaction between those in dominant "core" areas and those in dependent "periphery" areas, that we can expect one of a variety of forms of religious activity to be taking place -- the exact form depending on the type of trans-national process actually involved.

It is, of course, a very broad brush with which Wuthnow paints, and he is the first to insist that considerable historical testing of his typological offering has yet to be done. But the principle and undoubted value of such an ambitious exercise is, to borrow the words of his final sentence, that it affords a systematic basis for comparing the kinds of watersheds that religious movements may portend.

II NOW AND THEN: THE INDIVIDUAL AND SOCIETY

In this second section two themes are intertwined. The first one introduces some of the issues associated with the time-honoured debate about the relationship between the individual and society -- issues which abound in apparent paradoxes and pose dilemmas such as the relationship between free will and determinism, individuality and conformity, self-realization and transcendence. To those who are overly familiar with conventional western religiosity it may at first seem that the contemporary new movements discussed in this section could have little to do with religion. It is, however, possible to recognize that Heelas' neologism "self-religion" may lay claim to more than a merely definitional statement, and this may become even more apparent when one turns to Oden's comparison between modern encounter groups and the pietism of the seventeenth and eighteenth centuries. Through this analysis Oden introduces the second theme of the section -- what we might learn about a society through a longitudinal or historical comparison of a particular motif or "resource". Both he and Martin (who analyses old and new types of pacificism) show how different movements, displaying different forms of the same motif, can

appear in either secular or in more traditionally religious
forms, according to the times, displaying certain peculiarities
which reflect the characteristics of the society at that particular period.   Martin's paper also deals with further aspects
of the relationship between the individual and society, leading
us to consider, among other things, a possible incompatability
between individual and societal morality.

For Heelas the self-religions are "those which exemplify
the conjunction of the exploration of the self and the search
for significance".   They fall mainly into the category which
Wallis would call world-affirming religions (Section IV).   It
is through the study of such movements that Heelas attempts
to show a way out of a dichotomy between, on the one hand,
the self identity of a free-floating psyche which, having no
firm basis in the reality of society, floats itself into chaos,
and, on the other hand, an identity which, having surrendered
itself to a totalitarian, totally other, social definition of itself has surrendered any potential for individual autonomy.
A first glance, perhaps that of the potential convert,would suggest
that the self-religions are in business to free the subjective
self from any trace of nasty, social accretions; the pure ego
will rise phoenix-like from the ashes of society.   A second
glance might make one wonder whether such movements might
in fact not be more constricting that liberating.   A forceful
proponent of such a view would be R.D. Rosen, author of Psychobabble.   To elaborate a quotation from Rosen which appears
in Heelas' paper: "Their jargon seems. . .to free-float in an
all-purpose linguistic atmosphere, a set of verbal formalities
that kills off the very spontaneity, candour and understanding
that it pretends to promote.   It's an idiom that reduces psychological insight to a collection of standardised observations,
that provides a frozen lexicon to deal with an infinite variety
of problems."

Heelas, however, wants us to take a third look at the
self-religions.   It is, he believes, because they use techniques
which socialise the subjective that they can lead to freedom
for the individual.   The individual is neither left to the anom-
ic emptiness of floundering without social definition, nor has
he had to give himself up to a publicly defined, totalitarian
slavery.   Through the social, especially the psychological institutions of the self religions, he can transcend the social.

The historical dimension is added with Oden's likening
of the pietistic encounter styles of free-church protestantism
with those of the current encounter culture.   This he does a-
long five different dimensions: the small group format; the
zealous pursuit of honesty;the focus on here and now experiencing; the nurture of intimacy; and revival as marathon.

For each of these areas he places quotations taken from eighteenth and nineteenth century pietistic writings (e.g. Wesley,
Newstead, Rosser, Finney and Lee) beside statements from the
principal encounter leaders of today (e.g. Perls, Rogers,
Maslow and Schutz). The reader is unlikely to need much further persusasion to recognize the existence of some striking
similarities between the two styles.

What Oden illustrates in his paper is not only the way
in which a society can resuscitate a mode of experiencing with
which it has experimented in the past, but how, when that experience is one which emphasizes the here-and-now and the
novelty of experience, there also develops a denial of past discovery -- "the tradition against tradition". By using the concepts and language of Eastern religions, it is possible for the
encounter clientele to believe that they are rebelling against
the very tradition which they are in fact confirming. "Much
that the encounter culture is protesting is a result of basic
inadequacies in Western society. But its protest is as Western
as the Western distortions against which it is protesting".

Martin too explores the ways in which new religions have
drawn upon history for a particular "resource" -- the peace
sentiment -- but he concentrates on how, in the process, the
resource has been realized in a very different way. In the
contemporary Anglo-American context, Martin argues, an education which has emphasized the search for each and every kind
of expression has eroded the Protestant ethic of integrity, self-
respect and self-control: "To young people, reared on doctrines
of self-exploration and on adjustment to purely personal environments, the demands of the nation appeared to have no
persuasive power. . . .Since neither national membership nor
personal discipline exercised an appeal, young people were
cast adrift from the ancient anchors of the state and the
psyche". It is these young people who form the pool of potential converts to contemporary new religious movements. The
new religious movements can be seen both as reflecting this
free-floating, groupless-group psyche and as a reaction against
its existence -- this being when it results in the search for,
or relieved response to, authoritarian movements which offer
certainty, identity, loyalty and definition.

In his contrasting of the new style and the old style
pacifism, Martin draws out what he sees as the internal logic
of each style and in so doing offers us a glimpse of possible
views of society from within the perspective of those movements.
These are logics which embody a series of implications and
contradictions, not the least of which is the disjunction between an extreme pessimism about the actual workings of the
individual and society, combined with an extreme optimism a-
bout their potential.

III IMPACTS OF EXPORTS: ACCOMMODATION, REJECTION, INNOVATION, ASSIMILATION AND DISINTEREST

While the preceding section was concerned with some of the ways in which movements can reflect social continuity and change over time, this section is concerned with the ways in which imports will produce different types of reactions and themselves react to the host society.

King's paper shows how a totalitarian Nazi state could force movements into polarized positions of accommodation and compromise on the one hand, and outright antagonism on the other. She follows the fortunes of the Mormons, the New Apostolic Church, the Seventh-Day Adventists, the Christian Scientists and the Jehovah's Witnesses during the period of the Third Reich which was producing what, she says, was in some senses itself a new society. By comparing the dynamics of accommodation to or rejection of the Nazi regime, King demonstrates both the potential flexibility of dogma and practice which is possible in the face of a particular social situation, and the extraordinary resistance that can be offered to any compromise -- the ideological battle being fought in this case literally to the death.

King further argues that the reaction of the Nazi regime to these religious movements revealed both its strengths and its weaknesses -- what it could tolerate, and what it could not. The outsidedness of the Jehovah's Witnesses exposed with a frightening clarity just what it was that a Nazi society demanded in commitment and submission. Indeed, King's analysis almost suggests that reaction to a group like the Jehovah's Witnesses can provide a sort of litmus paper test of what might be called a society's Totalitarian Quotient. The Witnesses are not intrinsically anti-society, and up to a certain point they will go their own way without appearing to be more of a nuisance or threat than, say, being the cause of the milk boiling over when they ring the doorbell to sell Awake or Watch Tower. But once that certain point is reached there would appear to be not just a change in degree in the type of relationship the movement will have with society, but a qualitative change which might best be described with the language and concepts of catastrophe theory. The process of control described by Bromley, Busching and Shupe (Section V) may be seen to operate for the early stages of a spiral of antagonisms, but the story King tells reveals a further ironic twist to the process when "the time-honoured methods of persecution, torture, imprisonment and ridicule were not resulting in the conversion of any Witnesses to the Nazi position but were in fact backfiring against their instigators." Germany, King declares, could not contain two systems so similar in their uncompromising and totalitarian claims.

In Smart's paper the import is westernization. By comparing the fate of new religious movements -- those which were successful and those which failed -- as they arose in response to this outside threat to the identity of Indian and Chinese cultures, we can understand more of the nature and needs of their respective societies.

Christianity (in its many different guises) has of course been the "new" religious movement which Europe has made repeated attempts to impose upon the rest of the world over the last few centuries. But the missionary zeal with which it has gone forth has met with widely assorted responses according to the ground upon which it has been disseminated. In much of Africa it found a firm foothold, although it was frequently transformed almost beyond recognition into one of the "New African Religions". This, however, was not the case in either India or China.

By examining why new religious movements such as Ram Mohan's Bramo Samaj or Dayanand Sarasvati's Arya Samaj failed, and the new Hinduism prospered in India; why the Taiping movement collapsed, and Marxism succeeded in China, Smart indicates the tensions and pressures being brought to bear on these two great societies in their struggles to cope with the impact of the west. He examines the different "psychic deals" that can and cannot be negotiated within different social contexts -- deals which can, given different initial conditions, veer in fundamentally different directions. Yet, despite the fact that the content of the beliefs and indeed the practices of Hinduism and Maoism could hardly seem to be more opposed to each other, Smart argues that both were successful because they managed to perform the function of providing a cultural identity for the new nation states. Seen from such a perspective, the role of the new religious movement in the understanding of a society is not insignificant.

Reversing the direction of the migration, Whitworth and Shiels show how two new religions with their roots in India have come to meet the needs of certain individuals in North American society and, in the process, have become absorbed, and even generally accepted (at least in the case of the Vedanta) into the general cultural milieu of the society.

Unlike the other contributors to this volume, who tend to draw on selected apsects of new religious movements to illustrate particular theoretical points or generalizations about society, Whitworth and Shiels provide fairly detailed accounts

of the beliefs, practices and membership of the International
Society for Krishna Consciousness (the Hare Krishna movement)
and the (not so new) Ramakrishna Vedanta Society. Whitworth
and Shiels reject any over-simplistic brainwashing or personal
inadequacy theory to explain the existence of the movements,
but, like some of the other contributors, look to personal experiences of the societies in which the movements flourish and
the alternative which they offer for an understanding of their
membership. The main conclusion of their analysis is that the
movements they have studied are "offering refuges from culture
rather than contributing to it".

But the two movements, although similar in certain respects, are in several other respects very different from each
other and appeal to different sectors of the community who
have had different experiences of society. While the "Hare
Krishnas can be conceived of as inhabiting a haven protected
by a <u>cordon</u> <u>sanitaire</u> from the corruption of the world, the
<u>Vedantist   societies</u> can perhaps be compared to oases where
the sectarians believe true spirituality flourishes in the midst
of a desert of materialism, sensuality, error and lack of purpose". Whitworth and Shiels predict, moreover, that the Hare
Krishna are unlikely to persist in the way that the Vedanta
societies have already succeeded in doing. But, whatever the
differences between the movements, they are seen to perform
a function for the individuals who join them, rather than for
the society from which the members turn.

The interest in Nordquist's paper lies not in what we can
learn about a society from its interest in new religious movements, but rather what we might learn from the relative
<u>absence</u> of interest in such groups in contemporary Sweden.

It is indeed a salutory exercise to take Sweden as a
"control group" with which to test some of the more sweeping
generalizations which have been made about the current rise
of new religious movements in the west. Nordquist's analysis
of the lack of interest experienced by six groups which have
been imported into Sweden, led him to pose the question: "Since
most of the research on new religious movements has linked
their growth in the 1970s with youthful discontent over secularization and the bureaucratic state, the question arises as
to why the movements are so relatively "unsuccessful" in Sweden, which by most international standards is one of the
world's most secularized countries?" It is not that the Swedes
do not share with the Americans many of the difficulties of a
modern industrialized society -- what studies there have been,
suggest that they do. But the cultural milieu would seem to
be such that it will not be to religion that the Swede will turn

to look for solutions to -- or even the articulation of -- his problems. By exploring some of the reasons for the peculiarities of the Swedish situation (in particular the monolithic role of the Lutheran Church and its close historical connection with the state), Nordquist's analysis forces us to pay more attention to a society's historical circumstances (such as the role of pluralism and the traditions of dissent that have existed in North America and some parts of Europe), if we are to increase our understanding of the kinds of responses a society might make to economic, technological and other social changes.

IV NEW RELIGIOUS MOVEMENTS: SOCIAL RESOURCES, INDICATORS OR REFLECTORS

This section deals with the thorny question of the extent to which the new religious movements can be seen to indicate a reflection of, or a reaction to, a particular social context -- whether or not they can be interpreted as arising in response to "needs" which are not being adequately met by the wider society. It is a subject which is touched upon in the introduction and in several of the other papers, most notably in those by Wilson, Wuthnow, and Whitworth and Shiels. The four papers in this section focus on the problem directly and from very different theoretical perspectives. Lewis sees the new religious movements as performing a function for the society as a whole; Wallis sees them as more likely to be indicating the needs of particular members of a society; Campbell sees them as reflecting a far wider process that has been occurring within the society; Anthony and Robbins see them providing, in their diverse forms, a response which can be either a reflection of, or a reaction to a situation in which moral meanings have become increasingly problematic.

Lewis' thesis is that the new religious movements either meet (or, disastrously, fail to meet) the needs of society in which they emerge or take root -- needs which the society is unable to deal with itself. This the movements do not do directly -- rather they are brought into being to function as a laboratory within which social problems experienced by the society can be worked out. It is unlikely that society will thank them for their efforts -- it is more likely to persecute them -- but the movements can "come-again" in some form or other to provide the content or justification for a solution to a particular social need.

Of course new religious movements can be seen to develop in a variety of ways, but, being perhaps more adventurous than most sociologists, Lewis is prepared to proclaim that there is, underlying the variety, a "social-historical 'law' of religious homeorhesis". Borrowing concepts from C.H. Waddington, Lewis uses the analogy of a stream flowing down a hillside; it may be diverted in its path and follow diverse routes, but it is inevitable, the law of gravity decrees, that it will eventually, somehow, somewhere, reach the bottom of the hill. Thus, although they may arise in different situations and meet divers environmental hazards, new religious movements will inevitably, somehow, someway, pass through certain stages and reach a final position in relation to the (social) environment.

There is a theological tinge to Lewis' argument in that he suggests that the role of religion, while certainly functional for society, is not merely a social phenomenon -- it can be seen as one of His Ways.

Lewis illustrates his general theological position with examples from nineteenth century America. He then moves into his predictions for the twentieth century. What Lewis sees the Unification Church (among other movements) doing (among other things) is to provide a religious and moral justification to America for the social necessity of a Third World War in opposition to communism. It is not that the Unification Church itself will start or even want the use of military power; it is just that American society has given rise to and will use the new religious movement in order to assist in the task of working out and confirming the divine righteousness of its cause.

Wallis distinguishes religious movements which developed in the west in the 1960s by placing them into two broad categories, defined according to the attitude expressed by the movement towards the society of which it is or was a part. On the one hand, there are the "world-rejecting movements" (e.g. the Children of God, Hare Krishna and the Unification Church) which react against their society, and on the other hand, there are the "world-affirming movements" (e.g. Scientology, Primal Therapy and encounter groups) which celebrate their society. Having elaborated a range of possible characteristics which might be found within each of his two types, Wallis looks at some of the features of western society which could be conducive to the development of, and provide sources of support for, the movements. "Undoubtedly", he claims, "the major long-term trend underlying the emergence of the new religions. . .is. . .that of rationalization." There follows a discussion of the kind of changes in the relationship between the individual and social institutions that rationalization brings in its wake (in particular the de-institutionalization of identity and the attenuation of community) -- changes in response to which, Wallis argues, the new religious movements have developed.

Wallis then narrows the focus of his analysis to examine the more specific factors which have led to the development of his two polar types. To assume that one can explain the frequently rapid conversion to "world-rejecting movements" as being the result of brainwashing or hypnosis is, he says, entirely to misunderstand the process. The main attraction of these movements lies, according to Wallis, in the salvation in community from the loneliness and impersonality of the world the members had been experiencing. The "world-affirming movements", on the other hand, offer not a refuge from, but a way of coping with the demands of modern society. There is, Wallis points out, a curious twist to be found in understanding the role of society in such situations: "at the same time as the emergence of a market for recipes for worldly success, there has emerged a need for methods of escaping the constraints and inhibitions usually required in order to achieve that success".

In Campbell's paper we find a sharp critique of overly functionalist perspectives. He argues that accounting for the origins or growth of new religious movements by pointing to some individual or collective need does not answer the more pertinent question "Why are they plausible?" and has the major disadvantage of "deflecting attention away from the larger cultural context in which these movements flourish and from the specific cultural trends which can be identified as conducive to their growth". If one were to turn away from the internal features of the movements and look instead at the larger cultural context from which the membership is recruited, one would notice that a far larger population had emerged as the critical and necessary condition for the creation of new religions. The evidence, Campbell believes, points to a major shift in society "not so much from belief to unbelief as from belief to seekership. That is, away from any commitment to doctrine and dogma towards a high valuation of intellectual growth and the pursuit of truth coupled with a preparedness to believe in almost any alternative or occult teaching".

It has been widely claimed that rationalization can be expected to lead to secularization -- a process that the very existence of the new religious movements (and indeed the current wave of evangelical revivalism) would seem to throw into doubt. But if, Campbell argues, we distinguish between two kinds of rationalization we might better understand what is happening. For while rationalization may refer to the process whereby the values of technical efficiency and calculability take over from traditional or intuitive (including religious) values, there is also a process of rationalization which can lead to greater systematization, coherence and the subsuming of a set of cultural symbols under a higher order principle. This latter kind of rationalization can include, and even in

some cases promote, non-rational values within the rational
system.   An examination of the new religious movements can
show, Campbell concludes, how mistaken it was to assume that
a secular culture, independent of religion, would automatically
be hostile towards religion -- or that freeing areas of culture
from religious dominance would necessarily mean their submission to rational criteria.

Anthony and Robbins see much of the spiritual flux experienced in the west during the last decade or so being the
result of the disintegration of a traditional, dualistic moral
absolutism and its associated ethos of individual freedom and
responsibility.   For various reasons there is no longer agreement on a clear-cut division between right and wrong.   In the
past, they argue, Americans had accepted a traditional biblical
morality which proscribed certain "bad" actions, thereby in-
timating that other, non-proscribed, actions would be "good".
It is not merely that erstwhile bad actions have become permissible in a permissive society, erstwhile "alright actions" have
also acquired a questionable moral status. The relativism of
this moral ambiguity is further confounded by a questioning
of the assumption of a ubiquitious possibility of free will.
Psychology and social science have played their role in undermining confidence in the concept of moral responsibility.   Not
only might it no longer be possible to know what is right,
one's genetic or environmental background, or one's social position might prevent one from doing what is right.

New religious movements have, Anthony and Robbins
argue, provided two contrasting responses to this situation.
On the one hand, monistic mysticism and the monistic perspectives of many of the therapeutic "self-religions" can be seen
to imply a moral relativism in which morality is instrumental
rather than obligatory and in which the emphasis shifts from
objective, external action to subjective, inner consciousness.
On the other hand, there has also emerged a large number of
movements which are actively reacting against relativistic tendencies and offering instead a clear-cut ethical dualism and
moral absolutism.   Anthony and Robbins then survey the available data on the membership of these two kinds of movements
and point out the ways in which people who have had different kinds of social experiences will associate with the different kinds of groups, thus reflecting, through their differential allegiances, something of the problematic and non-consensual situation of moral meanings in contemporary American society.

V SOCIAL PERCEPTIONS OF NEW RELIGIOUS MOVEMENTS:
REVELATION AND CONTROL

In this final section we are not so much concerned with the movements themselves as with the reactions of society towards them, and about what such reactions might indicate about the values and assumptions of society. Here it is not so much a question of having the gift "to see oursels [sic]as others see us" as the gift to see ourselves as we see others. The first three papers are all concerned with public reaction to the new religion which has probably received more adverse publicity than any other of the contemporary movements -- the Unification Church. Hardin and Kehrer analyse German reaction, Beckford analyses British reaction and Bromley, Busching and Shupe analyse the reaction in the United States. The final paper by Baker draws on the reporting of the tragedy at Jonestown, Guyana to illustrate the process of "media conversion".

Hardin and Kehrer give us a model for comparing the ways in which societies which teach tolerance and pluralism may nevertheless reject a new religious movement through ensuring that one or more of four different characteristics of a belief system are defined as illegitimate. These characteristics are, firstly, the content of the belief; secondly, the degree of commitment it requires of its members; thirdly, the type of action involved and the area in which it takes place, and fourthly, the nature of its carrier -- the organization, its internal structure and processes. The model then distinguishes four types of possible rejectors: the individual citizen (who may be a parent); organized alternatives to the new religious movement (such as the established churches); the mass media and fourthly, governmental institutions. Each of these rejectors has more or less power in the number of illegitimating tactics that it can itself use with legitimacy; the degree to which the four rejectors are able to work in concord will, to a certain extent, determine the likelihood of success of the rejection process.

Hardin and Kehrer then employ their model to evaluate German reaction to the Unification Church. The very fact that German society has specifically focussed its concern upon the Unification Church is seen by Hardin and Kehrer to be of some considerable significance in itself in that it does, like the actual strategies of rejection involved, clearly indicate the interests and concerns of the society. When, for example, it is realized the extent to which factors related to social security benefits are the focus of rejection one can, they suggest, begin to understand something of the dominant value system and preoccupations of contemporary Germany.

Beckford seeks for the clues that the hostility and suspicion engendered by new religious movements can give us about the beliefs and values of British society. In doing so he shows how the social definition of such concepts as rationality and freedom are thrown into sharp relief once taken-for-granted presuppositions are threatened. This he does by considering eight different points at which popular sentiment reacts against the Unification Church. These are not disparate points. His analysis shows a remarkable coherence due, he suggests, to an underlying logic which contains "a sharp and pervasive contrast between on the one hand the supposedly normal states of the person as an autonomous, rational and free being and, on the other, the allegedly characteristic states of the person in a cult as a dependent, irrational and controlled being".

Beckford finds that not only the anti-cult movement, but popular sentiment as a whole, will continually refer back to implicit cultural assumptions which define "normal" people and "normal" religious groups. "Unwittingly the cults expose the limits of normality allowed in (British) society to religious feelings, actions and institutions." Furthermore Beckford argues that, given the taken-for-granted assumptions that they hold about normality, the members of the society act quite rationally in using evidence provided by a new religious movement to accuse the movement of violating these assumptions. In other words, Beckford would seem to be pointing out how people can be perfectly rational about rationality within the context of a socially defined rationality. The trouble is, of course, that if one learns to put on an alternative pair of glasses with which to view the world, the new perspective of rationality can be seen as demanding quite different though (now) equally rational behaviour and beliefs -- which is, no doubt, part of the very real threat that the new religious movements can present to society.

In their paper Bromley, Busching and Shupe search for an understanding of North American society through its reaction to the Unification Church -- a reaction which they see primarily as an example of a generic process in which those with power in a society exercise social control in response to a perceived threat. The process gets under way as the two sides in the dispute (in this case the member of a new religious movement and his family) find themselves unable to continue to formulate and share acceptable symbolic definitions of the other's behaviour. The more powerful side then starts to define the other side into a position of deviance. Such a definition serves then to legitimate the kind of unilateral social action which is thought necessary to deal with the perceived challenge. In this way a practice such as "deprogramming"

which can involve actions that would, under other circumstances, be seen as a violation of an individual's right to religious freedom, can instead be defined as a means of liberating a hapless victim of brainwashing or mind control. What,
in other words, Bromley, Busching and Shupe are arguing is
that it is not the actual content, but rather the social context
of any behaviour which determines how it will be seen and defined: "Behaviour which is represented as illicit and maniacal
in one context may be defined as religious rebirth in another".
What Bromley et al illustrate is an example of such a process
and how, in this case, an analysis of the dynamics of confrontation between members of a new religious movement and
their families can highlight some of the cultural values and
structures of power to be found within contemporary American
society.

In his paper Baker argues that "media conversion" in
the form of brainwashing was imposed upon the public during
and after the mass suicide of members of the Peoples' Temple
in Jonestown, Guyana in 1978. By media conversion Baker
means a process that is quite distinct from religious conversion. It is the "process of absorption, self-accommodation and
self-identification that takes place when the mind enters into
the cognitive space of publicly-reported events". It is when
one is not merely an observer of, but also a pseudo-participant
in distant events, that one has become converted to the reported reality. While such involvement is usually passive, it may
take the form of "brainwashing" in which case one is put under pressure to act —as if decisively. When I am thus brainwashed my conversion "is to a new, emotionalised understanding of my own importance in the world. I am now ready to
polarize my conception of issues in such a way that I come
out either courageously "for" or "against" a dramatic action
or cause. . . .A neurotic desire for "more information" only
occurs after having abandoned a normal ego-identity as observer and after having taken on a new identity as a protagonist".

Drawing on the reporting of the Jonestown incident and
various other events, Baker illustrates the stages of what, he
says, can be identified as an observable, recurrent process
of media-induced hypnosis. The five stages he describes are:
news shock; identity confusion; media histrionics or "artificial
doing"; assimilation and, finally, recovery. Baker ends his paper with a plea for "a quest for community and metropolitan
ethics in matters of public information and programming". It
is necessary, he argues, to understand and question not merely
the content of media communication, but also the ways it
"works" –– the processes and consequences of these processes
at both social, institutional and at individual, psychological
levels. Analysing the existence of these processes with the

sharp focus revealed through an analysis of the Jonestown tragedy reporting does, Baker tells us, help us to recognize and understand and thus, perhaps, to tackle something more of the deeply complex moral dilemmas that underlie media consumption in a society with modern technological means of communication.

Although the general perspective of this book has been not to look at new religious movements so much as to look at society and social processes through the study of the movements, the book ends with a list of features which might characterize any movement and which could be taken into account for comparative purposes; and there is also a glossary in which several movements are described by those contributors who refer to them in the course of their papers. It should be stressed that these notes are not meant to serve as definitive statements, but rather to serve as a quick reference for readers who may otherwise be unfamiliar with the movements.

In conclusion, I would like to thank all those who have, in one way or another, helped in the production of this volume. They cannot all be named, but I would like to mention Karel Dobbelaere who first gave me the idea of editing such a book; Graham Howes and Herbert Richardson, both of whom made many helpful comments on early drafts; the contributors themselves who have, remarkably, remained my friends — even those who patiently rewrote their essays several times; Marge Blackwood and Jean Ridyard whose secretarial assistance was invaluable; the Social Science Research Council of Great Britain which has not only funded my personal research into new religious movements, but has always been helpfully there when wanted; and finally, and especially, Peter Barker.

Eileen Barker
London School of Economics
June, 1982

I

NEW RELIGIOUS MOVEMENTS:
THE WIDER COMPARATIVE PERSPECTIVE

FROM SECTS TO SOCIETY:
A METHODOLOGICAL PROGRAMME

Eileen Barker

In this essay I propose to outline some of the areas in which empirical data culled from the study of new religious movements might inform our theoretical and practical understanding of society. Many of the points I shall raise are dealt with in more detail by others .elsewhere in the book and where applicable this will be indicated by the insertion of the relevant contributors' bracketed initials.

One of the main advantages of drawing on new religious movements for empirical data in a quest for social knowledge is that, unlike most aspects of the generally messy and complicated world of social reality, the movements present us with comparatively neat, clear-cut objects of study. There are potential pitfalls for the unwary arising out of this very fact (which will be discussed below), and the movements may not, indeed they certainly do not, enjoy the clinically hygienic isolation of an experimental laboratory. But they do usually offer relatively clearly defined boundaries of membership and relatively clearly defined patterns of belief and action. Almost by definition the movements and their followers are "set apart" and visible for study because of their newness, their alternativeness, and because of this alternativeness they can throw into sharper relief and thus make more visible that to which they are an alternative -- which is one of the reasons they are frequently perceived as a threat by the wider society.

As the new movement will usually start as a small, relatively -- but only relatively -- self-contained unit, it can provide a useful basis from which to observe a wide spectrum of social processes which range from the individual to the international level. At the individual level one might, for example, study the process of secondary socialisation, observing, that is, the ways in which the newcomer consciously or unconsciously, actively or passively, accepts or rejects, welcomes, questions or negotiates (and contributes to changes in) the alternative visions of reality and patterns of behaviour offered by the movement (P.H). At the same time one might observe the processes of social control as these operate upon the individual.

At the group level the social scientist can observe a different set of social processes. How, for example, routinisation or bureaucratisation will seem almost inevitable over periods of time and growth (B.W.). How, once a critical size is reached, a particular system of communication and control, effective enough for a small membership, is no longer viable. A new kind of authority system may evolve and, in the light of these changes, new structures, such as those of communication or power, will emerge, endowing the group with new properties (potentialities and constraints) which cannot be reduced to the characteristics of the individual members.

But the social scientist need not, indeed cannot, limit his investigation to what is happening within the group. New (first generation) movements have to draw their membership from those brought up within a wider society -- from people who will bring with them, consciously or unconsciously, an acceptance or rejection of that wider society, thus reflecting, perhaps through the distortion of a mirror image, something of the mores whence they came (W. & S., C.C., B.W., R.Wa., R.& A.). And new movements themselves, even when they advocate total withdrawal from the "host" society, are in fact part of that society. They will usually depend upon it not only for recruitment, but also for economic support or exchange and, even when they are outlawed or their beliefs are rejected, for political status and protection (D.M.). How they react to the rest of society, and how society reacts to them, can reveal as much about the wider society as it can about the movements themselves (J.B., H. & K., B.B. & S., G.B., C.K.).

Then on an even broader level, the social scientist may observe the characteristics of those societies which, at certain periods, give rise to particular types and numbers of new religious movements and compare these with the characteristics of societies or periods which do not do so (B.W., N.S.). And finally, at the broadest of all levels, he may be alerted to look not just to what is happening within the societies themselves, but to their position within an international world order (R.Wu.).

A further dimension arises when we take seriously the fact that the movements which are being observed are religious movements. In some cases their religious character is denied by their opponents, but such a denial begs some very important questions. At the individual level it can deny the possibility of a genuinely religious conversion taking place in any particular instance. At a more general level, the denial can reinforce, without further empirical evidence, social theories which insist that ideology and religion are merely epiphenomenal, that is that they are fundamentally dependent on class interests or the economic structure. Such perspectives have led to the role of ideas being thought unimportant or even ignored altogether in much contemporary sociological analysis, but the presence of new religious movements would seem to present at least a prima facie challenge for too facile an epiphenomenalism.

To what extent can men and women really be motivated by ideas rather than by, say, economic or political interests? How can it be that some people are apparently willing to give up everything that the world has to offer them for the sake of some deviant ideology? How can something which is non-sense for the majority come to make sense for the minority? Studies of the Crusades, the Thirty Years War, contemporary Iran or Northern Ireland, would suggest that religion can, at the societal level, certainly provide a motivating focus for great sacrifices and far-reaching changes (not to mention bloody intolerance). But it is often difficult to unscramble the symbolic from the pragmatic, the religious from the economic or the political when all the complexity of a full-scale society has to be involved in the analysis. The new religious movement can provide a comparatively simple arena within which the social scientist might attempt to disentangle the various forces moving man to act; an arena within which the functioning and the strength of ideas, as well as of economic or political interests, may be more clearly coloured and thus more clearly observed.

Of course not all the generalisations made as the result of the existence of new religious movements are equally easy to test. Especially tricky are those very theories which make claims about the religious nature of man when those claims rest upon biological propositions, and predictions about the direction in which society is or ought to be moving. There are, for example, those who believe that the current outcrop of movements evidences an evolutionary development that has become manifest in the youth of the day. Youthful seekers (particularly the Californian variety) are seen as the vanguard of the super-race of tomorrow, capable of a sensitivity to and an awareness of the beyond in a way that their parents, a sub-species lower down the evolutionary scale, where denied. It is the dawning of the Age of Aquarius.[1]

The historian of religion may wish to point out to proponents of such theories that movements oozing spiritual enthusiasm have made a habit of spreading through various societies at various periods throughout the last few millennia (Z.W.), but it is difficult to see how one could convincingly refute those who would herald the New Age. An almost

diametrically opposed proposition is that the human race
has always enjoyed a sensitivity to the transcendent,
but, because of contemporary secularity, the "original
vision" atrophies during childhood and is likely to be
lost to consciousness.[2] Yet another theory would agree that
man has long had a religious nature, but this was not
due to some "divine flame";[3] it was, rather, an accident
arising out of a chance mutation in our genes which was
selected for its adaptive value during the early stages
of our development. Now, however, man can, in the light
of this knowledge, transcend his superstitious past and
embrace the present scientific ethic.[4] From such a perspective
any rise of new religious movements can be dismissed as
mere evolutionary "lag".

Possibly easier to assess are three popular, though
apparently contradictory theories about social processes
which give rise to new religious movements. The first of
these states that the movements come into being because
they meet certain "needs" and that they thus arise as
a reaction to the "host" society which has not adequately
catered for such needs (B.W., R.Wa., W.L.). The second
theory suggests that what are thought to be strange, new
beliefs and practices are in fact a sharply focussed reflection
of the beliefs and practices of that part of society from
which the movements draw their members (C.C., B.W.,
Z.W.). The third explanation denies that what is going
on in the host society is at all relevant. Here the assumption
is that once a person has become a member of a new religious
movement, or has even just come into contact with it,
it is possible, through the application of certain manipulative
techniques, to get him to believe or do anything that those
in a position of power want him to believe or do.

Used indiscriminately these three perspectives can
function merely to reinforce practically any existing beliefs
about society and social processes. This can be illustrated
by comparing some of the conclusions that have been drawn
about the significance of the diverse sexual practices to
be found in some contemporary movements. One is told,
for instance, that the long periods of celibacy practiced
by Krishna devotees and members of the Unification Church
have come into being as a reaction against an increasingly
permissive society. And one can hear that it reflects a
growing puritanism within society. And at the same time
(even, curiously enough, from the same sources) one is
told that the practice of "flirty fishing" (the promiscuous
behaviour of women recruiting for the Children of God)
or the highly publicised "love-ins" held by the followers
of Bhagwan Rajneesh can be explained either as a reaction
against the prudish society or as a reflection of the permissive

society -- only now, of course, the "reaction to" theory is producing a totally different conclusion about the nature of the host society, a conclusion which happens to be the same as that produced by the "reflection of" analysis of movements practicing celibacy. Finally, to complicate matters even further, one can hear that anyone joining such movements can be made to do, or to abstain from, anything, whatever their "natural" inclination.

None of these conclusions is intrinsically implausible. But if we want to investigate which, if any, or what kind of combinations of these potential explanations lies closest to reality our next question would have to be whether those who become Moonies or Krishna devotees are different kinds of people, who have had different kinds of experiences, from those who join the Children of God or who follow Bhagwan Rajneesh. If we find this to be the case to a significant degree we might then try to pursue the investigation beyond the fairly obvious fact that we live in a pluralistic society in which people can have significantly different experiences either because of the environment or because of their nature -- assuming the two are separable (R. & A.) We can then try to find out more about the differential composition of society. Alternatively, we may find that there does not really seem to be all that significant a difference between the backgrounds of the two groups of membership. This might lead us to ask further questions about the sort of social processes involved in the defining of reality and the promotion of certain types of action by the new religious movements themselves. We shall now be asking not the specific question about the specific society, but the general question about human potential for malleability and the sorts of conditions under which people can be influenced. We might, furthermore, observe that some societies or sections of society are more likely than others to notice and to remark upon the peculiarity of sexual practices in new religious movements.

What these examples have sought to illustrate is both the danger of overly facile generalisations and the importance of the comparative approach. As these points are of crucial importance let me briefly elaborate. It is an obvious error, but one that is made with suprising frequency, to assume that all new religious movements share the same characteristics. There is a sense in which the only characteristic shared by new religious movements is the label itself. This does not mean that the label cannot be a useful device for initially putting together a number of movements which bear a "family resemblance" to each other. It is a label which allows us to start the work of comparison -- comparing (1) the same movement in different places and at different times, and (2) different movements in the same society at the same time, seeing which characteristics are shared and which are peculiar to particular movements or clusters of movements; and (3) comparing different societies or a particular society at different times (i) with respect to the actual existence and fate of new religious movements and (ii) with respect to popular reactions to the various movements. The appendix contains a list of some of the characteristics of movements which might be selected for comparison.

The point here is to underline the vast number of ways in which any particular group can be viewed. Frequently one finds that people will characterise the movements by only one of their many features, such as their Eastern origin, recruitment methods, communal life style, an anthropomorphic conception of Satan, or fund-raising activities, and it is assumed that all movements sharing that particular characteristic will be similar in all other respects and that certain things necessarily follow from these inferred generalisations. It is of course perfectly legitimate to classify new religious movements according to particular characteristics -- such as world-affirming or world-rejecting (R.W.) -- so long as it is clearly recognized that the selection of that aspect will be fairly arbitrary. Any particular selection should be judged as more or less useful for investigating a particular problem. Different patterns, different regularities, different conclusions will emerge according to the particular characteristics selected.

Systematic comparison is the only reliable method which will allow us to test the theories which have, since the dawn of time, been entertained about the nature of man and society. Unless we have some idea of the direction and extent to which a particular characteristic will vary (or not vary) in the presence of another variable, we cannot hope to get beyond mere speculation as to what the relationship between the variables could be. Even less will we understand the nature of the connection. If we do not subject the disparate pieces of information which we collect to critical, comparative analysis we can find ourselves making wrong assumptions, drawing wrong conclusions, searching for non-existent influences or just not noticing what is going on under our very noses. Put more positively, the comparative method can open our eyes to the unexpected.

If, for instance, we learn that 3% of the membership of a movement committed suicide in a particular year it could be important to discover what it is about the movement that encourages the members to kill themselves. If, however, we also know that 6% of a control group -- that is of non-members of a similar age and background -- committed suicide during that year, then the investigation might more profitably turn to a search for ways in which the movement could be meeting problems which were not being met by the wider society.

If, to take another kind of example, one suspects that the current spawning of new religious movements in the west can be accounted for in terms of the secularism and materialism of society, then it might be instructive to consider the case of Sweden, arguably one of the most secular and materialistic countries in the world, and to ask why there is relatively little interest in the movements there (T.N.).

By observing either differences or similarities between contemporary movements and those of the past we may heighten our understanding of certain tendencies towards either stability or change. If, for example, it is noted that a characteristic usually taken-for-granted in modern move-ments (such as a monotheistic belief system) has by no means always been a characteristic of previous movements, then we may be led to recognise features, otherwise unremark-ed, about the general perspectives and assumptions of contemporary society (Z.W., T.O.).

Comparative analysis can also, paradoxically, show us what we cannot learn about social processes or the wider society from a study of new religious movements -- or rather, it can highlight the differences between small, sectarian type groups and other social phenomena. It is not wise to assume all truths or processes to be found in new reli-gious movements are merely those of society writ small but clear.

Socialisation, patterns of communication or power struc-tures in an open environment of pluralistic competition do not follow the same patterns as do socialisation, communication or power structures in a closed environment. Processes of communi-cation and control when mediated through face-to-face interac-tion have neither the same strengths nor the same weaknesses, neither the same possibilities opened up nor the same con-straints imposed upon them, as have processes of communication and control mediated through impersonal, institutionalised means. What might make sense or "work" in a small community does not necessarily indicate what might make sense or work on a larger scale. Structural and symbolic properties may exist at the more complex level that have no counterpart when sym-bolic meanings and structures may be more directly negotiable. The contingencies of national politics do not always reflect a morality of individual conscience. Interpersonal relationships do not operate in the same way as international relations. The small community which is likely to be economically, politically

and socially parasitic cannot hope to set the ideal example
by overcoming all the problems to be found in the host community, one reason being that it does not have to face all the
problems which the host community has to face (D.M.).

This does not mean that a new religious movement may
not solve some problems. As suggested earlier, it may well
meet needs which the society itself is failing to meet. These
may be the needs of the society as a whole (W.L., N.S.), or
those of sub-groups or individual members of the society
(B.W., W. & S., R.Wa). In the case either of the individual or
of society the need may be a universally experienced need or
one which is specific to that society. At the more universal
level one might, for example, suspect that man has a fundamentally basic need to express religious feelings but that in
a largely secular society neither a sympathetic social context
nor religious concepts are freely available for such expression
-- except perhaps in a new religious movement. One might also
suspect that man has a deeply held need to give as well as
to receive, but that in a highly organised welfare state in
times of peace such opportunities are restricted; but there a-
gain it may also be that it is only those who have been
brought up (socialised) to believe strongly in the ideals of
duty and service who are likely to be attracted to the sacrifi-
cial kind of life found in some of the new movements. Likewise
we may begin to see ways in which a society could have an
eductional system which induced needs for academic achievement
but because of the very nature of the system, not all of those
who have been thus socialized can realize their goal. [5]

It is important to recognise that, once the basic needs
of food and shelter have been met, the concept of need is a
slippery one to employ. There is always the danger of using
tautological reasoning; e.g. "he must have been needful because
he joined such and such a movement". We also have to be a-
ware of the extent to which the movements themselves might
induce or perhaps bring to the surface previously dormant feelings of need (B.W.). But it is, nonetheless, possible that
through observing some of the (latent and explicitly recognised, intended and unintended) functions of a new religious
movement, we can, cautiously, with the help of control groups
and the rigour of comparative analysis, "work backwards" to
see some of the gaps and tensions inherent within a social
structure.

Tensions are also revealed when observing the dynamics
of the relationship between a new religious movement and its
host society. A variety of sociological perspectives such as the
deviancy amplification model[6] and resource mobilization
models[7] have been put to good use in this area. Work on the
fate of alternative religions under Nazi Germany provides a

particularly telling story of the sort of characteristics which might allow a group to accomodate to heavy State pressure, and the sort of characteristics which will not. Such a study also illustrates with horrible clarity the extent to which men are prepared either to cause or to accept suffering or even death when monopolistic world views compete for legitimacy (C.K.).

On a much less drastic scale it is possible to observe a vast variety of continuing struggles to define the "proper", the "true", and the "natural", and to observe the consequences of either having or not having (and the strategies employed to acquire) the power to persuade others (J.B., B.B. & S.). While it is certainly a helpful extension of our knowledge to observe which aspects of a society a new religious movement might wish to change, it is, perhaps, even more illuminating to observe which particular characteristics of a new religious movement will be noticed and selected for criticism or (more rarely) praise by members of the host society (H.& K., G.B.). We might, for example, ask why a movement like the Soka Gakkai was the focus of so much hostility in its early days in Japan yet passes practically unnoticed (as Nichiren Shoshu U.K.) in Britain today. We might ask why it is that the Unification Church has so often been the prime target for criticism in the west. And we might ask why, in their criticisms of that movement, the Americans would seem to focus primarily on tax returns and brainwashing, the English on the break-up of the family, the Danes and the French on politics, the Germans on social security benefits and mental health and the Norwegians on theological claims to be genuinely Christian, while the Finns and the Dutch appear to be relatively unconcerned about the presence of Moonies in their midst.

It might also be worth mentioning two kinds of erroneous assumptions that can be made in looking for answers to such questions. First, it is frequently assumed that objections to the new religious movements are always directly in proportion to the distance which they are from the generally accepted decencies of belief and practice. This is perfectly correct in many instances -- the bizarre can be a cause of great concern -- but it is possible to argue that the greatest threat of some of the movements which are most villified lies in the fact that they are at, rather than beyond, the pale. Furthermore (if I may be excused for perhaps overplaying a metaphor) those movements which are frequently perceived as the most threatening are not just sitting on the fence, they are stridently staking out a boundary claim, demanding a radical redefinition of what belongs to what, and of what may be accepted as the true or natural order of things.

One boundary that a movement like the Unification Church threatens is that of Christianity -- a label which it has been vehemently denied by various Christian bodies. In an English court of law an "expert witness" from the Church of Scotland has testified that its beliefs were nothing but a blasphemy. On the other hand, a movement like the Soka Gakkai is quite inoffensive in a Christian community. It does not threaten to pollute any boundary. Being unequivocally beyond the pale, taxonomically speaking, there is no need to attack it for the "wrongness" of its beliefs. The members are tolerantly allowed to believe what they wish, despite, -- indeed because of -- the fact that their beliefs are completely different from those which the "real" Christian might wish to have taken for granted as the truth. [8]

A second type of erroneous assumption is to think that a societal reaction mirrors the society's interests in a straightforward manner. It may well be that what we are observing is a deflection, rather than a reflection, of values. A possible example of this could be found in the case of the United States where the First Amendment's guarantee of the right of all to believe whatsoever they wish is a revered and treasured part of the Constitution. In societies in which religious freedom is an explicit value, intolerance of others' religious beliefs cannot be overtly advocated without uncomfortably obvious contradiction. Those such as deprogrammers who wish to "rescue" a "victim" from a new religious movement have to show that no one could actually have <u>chosen</u> to join the movement of their own free will. [9]

This concept of choice leads us to some of the most difficult questions which lie at the heart of the idea of a science of man and the relationship between the individual and society. One area in which philosophical assumptions about the nature of man as a social animal (how far he is determined by society, and how society "gets into him") become crucially important issues is the area of conversion. In studying conversion some theoretical positions are considerably more helpful than others in that they can make more sense of the phenomenon. If a purely behaviourist approach is adopted then we have no means of talking about religious experience or the ways in which conversion is meaningful to the converts themselves. We have to ignore the fact that the converts may strongly believe they had a choice in the matter. If, on the other hand, we adopt a purely humanist approach and say that each man is completely free to make his own choice in all matters, or, at a more theological level, if we just agree with the convert that the Holy Spirit has entered into him, then we have no way of accounting for the remarkably differential social selectivity of the free individual or the Holy Ghost.

The point here is that it is quite clear that the movements tend to attract people within certain age ranges and

from particular kinds of social background. At some periods
in some societies it has been the economically deprived or the
politically oppressed who have been most likely to join new
religious movements. This is not generally the case in the contemporary west where recruits tend to come from the privileged
middle classes. Furthermore those who join the Divine Light
Mission are not, sociologically speaking, the same type of persons as those who become Moonies or who join the Hare Krishna or Scientology. Such people will, moreover, be significantly
different from those who join Vedanta societies (W.& S., R.& A.).

Thus, through comparative analysis and the use of control groups, we can begin to sort out the relative importance
of various factors -- those which the potential recruit "brings
with him" (predispositions, values, interests, ideas about society and his place in it, etc.), and factors with which he is
confronted (the social context of more or less persuasive believers and the alternative offered by the movement). Arguments
about the capacity of the movements to brainwash their recruits
have given an impetus to attempts to "operationalise" the concept of choice -- that is, to analyse, in ways which can be
empirically checked, whether or not it makes sense to say the
convert only converted because of manipulative techniques. It
is however interesting that despite evidence (1) that over 90%
of those who attend Unification Church workshops in Britain
do not become Moonies, and (2) of those who do become Moonies
the majority will leave of their own free will within a couple
of years, many of the Church's opponents persist in saying
anyone who comes into contact with the movement will necessarily be subject to mind control and will be unable to leave of
his own volition.[10]

There can, of course, be no doubt that conversions do
occur, sometimes with spectacular effects within a very short
space of time. No one who has witnessed a sudden conversion
can question the fact that something far more fundamental than
the mere acceptance of a new idea has taken place. The convert
can change to such an extent that his friends and relations
will insist that not only does he believe something quite different, he has actually become someone quite different. The whole
personality is quite different from his former self -- he is no
longer behaving "naturally".

There is a vast potential for further explorations into
the way people can change under such circumstances. Some of
the most exciting of recent glimpses into possible mechanisms
of the brain and mind have been gleaned not from the study
of man himself, but from the study of primates and of computer
behaviour. Fascinating and enlightening as such studies are,
however, they will always involve the problem of reductionism
-- that is of reducing man's behaviour to "lower" levels and
thus of loosing important compontents in the process. So far

as is known neither a primate nor a computer has yet joined
a new religious movement.   Further study not only of conversion, but also of apostasy, could illuminate important dimensions in our understanding of the human condition at the levels
of social interaction and symbolic meaning.

It has been suggested that the empirical study of new
religious movements can, in several ways, provide a peculiarly
helpful starting point from which to enlarge our knowledge both
of social processes in general and of particular societies.
There are of course limitations to such an exercise, some of
which have been mentioned, but it is hoped that this volume
can serve as a basis for further investigation, further comparisons, and further understanding of the ways in which men
operate as social animals. And if the volume raises more questions than it manages to answer this will not count as failure
in the editor's eyes.

NOTES

1.   Roszak, 1975.

2.   Robinson, 1977.

3.   Hardy, 1966.

4.   Monod, 1972.

5.   I have discussed such arguments more fully in "Who'd Be a Moonie?" in Wilson, 1981 and in "Identity within an Unorthodox Orthodoxy" in Shaffir and Greenspan, 1982.

6.   Wallis, 1976.

7.   Bromley and Shupe, 1979.

8.   This argument which owes much to Douglas, 1966 is elaborated in Barker, 1981.

9.   Richardson, H. 1977; Richardson, J. 1982.

10.   Barker, 1980.

THE NEW RELIGIONS:
PRELIMINARY CONSIDERATIONS*

Bryan R. Wilson

The very concept of "new religious movements" presents its own distinctive difficulties for sociology. New movements have been a recurrent phenomenon in the context of Christian cultures in the West. Most of these movements — ridiculed, persecuted, or suppressed — were destined in a relatively short time to disappear: some, however, persisted until they ceased to be "new". Thus, in England, the early divisions of Protestantism — the Congregationalists, Presbyterians, and Baptists — gradually came to be known as "historical dissenters". In Japan, what are contemporaneously referred to as "new religions" began as long ago as the mid-nineteenth century, and writers have distinguished them chronologically — old new religions from newer ones.[1] The paradox of the idea of "old new religions" brings into high relief the difficulty of using chronology as the point of departure for a sociology of religious innovation: but what other point ' of departure might we use?

Sociology as a discipline is committed to the search for broad explanatory schemes that summarize in general and abstract terms the probable course of actual empirical change. Yet, it is clear that there must be limits to the utility of encapsulating in abstract general terms intrinsically and empirically diverse cultural, social, and spiritual processes. The sociological task is to embrace, in analytical formulations of wide application, diverse cultural contents — and the unstated, but implicit, assumption of sociologists is that their concepts should, like those of natural scientists, be of universal applicability. Despite these high aspirations in the study of religious movements both in the West and in Japan, we have, none the less, had to resort to such weak descriptive terms as "new", and have had to qualify "new" with such apparently contradictory terms as "old new": and this indicates just how far we are from possessing a real sociology of religious movements. Perhaps the time has come to recognize the impossibility — in any terms that are not unduly vague — of any general theory of new movements. Certainly we should not aim — as sociologists have sometimes been wont to do — at a theory that seeks to be outside time and space, even though we wish our concepts to apply outside and beyond the confines of any one culture or historical epoch.[2] If sociology is not to abandon the

real world for purely theoretical artefacts, then, we are always likely to be in some degree captive to the empirical circumstances of given cultures, of geography, and of history.

New religious movements are a phenomenon that taxes
our existing conceptual apparatus. The concept of the sect —
widely used, not only with specific meaning by sociologists,
but also more loosely by laymen — does not meet the diverse
demands that are made upon it. To have any rigour, the concept requires specification, but such specification is all too
likely to carry the imprint of particular culture and particular theological tradition.³ Nor is the term cult, which Wallis
has usefully re-defined⁴, to indicate a movement that breaches
the exclusivism normal in the Christian tradition, adequate to
cope with the different assumptions of non-Christian cultures.
In other religious traditions, plural loyalties — characteristic
in the West only of cults — is a more general phenomenon.
It is not surprising, then, that, for want of a better concept,
sociologists have continued to use the term "new movements".
But what, apart from a denotative list of actual movements,
are we talking about: what do these social phenomena have
in common? We are led to three broad, related questions. What
is new about new movements? Do new movements fulfill similar
functions even in diverse cultural and historical contexts? To
what extent is any given new movement capable of maintaining its own intrinsic character as it spreads in space and per-
sists in time? It is to some preliminary considerations that
might eventually lead to partial answers to these questions
that I address myself in this paper. What I have to say is
exploratory, and I refer to specific movements illustratively
rather than analytically.

The very idea that movements are new indicates the importance of considering them in the context of an already-
existing religious tradition. All new movements of necessity offer something unavailable in older religions. Basically, they
offer a surer, shorter, swifter, or clearer way to salvation.
Whatever its specific cultural content may be, sociologically,
salvation is, in essence, present reassurance of the possibility of overcoming evil, in whatever way evil is theologically
or culturally defined. Salvation is the commodity in which all
religions deal, whether it is release from witches, illness, dis-
grace, bad luck, early death, punishment after death, or dam-
nation to recurrent lives of misery. Using salvation in this
sociological sense, we have a general phenomenon, a category
that encompasses many different cultural contents. The appeal
of new movements is the offer of a more convincing reassurance about salvation than was hitherto available. New movements are thus likely to encourage optimism, at least among
those who subscribe to them, about prospects of overcoming
the evil and the untoward. Even of movements that have sought

to rationalize experience, in which the deity becomes a more transcendent, less immanent, entity, this generalization holds. If Calvinism made God transcendent, removing him from the stage of life, none the less, for believers, the effect of Calvinism was to make God's will, if inscrutable, in some sense ultimately rational. Salvation became more certain — not in the sense that a man could assert his assurance of election (although even in pristine Calvinism the record is not unequivocal), at least in the sense of knowing his obligations in both faith and morals. Calvinism swept away the arcane, mysterious, and quasi-magical apparatus and activities, with respect to which the lay individual had neither knowledge nor control.

The fact that, in established religions, salvation is often prescribed as remote and difficult, is associated with the process of institutionalization of religious systems, which affects not only church activities and their relationship with other social institutions,[5] but which occurs also in ritual and doctrine. In the older religions, routines and rituals acquired increasing formality: activities, that once had intrinsic purpose, persisted even after purpose was lost and action retained only symbolic significance. The virtue of the deeds of the saints became transferred — by the latent but recrudescent disposition towards the magical — to their bones. But, when nirvana is a thousand lives away, or when schoolmen calculate the specific value of relics and elaborate the penalties of post-mortem purgatory with ever-increasing scholastic refinement, laymen are likely to look for a more ever-present help in their daily troubles. New movements cut through such routine: offering more proximate salvation. The successive development in Japanese Buddhism from Nara Buddhism to the doctrine of salvation by faith in innate enlightenment in Tendai, and its further extension to reliance on the mercy of the Amida Buddha in Jōdo Shin Buddhism, and then, with Shinran in Jōdo Shin Shu, to the concept that the Amida Buddha had already accomplished the salvation of all men illustrates a process in which salvation, initially more difficult to attain, is progressively made into a present reality. The supersession of Calvinism by Arminianism — from determinism to free will salvation by faith — and the doctrine of assurance in Methodism, illustrate a similar trend.

It is not only remoteness and obscurity in traditional soteriologies that prompt lay demands for shorter, surer paths to salvation, and so to present reassurance, it is often also the effect of spiritual elitism and its not infrequent concomitant — clerical scepticism. Old religions tend to encourage the evolution of spiritual hierarchies, and the elites that emerge protect their own interests as the possessors of what is usually claimed as at least a superior, if not an exclusive, wisdom concerning the divine by the cultivation of

specialized techniques and performances that are offered as
indispensable for the layman in search of salvation. With their
own indispensability established, priests have shown two divergent tendencies, each of which engenders lay discontent.
One is the elitist preoccupation with minutiae and metaphysical speculation, which are essentially narrow, clerical concerns
that distance priests from laymen, and which render the terms
of salvation obscure. Alternatively, priests themselves have
often shown a considerable capacity for scepticism about the
doctrines they are supposed to profess. Occasionally, a cleric
has spoken out against the claims of the religious system he
serves, sometimes even leading a new movement. More typically, priests have acquired a personal scepticism concerning
their own publicized spiritual claims. The phrase trahison des
clercs did not become a commonplace without the phenomenon
it denotes being widely observed. Priestly disenchantment,
apathy, indifference, spiritual laxity, and moral turpitude
have been widespread in established religions. These things,
combined with clerical elitism and the claims to a monopoly
of indispensable functions, have provided impetus to new religions.

New movements arise to offer more proximate salvation
and also to offer wider access to it. They have frequently attacked the distinction between priest and layman, whether in
asserting a "priesthood of all believers" as in Protestantism;
or in the contemporary radical claim in Catholicism to a
shared ministry of laymen and clerics, with Christ the only
priest; or in the diminution of clerical distinctiveness, as
when priestly celibacy is set aside as in Anglicanism, Luther-
anism, and in the Jōdo Shin Shu school of Buddhism. Thus,
spiritual elitism is assaulted, a now voluntarily-recruited public is given wider access to spiritual opportunities, and there
is prospect of more rapid spiritual mobility. Salvation is now
to be obtained by simpler techniques, and paradoxically they
become, by an iron law of institutionalization, the basis for
new distinctions between specialists and laymen. The simpler
techniques become an avenue for rapid spiritual— and social —
mobility for a new style of religious specialist.

When laymen seek reassurance — that is to say, when
they consider salvation — they tend to do so at the prompting
of urgent need. They are impatient of doctrinal refinements
and uncomprehending of abstruse soteriological considerations
that stand between them and the assistance and reassurance
that they seek. When doctrines become too metaphysical they
have typically had recourse to the palliatives, remedies,
prophecies, and panaceas of ancient magic, and such magic
has, even despite the type of hostility it encountered in Christendom, lingered on.[6] New religions cater to the same need,
sometimes by a virtual return to something like the same

nostrums, but at other times by new rationalizations of man's problems and the means to their solution. It should not, then, surprise us when new religions offer therapies for mental or physical distress. In doing so, they pick up an ancient function of man's concern with the supernatural, but they realize it by contrasting their claims with those of conventional religion. Thus, what is "new" may be something restored, reformed, or revived (as in revivalism, fundamentalism, or Charismatic Renewal); or it may be wisdom newly garnered from other, half-unknown cultures (as in Krishna Consciousness, the Divine Light Mission, or 3HO)[7]; or it may be presented as something modern and scientific (as in Christian Science and Scientology).[8]

The characteristics of new movements — the offer of a more proximate salvation; the implicit assault on spiritual elitism; their availability to a wider public; the accessibility of their techniques; the spiritual mobility they facilitate; and their use of therapeutic claims — may all be described as life-enhancing for the ordinary man. In some respects one might even postulate a broad, loose, evolutionary trend towards the demotic. Religions develop intellectual and metaphysical orientations, but old religions began in ways similar to the contemporary new movements in some respects — as is evident both in the appeal of physical healing, and in the promise of a new kingdom in early Christianity.[9] The new religions in America have been described as offering man a new partnership with God, in which man acquires an increased capacity "formerly reserved for the gods, of not only discovering reality and truth, but of creating them symbolically and experientially."[10] But the process is not unique to the new eastern mysticisms now popular in the United States: Mormonism, from the 1830s and 40s, declared that men had the opportunity to evolve into gods, and it reiterated the sentiments of another new movement of the time, Universalism, in claiming that practically everyone would attain the heavenly afterlife. Again, in the old new religions of Japan, Tenrikyo and Konkokyo, the highest Deity became more available and more concerned with the affairs of ordinary people, providing healing, solace, and the regimen of an ordered life in rapport with spiritual forces. The new religions offer more, and offer it more immediately, to more people: they overthrow the old scarcity mentality which older religions often manifest. In new religions there is prospect of spiritual abundance.

We may speculate whether such an offer is related to the general improvement in the lot of mankind. As higher living standards and greater life security make the religious repertoire of sacrifice and self-denial less compelling and less relevant, at least in the material sense, so it may be that the spiritual appetites undergo change, demanding different

titillation and different sustenance. The "transcendental Aus-
gleich" of traditional Christian theodicy is perhaps less necessary in a world in which the ills that men suffer are, in considerable measure, of a different kind from those experienced
in the formative period of the great religions. Men seek com-
pensations at different points of experience and in different
material and symbolic terms. The new religions are, in this
sense, adaptations to changing human circumstances, and the
changed expression of spiritual needs.

The anti-elitism and the open accessibility of new religious movements is often accompanied, when movements are in
their pristine state, by at least an element of the ecstatic,
whether or not that is a feature of the religious tradition
within which, and against which, they arise. New religions
tend to set spontaneity, immediacy, and sincerity over against
the cultivated and measured responses of conventional religion.
They call for total allegiance rather than for mere regular
and regulated attendance. Thus, they mobilize enthusiasm at
a level that is not usually attained in traditional religion,
and which, when, abnormally, it does occur there, is a
source of embarrassment to other believers, with their moder-
ated expectations concerning religious performance. Just as the
new religions are life-enhancing, so they explicitly enhance
emotional responses. In the longest run, they all face the
dual problem of how to maintain, but also how to contain, the
initial enthusiasm. That exercises intended to sustain enthusiasm may themselves become routinized is evident in the history of religions — whether in the sponsored revivalism of Finney and his successors; or in the recurrent invocation of the
Holy Spirit in Charismatic Renewal; or in the stimulated excitement with which the pilgrims of Soka Gakkai go to Taisekiji.

Yet containing, rather than sustaining, expressions of
enthusiasm often becomes the main concern of new movements,
and this within a relatively short time. The phenomenon of
routinization is well-understood. It begins as an initial following, is converted into a stable membership engaging in regular
devotions, making regular subscriptions, accepting specific obligations, giving public acknowledgment to specific teachings,
and obeying specific social, moral, and administrative stipu-
lations. Movements must balance the ecstatic (in however di-
lute a form it is permitted to persist), since it marks the
mobilization of emotional commitment, with the imperative of
orderly, systematic, organized, and sustained patterns of behaviour by which alone a new movement is assured of stability, unity, continuity, and growth. Whether the process of routinization is effected by social control within the movement —
that is by explicit rituals, the supervision of officials, and
sometimes even by magical sanctions — or whether it is

achieved through the encouragement of self–control, personal discipline and accountability of individual believers each to himself, are variables that may be culturally determined. Movements that fail to achieve routinization, and which fail to develop a sense of boundary maintenance, tend to fail as new religions. In such cases, where we perceive a loose, ill-defined set of practices and ideas spreading within a population that is never weaned of its traditional commitments, we have a fashion rather than a movement. Charismatic Renewal is an example of just such a congeries of beliefs, practices, and partial organization. It is not yet clear whether its ulti-mate destiny is to become a real movement, or to remain a party that will change the church, or to pass away as a fashionable style of worship of a limited period.

We may note, moreover, that boundary–maintenance is it-self subject to cultural variation. In cultures with a pluralist tradition, in which there is no emphasis on the exclusivity to any one movement of religious truth, or in which such exclu-sivity is heavily compromised, the ideal–typical construct of a new movement as a separate, self–contained entity, demand-ing total and sole allegiance of its members, is not substan-tiated by empirical fact. Indeed, even in western societies, where exclusivity is the norm, new movements may compromise: organizational principles rather than the claim to a monopoly of truth and the exclusiveness of correct practice may suffice to distinguish movements, e.g., the Methodist schisms of the nineteenth century, or the Pentecostal sects of the early twen-tieth. The newest movements in western societies have arisen at a time in which boundaries have increasingly been chal-lenged, and in which discrimination gives place to a vogue of indiscriminateness in a wide variety of social phenomena, and especially among the young, to whom in particular the new movements appeal. We must wait to see if movements which reject boundary maintenance, such as Transcendental Meditation and Charismatic Renewal persist, or wither, or are absorbed.

If routinization is a normal feature of the development of new movements, it arises because stability of commitment, consistency, and calculability of member dispositions are ulti-mately even more vital than enthusiasm to the persistence of any movement. Fervour and discipline must thus go together, the one justifying the other. In persisting movements, a new balance of emotional control is struck at a far higher level of dedication — at least as far as the generality of the mem-bership is concerned — than is encountered in all but excep-tional cases in conventional religions.

Discipline is itself an earnest of the new order which the new religion proclaims, intrinsically as a movement, in its own operation, and as a precursor of a worldwide order which, in one sphere of experience or another, is to come. It is by no means always the case that new religious movements represent more rational procedures than traditional religions. In the nature of the case, there must always be a strong non-rational element in any religious system, given the super-empirical nature of the goals that are canvassed, and thus the necessarily arbitrary nature of the procedures specified for their attainment. This said, however, we have noted that new religions tend to simplify the techniques and procedures that are stipulated for the attainment of super-empirical ends, and this simplification may, in certain circumstances, be something of a rationalization. Again, since new movements arise in conditions in which rationalization is increasing in the external secular society, where it is manifested most explicitly in increased technologization, they, too, are likely to be influenced by the availability of more rational techniques with which to attain certain organizational ends. New movements, being less inflexibly bound to traditional procedures and precedents, easily adopt more recent and more rational techniques. Particularly where their concerns transcend those of a local culture, or where essentially secular procedures of propaganda, recruitment, evangelization, fund-raising, member-deployment, and assembly, are available, new movements are likely to manifest the influence of rational organization. If teachings are arbitrary, organization is modern and often secular in its spirit. This may be seen in the stake organization of the Mormons; in the use worldwide of uniform Sabbath school materials by the Seventh-day Adventists; in the uniform printed lesson-sermons of the Christian Science Church; in the deployment of members on a strictly rational basis as canvassers by Jehovah's Witnesses; and in the cell and cadre structure of Soka Gakkai. Devices borrowed from secular culture give all these movements a more rational organizational style than that maintained by traditional religion, or than would be congruous to its spirit and ethos. It is not an accident that the first four of these movements originated in the United States.

Obviously, rational procedures may be variously mixed with entirely arbitrary elements that stem from the received supernaturalist doctrinal content of a new movement. Thus, in Christian Science, rational businesslike procedures of appointment of officials and arrangements for their remuneration are linked to essentially non-rational techniques of healing (even if these are set forth in terms that echo the rational, as the very name Science suggests). At a more primitive level, the establishment of band-meetings in Methodism, was an attempt to put system into the essentially non-rational sphere of devotion: again, the name Methodism, indicates the orientation. Even in the very new and more charismatic movements, the Unification Church and the Divine Light Mission, there are some guidelines of rational organization — not all of them conspicuous publicly.

In the foregoing, we have not attempted to construct an ideal-type of the new religious movement: the concept is too unspecific and too relative for any such exercise. New religions are too diverse for such a formulation, even when their main characteristics are denoted in terms of considerable abstractness. Different new religions adopt diverse organizational arrangements and espouse divergent values. A movement like Soka Gakkai is manifestly a mass movement with a vigorous public presence, taking its place in the national life of Japan; in complete contrast, Krishna Consciousness is deliberately a minority movement, appealing explicitly to one section of the community, and more or less self-consciously casting itself in the role of the exotic and outlandish, unconcerned about the general social order. Sects such as the Seventh-day Adventists and Jehovah's Witnesses reassert many traditional values in idealized form, in contrast with the explicit rejection of traditional values by a movement such as Scientology. The Children of God draws its members out of the wider society into segregated communities in preparation for the end of the present dispensation, whereas, in various ways, Transcendental Meditation, Scientology, and PL Kyodan offer principles and therapies to help their votaries to get more out of life within the existing social order. New movements, then, have in common only their newness at a given point of time. For any specific purposes of analysis and prediction, we should need refined typologies: even so there is some value in looking at new movements as a generic class. That so many and such diverse religious manifestations emerge more or less contemporaneously in itself points to inadequacies in traditional religion in the context of social systems and national cultures that are undergoing disruption, and points too, to the latent discontents prevailing within advanced societies. New religions indicate an area of need among the population: some of these needs may be spontaneously felt; others, some people may be easily induced to recognize within themselves. The new religions speak to a variety of conditions of men: their success indicates the spiritual, social, and cultural defects of the times. When traditional religionists say that new religions arise from a spiritual malaise, we need not gainsay them: but we should be clear that the new religions are not themselves that malaise — rather is it located in the current social situation. The new religions, however they might be evaluated — and evaluation is not our concern — are responses to the malaise, not its symptoms or its source.

The new religions do not, except in the most general sense, fulfill the same functions in the various cultural and historical contexts in which they arise. Thus, for example, the new religions in Japan appear to act as important loci of allegiance between the total society, including the state, and the individual. They undertake a variety of intermediate functions, providing welfare, education, medical care, a sense of involvement, a focus of loyalty, meaning and orientation, and a point of identity for people living in a newly urbanized world in which the older intermediate agencies of social structure, and particularly the traditional household, have largely disappeared. Thus, perhaps especially for those — housewives for example — uninvolved in the life of a company to which loyalty is to be given, a movement such as Rissho Kosei Kai provides such an encompassing focus. Springing up spontaneously, as they have, would it be too much to see in the new religions in Japan, the type of institution which Durkheim prescribed for modern society when he (mistakenly) ascribed to professional guilds the function of mediating between modern man and the state.[11]

These functions of Japanese new religions differ from those of new movements in the West, which cater to an individuated public, often recruiting isolated people searching for much less structural and much more metaphysical support, for personal therapy, encounter, and a lighter, often more contractual commitment of a more adventuring kind. To say more, we must have more detailed profiles of those who are recruited and closer accounts of the processes of induction and socialization. How are the predispositions of individuals who are recruited to a movement matched to its particular facilities and orientations? What is the fit between the previously felt needs of those who become members and provisions to meet needs in particular movements? On these questions, all our plausible theories, including the relative deprivation thesis, are weak.[12] Only with detailed individual studies, can such theories be put to the test. We cannot rule out the possibility that, in some measure, movements may awaken needs in particular individuals, giving them increased specificity in the terms of the movement's own ideology, and so defining the situation for prospective adherents, supplying both the sense of needs and the means of its fulfillment. One can see such a relationship in traditional religions, most conspicuously perhaps in the inducement of a sense of personal sin by evangelical Christianity, and the offer of techniques for the elimination of the sense of guilt and the control of conduct with the goal that what the religion defines as sin might be eradicated. Clearly, what is called sin must have some objective reality, and it might be argued, at another level, that this reality was indeed constituted of socially deleterious conduct: but the process of "consciousness raising" about needs and deficiences has always been a function of new religions. Stating the problem in these terms does not solve it: we still need to know why people should accept the proposed definition of their situation and the proffered solutions.

Functionalist explanations of new religious movements tend to relate to phenomena that are general in given cultures, but they usually fail to discriminate between the different postures of the new movements themselves. Thus, if urbanization; the new technology; the development of role-articulated social systems and the corresponding process of institutional differentiation; and the creation of impersonal social contexts — are all general circumstances in which new movements emerge, how are the discontents that these conditions precipitate related to the specific teachings, practices, styles, and orientations of the very diversified new religions? Of course, broad patterns of social change are mediated by multiform processes to particular regions, classes, groups, and individuals, and this allows for considerable variation of effect. Yet we cannot be sure that these effects are themselves related in any systematic or determinate way to the specific intrinsic orientations of the movements. Even employing a value-added logic of the kind advanced by Smelser,[13] takes us little further than the level at which action occurs: religious movements are all value-oriented movements. Our problem is to account for their differences in value-orientations. Can we even eliminate the element of randomness in the distribution of adherents to movements, which may obtain even though joining is voluntary? Individuals suffer situational constraints, and these constraints may propel them towards one movement rather than another, and may have nothing to do with their basic personality dispositions.

Obviously, certain broad facilitating circumstances condition the emergence of new movements. The diminution of religious persecution is a sine qua non. Toleration, initially for dissenters objecting marginally to the main tradition, gradually extended to permit choice that is limited only by considerations of conventional morality, and to protect individuals from constraint and from unapproved therapies. (Health is an issue on which such diverse movements as Christian Science, Jehovah's Witnesses, and Scientology have skirmished with the authorities.) Of course, official prohibition, as in the Soviet Union and some East European countries, does not eradicate religious movements: proscribed movements persist, and sometimes flourish. The break of the links between traditional religion and national, regional, local, and familial communities provides the gap in which new religions can grow. The impersonal contexts of modern society facilitate the attraction of socially anonymous individuals to new religious communities, whether those religions seek, as do Pentecostals, to revive personal relationships and affectivity; to celebrate impersonality and capitalize on it, as do Christian Science and Scientology;

or to heal its effects in the fashion of the human potential
movements.[14] The impersonality of the social context affects the
process of communication in religion. Literacy is the single
most important facility. Even though movements have from time
to time used radio and even television, neither of these media
appear to have been significant ways of recruitment. Jehovah's
Witnesses who once used radio gave it up and have found better methods. In Africa, Seventh-day Adventists broadcast their
Voice of Prophecy, but my evidence was that very few had
been influenced to join by radio. These mass media are, after
all, more ephemeral than the most feeble piece of printed
ephemera. Personal communication, face to face and by word
of mouth, appears to have special significance for movements
with a strong supernatural content. Door-to-door canvassing,
as undertaken by Witnesses and Soka Gakkai, work through
informal networks, and the augmentary circulation of literature, are the agencies of recruitment. In impersonal contexts,
the little touches of personal warmth and friendly association
are effective — sometimes leading to the creation of surrogate
communities.

Therapy has had a varying role both as a conditioning
factor, and as a function of the new movements. Physical healing has frequently been part of a movement's promise, but in
societies in which medical care has improved and has been undertaken as a recognized social obligation, so the demand for
healing through recourse to supernatural agencies has diminished. Faith healing of physical ills is less canvassed in advanced societies, except for ailments regarded as incurable
medically or too vague or too trivial for medical treatment.
In Japan, the new movements are less exclusivistic than those
of the West, with regard not only to doctrines but also to alternative curative practice, and some, such as Tenrikyo and
PL Kyodan, have increasingly combined the facilities of mate-
ria medica with their own resources for curative practice. In
the West, the emphasis has shifted from physical to psychic
well-being, and this not only in explicitly mind-healing curative movements and movements concerned to realize "human potential". Even among Jehovah's Witnesses, a movement without
explicit therapeutic provision or expectation, "peace of mind"
is perhaps the most common response elicited when Witnesses
are asked what are the principal blessings that they have experienced since becoming a believer.[15]

Especially in the West, there are marked variations in
the functions of new religions with respect to social control
and socialization. Both were important functions of traditional
religion: in societies where secular morality was underpinned
so centrally by religious sanctions, religion supplied the vital
agencies of attitudinal control. In Christian cultures, religion
increasingly defined the mores and in certain respects did so

even more powerfully after the Reformation: the moral man
was, for a time, the religious man. Subsequently, religion declined as an agency of social control, partly as it concentrated more on the internalization of values and as it emphasized the individual's responsibility for his own conduct in
an evangelical scheme of personal salvation. With the processes of secularization and the rationalization of social life,
social control became less a function of morals and more a
matter of techniques. Men were controlled less by inbuilt inhibition and external moral censure, and more by mechanical
instruments which measured or regulated in "objective" ways
the individual's obligations, and extracted performance from
him. So, works' clocks, conveyor belts, traffic lights, electronic eyes, and data retrieval systems belong, at different
points, to the process by which society is technically demor-
alized. The need for supernatural sanctions wanes, and even
reliance on internalized pressures of conscience apparently
diminishes — certainly in the economic sphere. As old religion
in the West surrendered its control and socialization functions, only the new fundamentalist groups sought to take them
up: for the newer mystical faiths, such things become irrelevant. If the new religions emphasize discipline, it is discipline not normally for the well-being of the wider society,
but rather a spiritual exercise for the benefit of the individual believer himself, and sometimes for the communal life of
the group.

New religious movements were once no more than devia-
tions from older traditions of the culture to which they were
indigenous: whatever was new about them, their continuities
with parent religions were far more evident. Today, national,
regional, and cultural barriers have been eroded, and new
movements spread very rapidly from their native culture to
others. By vigorous proselytizing Pentecostals, Mormons, Witnesses, and Seventh-day Adventists have become worldwide
movements, newer in some contexts than others. Sometimes they
have been very effective in other societies — the Witnesses in
Zambia; the Adventists in Western Kenya; the Pentecostals in
Chile. Clearly, there are questions to be raised about their
functions in different societies, and even about the cultural
identity of the movements themselves. Other movements appear
to flourish especially by transfer. Thus Krishna Consciousness
and 3HO are regarded as less than authentic in the societies
from which they sprang, and they subsist almost entirely as
alien growths, less transplanted than deliberately cultivated
as exotica in alien host societies. Some movements have less
capacity for transfer except among emigrants from the indigenous society who become ethnic minorities elsewhere. Ethnic
sects are always likely to be viewed with suspicion, as potentially subversive of a host culture which expected rather to
absorb immigrants than to house distinctive minorities that

use religion to reinforce alien ethnicity. But not only ethnic religious movements find themselves proscribed: all sects are likely to be seen as the purveyors of alien ideology or as agents of other societies, as evidenced by Soviet reaction to Jehovah's Witnesses, and the hostility to the Children of God and the Unification Church in several countries. Politicians recognize the implicit threat of alien values, even if, in practice, they need rarely fear that such movements will effectively challenge the operation of the state and the economy.

It has been a commonplace of modern sociological theory that social systems depend for their integration on value consensus, and that such consensus attains its ultimate expression in religion. The latest form of this thesis, perhaps in acknowledgement of the decline of supernaturalist orientations in both social structure and popular consciousness, locates these values in civil religion — the more or less explicit symbolic celebration by its members of their society, and often indeed of the state. Yet, today, states have tarnished reputations in the eyes of many of their citizens; and society becomes too amorphous in many ways, too similar, in its basic dependencies, to other societies, and too bound up with them economically for "our society" to be much of a focus of identity, much less of pride. It is difficult to say just what are the supposed values of given social systems, or how they are rooted in traditional religion. The prevalent values of modern society appear to be procedural rather than substantive, and to be sanctioned and legitimized by pragmatic considerations rather than by absolute standards derived from the supernatural. When intrinsic societal values are surrendered to the purely technical imperatives of economic efficiency, and when states and their rulers fail the test even of honesty and common decency, then the social system itself ceases to be a focus of loyalties. The old religions — whatever the virtues they canvass — lose all influence on social and political structures. Like Protestantism, they fall into palsied desuetude, or like Catholicism, they manifest overt internal value-conflict and accelerating decline. The emergent new religions provide new focal points of commitment, and even if they are marginal, as they certainly are in the West, their existence is itself of the utmost sociological significance. But will such new movements become a source of new values for society as a whole? Not, certainly, if they appeal only to sectional minorities, nor if they remain so widely diverse in orientation and structure; nor yet again if they fail to acquire purchase on any facet of the institutional structure. They persist in offering their solutions in what may be called the evangelical mode, as if private virtue and personal discipline could transform modern society. That vision might have been plausible in Victorian England: it is scarcely so now. Making men new appears to have little impact on the inexorable cost-efficiency processes of modern economics and technology: private virtue appears to be irrelevant to public performance and to modern organization. The new religions may achieve much for individuals in their personal lives, they may even create new subcultures into which some men can permanently, and others occasionally, retreat from the abrasiveness of the impersonal society of the modern world. But as yet we have little reason to suppose that they have any likelihood of transforming the structure of society and the alien experience that it produces into the encompassing community of love, of which — inside the new religions and out — men still so vividly dream.

NOTES

*   This paper was presented to the Tokyo meeting of the International Conference on Sociology of Religion, December 1978 and first published in the Proceedings of Tokyo Meeting of The International Conference on Sociology of Religion by the Organizing Committee for Tokyo Meeting of C.I.S.R. c/o Department of Religious Studies, University of Tokyo, Japan, 1978.

1.   See the distinctions discussed in the chapter "New Religious Movements" (Hori Ichiro et al. [eds.] 1972, pp. 92-4).

2.   Max Weber wrote, "The more comprehensive the validity, — or scope — of a term, the more it leads us away from the richness of reality since in order to include the common elements of the largest possible number of phenomena, it must necessarily be as abstract as possible and hence devoid of content. In the cultural sciences, the knowledge of the universal or general is never valuable in itself." (Weber, 1949, p. 80).

3.   For a fuller discussion see Magic and the Millennium (Wilson, 1973, pp. 9-18).

4.   See "The Cult and Its Transformations" (Wallis, 1975, pp. 35-47). I am more convinced by this formulation than by the more recent position adopted by Richardson (Richardson, 1978a).

5.   The locus classicus for the discussion of institutionalization is in "Five Dilemmas in the Institutionalization of Religion" (O'Dea, 1961, pp. 30-9).

6.   The evidence is particularly impressively presented for Ceylon (Gombrich, 1971).

7.   On Krishna Consciousness, see the paper by Gregory Johnson, "The Hare Krishna in San Francisco" (Glock and Bellah, 1976, pp. 31-51) and Francine J. Daner, "Conversion to Krishna Consciousness" (Wallis, 1975, pp. 53-69); on the Divine Light Mission, see the essay by Jeanne Messer, "Guru Maharaj Ji and the Divine Light Mission" (Glock and Bellah, 1976, pp. 52-72); and on 3HO, see the paper by Alan Tobey, "The Summer Solstice of the Healthy-Happy-Holy Organization (Glock and Bellah, 1976, pp. 5-30).

8.   For a discussion of Christian Science, see Sects and Society (Wilson, 1978, pp. 119-215); on Scientology, see the most thorough discussion in The Road to Total Freedom: A Sociological Analysis of Scientology (Wallis, 1976).

9.   On the significance of the kingdom promise, see Kingdom and Community (Gager, 1975, pp. 20-65).

10.   Wuthnow discusses this point in dealing with religious populism (Wuthnow, 1978, pp. 191).

11.   See the discussion in "Professional Ethics" (Durkheim, 1957, pp. 1-41).

12.   The relative deprivation thesis is set forth most cogently in "On the origin and evolution of religious groups" (Glock and Stark, 1965, pp. 242-59).

13.   The idea of a value-added logic in sociological analysis is developed in Theory of Collective Behaviour (Smelser, 1962, pp. 80-123).

14.   On these movements, see the essay by Donald Stone, "The Human Potential Movement" (Glock and Bellah, 1976, pp. 93-115).

15.   This finding derives from my own research on American religious movements in various cultures (as yet unpublished).

RELIGIONS NEW AND NOT SO NEW:

FRAGMENTS OF AN AGENDA*

R.J. Zwi Werblowsky

The "new religions" are "in". Some pundits even assure us that they are the harbingers or evidence of a "new religious consciousness".[1] Other writers, casting themselves in the role of prophet-preachers with a faintly academic halo and disdaining the false objectivity of the big, bad professionals arrogantly surveying the cult-scene from their scholarly grandstand, offer us enthusiastic or, alternatively, moderately temperate analyses of the long overdue transvaluations of western, instrumental, rationalist, manipulative (other pejorative epithets to be added ad lib) values effected by the young (or not so young) in Berkeley, California (or elsewhere). It is not surprising to find kerygmatic journalism stopping short where it finds it most convenient: a tulku[2] may be extolled as the new spiritual light of the world whilst his record of alcoholism and other unsavoury derailments is studiously ignored. A learned author[3] may praise his favourite Tibetan incarnation for having brought with him to the spirit-starved West "rare Tibetan manuscripts", but unfortunately fail to satisfy the regrettable curiosity of his less euphoric and more academically petty-minded fellow-scholars who may want to know exactly what kind of Mss. and in what sense "unique". (Have their titles or existence been unknown? Have they never been catalogued? Are no other copies to be found in any western library?) Alas, hot-gospelling is no alternative to scholarship, yet students of religion will be excused if in the prevailing climate they are occasionally tempted to interrupt their serious researches and to follow the lure of the sociology of current scholarly as well as pseudo-scholarly activity. Why do certain subjects suddenly become fads? Why is everybody taking to writing on this or that particular subject? Why did every half-baked journalist or graduate divinity student become overnight (after the Jonestown massacre) an authority on "cults"? Of course, every journalist, including some respectable university professors, wants to cash in on a subject while it is "hot". After all, no publisher could hope to turn even the best researched study of Vatican II into a bestseller if sent to press three years after the Council. The rash of "quickie paperbacks" about the People's Temple and "the unaccountable millions of words devoted to Jonestown"[4] are not really all

that unaccountable. Still, one wonders why it was precisely
in the sixties that so many books and studies appeared on the
so-called "new religions" of Japan. The Rush-Hour of the Gods
(thus the title of H. Neill McFarland's fine book of 1967) was
also the rush-hour of books about the shin shukyo.[5]

The trouble with most writings on the new sects viz.,
cults viz., churches viz., movements viz., denominations viz.,
religious groups[6] is that their authors seem to have forgotten,
or never learned, history. After all, practically all the great
religions of the world began as quaint sects. We cannot help
thinking of those odd Jewish sectarians in Jerusalem and Gali-
lee who followed Jesus (and subsequently gave rise to Christianity), or the strange and small group of Arabs in Mecca
listening to Muhammad.[7] Perhaps the interesting thing is not
so much the phenomenon of sects as the problem why and how
some managed to "make it" (e.g., Buddhism) whilst others did
not (e.g., Jainism). An even more interesting problem concerns
the forms and degrees of hostility provoked by new sects and
movements (when, where, in what social i.e., cultural and
political contexts?). One thinks of the violent opposition in
Japan to the Soka Gakkai (at least in their early aggressive
shakabuku[8] stage), or the staggering shamelessness with which
kidnapping parents, employing paid professional "deprogrammers" accuse the Unification (Moon) Church of "brainwashing".
Historians of medieval Europe are still busy writing about the
rise and decline (or extermination) of heretical sects in the
late middle ages, trying to typologize these movements into ec-
clesiastically structured counter-churches (like the Cathars),
and spiritual anarchists (like e.g., the Brethren of the Free
Spirit[9] who also represented a kind of "new religious consciousness"). Students of traditional Chinese (folk) religions
are doing, mutatis mutandis, the same. Anthropologists are
scouring North and South America, Africa, Asia, Melanesia,
and Polynesia in quest of millenarian, prophetic, revitalization, or crisis cults. There is no end to the typological vocabulary: cargo-cults, mahdism, Brazilian messianisms, Indian
revivals form the Pueblo revolt to Pope and Tenkswatawa to
the Sun- and Ghost-Dance outbreaks, African native or "prophetic" or "Zionist" churches (whether in Bantuland or in West
Africa) and so on and so forth.[10] Fortunately for the study of
modern western sects, the nineteenth and early twentieth centuries are still close enough to prevent even completely unhis-
torical minds from forgetting them completely. Aimee Semple Mc-
Pherson may now be forgotten by the prophets of the California "new consciousness", and Father Divine may no longer
be with us, but the Mormons, Jehovah's Witnesses, Seventh-
Day Adventists, Christian Scientists, Bahais, Philadelphians,
and perhaps also Mazadaznan and Abd-ru-shin's "Movement of
the Grail" still are. Thus Scientology, the Rev. Moon, and

Mr. H. Armstrong's Pasadena-based "Worldwide Church of God"[11] can at least be seen in perspective. And if sects multiply by the "natural" process of schisms and split-offs, the sociologists are always at hand with their jargon about "fissiparous tendencies".

Perhaps a parenthesis should be added here to the effect that the proper perspective for viewing the Unification Church is the Far Eastern one. Comparisons, if any, have to be made not with Oral Roberts but with the Soka Gakkai, Tenri-kyo, Meshia-kyo, Tensho-Kotai-Jingu-Kyo etc. as regards eschatological orientation, (near) divine status of the founder, authoritarian structure and the combination of church organization with business enterprises. The comparison also makes it highly probable that after Mr. Moon's demise the mantle will fall on the shoulders of one of his descendants (child or grandchild). Long before American study of religion discovered, and jumped on, the bandwagon of the "new religious cults", the first edition had appeared of a German classic: K. Hutten, Seher, Grübler, Enthusiasten: Das Buch der Sekten (1950), discussing over fifty groups and cults according to a typology which is not our present concern. The tenth, considerably revised and augmented, edition appeared in 1966!

It is a tautology to say that new religions arise because the old ones are no longer perceived or experienced as satisfactory (very often because new factors or situations have arisen: mass-culture, urbanization, secularization, colonial domination or other forms of dependence, shifts in the threshold of expectations and hence of frustrations etc.). Historians and sociologists are therefore interested in finding out about several things.

1) Who are the alienated elements in society capable of becoming the bearers and followers of the new message viz., the disciples of the appropriate charismatic leader?

2) Are the followers statistically or in terms of their social location significant enough to provide the "critical mass" necessary for cultural transformation (of the kind exhibited e.g., by Methodism in eighteenth-century England or, in the twentieth century, with a view to the quantitative and qualitative change in the social locus of youth, by the latter)? Or are they content with creating subcultural ghettos or utopian closed micro-societies? It should be added that occasionally a subcultural ghetto can have a catalytic or exemplary function with regard to the larger society such as e.g., the monastic institution in the Catholic middle ages in Europe or (in a secular transformation) the Israeli kibbutz.

The social role of the new sects is relevant also from another point of view. The alienation that drives believers into their arms, especially the young ones, is largely a social alienation and not merely spiritual confusion or religious quest. The Moon "family" is only one example. In fact many sects have evolved ritual or semi-ritual patterns reminiscent of group therapy, "encounter", and similar forms of koinonia (the latter being not only a venerable Greek word with theological associations but also the name of an extant American sect). One thinks e.g., of the hoza meetings of Rissho-Kosei-Kai and Reiyukai, or of the shared mediumistic experiences (kojo-sesshin) practiced in the Shinnyo-en.

3) How much of the "message" is new wine in old bottles, old wine in new bottles, old wine in old bottles, or new wine in new bottles? Or perhaps no wine at all?

4) To what extent does the "alienation" character of the cult help to explain the social composition of the followers (sex, colour, age; the disadvantaged or dispossessed; in the West the college-educated, affluent, middle-class young are often more sensitive and intelligent, and hence react particularly strongly against what they perceive as the hypocrisy of their parents' culture — this may also explain, at least in part, the disproportionately high percentage of Jewish youngsters in many cults). Last, but not least, there is also the decisive factor best described as "the lure of the exotic". It will be Harvard and Berkeley students who fall for Zen and assorted Tibetan lamas and not students of the universities of Tokyo or Kyoto (as Messrs. Needleman & Co. undoubtedly know).

5) Are there clearly analyzable psycho-social lines of demarcation along which the much overworked typological dichotomy of inner-oriented self-realization religion versus society-oriented world-salvation types of religion can be operationalized?

6) How representative are these typological "ideal types" in view of the far more frequent intermediate phenomena?

7) This leads to the related problem of eschatology, millenarianism and chiliasm. I am not referring here to the commonplace that political liberation or revival movements tend to have a strongly eschatological streak (whether connected with the Second Advent of Christ, the coming of Maitreya, the return of the Ancestors, the arrival of T'ai P'ing (the "Great Peace"), or the dawning of a new age — Aquarius, or Omega Point, or the Su-God — matters little). Far more interesting is the combination of eschatology with non-political or only implicitly political orientations — from the Early Church to Jehovah's Witnesses to most modern Japanese shin shukyo to

the Flying Saucer cults or the group studied by Festinger et al. in When Prophecy Fails. The Japanese "new religions" [11a] (many of which are no longer all that new, having begun long before Meiji and being now in their third or fourth generation), like so many others, well illustrate the development aptly described by Raymond Hammer (in Japan's Religious Ferment, 1962) as the "retreat from eschatology". But there are also forms of completely non-political eschatology (e.g., the dawning of the new spiritual age, either for mankind or for the elect), even as there are "restorative" politico-religious revivals utterly non-utopian and non-eschatological in character. Like many contemporary Islamic movements, they desire the restoration of the lost glories of a past ideal and righteous age rather than the creation of a totally new reality. Some western, especially American students of religion appear to be slightly puzzled, embarassed, or even upset by the spectacle of religions "turning political". The average historian of religion, brought up on Judaism (Moses or the Pharisees), Islam (Muhammad's or that of the Ayatullah Khomeini), Confucianism, Nichiren-Buddhism in Kamakura Japan etc. is far more puzzled by that strange animal called the "separation of church and state".

8) The relationship to science viz., technology — genuine or mythified -- presents another dimension of the problem. Many decades ago the late Prof. H. von Glasenapp, writing about modernization in India, drew attention to the strange mixture of spirituality and pseudo-science (Afterwissenschaft) which it exhibited. The eminent orientalist wrote long before Scientology, Flying Saucers, "Black Boxes" of diverse kinds, Alpha Waves, and Biofeedback had burst upon the world,[12] but he must surely have been aware of the strange antics of some of Europe's foremost scientists — evidently overcompensating for their conscious "scientism" by a subconscious hankering after what they mistook for "spiritual" — falling for the most palpable frauds of psychic media, or constructing cameras for photographing ectoplasms and the like. Dr. Rhine, it should be evident, far from being a pioneer, was the successor of a long line of "research", including the contributors to the Journal of Psychical Research in England and the von Schrenck-Notzings in Germany. His declaration that if his studies established the existence "of disincarnate spirit personalities" then there would be "dramatic proof of spiritual realities...the machine theory would be wrecked once and for all" eloquently says everything. In fact, "proof of survival would squelch forever the dreadful error of the materialistic view of man on which Communism and other gross misconceptions about humanity rest. On the other hand, certainty about it could revitalize religion...". Here, if you want, is the ultimate triumph of crude materialism and the ultimate misconception about the nature of religion! But however that may be, a great many

contemporary eastern spiritual masters owe their success not
merely to their exotic associations (the fact that for many years
they may not have seen the Himalayas which they sport in
their titles is neither here nor there) but to their claim to
combine spirituality with testable "scientific" procedures --
whether Black Boxes or EEGs is immaterial. The enthusiasm of
Komazawa (the Soto-Zen Buddhist university in Tokyo) for
their Alpha-Wave laboratory[13] may have abated a little, but
many Japanese shin shukyo exhibit a strong symbiotic relationship with "science". They are not simply "faith healing" religions (see below) — though the roots of many founders in
traditional shugendo type magic is well documented — but complicated systems and doctrines concerning the structure of the
universe, the physico/spiritual forces operating in it viz., on
its different levels (sometimes combined with traditional conceptions of karma), and the "scientific" methods of concentrating and focusing the cosmic energy and light (by means of
a consecrated amulet) and radiating it (by means of the raised
hand of the practitioner, as through a lens) to the ailing person or to the object needing repair.[14] Of special interest is
the gradual acculturation of some original faith-healing sects[15]
to the mores and values of our technological society. (I leave
it to others to discuss Christian Science.) Denominations like
Tenri-kyo which fifty years ago would still have indignantly
rejected the very idea of medical intervention — believing in
the exclusive efficacy of their amulets and healing ceremonies —
now proudly show off their newest and "most modern" hospital.
The Mahikari organize medical congresses at which slides and
photographs are shown, proving the efficacy of the okiyome
exorcism viz., treatment on severe wounds, burns, cancer,
and even plant growth. (The Meshia-kyo case is slightly different because of the doctrine of "nature farming", shared also by some other sects. The system, which is akin to mulch-
ing, is conceived as the divinely willed method to keep the
world and the environment beautiful, clean, and "natural",
and to prevent environmental pollution and topsoil erosion.
Here the scientific research is designed to prove that nature
farming does, in fact, achieve the results claimed for it). Mention should also be made in this connection of Mrs. Kitamura's
Odoru Shukyo (as it is popularly but inexactly called), which
is remarkable for refusing to promise health-cures or worldly
success, though it implies that these will almost inevitably
follow. The point is that the teaching does not want to dis-
pense cures but to put a person's spirit right. If you genuinely labour for God's kingdom (kami-no-kuni), then the rest
will follow. The Mahikari doctrine, on the other hand, seems
to assume a kind of ex opere operato notion of okiyome.

    9) Not all healing cults surround themselves with "scien-
tific" paraphernalia. Some seem to believe in the direct activity of the spiritual powers (viz., of the Holy Spirit) cutting

through the material and worldly realities. Since sickness is
not just an incidental negative condition but often serves as
a major symbol of the fact that something is morally, spiritually, or karmically wrong viz., "out of joint" (i.e., sickness as the physical mirror-image of sinfulness), healing is
essentially a righting of things and hence (like death and resurrection in a minor key) properly the province of the Holy
Spirit or, in the Far Eastern version, of karmic reparation.
Hence also the logical connection between "speaking tongues"
(as one of the principal manifestations of the presence of the
Spirit) and healing, as exhibited by ever so many charismatic
and pentecostal movements, both Catholic and Protestant. The
content (if any) of the glossolalic message is immaterial. Very
often "the medium has no message" but it is the manifest presence of the spirit that counts.   Mutatis mutandis similar considerations could be applied to the mediumistic group experiences practiced in some of the Japanese "new religions", e.g.,
the kojo-sesshin of the Shinnyo-en sect.

10) Of considerable interest for any phenomenology of religion is the understanding viz., self-understanding of the personality, authority, and role of the founder. Most Christian
sects, committed to the dogma that only Jesus Christ as the
Son of God can claim divinity, are content with preachers, reformers, forerunners, announcers etc. Those who claim to be
more tend to be dismissed automatically as cranks or pathological cases of megalomania (cf., John of Leyden). This phenomenon is doubly interesting in our contemporary, ecumenical
age. Earlier generations of Christian scholars and missionaries had no hesitation to say what they thought about the
Prophet Muhammad, though he claimed prophecy only and no
divinity. To say the same things today would be considered
to be in very bad taste. Yet nobody seems to have any
qualms about qualifying Messrs. Reeve and Muggleton as psy-
chopaths. The reason seems to be that the sect of the Muggle-
tonians no longer exists and that hardly anybody knows that
in the seventeenth and eighteenth centuries there were Christians who used to sing

> I do believe in God alone
> Likewise in Reeve in Muggleton.
> Christ is the Muggletonian king
> To whom they evermore will sing.

The Eastern experience is different. Gods there are galore,
and where every brahmin or guru is a god, or almost so, divinity is cheap (in the words of Prof. A.L. Basham) and even
the divinity of kings need not weigh too heavily on their subjects. Hence the student of Indian religions reacts with greater composure to masters sporting in their titles such impressive (or ridiculous?) epithets as "His Divine Holiness" — unlike

their western devotees who are, undoubtedly deeply moved by
the exotic exaggeration of it all. The Japanese case [16] is different again because of the traditional background of shamanism, spirit possession, and the notion of ikigami (living, present kami). Hence an interesting distinction exists in the typology of the founders of new religions. Whilst most of the Lotus
sects were founded by inspired or even possessed teachers but
not by incarnations of the divine — after all, the locus of
the sacred is a Buddha, Bodhisattva (viz., his manifestation
in a Prophet-Teacher like Nichiren) or a Sutra — matters are
different with the founders of most other shin shukyo. They
were not merely inspired teachers, nor prophets, not even
"spokespersons" (since many of them were women — further evidence of the shamanistic tradition), or representatives of the
deity that had chosen them, but actual representations, incarnations, indwellings, manifestations, or what-have-you, in
the Japanese tradition of living, present, and earthly kami.
This is true of the Foundresses and Founders of Tenri-kyo
(Nakayama Miki), Tensho-Kotai-Jingu-Kyo (Kitamura Sayo),
Sekai-Kyusei-Kyo (Okada Mokichi), and many others. This might
seem to create problems in the matter of succession and for
the definition of the spiritual role of the successor. Generally,
however, the hereditary principle is accepted as a matter of
course (with the notable exception of the Soka Gakkai), and
power struggles or schisms, to the extent that they take place
(as was the case in the Mahikari sect) are, more often than
not, concerned with deciding not who will be the "emperor"
but who will be the "shogun". Seen from a Far Eastern perspective the role attributed theologically to the Rev. Moon
makes perfect sense. It is equally obvious, as has been remarked before, that after his demise the mantle will fall on the
shoulders of one of his descendants — whether child or grandchild is immaterial.

11) The monotheistic tendency of some new religions
should be briefly remarked upon. Evidently monotheism is a
matter-of-course for Christianity-derived movements — whether
in Europe, the Americas, or Black Africa — and hardly calls
for special comment. Indian cults tend to be more henotheistic
viz., monolatrous, but their monistic proclivities can bring
them close to what is usually called monotheism. (Pseudo)-
science based cults similarly have as their point of departure
some abstract or concrete unifying principle. The real surprise is provided by the Japanese shin-shukyo — leaving
aside, for the present, the Lotus sects with their different
(Mahayana) metaphysical presuppositions, no matter whether
we describe these as "monistic" or as "non-dualistic", though
some of our considerations would be applicable to them as
well. The increasingly unified world view of modernity (one
world, one humanity, one history, one destiny, one universe,
one salvation — or none at all — for humanity and the

world) encourages monotheistic tendencies. Hence the "ten thousand gods" of the Shinto tradition (yao-yorozu) are out as far
the new religions are concerned, and each new sect preaches
one specific god. His name is, of course, as important to the
sect as it was to Moses (cf., Exodus 3:13), but to the historian of religion interested in the phenomenon as such it matters relatively little whether the deity concerned calls itself
the Su-God, or Tenri-o-no-mikoto or Tensho-Kotai-Jingu, or
Miroku-o-mi-kami.[17] Japanese religions, unlike "biblical religions" are generally not militantly and aggressively fanatic,
though they may be "implicitly exclusive" in spite of their
much talked-about syncretism. Hence also their monotheism is
a low-key one, and only very few shin shukyo feel impelled
to make repeated public statements on the subject. Oomoto-kyo
likes to refer to itself as the only Japanese monotheistic religion and in this capacity (and aided by Christian ecumenical
fervour) has installed a (shinto-type) Oomoto altar in the
(episcopalian) Cathedral of St. John the Divine in New York.
To the writer's admittedly limited knowledge this is an exceptional case.

12) Another aspect inviting closer study is the political
tendency of the new religions[18] — right or left (which are
utterly misleading and almost meaningless terms, but used
here for the sake of brevity). The counterculture type movements of blessed memory were, in the nature of things, aligned with what is broadly designated as the left. The same holds
true of most of the contestataires in the great establishment
churches, not to speak of the "Liberation Theologies" in Latin
America and elsewhere. On the other hand most fundamentalist-
revivalist type of sectarian movements tend to the right or at
least to conservative value systems. Most of the Japanese shin
shukyo too are very much to the right, many of them in fact
refusing to admit members with Communist affiliations or sym-
pathies, though few of them are as extreme in their anti-
communist crusading fervour as the genri undo (i.e., the Rev.
Moon's Unification Church). It is still too early to judge
whether the Soka Gakkai's flirtation with the People's Republic of China is a matter of religious-moral-political convictions or a matter of political expediency and jumping on a
fashionable bandwagon. Generally speaking the reason seems
to lie not so much in an inherent inclination to fundamentalist orthodoxy (as in American evangelical groups) as in the
fact that the Japanese counterculture students are not sufficiently interested in what the West calls "religion" or "spirituality" to go in for new religions. As a result, those who nevertheless do, evidently prefer the right-of-centre counterculture,
"counter" in the sense of rejecting the mindless materialism of
modern Japan.

13) A brief observation should be made about the non-sacerdo-
tal (lay) character of many new religions, especially in Japan.

Of course, the gradual emergence of a clergy-like class is inevitable wherever the development of a religious group requires the
services and availability of full-time teachers, practitioners, or
other types of leaders. Nevertheless, it is a fact that practically
all new religions (the exceptions are very few indeed) were founded
by "laymen" viz., laypersons who suddenly experienced a calling,
and that many such groups still continue to insist on describing
themselves as "laymen's associations". These facts are not without
significance, and they indicate an emancipation of religious consciousness from ecclesiastical institutions and sacerdotal authority as such. The phenomenon is particularly striking in
the case of the Japanese Buddhist revival groups, and
especially the Lotus sects (Rissho-Kosei-Kai, Reiyukai etc.)
which even provide the proverbial exception that proves the
rule. The Soka Gakkai, as a laymen's organization (i.e., an
organization of lay followers devoted with special zeal to the
Lotus doctrine as preached by Nichiren and handed down by
the temple and priesthood of one particular sect, the Nichiren-
shoshu) has a strong bond, in fact religious dependence, on
the main sanctuary of the Nichiren-shoshu, the Daiseki-ji. In
due course the excessive and powerful charisma of the Soka
Gakkai leader (and the implicit danger of his embarking willy
nilly on the road towards Bodhisattvahood viz., the role of
"the Nichiren of our age") became too much of a threat. Suspicion on the part of, and conflict with, the Daiseki-ji priesthood became inevitable, and a schism was averted because
(this seems the most probable explanation) Mr. Ikeda was a
genuinely faithful son of the Nichiren Church and as such did
not wish to found an independent denomination. He, therefore,
preferred to resign as President (1979) and to become "Honor-
ary President" of the Soka Gakkai. Other sects, which do not
have such a strong tie to a traditional ecclesiastical institution have a much easier time in maintaining their characteristic combination of revivalist and lay. Since lay movements are
nowadays a major feature in the life of also the great establishment churches in the West, this aspect of modern religiosity would seem to deserve more attention, due notice being
paid, of course, to one major distinction: the value-system
espoused by most western establishment contestataires (unlike
most fundamentalist sects) tends to the "left", whereas the Japanese shin shukyo, Buddhist and non-Buddhist alike, seem
committed to conservative values.

14) A final word should be devoted to the sociology of
hostility to new religious movements. The persecution of the Japanese shin shukyo by the pre-1945 regime belongs to a different category altogether -- as does the persecution of Jehovah's Witnesses
by the Nazis (described by Christine King in Chapter 8 of this volume). The hostility to the shakabuku practice of the Soka Gakkai
was largely provoked by the obnoxious and agressive proselytizing methods which were part of it in earlier days, before the
movement became domesticated and more respectable. Even accu-

sations of criminal activities were not lacking. In the West only Scientology and the Unification Church provoked reactions of
similar violence. Even right-wing sects in Japan hesitate to enter
upon too visible alliances with the genri undo.The American hostility is particularly fascinating in view (as has been remarked above)
of the mind-boggling shamelessness with which kidnapping parents employing paid professional deprogrammers accuse the
church of brainwashing. Also the accusation of aggresive proselytizing is extremely interesting. After all, most churches
and denominations have at one time or another aggressively
proselytized. It is true that former missionary churches have
become more civilized in the modern, secularized, pluralistic
setting and prefer to speak of "testifying". (The Jewish case
of retreat into their shell after facing a hostile world, and
their allegedly universalist solution of providing a kind of
ethical unitarianism [Noahite religion] as their message to the
lower breeds, is a different subject altogether.) But no sen-
sible historian of religion would expect a new evangelizing
movement to exhibit the "old age" (not to say senility) symptoms of traditional denominations trying to come to terms with
secular pluralism. Hence several other hypotheses should be
considered and, of course, carefully tested. There is the possibility of a racial component. Rev. Moon is Korean, and Ko-
reans are not particularly well-liked, neither in Asia nor in
the United States. Things might have taken a different turn
had the Rev. Moon been a Tibetan tulku, or an Indian guru
(with or without the title "His Divine Holiness"), or a Japanese Zen master. The street-begging, soliciting, and fund-
raising ("testifying") of the young devotees do not go down
too well with the ethos of an American society which in this
respect duplicates the characteristic Confucian reaction to
Buddhist mendicancy. Even Catholic "mendicant" orders have
learned to make money by other methods than begging on
street corners or on doorsteps. The Salvation Army do, indeed,
solicit in the streets but within a socially acceptable motivational framework: donations are visibly converted into hot
soup and shelters for the down-and-out and not used for the
benefit of the church or for public relations operations such
as the International Cultural Foundation. The American public
condescendingly forgives its Sikh-type "kids" their "funny"
dress and turbans, and the "divine music" wafting through
their Golden Temple vegetarian restaurants, not to speak of the
comfortable shakti-sandals sold in their Golden Emporium
shops — these guys clearly live up to the sacred American
ethos. They do not beg but work hard for an honest living,
and their outlandishness (unlike that of the Hare Krishna) is
kept within acceptable limits — proof that even Gringo-Sikhs
can share the Protestant work ethic. Last, but not least,
there is the Unification Church's anti-communist crusading politics. It is more than probable that the average American liberal, churched or unchurched, loathes communism and is afraid
of it. It is, indeed, wonderful to live in the Bay Area, to encourage and even protect the "Reverend" Jim Jones, and to de-

nounce the "Establishment" and all the evils incarnate in the
American way of life — as long as one can do so cheaply and
at discount rates, and with the sure knowledge that one will
not end up in the Gulag Archipelago. How wonderful to be a
protesting student at Harvard, Chicago, Berkeley, Kent State,
or wherever (especially when the draft hangs over your
head), in the safe knowledge that the corrupt and unredeem-
able establishment will spare you the fate in store (in similar
circumstances) for your counterparts in Moscow, Prague, East
Berlin and Peking. The really unforgivable sin of the Rev.
Moon may have been to have let the cat out of the bag and
to have said the things which the average liberal would like
to say but will not, cannot, must not, dare not say because
looking in the mirror — like all narcissists — he is afraid
of the reflection of the late Senator Joseph McCarthy of Wiscon-
sin grinning back at him. And, as the Baker in Lewis Carroll's The Hunting of the Snark would have said, "this notion
I cannot endure". A mere hypothesis, but perhaps one worth
exploring.

It goes without saying that the "explanations" proffered
in the preceding paragraph are insufficient by themselves.
There are many local and regional variations that have to be
taken into account. This applies both to the activities of the
Unification Church and to the manifestations of hostility. Thus
it would appear that many of the accusations (e.g., bringing
youngsters into the communes under false pretences; using
"heavenly deception" — or less heavenly one; lowering the
resistance of the prospective converts by undernourishment,
lack of sleep, enforced isolation from the normal environment
etc.)[19] are specific to the Californian scene but not typical of
other Unification Church centres. (After all, everybody agrees
that it would be grossly unfair to judge the U.S.A. on the
basis of observations made in the Bay Area!) As regards hostility, for instance, the accusation that Mr. Moon "destroys
families" looms large in (at least theoretically) still family-
oriented France, whereas in Germany's vaterlose Gesellschaft
(to use Mitscherlich's term), other arguments are used. Nevertheless the fact remains that a general phenomenon also requires general explanations.

NOTES

* I wish to make use of this occasion to express my thanks
to the Kokusai Koryu Kikin (The Japan Foundation) for a
Research Fellowship granted to me in 1978 and which enabled me, over a period of six months, to pursue
my earlier studies of the "new religions". Many

of the implicit or explicit references to Japanese religion contained in this essay are the product of that
fruitful period of research. The first draft of this paper
was written during a month which I spent as a "resi-
dent scholar" of the Rockefeller Foundation at their in-
comparable study centre, the Villa Serbelloni in Bellagio.

1.   Cf., Glock and Bellah, eds., 1976, and the review by
Eileen Barker in Numen vol. XXVI, 1979: 274-7.

2.   In Tibetan Buddhism: a reincarnation of a very high
order.

3.   Needleman, 1970.

4.   Both phrases are taken from Decter, 1979 -- the only
sane and really instructive piece of writing on the subject.

5.   The literature on the Japanese "new religions" is enormous. A good guide is Earhart, 1970 (96) which takes the
bibliography up to the date of publication. A revised and up-
dated edition is currently (1980) in press.

6.   This string of nouns is not meant to be facetious. We
are all conscious of our debt to Weber, Troeltsch, et al., and
these giants would be the first to acknowledge that ideal-type
concepts are not labels to be stuck on bottles in a chemist's
shop. If there is one thing more objectionable than the obsession with labelling, then it is the obsessive Troeltsch-flogging
indulged in by some would-be sociologists.

7.   An interesting point is raised by these small fringe
sects which want to become world religions.   How does a small
sect which knows that it is (at least relatively) small, yet
at the same time also believes itself to be the only true religion and way to the salvation of the world, relate to its
size? On the one hand there is the immanent and necessary
drive towards expansion viz., missionary activity, and on the
other hand the (conscious or subconscious) knowledge that in
our pluralistic world of competing denominations they will always remain smaller or less small minority groups but —
unlike Christianity, or Islam, or Buddhism — never become
world religions.

8.   A Buddhist term signifying the militant and aggressive (as opposed to the mild and persuasive) conquest of evil.
In the Nichiren tradition it meant aggressive and violently
threatening preaching. The Soka Gakkai in its beginnings took
up this concept as the guiding principle of its proselytizing
techniques.

9.   A penetrating analysis of these groups is given by Scholem, 1974: 13ff.

10.   A good, though already out of date bibliography can be found in La Barre, 1971: 3ff. Personally I happen to disagree with some of the arguments in this article as well as with the term "crisis cult" which is almost meaningless since most religions started as "crisis cults".

11.   Cf., Hopkins, 1974.

11a.   Cf., Blacker, 1971, pp. 563–600.

12.   Cf., for example, Evans, 1973.

13.   Cf., for example, Akishige, ed., 1968.

14.   Cf., the gojorei of the Sekai-Kyusei-Kyo, or the okiyome of the Mahikari sect. The practice did not, of course, originate with these groups but goes back to earlier movements; cf. Davis, 1980. In many respects the Oomoto-Kyo is one of the most important and interesting — not only because it is one of the "older" new religions, but mainly because it exhibits some of the "ideal type" features: the founders are considered — or even considered themselves — as divine (as evidenced by their imperial-type burial mounds or by the fact that Onisaburo Deguchi rode about on a white horse); the millenarian element is emphasised by the role which Miroku (the Japanese form of Maitreya, the future Saviour-Buddha in the Buddhist pantheon) plays in this "Shinto-type" religion. It is from Oomoto that Miroku-o-mi-kami was taken over by the Sekai Kyusei Kyo.

15.   Cf., the title of C.B. Offner and H. van Straelen, Modern Japanese Religions, with Special Emphasis on their Doctrine of Healing, 1963.

16.   The enormous amount of work done on the Japanese shin shukyo has diverted attention from the Chinese material. On Chinese sects and folk religions until the twentieth century cf., the work of de Groot, D. Overmeyer, and the volume edited by C. Chesneaux. A recent Chinese "new religion", the T'ien-te Sheng-chiao is described by Welch and Yü in Numen vol. XXVII, 1980.

17.   Usener's classic work (1896) pursued other aims both substantively and methodologically. Our interest here is focussed on the monotheistic character of the new sects, no matter what the genetic background of the deity's name.

18.   This is not the place to go into all the complications generated by the presence or absence of the American-type separation of church and state. Suffice it to say that church and state are not identical with religion and society. In fact, the official and legal separation of the first pair can function as a convenient mechanism for promoting the symbiosis of the second pair. This, I suspect, has taken place in the U.S. On the other hand even cynics should (at least temporarily) suspend their cynicism and pay homage to the, at times, heroically obsessive tradition of civil liberties in the U.S., a tradition which accounts for a great many abuses as well as hostilities encountered in the field of organized religious life. The price which American society pays for its commitment to civil liberties, particularly with reference to the religious and sectarian scene, at times appears to be rather high.

19.   These practices   viz. allegations are described in several, partly autobiographical books reviewed in the New York Review of Books, Oct. 25, 1979, by Francine du Plessix Gray ("The Heavenly Deception"). In order to see this accusing and condemnatory article in proper perspective one should bear in mind that Ms. Gray is herself a cultist -- though her cult-heroes are not the Moonies but the dissenting radicals and contestaires in the great establishment churches like Ivan Ilic or the Berrigans; see F. du Plessix Gray, Divine Disobedience, 1969. On the whole issue, especially with reference to the Moonies, c.f. Bryan Wilson (ed.), The Social Impact of the New Religions, New York, 1981 and especially the chapter by A.D. Shupe Jr. and D.G. Bromley (ibid. pp. 179-215) "Apostates and Atrocity Stories: Some Parameters in the Dynamics of Deprogramming". See also J. Richardson (ed.), The Brainwashing/ Deprogramming Debate: Sociological, Psychological, Legal and Historical Perspectives, 1982, and especially Eileen Barker's chapter "With Enemies Like That. . .Some Functions of Deprogramming as an aid to Sectarian Membership". See also H. Richardson (ed.), New Religions and Mental Health, New York & Toronto, 1980.

WORLD ORDER AND RELIGIOUS MOVEMENTS*

Robert Wuthnow

Typically the consideration of new religious movements leads to questions about the social conditions facilitating the emergence of these movements. These questions, in turn, require an investigation of the structure and connections among broader social patterns. At any particular historical juncture, such as the past decade, it is difficult to generate a convincing analysis of these larger patterns without some reference either to spatial or to temporal comparisons. From this perspective, the new religions have provided an incentive for reexamining in a broad comparative focus the social conditions giving rise to different kinds of religious unrest.

In my own work on the new religions I have been particularly interested in the claims that have been made in many social scientific discussions as well as in the writings produced by some of the movements themselves about the broader significance of these movements as indicators of social change. Such claims are generally supported with references to various historical antecedents, as evidenced, for example, by the use of the phrase "Third Great Awakening" to characterize the recent period in American religion or, during the somewhat more optimistic years of the early 1970s, by analogies between the current "age of Aquarius" and the Renaissance. For the most part, these analogies have remained superficial, rather than being rooted in a systematic comparison of the historical conditions surrounding different periods of religious ferment. Accordingly, it is not surprising that the conclusions drawn have varied almost without limit.

The present essay grew out of a period of extended reading on the history of modern European and American religious movements which was initiated by the frustrations just noted. This reading in religious history quickly demonstrated a need to pay special attention to the dynamics of broad economic and political transformations as well. What emerged is not only an attempt to distinguish among some important types of historical religious movements, but also a preliminary formulation concerning these broad social transformations. Though the scope required to examine these broad developments in relation to one another means that many historical events have had to be surveyed, albeit in condensed terms, this essay should not be interpreted as an attempt to propose some new Procrustean

47

bed for the examination of history. It should rather be regarded as an examination of a particular analytic layer of history. With the exception of work in recent years concerned with the idea of world order, this layer has been relatively neglected. It seems particularly relevant, however, to a comparative analysis of the social conditions in which new religious movements have appeared.

Against all the predictions of nineteenth-century sociologists, religious movements have survived and flourished in the modern world. We need not seek their causes in benighted minds or in abnormal personalities. Nor need we posit superhuman charismatic leadership to explain their persistence and frequency. For religious movements have emanated from the central social processes of the modern world itself. Groups whose lives have been intruded upon by the expanding world-economy have sought refuge in the security of religion. Rising cadres have legitimated their new status with religious creeds. Basic changes in the structure of world order have characteristically produced, and in turn have been nurtured by, exceptional outpourings of religious activity.

But religious movements have been distributed neither evenly nor at random in space and time. The early sixteenth century stands out as a time of great religious experimentation. The early seventeenth century also is notable, less as a time of sweeping reform, than as a time for a vast number and variety of new religious movements. The period in between was one of intense religious activity, but did not spawn religious movements in the numbers or magnitude of either the preceding or succeeding periods. In the eighteenth century, definitions of ultimate reality were fundamentally transformed by the Enlightenment, much as they had been by the Reformation. But it was not until the 1830s and 1840s that religious movements began again to multiply in large numbers. From the 1860s to the end of the nineteenth century, there was a period of relative calm in religious movements, although the seeds of another world-shaking redefinition of ultimate reality were being sown in the gradual evolution of Marxism. In the twentieth century, every decade has witnessed religious movements, but these movements have varied greatly in kind and in location. Few decades have given rise to as many religious movements as the late 1960s and early 1970s. By the early 1970s, in fact, some estimates suggested that the number of local new religious groups in America might number in the thousands, with some of the larger movements claiming adherents in the hundreds of thousands (Wuthnow, 1978).

In light of their uneven occurrence, it has been tempting for social scientists to seek the causes of modern religious movements in some form of rapid social change and its accompanying tensions and strain (cf., Glock and Stark, 1965: 242-

-259; Wilson, 1970c). Efforts have been made to classify the various religious responses to social strain and to show that different kinds of strain produce different kinds of religious movements. But these efforts run into trouble when confronted with historical reality.

They fail to explain, for example, why the rapid industrial changes of the 1880s and 1890s in the United States produced relatively few religious movements in comparison with the 1830s and 1840s. They fail to explain why the disruptions of two world wars produced fewer religious movements than the 1960s, or why Britain experienced more religious movements in the 1840s than it did in the 1780s during the Industrial Revolution. They also fail to explain why different periods have nourished wholly different types of religious movements. There have been profound reformations and there have been ephemeral cults. There have been great religious revivals and sweeping religious defections. Movements have developed within the churches as well as outside of the churches and against the churches. Conventional accounts of religious sects and cults have said little about many of these kinds of movements.

RELIGIOUS MOVEMENTS AND WORLD ORDER

My reading of history convinces me that modern religious movements can be understood better in conjunction with major changes in world order than they can be by looking only at changes within societies. By "world order," I mean simply the presence of a transnational division of labor in which societies and members of societies participate, necessitating recurrent, patterned exchange (economic, political, and cultural) across national boundaries. World orders are stratified into dominant, "core" areas and dependent, "periphery" areas. As with societies, the status of these areas and the relations among them tend to be patterned and legitimated by broad definitions of reality.

The modern world order had its origins in sixteenth-century Europe as the various local and regional economies of the Mediterranean, the Hanse, France, England, and the Baltic came to be integrated into a single system of production and exchange (Wallerstein, 1974). At the outset of the sixteenth century, the European world order was politically dominated by the expanding Spanish Hapsburg dynasty. But what distinguished the European world order from the various world-systems that had flourished in antiquity, and from contemporaries such as the Ottoman Empire, was that the Hapsburg dynasty failed in its attempts to bring the European world order under the hegemony of a centralized political empire. By the middle of the seventeenth century, a new system of world order, which later critics would call "mercantilism," had come into being, dominated by a politically decentralized core (England, France, and to a lesser extent the Netherlands), and encompassing all of Europe (but not Russia), colonies throughout much of North, Central, and South America, and trading centers in coastal parts of West Africa, India, China, and the Indonesian Archipelago (Schmoller, 1896; Chirot, 1977). As the colonial and protectionist trade policies of this system became increasingly cumbersome, a system of free trade dominated by the British empire gradually susperseded the mercantilist system, resulting in a world-economy which included nearly all parts of the globe by the end of the nineteenth century (Polanyi, 1944; Fieldhouse, 1966; Hobsbawm, 1969). In the twentieth century, after the experience of two world wars, the establishment of a communist sector, and numerous nationalist movements throughout the Third World, the capitalist world-economy has continued to prevail and expand, but within a provisional diplomatic framework characterized by military tensions and economic uncertainty.

The main religious movements in modern history have been closely associated with periods of crisis and transition in the expanding capitalist world order so defined. Three kinds of periods, in particular, have given rise to intense religious activity: (a) periods in which the dominant world order has expanded rapidly to the point of producing strain in the basic institutions linking together core and periphery areas; (b) periods of overt polarization and conflict between core and periphery; and (c) periods in which newly stabilized patterns of world order are being reconstituted.

The first — expansionary periods — are best illustrated by the first half of the sixteenth century, in which the Hapsburg dynasty expanded to its farthest reaches; by the early eighteenth century, which saw the first wave of colonial expansion under the mercantilist system; and by the years surrounding the turn of the present century, in which the second wave of colonial expansion took place. The second — periods of polarization — are most evident in the late sixteenth, the late eighteenth, and the early twentieth centuries, all of which were dominated by international wars involving both core and periphery powers. The third — periods of reconstitution — are most clearly evidenced in the early seventeenth century, in the early nineteenth century, and in the period following World War II, in which the mercantilist, free trade, and contemporary (provisionally known as "detente") forms of world order, respectively, were in the process of formation. The differences in the political and economic processes prevailing in these three kinds of periods have led to major differences in the kinds of religious activity characterizing these periods.

The kinds of religious activity generated in each period also differ depending on whether it occurs among groups

whose relation to power is rising or among groups whose relation to power is declining (cf., Tilly, 1969). In expansionary
periods, the main groups whose power increases are new political and economic cadres in periphery areas, and the main
groups whose power decreases are members of the lower orders
in periphery areas who lose traditional rights vis-à-vis these
cadres. In periods of polarization, representatives of periphery areas struggling to secure independence from the dominant
core have tended to gain power, while representatives of the
core have typically lost power. In periods of reconstitution,
strata associated with emergent patterns of international exchange within each society have been most likely to gain power, while strata associated with decaying patterns of international exchange have been likely to lose power.

The perspective afforded by regarding the context of religious movements as world order, rather than societies, makes
it possible to better identify the major forms that modern religious movements have taken, and to specify the important social conditions that have produced them. This identification
is based on a simple argument: A population's place in the
larger world order strongly affects the manner in which it defines the major problems of its existence, and therefore, the
nature of its religious orientations. These religious orientations, for their part, channel the kinds of actions that people
take, and therefore, affect their influence upon the world order. Without too much difficulty we can place the forms of
modern religious movements in the following categories: revitalization, reformation, religious militancy, counter-reform, religious accomodation, and sectarianism. In the pages that follow I shall attempt to outline briefly the social conditions at
the level of world order that have facilitated the formation of
each of these kinds of religious movements. This will serve as
a context then for some brief observations about the relations
between world order and contemporary religious movements.

REVITALIZATION

The term "revitalization" is Anthony Wallace's (1956).
However, I would like to give it a more restrictive meaning
which is both more in keeping with the movements with which
Wallace was most concerned and more useful for discriminating
among kinds of movements. Revitalization movements are attempts involving some form of religious ideology to collectively
restore or reconstruct patterns of life that have been radically disrupted or threatened. The main varieties of revitalization movements include (a) nativistic movements, which attempt
to purify their members from the influences of alien persons
or customs; (b) revivalistic movements, which attempt to redis-
cover simple or natural styles of life perceived as being
threatened by modern culture; (c) cargo cults, which attempt

to import advantages supposedly available from alien persons
or ideas; (d) millenarian movements, which attempt to prepare
their members for the coming of an apocalyptic world transformation; and (e) messianic movements, which attempt to prepare for the coming of a divine saviour. Periods of revitalization may combine a number of these responses.

Conventional accounts of revitalization movements have
emphasized social disruption as their source, but not all sorts
of disruption produce revitalization. Natural disasters have
displaced entire communities, but seldom have they been the
source of revitalization movements. During World War II, much
of Europe fell victim to devastation, yet largely without such
movements developing. The kind of disruption that has produced revitalization movements most often has come from contact between traditional populations and a dominant cultural
system (cf., Worsley, 1968). Such contact occasionally has
been disruptive because of forced migration and resettlement,
or because of violent conquest. But these disruptions usually
have not produced revitalization movements, because they themselves impose new forms of social organization (e.g., Wolf,
1959: 176-201). The kind of cultural contact that has most often produced revitalization movements is that which creates
cleavages between local elites and the mass majority.

Cleavages of this sort have occurred on the widest scale
during periods of rapid expansion in the modern world-
economy. As trade flourishes and new markets become integrated into the world-economy, local elites who have previously been dependent upon local economies participate in the benefits of broader markets. Their new prosperity gives them greater power vis-à-vis subject populations, whose traditional
rights can now be curtailed or neglected. Cleavage between
local elites and subject populations is not only economically
disadvantageous but socially disorganizing for these populations, since local elites in such settings typically remain in
charge of distributing social services and enforcing the regulations that affect daily life. Revitalization movements provide
hopes that transcend immediate deprivations and inspire new
modes of social organization.

These conditions are clearly illustrated in the origins
of the Anabaptist movements of the early sixteenth century,
which developed during a period of rapid expansion in trade,
population, prices, political hegemony, and capitalist agriculture throughout Europe. This expansion brought to the territorial landlords and city magistrates of the German states,
the Swiss Confederation, and Hapsburg Austria new opportunities for production and exchange beyond the local market, permitting and encouraging the erosion of seigneurial obligations.
The sale or division of common lands, the replacement of land
tenure with contractual relations, and the centralization of

judicial functions resulted from this growth. In the wake of these infringements of traditional rights under the old "common" law, the Anabaptist movements occurred first and most extensively among those peasants who had enjoyed the greatest prosperity and freedom under these customs, and therefore, were most disinherited by their erosion (Williams, 1962).

Similar effects are again apparent in the early eighteenth century during the commercial and colonial expansion of the mercantilist system; for example, in the early Methodist movement among the miners at Bristol, in the religious awakening among the urban poor in Scotland, and in the various prophet cults among the Indians in North America. The same effects are also evident during the early years of the twentieth century in areas newly incorporated into the free trade system; for example, the Watchtower movement in South Africa, the widespread influence of Pentecostalism among the Toba Indians in Northern Argentina, the spiritualist movement in Singapore, and the cargo cults in Melanesia (Wilson, 1973).

The distinctive diversity of revitalization is a function, first, of the fact that these movements are aimed at restoring disparate local customs in the face of an expanding world-economy, and second, of the different forms in which this expansion becomes manifest. For example, revivalistic movements that stress individual salvation and piety, such as early Methodism, have been more common where individuals have been displaced from traditional groups and incorporated separately into new economic contexts. In contrast, cargo cults and nativistic movements have been more likely where whole groups have been collectively displaced, as among the North American Indians.

The evolution of revitalization movements has also varied with the kind of expansion experienced. Where commercial expansion has been accompanied by settlement colonies, revitalization movements have tended to be short-lived due to the reorganization or extinction of native populations. Where expansion has occurred through the incorporation of domestic lower classes into new occupational roles, these movements have generally evolved into established religious organizations, as in the evolution of Methodism in England. Revitalization movements have persisted as such on the widest scale among populations exposed to the dominant world order but not fully incorporated into its rights or style of life, as evidenced by the continued spread of these movements in the Third World.

REFORMATION

It has been suggested on numerous occasions that there have been three ideological reformations of unparalleled

significance since the inception of the modern world order: the
Protestant Reformation, the Enlightenment, and the growth of
Marxism. Each successfully institutionalized a fundamental redefinition of ultimate reality. Of all religious movements, reformations have been the most distinctively international and
can be understood only in the context of world order.

Reformations have been carried by rising elites in periphery areas during periods of rapid expansion in the world-
system. Overall economic expansion incorporates these elites
into wider markets and, as previously suggested, increases
their freedom relative to subject populations. In the extreme,
economic and political expansion has also created greater administrative burdens for core areas than for periphery areas,
significantly increasing the competitive advantages of periphery elites in relation to the core. The correlative decentraliza-
tion in the distribution of world power has afforded opportunities for the growth of new ideas, especially ones that challenge the hegemony of the core and legitimate the rising status of the periphery.

The Protestant Reformation occurred in the context of
rapid population growth, a long-term rise in grain prices,
great expansion in the volume and circulation of money due
to the importation of bullion from America, naval and military
innovations, and an intensification and broadening of trade.
This expansion greatly benefited the German and Polish nobil-
ity, the Swiss city magistrates, and the Dutch and English
merchants, all of whom prospered from the expanding trade
between the Baltic and the Mediterranean. It was among these
peripheral cadres the Reformation first became institutionalized. The reformers' attacks against the Church implicitly de-
sacralized the Hapsburg empire, whose legitimacy rested heavily in the defense of universal faith, and broadened access
to legitimate authority. In the periphery the Reformation
prompted the secularization of church lands, giving elites rev-
enues independent of church and other taxes, and encouraging
land reform beneficial to commercial agriculture. The net effect of this placed the periphery in a more favorable trading
position in the world-economy. After the middle of the sixteenth century, owing significantly to the financial burdens
which Spain incurred in combating the Protestant heresies, the
core of the European economy shifted increasingly to the
north, and with it the Reformation became firmly established.

Like the Reformation, the Enlightenment and the institutionalization of Marxism also took place during periods of de-
mographic, economic, and territorial expansion, the first during the years in which the mercantilist system had spread to
its farthest reaches through commercial, industrial, and colonial expansion, the second during the global explosion of
trade and imperialism after the turn of the present century.

The Enlightenment attracted the rising commercial and industrial classes in peripheral sectors of the world-economy, such as Manchester, Scotland, and North America, and was only later institutionalized in areas such as France and Prussia. Marxism was also most successfully institutionalized in areas peripheral to the European metropolis. Both challenged the legitimacy of prevailing patterns of world order and encouraged successful economic reforms, respectively of labor and capital, in the periphery. In all three cases, these were reformations from above, gaining institutionalization before achieving mass popularity.

The distinctive ideological coherence of each global reformation inhered in its opposition to the sacred assumptions underlying the prevailing world order. These assumptions were made the explicit objects of profanation: Church as Harlot, mercantilist protection as inimical to national wealth, bourgeois culture as false consciousness. Each reformation most vigorously attacked the rituals binding people to their most sacred institutions: the sacraments (for which Luther was excommunicated), the laws and tariffs of the mercantilist state, the fetishism of commodities in the free market. At the same time, each reformation posed a new definition of ultimate reality that liberalized access to the sacred: salvation by faith, freedom in reason, justice through proletarian revolution. The success of each reformation was determined by the conjunction of these ideas with the rising status of the elites that were attracted to new definitions of reality.

RELIGIOUS MILITANCY

Relatively little attention has been paid to religious militancy as a type of social movement; yet, some of the most familiar of modern religious and quasi-religious experiments — Calvinists, Jacobins, Bolsheviks — have been of this kind. I shall define religious militancy as any diffuse movement which in the guise of an ultimate definition of reality actively attempts to overthrow an established social order through violent or forceful means. Though the offspring of reformations, these movements have typically espoused a more radical doctrinal departure from received definitions of reality, have believed in a more avenging God, and have championed the authority of the minority over the majority. They have generally been highly organized into tightly knit, strictly disciplined struggle groups.

Although many religious movements have taken militant stands, the broadest and most successful outbreaks of religious militancy have been among cadres in the periphery during periods of deep polarization and conflict in world order.

These have been periods in which widespread economic instability and stagnation have produced divisive political strain within core areas, especially where these areas have been politically decentralized. Instability and strain of this sort have typically resulted in efforts on the part of the core to effectively tighten control over economically or politically strategic periphery areas. But these restrictions have seldom been received lightly in the periphery, particularly among elites having grown strong in autonomy during times of expansion and prosperity. The usual consequence has been conflict between periphery and core, as for example, in the revolt of the Netherlands against Spain, the American revolution against England, and the various anti-colonial revolts of the twentieth century.

The emergence of radically militant religious groups has been a function of the distinctive state of world order during periods of polarization. The weakened position of the core due to economic reversals and increasing military and bureaucratic expenditures has inhibited its ability to crush the formation of militant movements in the periphery. This has particularly been so when the resources of the core have been preoccupied with internal factionalism and war. Militant movements have been facilitated further by the social disorganization accompanying war, once war has emerged between core and periphery. An overwhelming number of the Dutch Calvinists who revolted against Spanish domination in the late sixteenth century, for example, were exiles from earlier purges in the Netherlands and elsewhere throughout Europe (Geyl, 1932). Beyond these conditions, a decisive circumstance contributing to the rise and spread of religious militancy has been the fact that periods of polarization in world order have usually followed upon the heels of successful reformations which have left the world divided ideologically and politically. The important consequences for militant religious movements have been twofold. First, these movements have been able to gain strength through international alliances and, indeed, have typically espoused highly internationalistic orientations (a fact that Troeltsch, 1960, emphasizes in his discussion of Calvinism, for example). Second, international political divisions have tended to promote competing domestic factions benefiting from, and therefore supporting, alternative foreign policies (the War of the Three Henrys being an extreme example). Internal rivalry of this sort has necessitated disciplined loyalty within the ranks of such factions. Militant religious devotion has been of strategic value to political mobilization in such periods of polarization.

COUNTER-REFORM

Counter-reforms may be characterized as movements among institutionalized representatives of ultimate reality to strengthen the moral obligations that bind individuals to the corporate order. The beliefs of these movements conceive of ultimate reality in corporate terms and stress the immanence of ultimate reality in institutions representing the corporate order. Attainment of a relation with ultimate reality is made contingent upon participation in corporate sacraments and ceremonies. Examples include the renewal of Thomism in sixteenth-century Spain, the Gallican revival in eighteenth-century France, and the religious nationalism of the interwar years in the present century.

Counter-reforms have tended to occur in core areas during periods of polarization in world order, usually at least partly in reaction to the challenge of reformations and militant movements. It was in the context of the Protestant revolts, military setbacks, price inflation, and imperial bankruptcy that the Counter-Reformation experienced its greatest successes in the Hapsburg domains. It was in the period of colonial revolt against the mercantilist system, accompanied by growing disaffection among the lower classes and increasing rivalry and conflict among the core powers, that the romantic reaction against the Enlightenment emerged with its Rousseauean emphasis upon the authority of the general will. Similarly, it was in the aftermath of World War I, followed by the collapse of the balance of power system and the international gold standard which had undergirded the free market world order, that fascist ideologies commanding quasi-religious devotion spread throughout much of Europe.

In each case, the geopolitical conditions were much the same. Increasing military and administrative expenditures on the part of the core, together with declining export markets and enlarged foreign debts, produced an unfavorable balance of trade for the core, weakening further its domestic economy. To maintain the traditional system of stratification under these circumstances placed greater burdens, especially in the form of taxation, upon the lower strata. Declining economic opportunities among the upper strata also produced pressures upon the polity to absorb excess members of these strata into the administrative bureaucracy, especially through the bestowal of honorific titles, military pensions, and — where available — ecclesiastical offices.

The incentive for counter-reform came most directly from the need to reinforce the loyalties of the lower strata to the social order in the face of declining material rewards. Thus, the activities of counter-reforms, while including proselytizing activities toward the periphery, have been focused for the most part on the lower strata within the core, directed especially at undermining local, family, and ethnic ties providing alternative sources of identification to the social order. The capacity for such reforms to be carried out successfully has been enhanced greatly by the influx of new personnel into the central bureaucracies representing the established order.

RELIGIOUS ACCOMMODATION

I shall employ the term "religious accommodation" to indicate movements that adapt mainstream religion to prevailing social conditions. The main varieties include (a) liberal reform movements within established religious organizations; (b) movements within these organizations to alleviate social problems; (c) the incorporation of minority or sectarian movements into the religious mainstream; and (d) movements of defection which strip religious organizations of certain traditional obligations.

Movements of these kinds have been particularly prominent in times when new patterns of world order were in the process of institutionalization. The emergence of the mercantilist system was accompanied, among other religious movements, by the Arminian movement in Holland, by the charitable movement initiated by Vincent de Paul in France, and by the incorporation of the Separatists and Independents in England. Similarly, the rise of the free trade system coincided with the Liberal-Catholic movement in France and Belgium and the great theological reforms of Schleiermacher, Hegel, and Strauss, the French monastic renewal oriented toward ministering to the poor, the incorporation of Protestant dissenters in England through the repeal of the Test and Corporation Acts, and with what Eric Hobsbawm (1962) has aptly called "the secularization of the masses" in speaking of the widespread religious defection that took place among the middle and lower classes during this period — to list but a few of the more prominent examples.

The social contexts nurturing these movements are far too complex to summarize in a few paragraphs, but at the level of world order the following conditions have contributed significantly to the prominence of these movements. These are the declining status of formerly dominant core areas during periods of reconstruction, the rising status of new core powers, new relations with periphery areas, and the temporary absence of a stable international monetary and diplomatic order. The major consequence of these conditions is an erosion of economic groups whose power has been protected by former patterns of international exchange and a strengthening of economic groups oriented to new patterns of international exchange.

This realignment, together with the overall economic instability deriving from the absence of an embracing international monetary order, generates civil conflict frequently resulting in some degree of political reform. This process occurs within the limits imposed by the interests of other nations and is conditioned by the presence of similar conflicts elsewhere. The net result consists typically not only of a change in the position of domestic interest groups but of a redefinition of government policy and of national role in the world-system. For established religion, especially where it has been in some measure subordinated to the polity, the consequences have usually included rising legitimacy for minority religions formerly critical of existing social arrangements, defection on the part of groups dissatisfied with the ossification of religious organizations, and efforts on the part of others to reform religious organizations in keeping with new political and moral climates. These have typically included social service activities functioning to alleviate hardships brought on the lower strata by the economic and political instability of the times.

As a brief example, the religious situation in England during the first half of the nineteenth century may be considered. By 1815 the mercantilist system of protective tariffs, colonial bilateralism, and state monopolies had been rendered obsolete by the successes of the American and French Revolutions, the high costs of the Napoleonic Wars, and the popularity of Enlightenment ideology. A new system of world order organized along principles of free trade was emerging creating pressures for changes in domestic social organization. Most urgently needed was reform of the protective tariff policies on shipping and grain which kept British food prices unnaturally high in view of cheaper sources from the United States and Prussia, thereby preventing wage levels from sinking to internationally competitive levels, creating unrest among the working classes, and maintaining undue privileges among the landed aristocracy (Knorr, 1944). Conflict between the landed aristocracy and the rising industrial, commercial, and financial interests came to a head in a series of Parliamentary clashes between the Whigs and Tories, culminating in the repeal of the Corn Laws in 1846 (Kammen, 1970). In religion the changing climate of political power and opinion led to increasing legitimacy for those minority bodies (largely Evengelicals and Dissenters) that had been early advocates of political reform and that could be counted upon for further support of the new government policies. It also led to the reforms of the 1830's, the purpose of which was to effect changes in the Anglican church, both in theology and organization, making it more compatible with the views and interests of the new commercial classes, many of whom had defected from the church over its support of aristocratic privileges. Finally, this period saw increasing efforts on the part of the church -- especially among its more evangelical elements -- to minister to the needs of the urban poor. Similar movements took place throughout the European system during this period.

SECTARIANISM

The final kind of religious movement to be discussed is
sectarianism, also most prominent in periods of reconstitution
in world order, but occurring more among groups whose relation to power is declining than among groups whose relation
to power is increasing. Sectarianism includes what might be
called "backlash" movements, which occur in response to efforts on the part of religious organizations to accomodate themselves to new social circumstances, sects that arise among the
lower classes, and the radical and utopian movements that
typically arise among intellectuals and students. Sectarianism
encompasses a variety of doctrinal styles and orientations, as
Bryan Wilson (1970a) and others have pointed out.

I have already traced the processes leading to liberal
reforms within established religious organizations. The accom-
plishment of these reforms characteristically occurs in the face
of opposition from those whose interests were better protected
by previous patterns of world order and domestic policy. When
this opposition contains moral as well as political dimensions,
it frequently results in religious schism and, if not contained, the formation of new minority religious bodies. The devot
movement in France, arising in opposition to Richelieu's policy of cooperation with the German Protestants, affords a
clear instance of this kind of movement during the early mercantilist period. The Oxford Movement which developed in reaction to the liberalization of the Church of England in the
1830s provides a similar case during the early free trade period. It was largely contained within the church. Among those
movements that could not be contained were the "great dispute" in Scotland in 1843, the secession of "Old Lutherans" in
Prussia, and the birth of the Christian Reformed Church in
the Netherlands. In each instance, these movements were predominantly populated by interest groups whose privileges were
being undermined by the emergence of new patterns of international exchange.

The conditions leading to the rise of sects among the lower classes during these periods result in the largest sense
from a lack of stable international monetary and political relations. These precipitate and worsen domestic economic crises
which create temporary unemployment and economic hardships
for the lower strata. These deprivations are aggravated by
the efforts of both rising and declining elites to maintain
their share of scarce economic resources. In addition, the likelihood of new sects emerging among the lower strata is enhanced by their physical migration away from established religious organizations due to economic difficulties and changing
opportunities for employment. The kinds of movements that result are illustrated by the diffuse spread of what G.L. Mosse

(1970) has termed "popular piety" among the peasants of England, Holland, and Germany during the early mercantilist period, and by the efflorescence of Baptists, Methodists, and Adventists in the new grain-growing regions of North America and among the new industrial workers of Britain during the early free trade period. The diffusion of these movements is significantly enhanced by the presence of political and economic instability throughout the world-system during such transitional periods.

This instability, together with the fluctuating moral climates it produces, is also an important factor contributing to the radical and utopian sects that have frequently developed among intellectuals and students during these periods; for example, the Cambridge Platonists and the Rosicrucians in England and the Socinians in Poland during the seventeenth century, and the Christian Socialists in England and the Transcendentalists in America during the nineteenth century. In each case, consciousness among intellectuals of domestic injustices to the lower classes and of foreign struggles for political reform were significant factors in the inspiration of these movements.

THE CONTEMPORARY PERIOD

Only some of the relations between religious movements and world order have been sketched here. It should be apparent even from this necessarily condensed discussion that religious movements in the past have been deeply conditioned by the prevailing state of world affairs. To an even greater degree this has been true of the contemporary period.

By the end of World War II the basic institutions undergirding the free trade system of the nineteenth century — the international gold standard, the British dominated balance of power, laissez faire government, and extensive colonial dependencies — had been mortally weakened (Polanyi, 1944). In their place a nascent system of world order dominated by the United States and the Soviet Union has emerged. But the operating principles of world order have yet to be fully reconstituted. Repeated attempts to create a stable international monetary system have met with only limited success (Block, 1977). The threat of nuclear war has proven only marginally capable of maintaining a stable international balance of power. Relations between the superpowers themselves have changed markedly, especially with the emergence of China as a nuclear force. In the Third World, the repercussions of anti-colonial revolts are still being felt.

The result of these instabilities has been a nearly continuous succession of domestic crises and political realignments in the world's major nations. In the United States, the
more vivid of these adjustments have included the Korean
war, the McCarthy era, the Cuban missile crisis, and the Vietnam war. Less visible, but perhaps equally important, have
been the United States' changing relations with Japan and
Western Europe, with China, and the changing relations between the government of the United States and its multination-
al corporations. For other parts of the world — for Vietnam,
Czechoslovakia, Israel, Cuba — the consequences of a world
order in transition have been dramatically more pronounced.

This period of reconstitution has been highly conducive
to the kinds of religious movements that America has experienced in the past quarter century. Successive shifts in the relations among nations have created successive shifts in the
statuses and ideologies of domestic interest groups which, in
turn, have occurred amidst a chorus of responses at the level
of our deepest spiritual and moral convictions. There have
been reform movements within religious organizations and sectarian reactions against these reforms. There have been religious defections, social service and civil rights campaigns,
and radical and utopian movements. These have been deeply
conditioned by the instabilities present in the larger world-
system. This is perhaps most evident in the crisis of the 1960s.

The crisis of the 1960s was, in an immediate sense, the
Vietnam war. But it was also a crisis in world order and in
the positions of domestic interest groups connected to that order. Insofar as the United States was concerned, the world order of the 1950s and early 1960s was oriented chiefly toward
military containment of the Communist bloc and the strengthening
of America's stabilizing influence within the free world (Schurmann, 1974). This system was predicated upon the monopoly
of effective nuclear strike capabilities by the United States
and by the Soviet Union, the dominance of the Soviet Union in
the Communist world and its ability to exert control over member nations, the ability of the United States to maintain security within its sphere of influence, and the tacit agreement on
the part of both superpowers as to the boundaries of their respective spheres.

The containment system also meshed neatly with the interests and ideologies of America's major power groups, even to
the extent of limited wars. In the South, strong military commitments to the defense of the free world strengthened the political power of old-guard hawks, fed money into Southern military training camps, provided career opportunities for both
blacks and whites, and wedded the conservative religious orientations of the South to the national interest. For agriculture, the same forces that kept Southern politicians strong also

helped ensure a stable farm subsidy program which, in the short-run, appeared better than the vagaries of an open international market, and again coincided with the religious and moral convictions of farmers and townspeople in the rural areas.

For the largest corporations, containment politics were scarcely essential to their prosperity. But for many of the weaker corporations (and in turn, labor) continuous demands for new weapons systems, the role of a large standing army in minimizing unemployment, and formal encouragement of foreign subsidiaries and joint ventures with Japan and Western Europe were by no means without importance. Even for the larger corporations, and certainly the universities, the scientific and technological efforts inspired by the arms race, and increasingly by the space race, contributed significantly to their overall well-being.

Vietnam was both symptom and cause of the changes in world order that witnessed the demise of containment politics. Included in these were the rise of China as a nuclear power, the Sino-Soviet split, economic tensions among the Western allies, and post-colonial instabilities in the Third World. Under these circumstances Vietnam became the catalyst which precipitated far-reaching realignments among domestic interest groups. For the South the increasing costs of the war, and hence its growing unpopularity, undermined the power of the old-guard and facilitated the rise of the so-called new Southern politician. Increasingly the war divided the interests of blacks, who saw the Great Society usurped by the costs of defense, from those of the white establishment, further eroding the traditional base of Southern politics.

Ideologically, the war drove a wedge between the more liberal advocates of containment and the more conservative champions of a rollback policy. For the corporate community, the worsening balance of foreign payments as the war dragged on precipitated a re-evaluation of its commitment to a firm containment orientation. In the universities, the war brought to a crisis the basic inconsistency of interests wedded to the export of military technology and ideology espousing universal humanitarian ideals. In short, the 1960s witnessed a major realignment of domestic interests, not just because of internal unrest, but because of larger conditions in world affairs associated ultimately with the breakup of the free-trade system and the transition to a new pattern of world order.

In religion, the most immediate consequences of this realignment were the radical and utopian cults that emerged among intellectuals and students, generally espousing anti-war and anti-technological orientations, and deriving popularity from their rejection of Western religious traditions. But the religious repercussions of Vietnam ran far deeper than these. The shifting moral climate and definitions of national purpose associated with the protests and realignments of the 1960s nourished liberalizing and social reform movements within the mainstream churches, including Christian-Marxist dialogue, civil rights activism, anti-war efforts, experiments in liturgy, and re-evalutions of traditional political and moral postures. They also contributed to widespread defection from the churches among the better educated classes for whom the events of the 1960s symbolized a growing gap between world conditions and the traditions of the church.

As in the past, religious accommodation of this sort brought forth other movements in reaction among those for whom the emerging pattern of world order meant declining power -- new denominations in the South and in the Midwest, such as the National Presbyterian Church and the reconstituted Missouri Lutherans; movements among Vietnam hardliners within the churches (the Presbyterian Laymen's Association, for example); and diffuse defection from mainline denominations into the more politically circumspect evangelical churches (cf., Kelley, 1977). Though generalized affluence and the welfare state prevented the kind of extreme hardships that had given rise to widespread sectarianism among the lower classes in the past, those caught at the margins of society during this transitional period, particularly minorities and less privileged young people, followed predictable patterns in their attraction to movements such as the Children of God, Pentecostalism, the Unification Church, the Black Muslims, and the Black Christian Nationalist Movement.

The religious accommodation and sectarianism of the contemporary period, like that of the early seventeenth and the early nineteenth centuries, has been a product of the transitional state of world order. Though the current transition has not produced civil conflict anything like the English Civil War or the revolutions of 1848, the social unrest brought to a climax by the Vietnam war was part of a major realignment in the relations between domestic interest groups and world affairs. The contemporary unrest in religion, both in America and abroad, has been symptomatic of the extensiveness of this realignment.

Periods of religious unrest like the one through which America has recently passed have, of course, been regarded as portents of change — as historical watersheds — at least since Herodotus. There has been much speculation about what the present religious unrest may signal for the culture. And, in this sense, this chapter must also remain speculative. Typological approaches like the one adopted here are of necessity limiting and a great deal more historical work would be required to demonstrate how well or how poorly specific historical events may correspond to these typological distinctions. Let

me suggest in closing, however, that the principle value of
considering religious movements in the context of world order,
as I have attempted to do here, is that it affords a systematic basis for comparing the kinds of watersheds that religious
movements may portend.

NOTE

*   This paper is reproduced with permission from Studies
     in the Modern World-System, edited by Albert Bergesen,
     copyright Academic Press, New York, 1980.

II

NOW AND THEN:
THE INDIVIDUAL AND SOCIETY

CALIFORNIAN SELF-RELIGIONS

AND SOCIALISING THE SUBJECTIVE

Paul Heelas

Two of our major cultural obsessions are with psychology and with meaning. I use the term 'self-religions' to character- ise those movements (including Kerista, The Farm, Primal Ther- apy, Rebirthing, est, and Co-Counseling) which exemplify the conjunction of the exploration of the self and the search for significance. They take a religious form because of an addi- tional ingredient, namely the obsession with perfection. Per- fecting the self leads almost inevitably into the religious, in- to the language of the ultimate, the metaphysical, the uni- tary, the complete. Two decades ago Mowrer could say of many works that they promise '"peace of mind" to the reader on the premise that psychiatry is wonderful, religion is won- derful, put them together and you get something better still!' (Mowrer, 1961: iii). The impact of eastern religions has made this promise more powerful.

Thus the self-religions, with their various syntheses of mind cure, psychotherapy, eastern religious ideas, and as- pects of the human potential movement and humanistic psychol- ogy, combine and highlight major cultural themes.: the psycho- logical, the religious, the meaningful, and the perfectability of man. Participants believe that psychological techniques en- hance experiences, provide the basis for authentic social sys- tems or interpersonal relationships, and in general function to fulfill human potentialities. Kerista (a small group in San Francisco) emphasises gestalt; Primal Therapy favours cathar- sis; Rebirthing, est, and, especially, The Farm, attach great importance to positive thinking.

Although these movements obviously provide a number of perspectives on society, I concentrate on one theme. Sociology is ultimately concerned with studying the diversity of ways in which people organize themselves and live together, and the kinds of effects that these have on the individual. I ar- gue that the self-religions shed light on a distinctive social response which is open to mankind. The response has to do with what I shall call the socialisation of the subjective, namely, the maintenance, in social life, of an emphasis on

69

psychological and 'inner' experiential states. I thus disagree
with those, for example Luckmann and Berger, who treat the
subjective realm of identity as inherently 'unstable' (Luckmann and Berger, 1964: 342).

The subjective, meaning 'existing in human consciousness', is, more specifically, the realm in which many
Californians explore experiences of self, emotions, altered
states of consciousness, and experiences in (sometimes 'con-
trived') personal relationships. The realm of the subjective is
not absent in organised, more traditional, social life, although, precisely because of the organisation factor, exploration by the individual is generally held well in check. To give
an example from British society, the city gent does not characteristically explore or emphasise the subjective, his experiences being in a sense objectified, structured, and externalised by his predominantly public way of life.

Indeed, concentration on the realm of the subjective
seems to imply the antithesis of organised social life. Here the
individual counts. Spontaneity, authenticity, the casting aside
of socially defined roles or masks, heart-to-heart communication, are all-important. Hence the longstanding tendency to
think in either-or terms: either unstable and transitory attempts to explore and enhance the subjective, or the development of social organisation which, for fear of losing control
of the individual, holds exploration of the subjective firmly
in hand.

My basic argument — that the self-religions have developed techniques which locate or construe the subjective in
such a fashion as to help make this realm predictable, secure, liveable, and, in a nutshell, social — therefore runs
contrary to a well-established dichotomy. Because they fuse
the social and the psychological, the self-religions also afford
a useful perspective from which to view another traditional dichotomy, that between sociological and psychological explanations. In short, I use the movements to examine the processes,
both psychological and sociological, which bind individual subjectivity in terms of constructed realities, meaning systems,
and institutions.

ETHNOGRAPHIC CONTEXT

The self-religions must be distinguished from the earlier
countercultures of the Woodstock generation and from more totalitarian and fundamentalist movements such as The Children
of God and The Love Family. They are grounded in a distinctive way of life, exemplified by middle class, and increasingly middle age, inhabitants of the Bay area of California. The

'Marin lifestyle' (see McFadden, 1977) is decidely not counter-
cultural, and does not appeal to the disturbed, impoverished,
or lower class members of society.

Marin culture is marked by a whole range of activities
designed to promote the exploration of experience, especially
feelings. Drawing on Reed's ironic commentary, 'Sometimes
Marin's Coast resembles parts of Cornwall, if the Cornish all
owned a car, a $72,000-plus house with patio and pool, and
a sailing boat, two big dogs, and at least one cat'. With this
basis,

> Ascetic and aesthetes all, they are also heavily
> into lentil soup and grande cuisine, second-hand
> clothes and tennis parties, herbal tea and large
> Tequila Sunrises, getting rid of body toxins and
> taking cocaine, puffing pot, and a no-smoking
> zone from Monterrey to Cape Cod. This is where,
> on a bright Saturday morning, you clip your ten-
> speed Tour de France Special on the MGB's grid
> and roar up the hills, where, after some brisk ped-
> alling, you roar back and enthuse about the 'to-
> tal physical experience' and the importance of not
> 'destabilising the environment ' (Reed, 1978:223).

Inhabitants retire to their sensory deprivations baths; they
take a course in est, Silva Mind Control, orgonomy, or one of
the many self-religions;[1] they compete at 'mellowing-out' or
at displaying their innermost thoughts whilst 'gestalting'; or
they spend their time with ecologically, experientially, and
economically appropriate pursuits such as urban planning,
psychologising, and catering.

The advertisement pages of the Pacific Sun help paint
the picture of affluent, hedonistic (if not narcissistic) self-
exploration:

SAMADHI ISOLATION TANK

> Float in silence, darkness. Experience centered-
> ness, profound relaxation, well-being. Explore in-
> ner realms with no distractions. More information
> and appointments by phone.

So too does their language, what Rosen (1978) has aptly called 'psychobabble'. I take an example from Utopian Eyes , the
journal of the seven-year-old Kerista self-religion:

> I sure hope you don't schiz-out of the group, Eve!

> I consciously push thought of wat [sic] to say aside.

I want to speak from my stream-of-consciousness
tonight. It's new territory for me, but lately my
confidence levels have been rising and I feel
ready for this kind of 'experiment'.

The only way to deal with paranoias is to get
them out in the open. This community is built on
the gestalt-o-rama process: total openness and honesty. How can people build trust if they're into
hold-back? You have to trust what you're feeling
at the moment and the ability of the group mind
to deal with it and come to clarity on issues.[2]

It should be apparent that the self-religions do not so
much reflect Marin lifestyle as constitute it. They are part
and parcel of a socio-cultural system which facilitates the exploration, communication, and fulfillment of personal experiences, emotions, and relationships. To summarise the main features, an important characteristic is that 'a sense of well-
being has become the end, rather than a by-product of striving after some superior communal end' (Rieff, 1973: 224), or,
to be more up to date,

These days, fewer seem willing to settle for anything so quaint as ordinary human suffering. Consumer expectations have risen.... The idea of being 'cured' has been fetishized; mental health is
thought of less and less as the capacity to confront, explore, and transmute the sometimes irre-
ducible contradictions of living, and more and
more as a total triumph over all that threatens the
autonomy of the individual (Rosen, 1978: 204).

Consumer expectations have risen and, with the perceived failure of the American dream confined to the material
world, the dream has been relocalised in the mind. Primal
Therapists expect nothing less than 'complete consciousness'.
The self-religions have developed a number of indigenous psychologies (culturally embedded models of the self) in order to
fulfill their respective 'dreams'. Marinites optimistically engage in mind cure psychologies or cathartic techniques to perfect the subjective. With respect to personal relationships, the
theme is to prevent individual isolation or masked role playing. Rosen speaks of the 'insistence on preventing failures of
communication' (p. 4), individuals employing psychobabble to
present their authentic subjective selves to each other.

THEORETICAL CONTEXT

Although many theorists have provided insights into the
broader context of which the self-religions are an expression,

I do not want to develop this theme here. The empirical basis of much large-scale theorising tends to be rather suspect,[3] and few theories help in explaining the details of the process of socialising the subjective. This last consideration is due to the fact that most students of the new religions have concentrated on fundamentalist, totalitarian movements, such as the Unification Church. There the picture is of the individual who has to be purified or saved, salvation being attained via powerful group organisation taking precedence over the autonomous ego. Theories of social and psychological control have little relevance to the self-religions. Here the assumption is that the individual is basically pure, perfection being arrived at when the autonomous self of what Tom Wolfe has called the 'Me Decade' is allowed full expression or liberation. Instead of authoritarian 'cultism' we find the aggressive individualism of an affluent and highly educated society which is in the position to experiment, try anything. With the 'epidemic of sudden personality change' (Conway and Siegelman, 1978) taking such proportions, individuals have an openness which precludes theories of indoctrination or radical control of the self. Indeed may of the features characteristic of fundamentalist movements are absent, including supposed brainwashing, scapegoating, and the like, together with millenarianism and segmentation from the outside world. The self-religions are part of society, often, as with est, being used to improve and transform overall social performance.[4]

What we need, then, is a way of explaining how the subjective can be socialised when this does not result in the social self taking precedence over the autonomous individual. I have been attracted by the work of Berger and Turner, Berger because he argues, in effect, that the subjective cannot itself be socialised, and Turner because he indicates how this can occur. According to Berger, the modern individual is not able to realise himself in terms of the institutions and meaning systems of the 'public world', the world of traditional society. It follows that

> the individual seeks to find his 'foothold' in reality in himself rather than outside himself. One consequence of this is that the individual's subjective reality (what is commonly regarded as his 'psychology') becomes increasingly differentiated, complex
> — and 'interesting' to himself. Subjectivity acquires previously unconceived 'depths' (Berger et al, 1974: 74).

Dichotomised between the 'private' (or subjective) and public worlds, 'modern man is afflicted with a permanent identity crisis'. The problem is exacerbated if the individual seeks his identity and values in the subjective. This domain is 'underinstitutionalized', having a 'shortage of institutions that firmly

and reliably structure human activity'. The reason is that
'something that is constantly changing is supposed to be the
ens realissimum'. The only alternative, it appears, is for the
individual to capitulate to the 'totalitarianism' of traditional
public institutions (Berger et al, 1974: 74, 167, 190). The either
-or is stark.

It is perhaps curious that Berger did not pay more attention to how dichotomisation can be resolved by institutionalis-
ing, whilst maintaining, the subjective. It is curious because
although we read 'the most obvious thing is that most individuals do not know how to construct a universe and therefore
become furiously frustrated when they are faced with a need
to do so' (p. 167), Berger had earlier indicated the role of
'secondary institutions' (including psychotherapies) in providing 'social maintenance and repair services for this precarious private universe' (Luckmann and Berger, 1964: 342). In
another article, he came yet closer to the theme of socialising
the subjective. Claiming that 'psycho-analysis has become a
cultural phenomenon, a way of understanding the nature of
man and an ordering of human experience on the basis of this
understanding', he argues that this model functions to provide
identity, self-explanations, and control in the private or subjective domain. However, even here Berger did not take his
theme very far: 'The understanding of the self as an assem-
blage of psychological mechanisms allows the individual to
deal with himself with the same technical, calculating and "objective" attitude that is the attitude par excellence of industrial production' (Berger, 1965: 27, 40, my emphasis).[5]

Whereas Berger draws back from examining, in detail,
how secondary institutions work on the subjective, Turner is
captivated by the existential and psychological state of un-
masked humankindness, which he calls communitas. He provides theoretical justification for the theme of the socialisation of the subjective, arguing as he does that 'the ultimate
desideratum...is to act in terms of communitas values even
while playing structural roles, where what one culturally does
is conceived of as merely instrumental to the aim of attaining
and maintaining communitas' (Turner, 1969: 167). This is not
the place to examine in detail how the experience of communitas, of an affectively laden, authentically construed aspect
of the social process, might help explain the grounds, symbolism, ideas and general nature of the self-religions, although
I do make further use of what Turner has to say about maintaining the subjective as social life.

SOCIALISING THE SUBJECTIVE

Self-religions are clearly examples of secondary institutions. How then do they function to provide a middle way

between the unstructured, unstable, uncertain, and private subjectivity of anomie, and the systematized, bureaucratic, anonymous, impersonal, and rigid domain of traditional public institutions? To be meaningful, let alone existentially and socially valid, models have to be provided for the subjective. In general terms, the self-religions provide models for conceptualising and organising the exploration of self, thus facilitating communication, experience, and action, as well as ways of responding to inadequacy, uncertainty and suffering. It is, of course, obvious that we need to know what we are experiencing or feeling, that we need to know how to communicate inner states, and that we need to know how to handle them, enhancing some and diminishing others. It is also obvious that Marinites have to organise potentially idiosyncratic subjective states to suit interpersonal relationships and 'communal' living: their ideology demands that the self is explored within culturally defined parameters and ideals.

The important models are provided by indigenous psychologies or culturally held assumptions about the nature of the self. With the demise of traditional, externalised forms of Christianity and other institutions which provided a focus, a way of organising, articulating, and communicating experiences in the public realm, widespread psychologisation has occurred. [6] For Marinites, indigenous psychologies articulate various goals (for example, fulfilling the self), describe the predicaments (absence of self-harmony), and provide the remedies (catharsis, mind cure, gestalt, psychobabble, insight, meditation, confession, bodily expression, and so on). These systems are the means for externalising or imaging subjective states, allowing participants to have faith in themselves, as well as being suitable for maintaining (whilst socialising) the subjective. They provide public or externalised models which allow the exploration of self and interpersonal relationships. Anomie and totalitarianism, it is believed, are avoided.

In greater detail, two main indigenous psychologies are operative, the 'idealist' and 'modified passiones' models. [7] The idealist variety emphasises the power of the individual, who is regarded as being able to use his will (or whatever) to act on the world and himself. Given the Marinites' faith in themselves, this model is well in evidence. Thus, Orr, the founder of Rebirthing, teaches that thoughts create reality and that by changing one's mind, one changes the world; good thoughts, he continually argues, produce money, friendships, and indeed purify the self (Orr, 1977).

The term passiones means 'instances of being acted upon' (Collingwood, 1944: 86). When this is modified, the self is seen as dependent on 'external' (that is, to the conscious self) agencies and as autonomous (the conscious self being envisaged on idealist lines). Thus the psychoanalytic model of

man, so characteristic of the self-religions, holds that the conscious individual is an agency in its own right but also sometimes comes under the control of an 'external' agency, namely
the unconscious. In Co-Counseling, for example, suffering on
the part of one's client is attributed to the fact that 'each
time your client was hurt, he lived through the experience
and stored up in some way everything that went on during
that experience of being hurt' (Jackins, 1970: 2).

A CASE EXAMPLE: KERISTA

To demonstrate how these two general models, together
with psychobabble and other institutionalised techniques, operate to socialise the subjective, I examine the Kerista self-
religion, drawing on other movements when appropriate. Life
for members of Kerista is organised so that they can obtain
as many experiences as possible. During weekends in the country (for most members have jobs in San Francisco), each
seeks out his or her own activities (hiking, bathing, 'schmooz-
ing schnoozing') and savouring them to the fullest (the sun
does not rise, it 'is peaking over the top' -- an early morning swim is 'a daring, breathless plunge into the cold pool,
then back to the hot, hot, producing a curious tingling sensa-
tion that fully wakens me') (Utopian Eyes,1978:12).But despite
this extreme individualism and emphasis on the subjective,
members are treated as being 'part of what we think of as a
group mind' (p. 3).

Kerista socialises states of mind by regulating and organising them in terms of a socially envisaged ideal self. Participants do not remain private and idiosyncratic in their subjective experiences because, having first self-consciously re-
membered these (p. 9), they employ an established psychological model to mesh them into the communal whole. The meshing
comes about 'by virtue of the gestalt process (Gestalt-O-Rama)
that we employ, a process of communication, growth, attuning
each separate mind to the overall currents of the larger
whole' (p. 3). The process — essentially a communal form of
stream-of-consciousness — is aided by the use of psychobabble. There is surely some truth in Rosen's claim that this is
'an idiom that reduces psychological insight to a collection
of standardised observations that provides a frozen lexicon to
deal with an infinite variety of problems' (Rosen, 1978: 11,
my emphasis). In other words, psychobabble allows participants to believe they are communicating their own unique experiences when they are perhaps primarily engaged in ritual
affirmations of generalised types of experience of self-
identity. Idiosyncratic subjective experiences are conceptual-
ised by means of notions embedded in the standard code of
psychobabble, these notions obscuring possible divergences in
experience. The sun has to 'peak'.

Another crucial aspect of the meshing process concerns
what is perhaps the main issue in the socialisation of the subjective, namely the avoidance of the discord, anxiety, and

and anomie which readily result when the individual explores
his own subjectivity. 'Theodicies', so vital for taking the
sting out of idealist self-responsibility, for handling guilt
and bad experiences, are provided in general by modified passiones indigenous psychologies. The unconscious is used to socialise bad feelings. Adversity is explained and handled by
being attributed to unconscious forces. The emphasis is on catharsis, on exorcising bad influences, on blaming them onto
prior states of affairs which can be got rid of:

> Disturbing behaviour, unwanted feelings, and de-
> structive impulses are perceived...simply as acces-
> sories to the self. You just sort of work off the
> problem like a wedding ring that hasn't been re-
> moved in years and — voilà! — you are psycho-
> logically single again, free of old attachments
> (Rosen, 1978: 207).

When a member of Kerista experiences 'paranoia' or
'anti-gestalt', to his or her dismay being unhappy and anti-
social, recourse is made to confessional 'talking it out' combined with something akin to catharsis. Thus Lil O'Lee's paranoia is 'gestalted': 'I could feel it bringing us all closer together as we realised the solidity of our friendship and also
became aware that if these paranoias had gone unsaid, comparison might have resulted in subtle insecurities about our
union' (Utopian Eyes, p. 20). As this indicates, however, the
emphasis in Kerista is more on the 'group mind' dealing with
problems by arriving at acceptable explanations than it is on
more fully-fledged modified passiones means. Marinites in general tend not to be quite so content with the powers of sensi-
ble positive thinking, supplementing this with techniques designed to purify the unconscious. Primal Therapy, for example,
holds that 'Primal Pain' must be released via the cathartic
activity of 'primaling'. The theodicy function is met, the ritual
of catharsis bringing the aberrant and perplexing (how can
I possibly be unhappy?) into the public world where it can
be exorcised and the individual brought into social and experiential conformity.

Needleman has argued, 'if the new religions are to influence our society in a serious way, they will do so by reviving the idea of the psychospiritual instrumentality of moral
behavior' (Needleman,1970:229). Kerista gestalt sessions also
function to socialize the subjective by virtue of the fact that
they are imbued with a psychomoral code: 'any individual who consistently follows a certain set of beliefs and behaviors, who
adheres to a specific path, will in return experience subjectively a correspondingly unique, or specific, mindset or consciousness' (Utopian Eyes, p.18). When Fullo Pep forgets some
journals, 'There was some gestalt at my and other's inefficien-
cy and spaceoutedness that alerted me to this weak point in

myself' (p. 9). Gestalt sessions are used to affirm social values, modes of behaviour and assessments of experiences. Their
relatively strict moral code comes into play, as do the assessments embedded in psychobabble (e.g., what it is to be 'mel-
low' or 'anti-gestalt'). The moral code affects 'mindsets' because of 'the tremendous extent to which our language...af-
fects our total consciousness' (p. 17). Divinity must be con-
ceptualised in the right way because it provides 'an emotional
focusing point' (p. 18) and therefore an important basis for
action. Since divinity is neutral with respect to gender, participants ought not to adopt sexist emotional responses to one
another.

Discussing The Farm, Hall has examined the socialisation
process in a self-religion which, following Turner (1969) ap-
proximates more exactly still to 'spontaneous communitas'.
There is even greater emphasis than in Kerista on 'attending
to the vivid present, as an individual in a social situation'
(Hall, 1978: 61). The problem of combining immediacy with social interaction is met by defining truth in terms of collective, renewable, agreement, rather than in terms of generalised rules. Communal activities are designed to 'plug in' individuals. This occurs when they 'intersubjectively constitute
objects of attention', that is, when they collectively affirm
and certify that they have had shared experiences. Accordingly, 'the shared moment in all its uniqueness constitutes a now
of communion and salvation' (p. 62). Subjectivity is also
brought into line by leaving little room for private thought,
activities being organised so that social pressure can be
brought to bear on those who are 'laying back' (p. 64; compare also Whitworth, 1975: 229). Holding feelings back is taboo, and abstract thought, which might encourage individual
idiosyncrasy, is criticised. Indeed, psychobabble operates to
direct subjectivity by providing 'a shorthand description of
collectively grasped situations, themes and relevances' (Hall,
1978: 96). Finally, as in Kerista, a modified passiones model
is employed to ensure that participants are not influenced by
anti-social and unspontaneous repressed feelings. Recognising
the 'subconscious', confessional means are employed to help
eliminate 'laying back'. Ultimately, however, the idealist model takes precedence: by coming to think in the right way under the guidance of group commentaries or 'witnessing', the
individual thinks he has freed himself from his subconscious
(pp. 98-99). The subjective is collectivised, for, as members
put it, 'There's no cover at The Farm' (p. 101).

A BROADER PERSPECTIVE

I have only been about to hint at the many ways the
self-religions stabilize, organise, amplify, and control the

subjective. To summarise: the goals provided by the subjective
(e.g., purity and love) are symbolically and publicly affirm-
ed. Means are provided to realise the goals, modified passiones models both handling bad experiences and making
ideals plausible, while idealist models suggest that positive
thinking can improve the self. Furthermore, the powers of language (psychobabble) are used to bring people together and
create at least a semblance of social togetherness and conformity. We must also bear in mind that moral and ritual rule systems are generally well in evidence, and that the communal,
small-scale, affluent nature of Marin lifestyle provides an excellent basis for the maintainance of self-religions by holding
Berger's public, strongly institutionalised sector at bay.

A more comprehensive analysis of the socialisation process would lead us to consider the many theories which examine the role of symbols, ritual, psychological and psychi-
atric techniques in handling the subjective. For instance, there
is considerable literature on the organisation of emotions
(Schachter, 1971; Gordon, 1974; Ortner, 1978; Scheff, 1977) and
on the functioning of 'dynamic psychiatries' (Ellenberger, 1970;
Lévi-Strauss, 1968). In particular, though, the work of Turner
serves to remind us that there is nothing new about the attempt to socialise the subjective (or communitas). As we have
seen, Turner regards the 'ultimate desideratum' to be a synthesis of social structure and communitas. He also holds that
communitas 'differs deeply, even abysmally' from life in social
structure (Turner, 1969: 127). The reconciliation is brought
about via spontaneous or existential communitas developing
moral and symbolic features, that is, by being transformed
into normative or ideological varieties (p. 120).

It is true that Turner claims that modern communitas orientated groups 'have not yet developed a structure capable
of maintaining social and economic order over long periods of
time' (p. 193), but this is not to deny that his examination
of those movements (such as the early Franciscans of medieval
Europe) which have developed moral and ideological structures
to socialise and maintain the subjective is not of great pertin-
ence to our theme. Thus he investigates how rituals function
to liberate, organise, and control the subjective, how symbols
'confer some degree of intelligibility on an experience [com-
munitas] that perpetually outstrips the possibilities of linguistic... expression' (Turner,1974:240) and how symbolic action permits participants to grasp, and thereby master, inauspicious
states of mind (Turner, 1969: 27).

ASSESSMENT

The strategic importance of Turner's work is that by refusing to identify 'the social with the social structural'

(Turner, 1974: 269) he has been able to take seriously the social or institutionalised possibilities of the subjective. The picture I have painted is that the subjective can indeed be socialised without swinging radically towards the totalitarian
public sphere. The subjective appears to be neither under nor
over institutionalised, and it seems to be the case that the
'identity crisis' is less marked among those who espouse the
self-religions than among those who live solely in the fragmented, relativised 'public' domain.

This picture, I now must make absolutely clear, relies
very heavily on the participant's frame of reference. Thus when
I wrote, 'I have only been able to hint at the many ways the
self-religions stabilise, organise, amplify, and control the subjective' I was taking the word of participants that catharsis,
for example, actually functions in this way. But this is by
no means self-evident: as I have argued elsewhere, experimental psychologists have not been able to establish, with consensus, that catharsis really works, perhaps the weight of the
evidence suggesting that it does not (Heelas, 1982).

What is not so obvious, in other words, and what is indeed one of the great issues facing the study of man in society, is the extent to which the nature of the subjective is
dependent on, modified by, socially and culturally given
models. Taking Whitworth's analysis of utopian sects as an
example, sociologists often assume that participant models
operate on members (cathartic techniques here permitting the
expression 'of accumulated tensions') (Whitworth, 1975: 230).
In the absence of experimental psychological evidence, this is
not justified. Since the self-religions bear on psychological
states, assessment must include the possibility that their techniques (cathartic or whatever) are cultural artifacts and do
not really achieve their ends. Experimental psychologists
might very well want to say that many of the psychotherapies
and self-improvement techniques which I have portrayed fall
into this category.

The situation, as I see it, is that sociologists interested
in the impact of small-scale communities or movements on the
self cannot ignore psychological evidence. However, we know
so little about this impact (witness the debate about 'brainwashing') that although adequate assessment of my theme of
socialising the subjective should make recourse to psychological evidence, I prefer, at least for the moment, to remain agnostic with respect to the issue. How else, then, are we to
draw conclusions from self-religions, in particular, conclusions which provide a perspective on society and the social
process?

The first point to make is that many features of the subjective are inherently meaningful, belonging to the sociocultural, which entails that participant reports are part of their
reality and are therefore to be accepted. Self-identity is self-
identity, and if Rebirthers believe that good thoughts 'clean
out' their lives and report positive feelings and actions, it
is difficult not to conclude that their idealist psychology has
worked. Despite psychological agnosticism, it is thus possible
to maintain that the subjective has been socialised if participant beliefs and activities indicate that their individual meaning systems or experiences have been brought into social and
cultural conformity. What happens in the subjective is in
large measure socioculturally defined or constituted (see
Heelas, 1982; Heelas and Lock, eds., 1981).

The second, more sociological, way of assessing the self-
religions is to show that, as meaning systems, they have obtained a fair degree of equilibrium or balance. It is perhaps
too soon to tell how successfully they have managed to handle
inherent strains, such as that between spontaneity and morality or between the autonomous and the socialised self.   But
there certainly seems to be a coherence in the Marin lifestyle,
as is shown by briefly introducing a contrast with   earlier
counterculture movements which did not obtain equilibrium.

Drawing on Meyerhoff's analysis, members of the counter-
culture sought to obtain 'ecstasy' by destructuring the individual, leaving him entirely free. As a consequence, there was a general 'paralysis of action' (Meyerhoff, 1975: 51), a general
lapse into something like anomie. The self-religions have not
lapsed in this fashion precisely because they are based on
the premise of the autonomous individual who has to be organised or structured to be fulfilled or explored. Because the
autonomous, structured   individual   is   not   opposed to the
search for ecstasy and fulfillment (The Farm even manages to
maintain the subjective and the spontaneous within a closed
and socially conformist setting), but rather goes hand in
glove with it, anomie is not seen as a threat. What matters
is that the self is fully expressed and developed, and to that
end the structured techniques I have outlined are quite in order.

Neither do the self-religions appear to have lapsed into
the opposite of countercultural anomie, there being no need to
rectify their state by means of totalitarian, bounded   forms
of organisation. Granted that the autonomous self has to be
structured or organised if self-development is to occur, the experimental orientation of participants means that their techniques or organisations do not become closed. Kerista participants, for example, are continually modifying and changing
their techniques for self-development and so amplify their

sense of autonomy. Marinites use organised systems, in particular indigenous psychologies, to fulfill the self. There are
few signs of these systems turning on the individual to threat-
en the traditional and, among Marinites, powerfully defended
values of self-freedom, self-dignity, and self-responsibility.

It appears, then, that because they are neither counter-
cultural nor fundamentalist and closed, and because they are
based on the premise of the structured, autonomous individual, the self-religions have reached an equilibrium. Because
they do not operate with either-or premises (either total freedom or total organisation of the self) the exploration of the
individual neither lapses into anomie nor into strong totalitarianism. The social self does not take precedence over the autonomous individual to the extent of oversocialisation as defined by current American standards; the subjective and autonomous is emphasised without being unstable, precarious, or
dangerous.

However, if assessment were to stop here we would be
left with a misleading picture. For there is a sense in which
Marinites are thoroughly socialised, and, although I think
they implicitly recognise this (by using many techniques to
structure or socialise the subjective), I would like to make
more explicit the 'paradox' that their freedom and autonomy
are socially and culturally derived. My concluding notes on
this point will also allow me to return to the Bergerian dichotomy between free, anomie-like subjectivity and public, totalitarian self-hood, to argue that this dichotomy falls down in
that freedom must be obtained via the sociocultural.

Dorothy Lee has made the point with sensitivity:

> Many people in our society have been apprehensive
> of the implications of personal autonomy, because
> they have felt that it is apt to lead to lawlessness
> and chaos. Yet actually it is in connection with
> the highest personal autonomy that we often find
> the most intricately developed structure. For
> example, the Burmese novices could proceed without
> receiving orders only because the structure clearly
> indicated what could and could not be done....
> (Lee, 1959: 9)

Subjectivity can never be entirely free — meanings are rule-
governed. Self-exploration and transcendence, the experience
of subjective freedom, is socioculturally dependent. Intricate
structure, as Lee observes, need not rule out the experience
of freedom. Marinites, so to speak, have put into practice
Lee's observation. Berger's dichotomy falls down: free subjectivity occurs because of -- not because opposed to -- socio-
cultural organisation.

At the level of sociological analysis Marinites are not
free; their subjectivities are inherently sociocultural.   At the
level of experience, or of participant reports, they are free;
the 'open-ended' nature of their techniques and institutions,
together with their beliefs in the nature of the individual,
positive thinking, and the possibility of freedom from the unconscious makes sure of this.[8] At least in this context — and
I suspect that much the same case could be made even for
groups like the Moonies — the invasion of the subjective by
the sociocultural cannot be polarised against the experience
of freedom. The self-religions must be clearly distinguished
from those movements where sociocultural institutions determine
the subjective by providing meanings and techniques which
take away the experience of individual autonomy or selfhood,
which 'foster the destruction of the ego and...bring about its
replacement by, literally, a collective consciousness, or almost
total otherdirectedness' (Whitworth, 1975: 229).

SOME REMARKS IN LIGHT OF OTHER CONTRIBUTIONS
(References are to pages in this volume)

My doubts about introducing the term 'self-religions'
have been alleviated on reading other contributions: Oden and
the parallels between pietism and encounter culture (although
I wish he had considered the possibility of independent invention, and the differences due to twentieth-century psychology);
Wallis on the self as the only God; Werblowsky on koinonia
and inner-orientated, self-realisation religion; and Wilson on
the importance of therapy in the West.

My worries about how to access the impact of self-
religions, which led to asking whether it is possible to explain their occurrence in terms of their meeting psychological
needs, are also diminished — particularly by Campbell's chapter. Plausibility with respect to cultural orientations, especially those which reflect general needs for an 'expressive logic'
(239,240) goes a long way in explaining how and why the self-
religions work (see also Nordquist and Oden).

Wallis' contrast between world-affirming and world-
rejecting religions is useful with respect to my distinction between self-religions and fundamentalist organizations. His observations on world-affirmation have also prompted me to
think more clearly as to how this term can be brought to bear
on characterising self-religions. He writes that world-affirming
religions take the 'anonymity, impersonality, achievement-
orientation, individualism, and segmentalisation of modern
life...for granted', but we also read of 'liberation...from constraints on his thought and behaviour from conventional ritual....' (227). He attempts to resolve this tension by referring to 'a major contradiction of modern Western life'; that

acceptance of the Protestant Ethic goes together with 'a need
for methods of escaping the constraints and inhibitions usually required in order to achieve that [Protestant envisaged]
success' (229). Some self-religions (see my note 4) do appear
to take their goals from the results of what Wallis describes
as the rationalization process, and so are devised 'to experience the world's benefits more fully' (218). However, Campbell's distinction between two senses of rationalization serves
to indicate that there is an alternative to world-affirmation
when this is seen as successfully coping with the demands of
modern (Protestant Ethic) society. Instead of being open to
and celebrating this world, following the process whereby 'the
values of rationality, technical efficiency, and calculability
are introduced into areas formerly governed by traditional or
intuitive values (239), a number of self-religions do not take
'for granted' anonymity and the other characteristics of the
public domain.

As I have tried to show, by being self rather than
world-affirming, and by living in a world (exemplified by
Marin County) or by creating their own, closed worlds (e.g.,
The Farm), they operate in terms of their own distinctive
goals — goals which do not raise the need for escape from
the consequences of pursuing Protestant values.

Perhaps there are two kinds of self-religions: world-
affirming (Campbell's first sense of rationalization, Werblowsky's society-orientated variety) and world-creating (Campbell's
second sense, Werblowsky's inner-orientated, self-realizing
variety). The latter kind — which predominates — cannot easily be handled by the distinction between religion as coping
with the modern world and religion as providing an alternative refuge (Whitworth:168). World-affirmation and rejection are
complex phenomena, depending so much on which world religions
are addressed. Thus the self-religions tend to reject some of societies' characteristics (anonymity); they transform what it is
to be an individual (e.g., Oden on the role of the group; see
also Martin:117, 119; Beckford:290); they affirm the self in
their own worlds; and they celebrate these aspects of the
world (e.g., Marin County) which suit their values. In general, they affirm a world, but a world of the autonomous self
rather than that of public man and the Protestant Ethic. Wallis
writes, 'They have joined such a [world-affirming] movement
not to escape or withdraw from the world and its values, but
to acquire the means to achieve them more easily and to experience the world's benefits more fully' (218; see also
222, 223). It is his contrary theme, concerning 'liberation',the
private alternative (229), which has prompted me to stress
that world-affirmation can in a sense be escapist — or at
least alternative. I prefer to see 'liberation' as from traditional society, rather than within it.

Finally, two small points. Concerning the last section of the book, it would be interesting to know more about the attitudes of society at large to est, Primal Therapy, and other self-religions. And concerning Wilson's mention of discipline (28), it will be instructive to see how the recent Californian emphasis on self-discipline will come to bear on how the self-religions maintain themselves.   How will this affect their routinization?

NOTES

1.   There are a great number of these movements, the list given in Common Ground, 1979, ranging from Astro*Carto* Graphy to Workshops with Master Yeh.

2.   Utopian Eyes, Vol. 4, 3, (San Francisco: Performing Arts Social Society, 1978), p. 11.

3.   When academics come to consider 'modern man' their imaginations tend to run wild. Carroll, 1977: 59, for example, suggests that 'remissive man' of modern America 'is a depressive trying to keep afloat by clutching at the straw of hedonist ideology'.

4.   See Gerzon, 1977 on 'counterculture capitalists' who are taught, among other things, to become 'Castenada-like warriors of the marketplace'.

5.   Luckmann goes somewhat further in delineating the major themes of the private sphere, treating secondary institutions within this context rather than viewing them as defusing it. But even he has little faith in this 'loose and rather unstable' domain (Luckmann, 1967: 117). See also Douglas, 1970; Jacoby, 1977; McFadden, 1979; Rosen, 1978.

6.   See Berger, 1965: 41.

7.   A number of the ideas which follow have been worked out in conjunction with Andy Lock (see Heelas and Lock, eds., 1981).

8.   Whereas in many fundamentalist movements passiones conceptualisations are important (thus minimising the experience of freedom), self-religions blame what is bad on the unconscious or similar notions. This prevents passiones elements taking over from the experience of being autonomous; the unconscious is within the individual self and so, given the basically idealist orientation of the self-religions, positive thinking, together with catharsis, is believed to cure the self, freeing it from harmful forces orginating in the unconscious.

THE NEW PIETISM*

Thomas C. Oden

THE TRADITION AGAINST TRADITION

Carl Rogers views the basic encounter group as "the most rapidly spreading social invention of the century."[1] Although it is admittedly spreading rapidly, we doubt that it is an invention of this century. For although it indeed has returned in a powerful new focus in our time, its basic shape is a recurring pattern in the history of religious communities. We can see similar small-group encounter flourishing in the seventeenth and eighteenth centuries, especially among the radical, dissenting groups of Jewish and Protestant pietism.

The current encounter group is a demythologized and secularized form of a style of interpersonal encounter and community that is familiar to the history of religious communities in the West. The basic prototype of the encounter pattern is found in Protestant and Jewish pietism, which emphasized "here and now" experiencing, intensive small-group encounter, high trust levels in group interaction, honest confession amid a caring community, experimental mysticism, mutual pastoral care, extended conversion marathons, radical accountability to the group, an eclectic amalgam of resources for spiritual formation, gut-level self-disclosure, intimate personal testimony, brutally candid feedback procedures, anti-establishment social attitudes, and the laicization of leadership.[2] All these are the staples of the intensive group experience today. My purpose will be to demonstrate that there are direct analogies, too numerous to be accidental (and, I would also hypothesize,[3] a definable stream of historical influence), between small-group encounter in Protestant and Jewish religious movements, and the current encounter culture.

One of the things that has fascinated me about intensive group experiencing in its popular form today is its determined antihistorical bent. So single-minded is its focus upon the here and now that it tends to neglect any sort of dialogue with the past. So determined is it to create a new future that it imagines that it has no past. Of course this is just historical ignorance. But it says a great deal about the very history out of which it has come, namely, the history of individualistic, pragmatic romanticism, which is paradoxically a tradition against tradition.

Facilitators who work with group processes are not accustomed to thinking historically, yet their work inevitably
exists in a historical continuum that deserves to be made
much clearer. So busy have the encounter culture gurus been
in turning people on to "the now" that it has not occurred to
them that anyone else ever could have done this before them.
Not uncommonly we find among them a flippant polemic even
against the raising of historical consciousness. One might suspect that some fear being discovered as "old hat." The most
damning description that can be addressed to any encounter
group or encounter group leader is that they are doing something old-fashioned. There is an insatiable hunger in the
movement for novelty. There is a corresponding embarrassment
and disgust with history. There is a common assumption that
the future is all that is worthwhile, the past merely an obstacle to be transcended. Thus it is not surprising that there
is a dire neglect of study and lack of awareness of the antecedents and historic prototypes of the encounter movement.

Henry Ford's unforgettable maxim "History is bunk" captures a characteristically American pragmatic attitude that is
deeply engrained in the group processes movement. There is
not only a general dearth of historical awareness (a kinder
term than historical ignorance) but also smug self-satisfaction
among groups that "we" have discovered something fabulously
"new" (the real magic word of the twentieth century). It is
a curious form of modern hubris, which surely someday will
be viewed as myopia. With astonishing self-assurance, the
movement assumes that the only significant moment of history
is the present, that the last single decade is of more value
than the remainder of the past century, and that the past century is of infinitely more value to knowledge than all previous centuries combined.

Accordingly, the limited attempts to account historically
for the encounter group movement and group psychotherapy
make no attempt to reach back more than a hundred years,
and most of them go back only fifty years or less.⁴ Various
accounts date the beginnings of the group processes movement
with Jacob Moreno in 1910, Joseph Pratt in 1905, Cody Marsh
in 1930, or Kenneth Benne in the early 1940s.⁵ Standard texts
in group dynamics attribute the earliest innovations to Kurt
Lewin in the 1930s, Muzafer Sherif in 1936, W.R. Bion in the
1940s. Some interpreters venture to go as far back as Durkheim, Simmel, Comte, Spencer, Cooley, Mead, Ward, Freud,
McDougall, F.H. Allport and others. None of these sources,
however, addresses the eighteenth-century religious societies
where the basic prototypes of the current encounter group are
clearly to be found on a vast scale in a highly refined form
as a vigorous and popular lay movement.

To say that the encounter culture is unconscious of its sources does not mean that it must be exhaustively conscious of those sources in order to function effectively at the operational level. But we would suppose that some heightened awareness of its historic origins would help it to avoid some of its messianic illusions or romantic conceptions of its own novelty. A part of what makes the group processes movement a "movement," however, is its curious conception of itself as something entirely new and uniquely promising for the future. Without this persistent historical narcissism, it could not have developed the strong "movement" character that it now has.

The encounter impresarios have extended the helpful therapeutic dictum of "staying in the here and now" into a general maxim of historical awareness. The only history they know is the history they are pretending to make. Yet, sadly enough, they remain blind to the very historical forces that enable them to think the way they think and to frame the issues the way they frame them. One never hears mentioned among them the names of Renaissance men such as Pico della Mirandola or Leon Battista Alberti, who, like them, were supremely confident of the capacity of man for self-transformation, and who inaugurated another vast "human potential movement", which we call the Renaissance. They know or speak little of the "heavenly vision of the eighteenth century philosophers" of which Carl Becker has so delightfully written, which in so many ways shapes the philosophical underpinnings of their romanticisms. [6] They have not studied the utopias of the sixteenth or nineteenth centuries, which in decisive ways predate their own utopian hopes.

So there remains a vast historical labor that needs to be done in order to bring the movement into clearer self-awareness. But my focus here will be on one principle pattern from which the encounter culture today has most decisively borrowed as a model for social interaction and growth, viz., the encounter style of Protestant and Jewish pietism in the seventeenth, eighteenth, and nineteenth centuries.

THE DEMYTHOLOGIZING OF PIETISTIC ENCOUNTER

A highly mobile charismatic itinerancy was the prevalent model for ministry in frontier American pietism. Faced with a frontier in constant flux not unlike our "temporary society," these itinerant charismatic leaders moved constantly on horseback from small lay group to small lay group, facilitating their growth. Energized by visions of vast and rapid human change, armed with eclectic resources, and fascinated by experimental social interaction, they were accustomed to brutally honest feedback procedures. [7]

Similarly today the encounter change agents have combined a broad spectrum of resources with tough-minded feedback procedures to facilitate rapid growth in a mobile social
context. The frontier model of itinerancy has been reappropriated as the prevalent model for leadership among the group
facilitators today. From weekend to weekend they go on the
"sawdust trail," converting, turning people on, building communities of growth and trust. They move from growth center
to growth center, from happening to happening, from revival
to revival, trying to re-energize the movement, teaching the
latest techniques, ever faithful to the apostolic witnesses of
the encounter culture (the canonical saints Perls, Maslow,
Rogers, Reich, and Watts), encouraging pilgrimages to holy
places like Bethel (!) and the healing waters of Esalen.

The social conditions to which the encounter culture is
responding (mobility, depersonalization, emotive paralysis, the
breakdown of authoritarian traditions) are almost identical to
the conditions against which Protestant and Jewish pietism
were protesting.[8] Rogers correctly observes that the small-
group movement "has grown up entirely outside the 'establishment.' Most universities still look upon it with scorn.... The
established professions of clinical psychology and psychiatry
have stayed aloof, while the political right wing is certain
that it represents a deep-seated Communist plot." Each of these
has its parallel in the anti-establishment mentality of left
wing experiential pietism, which was looked upon with deep
suspicion in its day by the Lutheran, Anglican, and Jewish
religious establishments and by the universities. In some cases
it was literally driven out of the land because of its seemingly radical character. It too was interpreted as an extremist
plot against common order.

The Jewish form of pietism is Hasidism. Hasid refers to
the righteous or the pious. The Hasidism that arose among remote Polish and Ukranian Jewish communities in the eighteenth
century is remarkably similar to the spirit of Protestant pietism. It too was not primarily concerned with correct dogma or
ritual but with the actual appropriation of the life of faith
in community.

By the eighteenth century, Judaism was ready for a reaction against certain ascetic forms of rabbinical orthodoxy
that emphasized fasting, penance, and "spiritual sadness." Hasidism was a response to the desire of ordinary people for a
joyful, emotively satisfying faith applied practically in a social context. The aim of Hasidism was not to change belief
but to change the believer. Concrete experiencing in the here
and now was more important than abstract conceptualizing. [9]

A prominent feature of all forms of pietism, as well as
of the current encounter culture, is the concept of a spiritual

breakthrough of intense emotive depth that changes behavior radically. The literature of pietism is filled with testimonials of persons who have undergone sudden and radical conversion experiences.[10] Typically, after having first experienced themselves as being crushed by guilt and despair, they then describe how, within a supportive group, a radical turning point is experienced in which they feel deeply the acceptance and grace of God, whereupon a rich flow of gratitude and freedom motivates them to reshape their behavior. This is the center of the pietistic conversion experience, epitomized best by John Wesley's feeling his heart "strangely warmed" when an assurance was given him that Christ "had taken away my sins, even mine."

Compare this with an account written by a member of a basic encounter group (quoted by Rogers): "I had really buried under a layer of concrete many feelings I was afraid people were going to laugh at or stomp on, which, needless to say, was working all kinds of hell on my family and on me.... The real turning point for me was a simple gesture on your part of putting your arm around my shoulder one afternoon when I had made some crack about you not being a member of the group — that no one could cry on your shoulder. In my notes I had written the night before, 'There is no man in the world who loves me!' You seemed to be so genuinely concerned that day I was overwhelmed! . . . I received the gesture as one of the first feelings of acceptance — of me, just the dumb way I am, prickles and all — that I had ever experienced. I have felt needed, loving, competent, furious, frantic, anything and everything but just plain loved. You can imagine the flood of gratitude, humility, release that swept over me. I wrote with considerable joy, 'I actually felt loved.' I doubt that I shall soon forget it."[11]

In probing these striking similarities, I am not arguing that modern group process leaders have been overtly or even secretly reading the literature of Protestant or Jewish pietism. The fact that they would not wish to be caught dead doing so, however, interests me immensely. A curious part of the task of historical inquiry is to show why they have preferred not to behold their own history, and why they have not analyzed the subtle and indirect forms in which they have unselfconsciously reappropriated and transmuted an available religious tradition. These pietistic patterns were quietly and inertly "in the air" as available social models for the progenitors of current group encounter such as Lewin, Moreno, Rogers, and the National Training Laboratories innovators.[12] The fact that they were borrowed and applied unconsciously rather than consciously is noteworthy, to say the least, especially among therapists so deliberately committed to "making the unconscious conscious."

I want to avoid the reductionist impression that current encounter group processes can be boiled down essentially to what was taking place in the eighteenth-century religious societies. I am trying, rather, to unveil the striking similarities between the two movements, and in a modest way to hypothesize that there may be some discernible flow of influence from the pietistic encounter style to the current encounter style.

Jewish and Protestant pietism have both been, like current encounter groups, highly syncretistic movements. Wesley's movement, for example, was a practical synthesis of Puritan and Anglican (or more broadly Protestant and Catholic) traditions of faith and practice and communal life. Few of the parts of the synthesis were original with him, but his putting them together in a practical focus, easily implemented in small groups, was a unique and gifted contribution.[13] Likewise, it is of the essence of the encounter culture today that it is syncretistic, putting a broad range of change strategies together into a working, practical synthesis of resources for human growth in small groups.

A system of approaches so eclectic can hardly be the work of a single man or narrow group of men. Nor can it be the product of a single generation. Rather, so complex and varied are these resources that it seems more plausible that they have emerged through a long series of cultural mutations and only through the achievement of several generations of intensive communities experimenting with personal growth.

It is regrettable that we are compelled to use the historian's term "pietism" to describe a movement so creative and variegated since that term has been so badly abused by a long tradition of religious experience which often bordered on fanaticism and anti-intellectualism. Some historians distinguish between classical pietism of the seventeenth and eighteenth centuries and a later or deteriorating pietism of the late nineteenth and twentieth centuries when the original genius had long been spent.[14] It is regrettable that when the term "pietism" is currently used, it usually points not to that classical movement which spawned so many creative impulses in Western history but rather to that deteriorated form of introverted, self-concerned, self-righteous fanaticism in its most undesirable and caricatured forms. Although classical pietism is still the nomenclature preferred by historians who mark the developments from Spener, Zinzendorf, and the Baal Shem-Tob to the Blumhardts, Finney and Mordecai of Lekhovitz, we might also correctly refer to this period as a movement of "experiential small group religious innovation."[15]

My intent is not to debunk encounter groups by showing their supposedly embarrassing historical origins. Doubtless some who are only willing to deal lightly with our hypothesis may draw that erroneous conclusion. Rather, I am attempting to be positively supportive of the encounter culture precisely through showing that its historic origins are unconsciously in touch with rich Western religious resources from which it now considers itself to be estranged. Though often despised and vilified, the classical pietistic tradition was far more innovative than its reputation for rigidity would indicate.[16] Both Jewish and Protestant pietism have been profoundly instrumental in liberating the Western tradition from the strictures of scholastic orthodoxy and in helping to introduce it to the modern world, focusing on the experiencing moral subject, which became the overriding theme of liberal theology from Kant and Schleiermacher to the present.

The question remains as to why the otherwise intelligent proponents of the intensive group experience in the twentieth century have not mentioned or even recognized their Protestant and Jewish pietistic origins. If we reflect carefully, however, their reasons for not wishing to discuss this relationship have been, from a practical point of view, understandable. Quite simply, the tradition of emotive and quasi-fanatical pietism has long been out of favor with the socially mobile intelligentsia and cultural avant-garde who form the clientele of the encounter culture. In fact, the pietistic tradition is radically out of favor today with almost everyone, including not only the universities and the historians but also the seminaries, and even the churches and synagogues that pietism has spawned. Pietistic words such as "revival" and "religion of the heart" and "conversion" and "testimony" are repulsive to self-consciously modern persons. The irony, of course, is that although the words are no longer acceptable, all the meanings that those words freighted have been taken right back into the heart of the encounter culture.

In a similar vein, David Bakan has shown that Freud had convincing practical reasons for not wishing to reveal his roots in Jewish mysticism, since anti-Semitism was rife in his Viennese context and "to indicate the Jewish sources of his ideas would have dangerously exposed an intrinsically controversial theory to an unnecessary and possibly fatal opposition."[17] Bakan plausibly demonstrates that "Freud would have had good reason to deliberately conceal his sources if he were conscious that psychoanalysis was a development in the tradition of Jewish mysticism."[18] Likewise we believe that the encounter leaders would have good reason deliberately and circumspectly to hope that their roots might remain hidden (even if inadvertently by failing to inquire into them), if they suspected that those roots might have made them look scandalous, fanatic, anti-intellectual, or, in a word, "pietistic" to their upwardly mobile liberal clientele.

We cannot ignore a curious form of dissimulation in the movement. If you can convince the encounter clientele that the meditation they are doing comes from Eastern religions, and not from the West, you can proceed amiably. If you can apply language like chakra, satori, and karma to your interpretations, instead of using their ordinary Western equivalents (which actually are more in touch with where the clientele is), you will find ready hearers, even though that language comes from authoritarian traditions which would be ipso facto rejected if they were Western. A group leader probably will be more acceptable if he can persuade his hearers that the "peak experiences" which he is programming have nothing to do with Western religion, and if Western, certainly not Protestant, and if Protestant, certainly not Calvinistic puritanism, and if Calvinism, certainly not pietism, against which they understand themselves to be most certainly rebelling.

Puritanism is doubtless the worst of words in the encounter vocabulary. The irony, of course, is that it is precisely the pietistic wing of the puritan Protestant tradition (so strongly influenced by English Calvinist dissent) which is being reappropriated in current encounter groups. Thus the deepest roots of the encounter movement are in the least likely of all places: in Calvinism more than in any other religious traditions, including all Hindu and Buddhist themes combined. In fact, the Zen and yoga themes which have been so overtly incorporated into the encounter culture have largely been absorbed into a world view decisively shaped by puritan Protestantism. In fact, the Americanized Zen and yoga often become unrecognizable to Easterners. So it is a curious self-deception to imagine that the deeper motivating forces behind the encounter culture come from Eastern religions. If and when the actual historical models are carefully clarified, this self-deception will be more and more difficult to sustain.[19]

COMPARISON OF THE PIETISTIC ENCOUNTER STYLES
WITH CURRENT ENCOUNTER

The following quotations are placed in two columns in order to clarify similarities between small-group encounter styles of free-church Protestantism and those of the contemporary encounter culture. Although a much more detailed analysis could be made, these quotations provide a brief sampling of the similar approaches in five basic areas:

    A.   The Small-Group Format
    B.   The Zealous Pursuit of Honesty
    C.   Focus on Here and Now Experiencing
    D.   The Nurture of Intimacy
    E.   Revival as Marathon

Statements from eighteenth- and nineteenth-century pietistic writings in the left column may be compared with statements in the right column from the principal leaders of the encounter culture today — Perls, Rogers, Maslow, Schutz, and others.

A. The Small-Group Format

Eighteenth- and Nineteenth-Century Religious Group Encounter Styles

Let each member of the class relate his experience with freedom and simplicity. The design of the classes is to ascertain the spiritual state of each member, in order that religious sympathy be excited, mutual regard promoted, mutual encouragement obtained.—Rosser, 1855.[20]

They have no need of being incumbered with many rules; having the best rule of all in their hearts. <u>No peculiar directions</u> were therefore given to them.... Everyone here has an equal liberty of speaking, there being none greater or less than another.... I often found the advantage of such a free conversation, and that "in the multitude of counsellors there is safety." — Wesley, 1748.[22]

Current Encounter Group Styles

All communication in the group should be as open and honest as it's possible to be.... Learn how to be more open with everyone, including yourself.... Talk directly to the person addressed. —Schutz, 1971.[21]

This group will meet for many hours and will serve as a kind of laboratory where each individual can increase his understanding of the forces which influence individual behavior and the performance of groups and organizations. The data for learning will be our own behavior, feelings, and reactions. We begin with <u>no definite structure</u> or <u>organization</u>, no agreed-upon procedures, and no specific agenda. It will be up to us to fill the vacuum created by the lack of these familiar elements and to study our group as we evolve.... With these few comments, I think we are ready to begin in whatever way you feel will be most helpful. — Seashore, 1968.[23]

I desired a small number... to spend an hour with me every Monday evening. My design was, not only to... incite them to love one another more, and to watch more carefully over each other, but also to have a select company, to whom I might unbosom myself on all occasions, without reserve. —Wesley, 1748.[24]

The deeper you go the safer it is. If you go deep the group gets close. People begin caring for each other and supporting each other. --Schutz, quoted by Gustaitis, 1969.[25]

They began to "bear one another's burdens," and naturally to "care for each other." As they had daily a more intimate acquaintance with, so they had a more endearing affection for, each other. —Wesley, 1748.[26]

A climate of mutual trust develops out of this mutual freedom to express real feelings, positive and negative. —Rogers, 1970.[27]

B. The Zealous Pursuit of Honesty

Do you desire that every one of us should tell you, from time to time, whatsoever is in his heart concerning you? Consider! Do you desire we should tell you whatsoever we think, whatsoever we fear, whatsoever we hear concerning you? —Wesley, 1744.[28]

Feedback is most acceptable when the receiver himself has formulated the question which those observing him can answer. It is solicited, rather than imposed. —National Training Laboratories, 1968.[29]

Do you desire to be told of your faults? —Wesley, 1744.[30]

Discover your resistances. —Perls and others, 1951.[31]

Rules of the Bands:
To speak each of us in order, freely and plainly, the true state of our souls, with faults we have committed in thought, word, or

The assumption in your groups seems to be, on the contrary, that people are very tough, and not brittle. They can take an awful lot. The best thing to

deed, and the temptations we have felt since our last meeting. —Wesley, 1744. [32]

Self-examination, severe, thorough, impartial. The class meeting will be productive of but little real, lasting benefit without this. —Rosser, 1855. [33]

Rules of the Bands: Is it your desire and design to be, on this and all other occasions, entirely open, so as to speak everything that is in your heart without exception, without disguise and without reserve? Have you nothing you desire to keep secret? —Wesley, 1744. [35]

What known sins have you committed since our last meeting? —Wesley, 1744. [37]

Rules of the Bands: To desire some person among us to speak his own state first, and then to ask the rest, in order, as many and as searching questions as may be, concerning their state, sins and temptations. —Wesley, 1744. [39]

do is get right at them, and not to sneak up on them, or be delicate with them, or try to surround them from the rear. Get right smack into the middle of things right away. I've suggested that a name for this might be "no-crap therapy." It serves to clean out the defenses, the rationalizations, the veils, the evasions and politeness of the world. —Maslow, 1967. [34]

The pursuit of honesty is begun by asking the couples to think of three secrets they have never told their mate and that would be most likely to jeopardize their relationship. During the course of the workshop they tell these secrets. —Schutz, 1971. [36]

I force my groups to be open, to tell me everything. —Schutz, 1971. [38]

Making the rounds. The therapist may feel that a particular theme or feeling expressed by the patient should be faced vis a vis every other person in the group. The patient may have said, "I can't stand anyone in this room." Therapist: "O.K., make the rounds. Say that to each one of us and add some other remark pertaining to your feelings about each person." —Levitsky, 1969. [40]

Falsehoods are many, but truth is one. —Rabbi Nachman Brazlaver, 1810.[41]

As open encounter proceeds and gets more profound, as intrapsychic methods get deeper.... I see man's unity and oneness more clearly. —Schutz,1971.[42]

C. Focus on Here and Now Experiencing

Let your expressions be clear and definite, pointed and brief, having reference to your present experience, so that the state of your mind may be easily apprehended. —Newstead, 1843.[43]

Realize (make real) the nowness of your experience. —Perls, 1969.[44]

Beware of resting in past experience. —Newstead, 1843.[45]

Nothing exists except the now. —Perls, quoted by Gustaitis, 1969.[46]

Prayer in the class-room is special, and is concentrated upon some present object, and this explains, to some degree, its power. —Rosser, 1855.[47]

Stay with the here and now as much as possible. —Schutz, 1971.[48]

An ingenuous account of our temptations is the surest way to subdue them. —Rosser, 1855.[49]

The principle is, "Can you stay with this feeling?" This technique is evoked at key moments when the patient refers to a feeling or mood or state of mind which is unpleasant and which he has a great urge to dispel.... The therapist says, "Can you stay with this feeling?" —Levitsky, 1969.[50]

Do you desire that, in doing this, we should come as close as possible; that we should cut to the quick, and search your heart to the bottom? —Wesley, 1744.[51]

I and thou; here and now. —Perls, 1969.[52]

Shun the very appearance of affectation. Let your words and your manner be perfectly natural. Do not... speak in borrowed nor hackneyed terms, lest it should become a merely formal exercise, and consequently a deceptive one. —Newstead, 1843. [53]

Words are special culprits in the effort to avoid personal confrontation.—Schutz, 1967. [54]

In the evening I went very unwillingly to a society in Aldersgate Street, where one was reading Luther's preface to the Epistle to the Romans. About a quarter before nine, while he was describing the change which God works in the heart through faith in Christ, I felt my heart strangely warmed, I felt I did trust in Christ, Christ alone, for salvation; and an assurance was given me, that He had taken away my sins, even mine, and saved me from the law of sin and death. —Wesley, 1738. [55]

Go to your core — focus, connect to yourself and then to the others with you, and surrender yourself fully to the feeling from your core. —Lewis and Streitfeld, 1970. [56]

D. The Nurture of Intimacy

Many, many a time, in immediate answer to prayer, in the class-room, so intensely burns the heart with love to God and man, that the whole class is quickened by the subduing and stirring testimony given, and the very class-room seems to be a mansion of glory. —Rosser, 1855. [57]

Participants feel a closeness and intimacy which they have not felt even with their spouses or members of their own family, because they have revealed themselves here more deeply. —Rogers, 1970. [58]

When a happy correspondence between the outward walk and inward piety of believers is discovered, which can be known only

Where all is known and all accepted...further growth becomes possible.... To his astonishment, he finds that he is more accepted the by the disclosure of the interior life, we are not only prepared to comfort, encourage and strengthen one another, but form an intimacy of the holiest nature, a union of the strongest character. —Rosser, 1855.[59]

If we yield to the suggestions that our distresses are the most deplorable, that our sins are so heinous that they ought not to be disclosed, or are so trivial that they need not be confessed, . . . or that we should give an unfair and partial account of our true state, . . . and refer in but an obscure manner to whatever in us is disagreeable and unfavorable...our testimony in all these cases amounts to nothing more than a hurtful illusion. —Rosser, 1855.[61]

Tell your experience; and tell your conflicts; and tell your comforts. As iron sharpeneth iron, as rubbing of the hands maketh both warm, and as live coals maketh the rest to burn, so let the fruit of society be mutually sharpening, warming, and influencing. —Rosser, 1855.[63]

We all partake the joy of one;
The common peace we feel;
A peace to sensual minds unknown,
A joy unspeakable.

And if our fellowship below
In Jesus be so sweet,

more real that he becomes. —Rogers, 1970.[60]

This willingness to take the risk of being one's inner self is certainly one of the steps toward relieving the loneliness that exists in each one of us and putting us in genuine touch with other human beings. A college student expressed this risk very well when he said, "I felt at a loss today in that encounter group. Very naked. Now everyone knows too much about me; at the same time I am more comfortable in the knowledge that I don't have to put on my 'cool.'" —Rogers, 1970.[62]

To discover that a whole group of people finds it much easier to care for the real self than for the external facade is always a moving experience. -- Rogers, 1970.[64]

One point at which open encounter and a mystical viewpoint are mutually helpful occurs when an encounter is going very deep. After hostility is worked through and differences acknowledged as people reach the deeper layers of personal-

What height of rapture
  shall we know
When round his throne we
  meet!
—Charles Wesley, hymn,
1979.[65]

Brother, is they heart with
mine, as my heart is with
thy heart? If it be, give
me thy hand. —Wesley,
1742. [66]

ity, the similarity of all
men becomes clearer. We are
all in the same struggle
but using different paths
with different defenses. The
notion that we are all one
is given great meaning at
these almost mystical mo-
ments in the group's life.
—Schutz, 1971.[67]

E. Revival as Marathon [68]

In this revival originated
our camp-meetings, and in
both these denominations
they were held every year,
and, indeed, have been
ever since, more or less.
They would erect their
camps with logs or frame
them, and cover them with
clapboards or shingles...
and here they would collect
together from forty to fifty
miles around, sometimes further than that. Ten, twenty, and sometimes thirty
ministers, of different denominations, would come together and preach night
and day, four or five days
together; and, indeed, I
have known these camp-
meetings to last three or
four weeks, and great good
resulted from them.... I
have seen and heard more
than five hundred Chris-
tians all shouting aloud
the high praises of God at
once. --Cartwright, 1856.[69]

The fountains of sin need
to be broken up. In a true
revival, Christians are always brought under such

The marathon is not unlike
a "pressure cooker" in
which phony steam boils
away and genuine emotions
(including negative ones)
emerge. The group atmo-
sphere is kept focused
every moment on the objectives at hand: to produce
change in orientation and
new ways of dealing with
old crucial problems.
—Bach, 1966.[70]

These experiences led me to
the conclusion that the
depth that could be reached in a concentrated workshop was so remarkable
compared to the other ap-
proaches that I have virtually abandoned all other
patterns.... I've found...
that one intensive week is
equivalent to two or three
years of periodic therapy
sessions, and that groups
are much more effective
than individual sessions.
—Schutz, 1971.[71]

A chronically contracted
muscle is in effect saying,
"no." ...Lying on a bed
with a foam mattress he is

convictions; they see their sins in such a light, that often they find it impossible to maintain a hope of their acceptance.... The first step is a deep repentance, a breaking down of heart, a getting down into the dust before God, with deep humility, and forsaking sin. —Finney, 1834. [72]

I have been at meetings where the whole congregation would be bathed in tears; and sometimes their cries would be so loud that the preacher's voice could not be heard. Some would be seized with trembling, and in a few moments drop on the floor as if they were dead; while others were embracing each other with streaming eyes, and all were lost in wonder, love and praise. —Lee, 1810. [74]

With regard to these prudential helps we are continually changing one thing after another. [This] is not a weakness or fault, as you imagine, but a peculiar advantage which we enjoy. By this means we declare them all to be merely prudential, not essential, not of divine institution. We prevent, so far as in us lies, their growing formal or dead. We are always open to instruction; willing to be wiser every day than we were before. —Wesley, 1748. [76]

asked to strike the bed repeatedly with his fists and say "no" with each blow in a loud and convincing tone.... At this point the group may encourage the subject to "let go," to pound with all his strength and yell with all his might. —Ruitenbeek, 1970. [73]

Participants almost unanimously speak of marathons, immediately afterward and a year afterward, as a worthwhile and moving experience. The words, "I felt reborn" are often uttered. —Mintz, 1967. [75]

The "open encounter group" ...implies that the method is always changing and evolving. The groups we run today are run very differently from last year's and next year's groups. —Schutz, 1971. [77]

CONCLUSION

Pietism never produced a respected theological literature. Speculative theology was less fascinating to it than live small-group encounter. What kind of literature did pietism produce? A literature that looks and "feels" much like the literature of current encounter culture. It was a literature of devotion and exhortation, of technique and practical behavioral change, of experimental mysticism and fascination with the occult. Its failure to produce a viable tradition of academic theology is paralleled by the failure of current encounter culture to produce a corpus of theoretical literature that would equal in impressiveness its actual innovative spirit.

Most historians of Christian thought have been immensely bored by pietism. The chief reason is that pietism has produced such a negligible amount of "systematic theology." What it did produce was an astonishing variety of communities experimenting with religious encounter, integrating faith into the whole of life. Since pietism itself was an experimental theology, there was a steady resistance to the very attempt to write any final or systematic presentation of theological systems, partly because it knew that whatever was written soon would have to be rewritten in the light of new experiencing. This is equally characteristic of the encounter culture with its lack of interest in systematic theorizing.

The principal medium of communication for both pietism and the encounter culture is the here and now verbal encounter in a small-group context with a high level of mutual trust. The medium is talk — experience-based talk, and that in small groups, with a strong emotive and experiential focus. It is not the academic treatise. It is not surprising that the academic establishment has been among the last to become interested in encounter techniques (despite their relevance for the educational process) just as academia was slow in seeing any value in pietistic radicalism.

The movement spawned by Moreno, Lewin, Rogers, Perls, Maslow, and Benne could not have occurred without the available models of societal interaction derived from the Judeo-Christian tradition. Over against the popular view that the religious inspiration of the encounter culture comes from Eastern religions, I am convinced that the basic "I-thou" model of interpersonal encounter was delivered to the encounter culture from Jewish theologians such as Buber and from Protestant thinkers such as Kierkegaard, Tillich, and Gogarten long before they became common currency in existential philosophy. The encounter model is only awkwardly and unconvincingly attributed to Hindu and Buddhist thought. This is not to idealize the West. Much that the encounter culture is protesting is a result of basic inadequacies in Western society. But its protest is as Western as the Western distortions against which it is protesting.

NOTES

*   This paper is adapted from "Chapter Two: The New Pietism," from The Intensive Group Experience: The New Pietism, by Thomas C. Oden. Copyright **O**   MCMLXXII, The
Westminster Press. Adapted by permission.

1.   Rogers 1970: 1.

2.   For further information concerning Jewish and Protestant pietism see Ritschl, 1880-1886; Lang, 1941; Ensign, 1955
and works noted below.

3.   A further attempt at corroboration of my hypothesis
could be made by pursuing the biographies of persons who
have shared the encounter culture. See Current Biography
(Yearbook, 1946-1968, published by The H.W. Wilson Company):
Carl Rogers, Dec., 1962; Alan Watts, March 1962; Martin
Buber, July 1965; Gordon Allport, Dec., 1967.

4.   Cartwright and Zander, 1960; 3ff; Bonner, 1959; 3ff;
Benne, "History of the T-Group in its Historical Setting" in
Bradford et al, 1964: 80ff; Dreikurs, 1959: 219-255; Ansbacher,
1951: 383-391; Moreno, 1969: 7-16.

5.   For accounts of the historical background of the encounter group movement, see Moreno, 1911; 1914; 1918; 1920;
1922; 1931; 18-19; 1941: 205-226; Moreno (ed.), 1960; Johnson,
1959: 42ff; Corsini and Putzey, 1957; Marsh, 1931: 328-349.

6.   Pico della Mirandola, 1956; Becker, 1950.

7.   For information concerning frontier American pietism,
see Bennis and Slater, 1968; Sweet, 1933; Asbury, 1852;
Muhlenberg, 1942-1958.

8.   Schmidt and Jannasch (eds.), 1965; Stoeffler, 1965;
McNeill, 1954.

9.   Scholem, 1941: 344; Newman, 1944; Buber, 1948(a);
1948(b); Buber (ed.), 1947; Schechter, 1896: 1ff; Dubnow, 1916;
Rabinowicz, 1960; Müller, 1946.

10.   Althaus, 1959: 3-25; Bodamer, 1961: 435-437; Dimond,
1926.

11.   Rogers, 1970: 34; cf. Moustakis, 1968; and Burke and
Bennis, 1961: 165-182.

12.   McLoughlin, 1965: 163ff.

13.   Telford (ed.), 1931; Emory, 1850; Outler, 1957; Simon, 1937; Nagler, 1918; Treat, 1967: 13ff.

14.   Gerdes, 1968: 257–268; Deeter, 1964: 18–49.

15.   Weinlock, 1956; Uttendörfer, 1935; Spangenberg, 1779; Arndt, 1868.

16.   Weigelt, 1970: 236–241; Tholuck, 1865.

17.   Bakan, 1965: 26.

18.   Ibid: 33 (italics mine).

19.   Watts, 1961; 1960; Northrup, 1946.

20.   Rosser, 1855: 282–283. For further study of the encounter style of the Methodist class meeting, see Atkinson, 1875; Christophers, 1873; Cordeux, 1820; Emerick, 1958; Fitzgerald, 1880; Janes, 1868; Miley, 1866; Wood, 1809.

21.   Schutz, 1971: 149–154.

22.   Emory (ed.), 1850: Vol. V: 184f (italics mine).

23.   Seashore, 1968 (italics mine); cf. Maslow, 1963: 7.

24.   Emory (ed.), 1850: Vol. V: 184f.

25.   Schutz, quoted by Gustaitis, 1969: 213.

26.   Wesley, 1974: Vol. II: 113; cf. Drakeford, 1967.

27.   Rogers, 1970: 7; cf. Culberg, 1968.

28.   John Wesley, "Rules of the Band" in Outler (ed.), 1967: 180.

29.   "Objectives of Human Relations Training," 92 (National Training Laboratories, 1968) (italics mine).

30.   Outler (ed.), 1967: 180.

31.   Perls et al., 1951: 40.

32.   Outler (ed.), 1967: 180

33.   Rosser, 1855: 284.

34.   Maslow, 1967.

35.   Outler (ed.), 1967: 180.

36.   Schutz, 1971: 39.

37.   Outler (ed.), 1967: 180.

38.   Schutz, 1971: xvi.

39.   Outler (ed.), 1967: 180.

40.   Levitsky:10.

41.   Newman, 1944: 488.

42.   Schutz, 1971: 63.

43.   Newstead, 1843: 17-18.

44.   Perls, 1969.

45.   Newstead, 1843: 19.

46.   Perls, quoted by Gustaitis, 1969: 49.

47.   Rosser, 1855: 286.

48.   Schutz, 1971: 149.

49.   Rosser, 1855: 283.

50.   Levitsky: 15.

51.   Outler (ed.), 1967: 180.

52.   Perls, quoted by Simkin in "Introduction to Gestalt Therapy," mimeographed paper: 1.

53.   Newstead, 1843: 18.

54.   Schutz, 1971: 140.

55.   Wesley, 1974: Vol. I: 465ff.

56.   Lewis and Streitfield, 1971: 18.

57.   Rosser, 1855: 287.

58.   Rogers, 1970: 9.

59.   Rosser, 1855: 151.

60.   Rogers, 1970: 8.

61.   Rosser, 1855: 283.

62.   Rogers, 1970: 114.

63.   Rosser, 1855: 47, quoted from a source "prior to the act of conformity."

64.   Rogers, 1970: 114.

65.   "All Praise to Our Redeeming Lord," The Methodist Hymnal (1966), Hymn 301.

66.   Telford (ed.), 1931: Vol. 2: 8.

67.   Schutz, 1971: 56.

68.   "Jewish Revivalists" (A Discussion of the Maggidim, or Itinerant Preachers), London Jewish World, July 28, 1932: 8-9; cf. Marsh, "Group Treatment as Psychological Equivalent"; Stoller, 1967: 28-33; Bach, 1967: 1163-1172; Lamott, 1969.

69.   Cartwright, 1956; McLoughlin, 1968: 46.

70.   Bach, 1966: 995-1002.

71.   Schutz, 1971: 127.

72.   Finney, 1960.

73.   Ruitenbeek, 1970: 158-159.

74.   Lee, 1810: 59.

75.   Mintz, 1967.

76.   Telford (ed.), 1931: Vol. 2: 298.

77.   Schutz, 1971: xv.

THE PEACE SENTIMENT: OLD AND NEW

David Martin

This paper is not concerned with a particular group, but
with a theme which was prevalent in the milieux drawn upon
by the current wave of new religions. That theme was peace.
However, this desire for peace was in some ways continuous
with the older versions of pacifism (some of them sectarian,
and some based on the individual conscience), and in other
ways discontinuous. Lots of features in the older versions
were reproduced by the newer ones, but transmogrified, ordered
in fresh combinations, given a different thrust and tone. The
social context of the sixties realised new potentialities in older
themes. So the paper has to begin by setting out the original
thematic material before contrasting this with the mutations
which that material underwent in the crucible of the sixties
from which new religions emerged. This original material is
analyzed in some detail precisely because this is the context,
the "resource", from which crucial attitudes and ideas were
taken and developed. The emphasis throughout is on Anglo-
American culture, since that is where the peace sentiment has
been most widely diffused. The last section is concerned solely
with what such mutations might imply about the society in
which they occurred.

THE KINDS OF PACIFISM

The classic manifestations of pacifism were of two principal kinds. One was Christian and sectarian, based on a principled withdrawal from the institutions of overt coercion whether within nations or between them. This Christian, sectarian
withdrawal had to build up a very distinctive and enclosed
pattern of socialisation, such as obtained amongst the Mennonites and the Quakers. This was necessary to maintain the integrity of social withdrawal, especially against state inter-
ference and/or the corrosive power of national enthusiasm.
The second classic manifestation of pacifism was rooted in the
autonomy of the individual conscience. It might be based on
a secular liberal principle, appealing to a Kantian moral imperative, or else on the typical stance of the free churches.
So far as a religious variant was concerned, it lacked the
comprehensive social backing provided by enclosed sectarian
socialisation and leaned rather on the general respect for personal conscience generated by evangelical Christianity. Perhaps this particular response occurred most where evangelical

religion had undergone some partial liberalisation. But whether secular or religious it rested on a conception of sensitive ethical autonomy nurtured in a vigorous self-discipline. It was high-minded and controlled.

However, there was a third variant of pacifism which existed alongside Christian sectarianism and religious or secular high-mindedness. This comprised a semi-anarchic hedonism, for which all constraint, whether exercised by the state or by the self, was inimical. The free self was the source of creation and delight, whereas the centralised authority of state or of the strong ego was repressive and destructive. Such a viewpoint could accept neither the discipline of high-minded conscientiousness nor the total long-term environment provided by the sect. Rather it depended on a broad, sensuous rapprochement with the world based on and induced by "permissive" socialisation. In the course of such socialisation the hard elements of social life, external coercion and self-control, were carefully avoided or kept at a distance by adults, and by a welfare state which provided indulgent protection.

Protected in this way the hedonistic ego is free to construct perspectives from which hierarchy, discipline and compulsion are absent. It can construct a responsive world where wish is -- almost -- law. Within such perspectives one may, perhaps, desire to build up a gemeinschaftlich community, but it will not usually require the taking of vows or obedience to rules because harmony and peace can be established naturally. Such peaceable communities may be joined by the children of pleasure at will and left at will. They need not assume any long-term commitment which can constrain and restrict their future options. A communitarian "kick" is just one temporary expedient among others. Inevitably in such a milieu there is no place for the concept of an ineluctable national loyalty and of military formations demanding absolute obedience. The psyche does not submerge itself for the sake of a "generalized other" embodied in a national group or admit subordination to an institution. Unchosen loyalty and invariant obedience are anathema.

This third variant of pacifism was precursor to the modern situation. This is not to say that all or most of the new religions adopted this generalised rejection of hierarchy and coercion. Indeed, some of the religious groupings were formed in reaction against just this slackened loyalty to the collective and loosened focus on achievement and discipline. It is simply that a particular version of the peace sentiment was diffused in the broad milieux out of which members of new religious groupings were drawn. It characterised the pool of broad orientations, ready for transmutation into the several varieties of overt commitment found in such bodies as, say, the Hare Krishna or the Unification Church or the Children of God.

One should not suppose that these orientations, characterizing the new peace sentiment and diffused at large in the recruiting sectors of the new religions, were totally distinct from
the attitudes informing the older pacifism. As I come now to
describe these older attitudes, it will be clear that many of
them were vigorously revived. At least there were enough
plausible resuscitations of the classical approaches to convince
some traditional pacifists that they had acquired new allies.
The difference lay, however, in new conceptions of self and
citizenship. Outside their specific rejection of war, the Quaker
or Mennonite sectarians, and indeed the liberal or Christian
devotees of conscience, were reliable, and self-consistent over
time, both as people and as citizens. The new generation was
not reliable in the same way, and might shift rapidly through
any number of psychic colourings which could even include the
momentary espousal of exemplary violence.

What the peace sentiment within the perspective of new
religions drew most from the liberal and sectarian utopias was
pervasive suspicion and the denunciatory style. The older liberal suspected the diplomats and secret diplomacy, the armaments manufacturers and the military interest. So too did the
most recent generation, focusing its suspicions on the military-
industrial complex with almost paranoid zeal. Old and new
displayed a common capacity to oscillate between impossible
optimism and total pessimism, simultaneously welcoming the new
age and announcing the Apocalypse. Both saw so much empirically wrong in "the world" and so much potentially right.
All the varieties of pacifism espoused a mutated version of the
Christian concept of "the world" in which the forces of evil
(or the "system") are concentrated, and which stands over a-
gainst the kingdom of the innocent and the good. The binary
view of good versus evil bound together classical pacifism and
the more modern rejection of war.

The above analysis has been concerned with a major mutation of the peace sentiment. It has relied on a contrast between a classic sectarian withdrawal as found in, say, the
Mennonites or the lonely Protestant or the Kantian conscience,
and the diffuse hedonism of today which finds certain kinds
of group loyalty and social demand unacceptable. This hedonism arises, as has been argued, in the broad pool within
which new religions fish for converts. It thus belongs to the
assumptions which govern the context of new religions, even
though certain of the new religions may be in sharp reaction
against those assumptions.

Nevertheless, the protest against automatic memberships
and ineluctable loyalties, against all hierarchy and the impersonal dynamics of coercion, within states and between them,

is a central part of the milieu where the new epiphanies make
their showing. By that, I mean that where the sense of self-
hood is governed by the empire of desire and the principle of
personal happiness, one cannot conceive of loyalty to the demands of the state or to the commands of the sergeant-major
as overriding. Young people in certain milieux just happen
to belong to a particular country and do not accord any sanc-
tity to its demands upon them. They have never felt that they
had to do anything, certainly not to obey military discipline
merely because the twists and turns of foreign policy might
from time to time require shows of military strength in Cyprus
or Kenya, in Korea or Viet Nam.

THE GENERAL LOGIC OF PACIFISM: OLD STYLE

Clearly there are problems in setting out any general,
principled objection to war. A Quaker who respects the divine
spark in every human being differs from a Jehovah's Witness
who rejects all secular wars and awaits Armageddon. Neither
a Quaker nor a Witness has very much in common with a Marxist who espouses revolutionary defeatism until such time as he
can openly and violently pursue the class struggle. One way
round this diversity is to set out the implications of an attitude to the state and to national loyalty which eschews violence. Thus one may attempt to set out a minimal logic of the
pacifist approach together with certain extensions which frequently follow. This logic will be distinct from the revolutionary defeatism of a Marxist or the apocalyptic attitude of
a Witness. It will also be distinct from the attitude of those
who hold that some particular war is ill-advised or evil, yet
nevertheless make such a judgment within the presuppositions
of "normal" politics. Those who would reject a particular intervention, say, in Saudi Arabia, but who nevertheless work
by the checks and balances of ordinary foreign policy do not
share the logic of pacifism.

What then follows from a principled rejection of inter-
state violence and what kind of perspective does that imply
in relation to national loyalty? The first and pre-eminent consequence is a rejection of tribalism. Perhaps it is wrong to
speak of "consequence" because the rejection of violence and
of tribalism are conjoined together at the core of the pacifist
approach.

Clearly there is here an extraordinary challenge to sovereignty, whether by reference back to New Testament norms
and Biblical authority, as was usually the case in Christian
pacifism, or by an appeal to a universal membership in Humanity over and above local attachments and national demands
for solidarity with fellow citizens.

From the viewpoint of the state, the nub of the challenge turns around the rejection of the magistrate's command to "serve in the wars" (to quote from Article 37 in the Anglican Book of Common Prayer). A nation is a tribe writ large, which demands that all within its boundaries defend its unity, honour, integrity and interests. The duties and privileges of the subject are articulated within the nation. He finds and receives his primary social place according to national laws and customs. To step outside national membership is to assert a personal judgement lacking social root and local sanction. This is why the psychic shift in acknowledging a higher loyalty to humanity is so profound. Both the demands of the state and the social foci of belonging militate against it. You have rejected the ultimate claims of the state and its laws, and resisted the pressures of local solidarity.

The objector must consolidate his stance against this huge contrary pull of centripetal social force. Except in a very few countries, like contemporary Britain, he is required to submit to national service. That involves a discipline of arms and accepting that enemies are defined by state decision. Choice of weapons and style of hostility are not up for nice, individual scrutiny. Armies are run on the conditioned reflex of automatic obedience, not on the conditional reflections of autonomous conscience. This means that the objector must work out a response both to the contingent local character of national loyalty and to the arbitrary, total nature of discipline.

The demands of the pacifist conscience require that no exceptions can be made for wars of self-defence, and that no place exists for the Augustinian concept of the just war. This means that a foreign policy based on tactical considerations and convenient military strikes becomes impossible. Likewise, a state would have to jettison alliances since these are based on international groupings of power and the threat of force. It would be impossible to threaten force and never to use it. For the pacifist true to his own logic, any pressure beyond moral suasion is inadmissible, however commendable the objective. The only possible form of foreign policy becomes moral appeal and broad dramatic gestures symbolising peaceability. Foreign relations are converted into a form of moral theatre.

The appeals and gestures of moral theatre may perhaps be accredited with redemptive potential, depending on whether the redemptive agent is able to carry out the gesture with a perfect heart. Here, there lurks, perhaps, a hidden eschatology, since a gesture must have once-for-all efficacy. Policy cannot possibly consist of a series of gestures, especially since the failure of the first gesture may mean that you are no longer at liberty to make the second. If your enemy does not quickly accept your peaceful, wide open arms, he may tie your arms behind your back.

There is another difficulty at this juncture which has
psychological correlates.   The difficulty relates to how a pacifist may expect moral gestures to emanate from social structures which he sees as deeply dyed in systematic evil.   The
psychology on which this expectation is based, combines intense
optimism with intense pessimism.   If the nation state is deeply
implicated in alliances and threats, bluffs and feints, lies and
subterfuges, it is hardly likely to achieve a reformed character
overnight, let alone a redemptive role.   Cynicism can hardly
be bedfellow to hope, though this is precisely the logic and
the psychology of the pacifist position.   One has to combine
a sad knowledge of what the state actually does, with fantastic
expectation as to what it may potentially do.

On the whole pacifists incline to an optimistic view since
a fully-fledged pessimism reduces pacifist witness to useless
protest and the pain of obscure, unnoticed crucifixions.   Perhaps it would be more true to say that the pacifist develops
a mind in two compartments.   One compartment deals with ordinary, mundane political transactions as depicted in daily
newspapers, about which he becomes more and more cynical.
He supposes that foreign policy is a noisome charade, played
out by consummate hypocrites.   Every item concerning mal-
practice at the foreign office is treasured as evidence of the
secret plots in which diplomats are always engaged.   The other
compartment, however, opens onto a quite different view.   The
pacifist sees a profound peaceability deep down in things, that
only awaits release to spring to life and power.   Whatever
states may do and statesmen may pretend, in Man as Man there
abides a yearning to unite with all men everywhere.   Man is
innocent; social organization   (and/or ignorance) is to blame.
In God or in Human Nature there lurks the untapped yet all-
powerful remedy.

It then becomes necessary to identify which aspect of social organization is the key to evil, or whether indeed social
organization is maleficent as such.   The process of identifying
the cancerous centre or core is not characteristic of all pacifists.   Some are content with a general negative characterization of the state and the organization of force.   Others, particularly those who believe that pacifism is a practical contribution to a better life, tend to look for the nigger in the woodpile.   Once found he is rarely let go again.   A fully-fledged
nigger in the woodpile is kept on continuous display.   The real
cause of war then becomes the activities of armaments manufacturers, or the needs of capital seeking outlets, or the psychic spiral of mutual fear, or the instinct of dominion over
others or the inculcation of a sado-masochist psychology.   It
is in this context that the pacifist may turn to the Marxist
arsenal of concepts, since the Marxist analysis is specially
useful for justifying deep pessimism about the present with

hope about the future. The pacifist dialectic of pessimism and optimism can find sustenance in the Marxist analysis, providing, however, one does not accept the necessity of class war. The pacifist swing to the left often comes to stop just where the Marxist analysis demands struggle and even violent revolution. Many pacifist consciences were exercised by left-wing demands to support the Republicans in Spain.

When the pacifist encounters the dilemma posed by the Marxist he is pushed towards an extreme doctrine of the relation of ends to means. This doctrine holds that what is morally wrong can never be politically right, or that the end never justifies the means. This view cannot be held solely with respect to the external relationships of states, but must necessarily be extended to the whole activity of law making and law enforcement. Thus it would be improper even to make an example of a criminal or a naughty child pour encourager les autres. Indeed, the very activity of law enforcement becomes morally questionable. Sometimes this extreme and implausible conclusion may be avoided by proposing a distinction between non-violent acts of legal suasion and acts of violent law enforcement. Alternatively, it may be held that law within states is based on a moral consensus which precludes the kind of war of "all against all" characteristic of fighting between states. Or again it may be argued that the police use the minimum persuasion necessary for compliance and that this suasion is aimed at identifiable individuals, not against some social mass, indiscriminately defined as the enemy. There are various ways of weakening the analogy between internal force and external war, so as to allow the former and preclude the latter. All the same it remains true that a pacifist will feel the pull of the anarchist position. He will lay stress on popular capacity for peaceful compliance without resort to external incentives or threats. Thus, the optimism generated by his broad view of foreign relations is transferred to internal relations. A pacifist will rely on the force of a moral appeal and seek out what William James called the moral equivalent of war in all the social relations in which he engages.

However, should it seem that people or groups remain recalcitrant and continuously resist moral appeals, then the pacifist has to save his optimism by claiming that people only resist because of their unhappy circumstances or because they are not accorded social justice. Thus the pacifist repeats an intellectual tactic developed in the field of external relations, which is to deploy a quasi-Marxist analysis of internal disputes. People are not activated by an inherent greed nor are they naturally disposed to power and the corruptions of power. They are, all of them, honourable men. Only the dishonourable disposition of society makes them appear dishonourable. Institutions have corrupted their natural goodness.

However, this itself generates a difficulty since the pacifist now feels a hostility towards all those who support the
current disposition of goods and rewards. He is caught between discerning the divine spark in all men and suspecting
that the divine spark has been dampened or been blown out
in the case of capitalists, military men, propagandists -- and
their dupes. Men must follow the highest when they see it but
a wretched claque have closed their eyes. If the majority goes
morally blind, and loses the natural gift of sight, then the
real villains have subverted it by propaganda.

With a little twist this view may degenerate into a conspiracy theory of history. In any case, there remains the
difficult question as to whether the revolution in social circumstances will come from men's changed hearts, or will be
brought about by structural upheaval. At this point pacifists
divide. If structural upheaval could occur in the course of
a peaceful and natural social evolution, then the structural
mode might be preferred. But it is well known that the mid-
wives of revolution are equipped with pincers for reluctant
births, and may resort to Caesarian operations. Thus with
the onset of any revolutionary crisis the pacifist will draw
progressively back, or if you prefer, he will regress to the
true reactionary logic of his beliefs.

Of course, in delineating such options and tendencies,
I am presuming a modern context. Nevertheless, the broad
logic tends to be similar across different periods, even though
the content and the precise formulations and vocabulary differ.
A pacifist in the past would have expected the Kingdom of God
to occur by a transcendent intervention aside from and beyond
his own efforts. He would, in short, have adopted an eschatological hope. This would be associated with the combination
of high optimism and profound pessimism already described.
Those who were entrapped in the present aeon had been handed over to the power of the Evil One. But precisely when that
power was most rampant and abominable, redemption would be
nigh. Whether the Evil One is the Devil or a socialisation
subverted by the military-industrial complex, the structure of
belief is broadly parallel.

Moreover, the logic of social withdrawal is similar in
very different periods. Once a pacifist (in either the twentieth
or the sixteenth century) perceives himself enmeshed in relations shot through with violence, then he will wish to withdraw
from them. In the sixteenth century the only way to withdraw
was to join a sect in which some enclave of a new and better
society already existed. For the sixteenth century believer,
this enclave might be conceived as God's Elect, a little flock
already saved out of the realm of darkness, awaiting the

moment of deliverance. For the twentieth century believer the
enclave may be an embryonic anticipation of a new way which
is soon to become universal. That will be the fullness, but
this is the taste. The twentieth century offers more scope than
the sixteenth for establishing embryonic communities which
establish in miniature what will soon be realised universally.
Indeed, ever since the eighteenth century some pacifists have
been able to set up communities where violence is eschewed,
the law abrogated, and brotherly love alone allowed to be the
binding force of society. It is difficult to be a pacifist on
one's own, integrally involved in the regime of violence and
law. The solution is found in the sect or the utopian community.

     Within such communities the logic of non-violence will
take various forms. It may, for example, be extended to in--
clude animal as well as human life. The brute creation was
no more established for the abattoir than was the human creation. Here the symbol of blood may come to play an important
role. War involves the shedding of blood. Blood constitutes
the sign around which the supreme evil is concentrated. Therefore, all activities which call for the shedding of blood are
to be condemned, and red meat itself becomes a symbol of raw
violence. Hence the varied connections between a pacifist
position and vegetarianism.

     In articles 37 and 39 of the Prayer Book directed against
Anabaptists, the controverted issues included capital punishment and the taking of oaths as a solemnity according ultimate
respect to the law. So far as capital punishment is concerned,
a pacifist will almost always be opposed to it. In capital
punishment the state arrogates to itself the right to take an
individual life and this is only marginally different from the
right to take collective life. The justice of the court may be
more discriminating than the justice of the pre-emptive strike
against some "enemy city", but the right of the state to exe-
cute "judgement" is present in both cases. The pacifist will
be disposed to say: "To the Lord alone belong the issues of
life and death." He will tend to adopt reformatory rather than
retributary theories of justice. He will also, by extension,
suspect or condemn corporal punishment, a position which in
the modern period he will illustrate with arguments drawn from
the psychology of aggression and sado-masochism. In the
extreme case, the pacifist is opposed to all violence against
children, animals, criminals and other states and he thus
participates in the generally progressive sector. (The reverse
does not apply: members of the Royal Society for the Preven-
tion of Cruelty to Animals are mostly not pacifists.)

     There are certain consequences which bear on the pacifist
perspective which follow from the overall impact of all the dis-

tinctive attitudes discussed above.   Clearly people who hold
such an ensemble of attitudes are going to form quite a small
minority and arouse the kind of hostility which defines them
as cranks.   The urge to consistency which leads to a total rejection of all violence, and even of police forces, feeds this
definition.   There is then set in motion a spiral of mutual
reinforcement whereby crankiness is attributed to pacifists and
the attribution helps to create or reinforce such crankiness as
may in fact exist . - Pacifists respond with an impaired sense
of their own normality and come to value abnormality as an
index of virtue.   They suspect the wider society of desire to
persecute.   Those in positions of power are regarded as   founts
of mis-information and the generality of mankind are defined
as dupes of propaganda.   Since propaganda is always operative to some extent, there is plenty of evidence to reinforce
the plausible view that nothing emanating from "worldly" sources is true, particularly if it reinforces the war-spirit.   Thus
pacifists in the Second World War were very reluctant to credit
the elimination of the Jews, equating such information with the
atrocity stories circulated about the Germans after the invasion of Belgium in 1914.   Inevitably, all these processes are
accentuated by war-time.   The sympathy felt for pacifists by
some ordinary denizens of the world tends to evaporate.   They,
after all, have had to submit to conscription, and the objector
is defined as a shirker or a coward.   A rather generalised
scepticism about the state and its purposes becomes converted
into a sense of shared deprivation and mutual comradeship.
The   pacifist is soon regarded as an outsider and a defector.

This means that pacifists try to cite instances of "realized eschatology" which contradict the normal view that war
is some kind of institutional necessity.   Pacifist lore teems
with examples of groups or countries who rejected the   weapon of violence and were the better off for doing so.   Thus,
a kind of sugared utilitarianism results.   On the one hand
sacrifice is the way to redemtpion, but on the other hand the
willingness to be sacrificed may mean that the cup will pass
away.   Not only is pacifism certainly right, but also probably
advantageous and useful.   The Utilitarian argument from the
greatest happiness principle sorts rather ill with the Kantian
objection based on the instrinsic wrong of taking life or offering violence.   Those who (like Bertrand Russell) deploy this
kind of Utilitarian argument can become protagonists of real-
politik should their estimate of the Utilitarian calculus tip in
the non-pacifist direction.   Russell recommended pacifism in
1937 and dropping the Bomb in 1947.   At any rate, the pacifist, confronted by the war-spirit animating the vast majority
of his fellows, is inclined to idealize some other country as
exemplifying a more moral approach to international relations.
India   played this role for a period and so also have Sweden,

Switzerland and Denmark.   This idealisation of countries other
than one's own finds its Marxist analogue in the way members
of the non-pacifist left persistently point to some new utopia,
as, for example, "Soviet Russia, a New Civilisation", or China,
or Cuba, or, nowadays, Albania.   The "True Land" has to be
created in the eschatological imagination if it cannot be demonstrated in reality.   Pilgrimages are made to the True Land
and excited accounts given of how much better things are
ordered elsewhere.   This knowledge of better things elsewhere
feeds the superiority felt by Marxist and pacifist alike towards
the unenlightened mass.   The "People", idealized by Marxists
and Pacifists, then become an imaginary point of reference con-
tradicted by every instance of how most people actually be-
have.   The feeling of sharing the Messianic secret amply compensates the feeling of being inferior or cold-shouldered by
the wider society.   Indeed, the sense of superiority and the
sense of persecution can mutually feed each other.

THE OLD LOGIC OF PACIFISM:
A RESOURCE FOR THE SIXTIES

To what extent, however, does such a group of attitudes
link with the phenomena of new religions and inform some part
of their outlook on society?   How did elements in the syndrome
just outlined mutate under the pressures and dissolutions of
the sixties?   How did the Campaign for Nuclear Disarmament
and the liberal Student Christian Movement, both of which
provided friendly environments for pacifism, feed into and dissolve within the psychic revolutions of that period?   (I merely
note in passing that the genocidal potentialities of modern weapons often accentuate the tendency described, although they
may also breed apathy by making individual protest appear
useless.)

Here after all we have a distinct sector of the progressive climate which loses a certain distinctiveness of outline,
and solidity or specificity of content under the dissolutions
of the sixties.   Once it had been a position (though linked
by congruity and affinity to all kinds of progressive attitudes), and then somehow this position started to free-float
as an element in a wider universe.   Pacifism lost the suffix
"ism" and began to bob about, suddenly salient with banners
inscribed "Make Love Not War", and, equally suddenly, lost
in the ensemble of attitudes -- or even submerged in waves
of exemplary violence.   Along with the Campaign for Nuclear
Disarmament and the Student Christian Movement it slid into
a melting pot.   The Peace Movement of the 1960's was not coherent in its sources, its ideology, or its psychic base.

The fire beneath the melting pot was individualism, but
an individualism of an odd kind because it had constant resort

to structural understandings of man's parlous state, and persistently erupted in "mass demonstrations". The atomised psychic reality appealed to the concept of a patterned, malignant social base; the whirling, individual atoms fused in masses and then diffused in a hundred grouplets and in sheer personal anarchy. And this made sense because these individual atoms were set free enough from constraints actually to notice structures (industrial or military) when they ran into them. The attempt to live "according to nature" had gone just far enough for the structure of society to seem as unnatural as it was glaring and obvious. Only personal exploration or loosely formed grouplets, dissolvable at will, or mass, temporary aggregations of shared fury and/or love, conformed to the state of nature. In such an atmosphere not only was loyalty to the state incomprehensible, but loyalty to any particular named organization with a stated creed or written-in attitude. The edge or boundary round such an organization, especially when large-scale, had to be rubbed out. Hence the near-dissolution of CND, and the practical demise of S.C.M. as it declared itself "open" to the world. Hence, also, the tight little groups, political or religious, which were eventually left as hard distillations within and after the Great Dissolution.

So the pacifism which coloured the post-fifties outlook was a free-floating element, loosely connected with intermittent searches for "community" and with a general slackening of national loyalties. The mobile exploration of the self undercut both a principled adherence to the Protestant conscience and a disciplined attachment to national loyalty. Every loyalty beyond the experience of the individual, except maybe to Mankind in general, was experienced as alien, even indeed as a consequence of machine politics and bureaucratic governance. To young people, reared on doctrines of self-exploration and on adjustment to purely personal environments, the demands of the nation appeared to have no persuasive power. Membership in the nation was a genetic accident, at best the nexus of certain utilitarian reciprocities: taxes paid for welfare services rendered.

Since neither national membership nor personal discipline exercised an appeal, young people were cast adrift from the ancient anchors of the state and the settled psyche. Their "pacifism" underwent a mutation into something more diffuse than traditional pacifism. It was part of the background, an unemphasized item in the repertoire of attitudes, and would only become active when challenged by some demand, particularly some dangerous demand based on the calculations and pressures of international politics. The impress of socialisation no longer bit deep enough for young people to sacrifice themselves to the contingent twists and turns inherent in international affairs. On the contrary, any national service de-

manded in the course of such political pressures aroused intense resentment towards both service and nation. This, of
course, leaves aside whether or not such demands were more
or less ethically justifiable. In other words, even had Viet
Nam been more justifiable than it was, the base of automatic
loyalty was no longer present. One incidental implication of
this is that the more tender minded and "democratic" a state
is, the less it can rely on its membership in the contingent
matters of foreign policy. A democratic, individualistic nation
conducts affairs in the semi-amoral arena of foreign politics,
weakened by the effect of its hedonistic mode of socialisation,
and facing grim adversaries whose whole effort emphasizes
automatic obedience and national fervour in the cause of totalitarian discipline.

That wider consequence apart, the pacifism of the post-
fifties was not so much a principled objection to war as a
state of mind which found national loyalty, and especially
obedience until death in the cause of policy, just incomprehensible. Young people revolted against such concepts of loyalty
and obedience with intermittent rituals emphasizing "Love Not
War". They made a kind of ritual war on conventional society
in the cause of love.

But there was no counter-collective to which the majority
of them adhered, such as a Hutterite community or a utopian
experiment or a Mennonite sect. Some did, of course, seek out
some peaceful bond of loving community. Most dipped in intermittent community as a partial baptism en route to other experiences and other kinds of chrism. They dabbled in liminal
"communitas." But they belonged to no single group, and they
travelled along loose networks in the interstices of the agencies of work and government. Their broad psychic tendencies
fostered loyalty neither to nation nor to any specific group
but only a mobile participation in loose, overlapping nets of
relationship. Ensconced in this way pacifism was not a matter
of principle with a logic of its own, but an item in a wider,
implicit, psychological set. War and the military constituted
an unthinkable intrusion, a visitation from real-politik without
a shadow of justification.

When the outer limits of this "unrealistic" set became un-
covered and visible, or when the psychic travelling and the
constant cycle of dissolution became intolerable, there had to
be a scramble for new bases of stability within which the dis-
tracted soul might re-form. If a base had previously been
laid down in the earliest years, then that might be re-utilised
in modified form to sustain and support the re-formation. Not
under the old name perhaps, though lots reverted to or discovered a neo-fundamentalism, but by way of a new cultic stabili-
sation.

WHAT DOES THIS SAY ABOUT THE SOCIAL CONTEXT?

What do such mutations imply about the societies in which they occur? Can we read back messages about the overall context which harbours and produces them?

First of all, something may be said about the social impress on the psyche with respect to the style of personal identification. Every society must stamp an impress on the mind, insofar as nobody can avoid culture and still realize their human potential. This stamp has, over the centuries of nationalism, included a sharp edge or margin distinguishing native from alien. To be "a national" was something crucial to the sense of belonging and it was built into the sense of identity. It was, so to say, a psychological identity card. Along with the identity card or identity disc went a near-automatic loyalty which could be called upon. Identity and loyalty were almost consubstantial. People might not be all that happy to take up soldiering, and would hardly welcome the press-gang, but they did not easily conceive how they might be divested of exclusive identity and loyalty. Yet this is precisely what has now started to occur in certain western liberal societies.

Alongside this partial undermining of identity and of automatic loyalty has gone a parallel tendency to dismantle all disciplines based on automatic responses. Psychic fluidity is not compatible with standing rigidly in rows immediately responsive to the word of command. The change is plainly observable in many spheres: school, church, and public assembly. In school, for example, rows are broken up, formal assemblies are discouraged, "esprit de corps" is devalued, and old-fashioned "drill" converted to physical education. Individualism militates against militarism, and against the ancillary disciplines which provide it with a base.

One may or may not regret such shifts with respect to identity, loyalty and discipline. Probably few will feel sorry that the state can no longer rely on "Your Country Needs You." But there are other implications about the moral sensibility characterising some contemporary western liberal societies. This psychology may embody a hedonism which resists any sense of cost or paradox. Good things are accepted very easily as part of the natural order, and their lack is treated with incredulity and horror. Frustration cannot be borne and rapidly issues in a sense of being ill done by. Moreover, in the fluid groupings based on loose, cultural affinities, so much has to be personally negotiated that alienation and a sense of chaos ensue. The individual becomes a nervous octopus constantly sensing out his environment for markers, points of stability, indicators of direction. The defensive margins of selfhood become susceptible to marauding explorations. The objective outer world also dissolves at the inquisitive touch of personal exploration. The lineaments of the "out there" (God, Society, and even physical constraints) collapse as the individual loses the markers which mediate meaning and provide his sense of "the given." The cultural images which might mediate meaning revolve or dissolve too rapidly for secure linkages between the self and the environment to be formed. This results, amongst other things, in the shared sense of a collective historical trajectory and lineage being corroded. History, as a donation given by the collective past, with markers and pointers for a future, loses its power. The idea of a classical, objective form ceases to be understood, whether as liturgy or poetic tradition or mode of government.

Such a situation generates certain kinds of explanations which either transmit the sense of disquietude in simple,easily swallowed capsules or else provide deliverances, also easily swallowed. This is not to claim that everything that lives demands a Weltanschauung, but it is to say that those nurtured in a world without sharp edges are likely to push at their environment for a solidity which will give them definition. Many, perhaps the vast majority, acquire tags which serve as interim guides to chaos. These tags are not worked up in coherent systems of ideas, but provide the materials for conversational ping-pong. They are expendable wisdom about male and female, job or career prospects, the over-world of politics, the nature of opinion itself. Everything tends to be reduced to opinion. The idea of a strict either/or becomes unintelligible, as does the idea of a demanding religion, and the idea of qualitative distinctions. Of course, in some sectors, quality and discipline impose themselves as they do in sport and music, but much of existence is handed over to mere preference and opinion. Faith is a "religious preference"; a variable liking for Shakespeare or Beethoven is just one subjective option among others.

Within these softened centres of liberalised society, there may emerge a very different reaction which seeks for edges and distinctions, which looks for comprehensive truths and explanations. In the past pacifism would have been one component in such explanations. It would have been woven into the fabric of a sectarian faith or else at the very least implicated in the overall "blik" of old-fashioned liberalism. Of course, pacifism can still arise in this way and become incorporated in a rigorous, or at least well-defined, dissentient viewpoint. But more frequently, pacifism now arises in the sector which lacks social and psychic definition, or historical trajectory and purpose. It has a kaleidoscopic life, mixing first with this element and then with that, temporarily tipping over into aggression and as quickly righting itself again.

It cannot give an account of itself, nor can it pass itself on except by contagion.

A society which exists over such incidental agglomerations of sentiment and feeling, finds the cultural content of education and socialization difficult to determine. It can, of course, emit just the contagious signals which arise from the collective calculus of immediate desires, but these do not provide solid psychic fare, shared meaning and being, a common symbolism connecting past and future, a language for mobilization. Furthermore, the necessities, costs and paradoxes of politics, especially of international politics, remain as unavoidable as ever. A population released from automatic loyalties and unequipped with a sense of political and social necessity is ripe for disillusion. It is the raw material of a crisis of legitimation. Legitimation in such populations turns immediately on the ability to meet desires and expectations, and has no positive, defined emplacement on which it may rest. It is perhaps arguable that this is just as it should be, but it means that societies which exemplify the desired situation are placed at risk; or else they must engender new obfuscations about their true nature in order to survive.

The point can, in conclusion, be put even more sharply. The survival of collectivities, such as tribes and nations, depends on a structure of decision and foreign policy which is resistent to moralisation, without necessarily being totally a-moral. The structure can be given an intellectual defence, but in order to work it requires a vigorous impress on the psychic substance of its membership. This impress is not provided by the hedonistic calculus of self-expression, and no viable foreign policy can possibly ever be erected on the net resultant of such a calculus. Thus, not only is legitimation placed at risk, but survival itself. Technical superiority is thereby made into the main defence option, and vacillation becomes the ground of policy.

III

IMPACTS OR IMPORTS:
ACCOMMODATION, REJECTION, INNOVATION,
ASSIMILATION AND DISINTEREST

THE CASE OF THE THIRD REICH

Christine King

Nazi Germany offers a particularly interesting case for the examination of the relationship between new religious movements and what was, in some respects, itself a new society. It is generally agreed by historians of the Third Reich that the claims of National Socialism to construct not just a new political system but a new German order were to a large degree fulfilled. Nazism can be seen, not only in its ideology and propaganda, but also in its operation, to have been an all-embracing world-view which influenced and directed German life from the cradle to the grave, from the workings of the state machinery to the realms of family, cultural and moral life.

In talking of German society as Nazi society there are obvious problems. Although little work has been done on the examination of public opinion in the Third Reich[1] and there is no easy way to assess public complicity in the ideals and policies of the new society, the presence of Germans in concentration camps as opponents of the regime would suggest that Nazism did not permeate German society completely. However, within this new order there existed many strands of traditional German society: the historical response of the Catholic and Protestant churches to the state, a conservative and anti-liberal judiciary and civil service, as well as a reactionary theme running through so much of German life extolling authoritarian government and rejecting the Weimar experience as a failed experiment. Not only had Nazism come into office with the tacit or open support of many conservative Germans, but it had the power to restructure society only with their compliance.

Those elements with which the sects came largely into contact were, apart from the few exceptional cases where public hostility to the Nazis resulted in respect for a sectarian opponent of the regime, the public bodies of society, the party, police, civil servants and judiciary. In discussing the relationship between Nazi society and the Christian sects we are, therefore, concerned primarily with society in its official and policy-making capacity. This examination may lead, however, to some clarification of the philosophy which informed the Nazis' attempt to remodel life and, by an analysis of the implementation of these policies, shed some light on the concerns, methods and problems of this new society.

However much it was linked to the past by its authoritarian traditions, this was a new society and relations with independent believing bodies like the churches and larger Christian sects had to be negotiated. The Christian sects, themselves founded so comparatively recently that they may be called "new", might reasonably be expected to appear to the Nazis as a particular problem. In their newness they were suspect, and in their largely American origins and international links they could be seen as potential enemies. The examination of the history and teachings of the sects which Nazi agents undertook during the early years of the regime[2] revealed the dangers inherent in sectarianism. The sects, on the whole, had a special role in their eschatology for the Jews, they preached universal brotherhood and enjoyed their own millenial, usually apocalyptic, world-view. Only one sect seemed to present no dangers. The Mormons were seen to have racial views acceptable to National Socialism and in their active pursuit of details of their ancestors, for the purpose of posthumous baptism, they were able to prove their Aryan background to such an extent that some members even received special awards for their industry in this area.

Only one other group, the Christian Scientists, presented a special case. Government documents indicate a suspicion of this sect's teaching and of its "non-materialist outlook", but they also reveal that the intervention of influential British and American Christian Scientists acted, until 1941, as a check against any move to be taken against them.[3] All other groups were regarded as potential enemies, all were observed by government spies, all were under suspicion.

Germany had proved a fertile ground for missionaries in the mid to late nineteenth century. Most of the larger sects had come from America and those indigenous German sects, so small that they were closed down by the Nazis without protest, had been founded either as schisms of larger groups or with some political or occult aim after the First World War.[4] After initial hostility from the public and government, sectarians had proved themselves loyal citizens and had fought in the First World War.[5] Under Weimar they had all been granted religious freedom and a certain amount of legal and financial protection. Under Weimar no sectarian was forced into any position where his loyalty to the state might be quesioned,and, since in matters of morality, sectarians were normally exemplary citizens, a degree of public tolerance appears to have accompanied their improved legal status. What criticisms there were, came either from the major churches, or from the yellow press, and the only physical harassment came from groups like the S.A.*

In 1933 then, both sects and society found themselves in a new situation. Ambivalent in its attitude to religion, the Nazi party was seen to accept for the time being, the support of the two major churches, which, with the exception of the Confessing church and some notable individuals, welcomed Nazism. The sects had two choices in the face of the government's suspicion of them; they could follow the major churches and accept the new society, its new policies and demands, or they could offer their resistance, if they felt their beliefs and freedom of worship to be in danger.

Most of the sects chose the former path. Not only the Mormons and Christian Scientists, who, it has been seen, earned themselves some kind of truce, but also groups like the New Apostolic Church and the Seventh Day Adventists behaved in a way designed to ensure their own survival and to convince the new government of their loyalty and their usefulness to society. Not that this response implied any subterfuge for the purposes of survival; indeed, many sectarians, like many Christians from the major churches, saw in Hitler, the teetotal, abstemious, upright hero, Germany's saviour. In welcoming Hitler as German society's defence against communism, anarchy and moral decay, they were behaving less like sectarians protecting their own world-view and more like patriotic, conservative German citizens.

Three brief examples may indicate the type of comments being made about Hitler by sectarians. In 1933 the editor of an Adventist journal wrote that "God sent our land a Führer who took strong command of the ship of state."[6] By the end of that year, the New Apostolic Community was already enlarging on that theme:

> The year is fast nearing its end . . . We look back thankfully, Germany is united, there are no split parties. Millions have found work and others have been helped so that they need not go cold or hungry this winter.

> We realise that it is all due to one man's love for the German nation. We New Apostolic followers will do all in our power to follow the orders of the Führer. He is best served with everyone knowing their place and their duties. . . God bless him and give him all the help with everything he needs to lead the German nation.[7]

As the regime progressed, the praise grew louder. On April 20, 1940, to celebrate Hitler's birthday, Adventist churches gave thanks for the Führer:

> Trust in his people has given the Führer the
> strength to carry through the fight for freedom and
> honour in Germany. The unshakable faith of Adolf
> Hitler allowed him to do great deeds, which decor-
> ate him today before the whole world, selflessly
> and faithfully he has defined the honour of his na-
> tion . . . Only very few statemen stand so bril-
> liantly in the sun of a blessed life as our Führer
> . . . [8]

Beside the pro-Nazi statements, prayers and sermons extolling the Führer and services to mark special occasions, like
the remilitarization of the Rhineland, these sects presented a
public support for the Nazis, both at home and abroad. All
the sects mentioned above sent letters or representatives to
brethren abroad, especially in America, extolling the virtues
of life in the new Germany.

A German Christian Scientist, for example, wrote to the
Board of Directors of the Church in Boston:

> What we have been going through these last weeks
> was a revolution. It was so splendidly organized
> that it was a bloodless revolution . . . What would
> have become of Europe if Germany had come under
> Bolshevism? It needed a strong hand to prevent this
> catastrophe and Hitler seems to have it. [9]

At home, the New Apostolic Church flew the Swastika flag over
its churches and held church parades for party members in
uniform. [10] More significant were the changes in liturgy adopted by many of these groups. The Adventists, for example,
particularly vulnerable to the attack of anti-semites because
of their celebration of the Jewish Sabbath, changed the name
of the day to "rest-day" and removed references to Old Testament words like Zion from their liturgy. In accordance with
the plans to remove from this new society all traces of the
"Jewish spirit", the sects all reviewed their use of the Old
Testament and its imagery, as well as their public policy towards Jewish converts. One Mormon church erected a notice
saying "No Jews Allowed."

Contributions were made to Nazi welfare schemes and the
Adventists turned over the whole of their extensive welfare provision to the state, and while Adventists still worked in the
clinics, hospitals and social centres, the apparatus was under
Nazi control and was administered in accordance with the "National Socialist spirit". No Jews or gypsies or "undesirables"
were now given shelter or charity. Some sectarians extolled

particular Nazi policies, even ones which were potentially at variance with their teachings. Adventists explained to their members in a contemporary journal, that the sterilization laws did not, as they appeared, contradict Adventist beliefs about life and health, but reinforced them.[11] New Apostolic Church officials examined their membership carefully to discover the identity of anyone who might be classified as an enemy of the state, and to expel that church member and report him to the authorities. Sectarians' children were encouraged to join Nazi youth schemes, and Adventist schools instructed their pupils to will and think in the National Socialist way.[12]

What is interesting is that the sects were allowed to make these gestures and that, in spite of their suspicion of the sects and their plans to close them along with the churches, in the next stage of Nazification, the Nazis temporized and allowed a stay of execution. It is clear that the survival of the sects indicates that the seemingly rigid and unbending Nazi state could be influenced in its behaviour by pragmatic considerations. The closure of the sects would not have been difficult since their numbers were small[13] and it would have been possible to represent them as enemies of Germany with dangerous American links or anarchist or bolshevik aspirations.

Was it then the practical use to the state that the sects offered which influenced their treatment? Certainly there were financial and propaganda benefits accruing from the sects' public support. Their propaganda role for Germany amongst foreign brethren has been noted, and when conscription was introduced, most sectarians undertook military or war-related work with enthusiasm. Such factors were not, however, enough to ensure that the state would leave these potentially dangerous groups alone, secure in their world-view and liable to criticize Nazi policies.

What saved these sects was their flexibility, their willingness to adapt their world-view to include Nazi policies. The Nazis did not bother to close the collaborationist sects because these had shown, in their support of the new order, that they were behaving not as rival world-views, but as institutions, anxious to accept and be accepted. In this lay a tacit recognition of Nazi superiority and of the "moral strength" of the new policies. Adventists were told, for example, that they must obey the new state, even if it ordered them to abandon their religious practices.[14] Since they were willing to make such sacrifices, closure was irrelevant and could be executed at some time more convenient for the state. Meanwhile these collaborating sects served two important purposes. Firstly they were, as has been seen, of practical use, and secondly, by their public acceptance of Nazism they joined the established institutions in giving the new order support and respectability.

The Nazis' initial suspicion of the sects may well have been based less on a fear that they would prove enemies, and more on a feeling that these groups were too new and lacking in roots themselves to offer the party any useful source of legitimization. This proved to be untrue, especially for those who could offer the added advantage of influential foreign connections. It is significant, however, that when these international connections were no longer an advantage, in 1941, and the Christian Scientists began to suffer harassment, that the group which had most lent its moral and theological support to the Nazis, the Mormons, remained untouched, immune even from the presence of government spies, and joined the closely observed Adventists and New Apostolic Church in the S.D.* category of "non-political sects." In Nazi terms, a non-political sect was one which made satisfactory political statements. In the collaborating sects the Nazis had found unexpected allies, groups who acknowledged the Nazis as victors, yet whose eventual suppression would be easy.

There was an alternative possible reaction and this was taken by the Jehovah's Witnesses.[15] As members of God's kingdom they stand outside any civil society, although they will obey its moral precepts as far as their citizenship of God's kingdom will allow. Co-existence with the state need not necessarily be problematical, and it is only in a time of crisis, like a war, or within a state which makes total demands on its people, that the Witnesses become a problem. They had experienced few difficulties in this area under Weimar, and in 1933, along with the collaborationist sects, were anxious to talk with government officials to assure them of their neutrality towards the state, and that they would do it and its members no harm. However, neutrality was not an acceptable posture to the Nazis, and they refused to talk, or to take note of the minor compromises and concessions offered by the movement.[16] Thus the Jehovah's Witness authorities were propelled from a moderate into an intransigent posture and by 1934 the tone of their communications with the Nazis was polite but unbending:

> We have no interest in political affairs, but are wholly devoted to God's kingdom under Christ as King. We will do no injury or harm to anyone. We would delight to dwell in peace and do good will to all men as we have opportunity, but since your government and its officers continue in your attempt to force us to disobey the highest law of the universe, we are compelled to now give you notice that we will, by His grace, obey Jehovah-God and fully trust Him to deliver us from all oppression and oppressors.[17]

To a certain extent, initial hositility towards the Witnesses was an outgrowth of views held about them before 1933,
and of the need to the S.A. to have yet one more easily identifiable enemy. What developed, however, took on a great deal
more significance than this initial clash might suggest, for
the Nazis found themselves engaged in a war with the Witnesses which took an ever-increasing amount of police time. That
Witnesses were not part of the new society became apparent
as they refused the public gestures of voting, giving the Hitler
salute, enlisting or celebrating national festivals. Not only
did they offer this civil disobedience, but, somewhat it seems
to the Nazis' surprise, they refused to accept the ban on their
activities, even at the cost of imprisonment or torture. Witness literature, widely distributed throughout German society,
continued to give details of the kind of treatment they were
receiving and to identify the regime ever more closely with Satanic forces. For example, the Witness journal "Consolation"
issued a rallying cry to all Witnesses to stand firm with the
following words:

> The apparent victory of the Devil's organization   is
> now virtually complete . . . (but) the power of God
> is infinite and in His own due time and way   Hitler
> and the Hierarchy will be destroyed and   righteous-
> ness and peace and truth will   triumph   and abide
> for ever. [18]

Suddenly the Witnesses were dramatically and obviously
revealed to be outside Nazi society. By being outside of it,
they highlighted in a way which might not otherwise have been
apparent, the nature of its new demands. Whatever the public
support for the Nazis, or however unwilling or frightened people were to resist, it may not have become obvious until a
work-mate was dismissed for refusing to give the Hitler salute,
that there was even a choice or a moral issue involved in giving the new greeting. A female Witness describes, for example,
the reaction of her neighbours when the Gestapo came to take
her children away:

> The window was open and a large group of persons
> gathered in front of the house and heard my loud
> screams of despair . . . I was questioned by the
> Gestapo for three hours . . . meanwhile, the ever
> growing crowd in front of the house increasingly
> began to indicate by their noise that they were not
> in agreement with what was going on. Finally the
> Gestapo withdrew . . . now they went about taking
> the children away secretly.[19]

What is more, the Witnesses made their work public; they continued door-to-door preaching and delivered vast amounts of smuggled literature through letter boxes, always trying to include in their surreptitious rounds the local party H.Q. The Nazi response was to increase the campaign of force, seizing property, arresting known activists and depriving members of jobs and their children. As this too met with little success, the campaign heightened, and after, 1935 Witnesses were subject to arbitrary arrest and detention without trial in a concentration camp. The camps, which provided in themselves a special kind of society, proved fertile ground for Witness work. Here torture, ridicule and death could not prevent conversions or persuade more than the smallest handful to sign the "denial" and purchase their freedom.

Inside and outside the camps the work continued and the position of neutrality gradually changed until Nazi society was seen as specifically identified with Satan's last throes and in which specific' elements of injustice and brutality to Witnesses and others were pointed out and commented upon in Witness literature. Therefore, the literature distributed to German homes, and the news of Germany smuggled out to Witnesses abroad, not only made Witness activity and thus police failure obvious, but also highlighted and criticized aspects of the new order in Germany. In one publication Hitler is referred to as a "beast of prey" and life in Germany is described as "worse than in Russia" with children taken from their natural mothers and with appalling and oppressive conditions for many German citizens, even those loyal to the Führer.[20]

By 1936 the police were devoting an inordinate amount of time to the pursuit of Witnesses and the courts were soon to become so choked with cases against them that they were either tried, en bloc, by special courts, or detained without trial. By 1935 there were so many Witnesses in camps that they constituted, for administrative purposes, a separate category. In 1933 there were twenty thousand Witnesses in Germany; by 1945 ten thousand had been imprisoned and some four to five thousand executed. The relative scale of this operation can only be compared to the war against the Jews.

The persecution of the Witnesses was raising all sorts of unwanted questions about the workings of the new society. There were protests from within the legal profession, that the law was being brought into disrepute by the treatment of these people. S.S.* men were seizing Witnesses after they had been declared "not guilty" by a court, in order to transport them to a concentration camp. A police internal memo rather tartly suggests that the officers in future wait until the accused is out of the dock before they seize him.[21]

The Witnesses were also acting as some kind of focus for anti-Nazi feeling. In a society where political protest is almost impossible, objections to the regime may well take the form of anti-government jokes, or of sympathy for a group identified as enemies of the regime. Whilst few citizens gave to Witnesses the private protection many gave to Jews, there is evidence to suggest that they refused to hand in or report literature, or to inform on Witnesses. Germans in camps and their relatives heard of the bravery of the Witnesses and how they were a special target for the brutality and mockery of the guards. Amongst some of these people, the Witnesses left a lasting impression. One camp inmate, herself a Catholic and hostile to the Witnesses' teaching, recalled the particularly vicious treatment members of this group experienced in the camps and how they alone would share bread and rations, keep the peace, help even the outcast Ukranian and Polish inmates and how they were seen by all the prisoners as "a rock in the mud."[22]

By investing the Witnesses with a political significance they did not deserve, the Nazis had created their own problem. Witnesses had entertained no thoughts of an alliance with Zionism or communism, or of overthrowing the new society; they had no concern with these things, which were in God's hands and which would find fulfilment in His eschatological plans. To a certain extent, conflict was inevitable, for in a totalitarian society, every issue assumes political significance. As the collaborationists were labelled "non-political", so the Witnesses appear in Gestapo reports as "political." By their refusal to validate Nazism, Witnesses became an enemy. By their treatment of the Witnesses, the Nazis helped them to develop new strengths. The group devised codes and strategies, a complex network in and out of camps, and a theology of martyrdom.

The nature and extremity of the Nazi response indicates a great deal about Nazi society. It was a new society, which, in spite of its attempts to construct roots from the myths of its Teutonic past, was essentially without an ideological or intellectual base. This society needed the approval and collaboration of existing institutions to give it respectability and to give credence to its claims to be restoring the true German way. Most established groups, from the churches to the civil service, for a variety of reasons, gave this support. In the sects the Nazis met not established but new groups whose response was unpredictable. Yet most sectarians had behaved like most members of the established churches, they had complied with the Nazis' view of themselves. Either by collaboration or by the willing acceptance of closure or a limitation on activities, they had accepted the new regime and by their cooperation in educational, welfare and cultural programmes, as

well as their religious recognition of Hitler as Germany's saviour,had provided an extra and unexpected source of legitimization. There were, of course, critics within the ranks of the
sectarians, but their voice was not publicly heard. In their
anxiety to appear as good, reliable citizens, the sects had
made themselves liable to ultimate closure and had, meanwhile,
provided the Nazis with one more moral weapon.

In their refusal to comply, the Jehovah's Witnesses offered a challenge to the totalitarian concept of the new society,
and this challenge, as well as the persistance of its survival,
demonstrably disturbed the architects of the new order. The
more the Witnesses were persecuted, the more they presented
a real ideological challenge. The time-honoured methods of
persecution, torture, imprisonment and ridicule were not resulting in the conversion of any Witnesses to the Nazi position and
were in fact back-firing against their instigators.

The Nazis panicked in the face of this unpredictable response. Any examination of internal police memos dealing with
the pursuit of the Witnesses after about 1935, when the failure
of the police campaign was becoming obvious, reveals the same
note of exasperation. Witnesses were finding more and more
ways around the bans; there was no cessation of activity,
none of these "cranks" could be persuaded to see the error of
his ways. In concentration camps the picture was the same.
Into the well-run block of women Witnesses at Ravensbrück,
the camp authorities moved a group of asocial prisoners, gypsies, prostitutes, and down and outs. So many converts were
made, that the new-comers, having failed in their mission to
upset the Witnesses, had to be moved out.[23] One observer has
suggested that the S.S. never got the better of the Jehovah's
Witnesses.[24]

Gestapo reports on the progress of the Witness persecution
reveal that there was more at stake here than the suppression
of a religious enemy who might harbour opponents of the regime
and this was confirmed by Kaltenbrunner, Heydrich's successor
as head of the S.D., at the Nuremberg Trials. This was a
conflict between two systems so similar in their totalitarian
claims, that Germany could not contain them both. Both were
new, both presented total world views and an authoritarian
system; both were millenarian, fundamentalist, Messianic,
anti-intellectual; both demanded fanatical devotion from their
followers; both were uncompromising. Between these two rival claimants on loyalty, the fight was bitter, even more so,
since the physically stronger Nazis were in many ways less
sure, less rooted in the firmness of their own conviction, less
certain of the survival of their 1,000 year Reich. Witnesses
did not doubt their own roots, for their faith had been evident

since the time of Abel. Whilst the Nazis had to suppress opposition and convince their supporters, often borrowing language and imagery from sectarian Christianity,[25] Witnesses were
sure of the total, unbending loyalty of their members, even
to death. Himmler once remarked that the Witnesses would provide a useful model for the S.S. in their fanatical devotion
to their movement and Messiah.

Not only did the Witnesses, therefore, challenge the Nazi
image of itself as an all powerful state, but more importantly,
in their ideological challenge they showed Nazism as insecure
and rootless, with its own internal certainties questioned by
a rival system, albeit numerically small and without political
influence. Since Nazism deliberately chose to use religous language in describing its own mission, the survival and growth
of a rival and banned religious system might make its own
metaphysical claims appear tenuous.

In conclusion, therefore, it can be seen that the experience of Nazi society would seem to suggest that any new order
faces a potential challenge from rival competing ideological
systems. In practice, in this case, most of these potential
rivals were happy to avoid conflict, to negotiate their own
survival and to accept the new society, thus conferring on it
an added element of legitimacy. The new society has the option whether or not to accept this opportunity and the acceptance may, as in this case, indicate a lack of real roots or
an ideological system.

The groups which accepted Nazi society were, on the
whole, established or anxious to become so, and in this context
even the support of comparatively new religious groups was
welcome because of the respectability gained by the new order.
It is also evident from the case of Nazi Germany that even a
totalitarian state is sometimes constrained in its treatment of
religious minorities by practical considerations. That the support of such groups as the collaborationist sects was accepted
does not, however, suggest that they would be tolerated on any
long-term basis. Since they had already bent the knee, their
ultimate closure would provide little difficulty.

In the relations with the non-collaborationists it is apparent that there was real conflict inherent in the meeting of
two aggressive, proselytizing, convinced systems of belief.
In attacking the Witnesses, even at great expense in time and
effort, the Nazis revealed what was most important to them and
where they were most vulnerable. Witnesses do not necessarily
come into conflict with society; conflict occurs only in those
situations where the state claims to represent and to be society
and to offer the only acceptable world-view. The persecution

of Witnesses by totalitarian states all over the world follows
the trend established by this, the first large-scale conflict of
the movement with a totalitarian regime.[26]

The Witnesses presented the Nazis with a special problem
in that the nature and scale of their response was unexpected.
This was no traditional enemy, like the Jews, Communists or
even Catholics. There were no precedents for dealing with this
group and none of the traditional methods worked. Witnesses
proved the "wild card" in the Nazi pack; they refused to accept the rules of the game. What is perhaps most apparent
is that the Witnesses, who provided one of the very few organised campaigns of resistance against the Nazis did so not as
anti-Fascist liberals, demanding toleration and freedom of
worship, but as conservatives, in their way, as traditionalist
as the Confessing Church, which fought not against Nazi tyran-
ny, but against changes in church government. The conserva-
tism of the Witnesses could, under different circumstances, have
served the Nazis well. Himmler saw in them German citizens
to be admired for their honesty, hard work and abstemiousness.
He made plans to settle them in eastern Europe as a vanguard
of Nazism after the war was won.[27] The S.S. had found them
useful servants: only Witnesses were allowed to shave the S.S.
guards using cut-throat razors, since only they could be trust-
ed not to kill. Political prisoners in concentration camps pil-
loried the Witnesses for being slaves of the S.S. It was the
sensitivity of the new Nazi order which initiated the struggle
with the Witnesses, but once initiated, this revealed, perhaps
more than any other area where opponents of the regime were
persecuted, the tensions inherent in the new society.

NOTES

*   S.A. Sturmabteilungen: Storm Troopers, paramilitary units
                            of the Nazi party.

     S.S. Schutzstaffeln: Protection Squad, elite corps of
                           Party, founded as a bodyguard
                           under Reichsführer S.S. Himmler,
                           their powers were considerably ex-
                           tended to include, amongst other
                           areas, police and concentration
                           camp duties.

     S.D. Sicherheitsdienst: Security Service of the S.S. formed
                             under Heydrich in 1932.

1.   See, for example Jeremy Noakes' discussion of the Olden-burg Crucifix struggle in Stachura (ed), 1978: 210-233.

2.   Boberach, 1971 passim.

3.   Bavarian State Archives, BayHStA, Reichsstatthalter 619, 11 August 1941.

4.   There was an interesting crop of new groups founded in the inter-war period. Note, for example, the Dinterbewegung, a group founded by Arthur Dinter, an ex-Nazi, who wanted to establish a new German religion; the Namenlose sect, founded by Joseph Mahl, a former member of the SPD who since 1934 had been prophesying a war and Liebe Vater habe Du Dank founded at the end of the First World War by Fürst Sels, who believed himself to be the reincarnation of Elijah.

5.   Even some of the Jehovah's Witnesses, whose German branch was isolated from the American leadership because of the war, accepted military service, unsure of the movement's stand on "neutrality."

6.   Sinz, 1933.

7.   Bavarian State Archives, BayHStA, Reichstatthalter 638, December, 1933.

8.   Morning Watch Calendar, 20 April, 1940.

9.   Canham, 1958: 286.

10.   Bavarian State Archives, BayHStA, Reichsstatthalter 638, December 1933.

11.   Gute Gesundheit, vol. 37, nr. 4, 1934: 170-171.

12.   See, for example Der Adventbote, vol. 14, nr. 16, 15 August 1935 : 249.

13.   In 1933 the population of Germany was approximately 65 million. Forty million were members of the Evangelical church-es and 21 million were Catholics. Of the remainder, some 620,000 Germans belonged to Free Churches or sects. (N.B. In January 1933, before the seizure of power, there were ap-proximately $1\frac{1}{2}$ million members of the Nazi party; by the end of 1934 it had increased its membership by almost 200%; Bracher, 1970: 294.)

14.   Der Adventbote, vol. 39, nr. 17, 15 August 1933: 1-4.

15.   It was taken also by the small Seventh Day Adventist Reform Movement, whose small membership was treated as harshly as the Witnesses on the grounds of their civil disobedience.   It is interesting to note that schisms from the main Adventist body have grown up in the Soviet Union, on similar issues of relations with the state.   The death of Vladimir Shelkov, leader of just such a break-away Adventist group, announced in January 1980, highlights this situation.

16.   The German Witnesses had, for example, offered in 1933 to change the cover of one of their publications which depicted a warrior holding a sword dripping with blood which the Nazis had found "political".

17.   Jehovah's Witness Yearbook, 1974, Watchtower Bible and Tract Society of Pennsylvania, New York :137; see also, Bavarian State Archives, B.Nr. 42274/ 34 I i B, 31 Oct., 1934.

18.   Consolation, 26 Jan., 1938.

19.   Jehovah's Witness Yearbook, op. cit.: 120.

20.   Bavarian State Archives, B.Nr. 50050/37 II I B/b 22 June, 1937.

21.   Ministry of the Interior, ref. 20, B. Nr. 51519/37 II i D, 20 August 1937, Document Centre, Berlin.

22.   Interview with Mrs. Werner Fett, 12 Oct. 1978.

23.   Buber, 1950: 237-8.

24.   Kogan, 1973:43.

25.   Hitler and other leading Nazis used religious language and imagery, and the state ceremonies developed under Nazism bore elements of both Christian and pagan symbolism.   The source of the Christian influence is normally seen to be the Catholic church, but an examination of the enthusiastic elements of such rituals as Party rallies, swearing loyalty to the Führer as well as the apocalyptic nature of religious language used seems to indicate a debt to sectarianism rather than Catholicism.

26.   The Third Reich saw the first serious conflict between the Witnesses and a totalitarian state.   More struggles were to follow, notably in the USSR, where the movement took a real hold only after the Second World War.   Russian prisoners of war had been converted by German Witnesses in prison and concentration camps and took the faith home with them.   The

Witnesses were immediately identified as enemies and have since been variously associated with Fascism or, as in Japan, with American capitalism.

27.   Ritter, 1954: 162-168.

ASIAN CULTURES AND THE IMPACT OF THE WEST: INDIA AND CHINA

Ninian Smart

It might seem a touch controversial to include a discussion of Hinduism and Maoism in a volume about the new religions. Is the one new, or the other a religion? But it is important that we should see new religions in the wider context of challenges to cultural identity. When a materially or culturally powerful force comes to threaten a different culture, there are various moves of adaptation which can be made. One such move is to reorganize older values into a new ideology, and this is what came to be the dominant solution in India, as it struggled both to digest and then throw off British rule. Another move may be necessary if for one reason or another older belief systems cannot easily cope with the new agenda: in such a case it may be possible to borrow a foreign system of values, but give it an indigenous face. The cases of India and China illustrate not only this symmetry, but another factor: the two cultures were sufficiently large and basically strong to be able to respond with a great degree of independence. In neither, for instance, did the religious values of the West, as expressed through missionary Christianity, achieve the dominance which the latter achieved in parts of Africa and among the Maoris, for instance. There the new religions such as Zulu Zionism and the Ratana had an overtly Christian form and arose out of a situation of previous conversions to "official Christianity". In India it was a resurgent Hinduism which proved the matrix of national revival; while in China the imperial powers' "opposition ideology" proved a strong system for the renascence of China. Thus the two cases which I here treat in a necessarily simplifed manner illustrate two kinds of responses to challenge. But it so happens that both movements occurred within the context of political struggle. Thus the question of the viability of an ideology within the framework imposed by political conditions and the need to change them, becomes much more important than it does in the milieu of new movements within, say, Californian society.

With culture contact, as with certain polarities within a given society, we can speak of cognitive and emotional distance.   Medieval Christianity and Islam were cognitively quite close; but emotionally (and socially, etc.) at a distance. The Indian move, an essentially conservative one, was to retain the older emotions, but mobilize them in new ways (the role of Ramakrishna and Gandhi), and to reduce cognitive distance through the new Hindu ideology (the role of Vivekananda and Radhakrishnan.)   But China's problem lay greatly in the fact that divisions within China and the specific character of its older spiritual and intellectual traditions meant that older emotions could not be mobilized in new directions;   while the cognitive distance between them and Western knowledge, though not unbridgeable, could not be reduced in a manner which engaged popular sentiment and needs.   This was an attraction of the West's opposition ideology, revolutionary Marxism.   Not only was it modern; but its very abrasiveness could serve to make the demands of revolution felt.   Revolution is like conversion.   As Aristotle said, the point of the mysteries is not to learn something but to experience a change.   Maoism proved to be a method of inducing a collective rite of passage: changing thus the whole frame of emotional attitude, and thus reducing dramatically the emotional distance between the two cultures.

I

The making of modern Hinduism was importantly the making of Hinduism.   It is of course true that the Indian subcontinent had come to possess a loose and incomplete federation of cults and belief-systems held together by the permeation of most of India by the Brahmin class.   Its sacred books and many of its sacred places were accessible only to part of the population.   If there was a name for it, it was the sanatana dharma and yet "the everlasting law" was a very partial expression of the varied ideas, customs and practices gathered together.   Negatively, it was not Buddhism or Jainism.   And from the 11th century, with the incursion of Islam, it was not Islam.

The coming of the British gave the impetus to a self-consciousness which was to express itself through a reshaping and absorption of the past into a new ideology, known as Hinduism. There were various ways in which the impact of the British was crucial.   First, there was the fact of the unification of the sub-continent under foreign rule and suzerainty -- a unification scarcely matched even by Asoka or Mughals.   The veins of India became the railways, the nerves the telegraph .   Second, the new all-Indian consciousness was developed through the imposition of a new language of education and administration.   The creation of the universities, partially through the

work of some great missionary educators, was in accordance
with the resolution of 1835 declaring that "the great objects
of the British government ought to be the promotion of European
literature and science" with a view to "imparting to the Native
population knowledge of English literature and science through
the medium of the English language".¹ After the Mutiny, implicitly India came to terms with the new culture, and this
implied the substitution of English for Sanskrit and the creation of a new middle class.   Third, the old Sanskrit heritage
was revived through the work of the new Orientalism.   The
parallel development of European scholarly labour amid the ancient fields of the Hindu heritage and the use of the printed
book liberated the texts from the grip of the old Brahmin tradition.   The juxtaposition of the Hindu heritage and modern
"British" knowledge stimulated reactions along the frontier between the two.   Fourth, from 1813, when the anti-missionary
policy of the East India Company was reversed by an Act of
Parliament, and especially after 1858 with the establishment
of the Raj, Christianity was perceived by Indians as having
privileged status: and it was through its exponents openly
critical of indigenous religion and society, especially Hindu.
The leaders of the Hindu community were on the defensive, as
regards idolatry (so-called), obscene practices connected with
festivals, temple sculptures, etc., social stratification, the
status of women and so forth.   The English Utilitarians and
Christian missionaries alike tended to a clear conviction of
the superiority of Western civilization.

Though Lord Macaulay could envisage a mental migration
into Christianity as a consequence of Western higher education,
characteristically the new Indian middle classes looked to a
way of transposing older indigenous values into the circumstances of the mixed culture which was forming.   The latter
part of the 19th century also saw the first beginnings of
Indian nationalism.   A new ideology had to deal with a number
of questions.

First, it needed essentially to be indigenous.   If Christianity was going to have a general effect it was more as an
inspiration to social reform and new styles of compassion --
through the figure of Jesus himself, the Sermon on the Mount
and the example of medical missionaries and the like.   To be
indigenous a new ideology needed to rest upon the Vedas and
Upaniṣads and on the rediscovered philosophical heritage of
India.

Second, it needed to contain a strong element of reform,
from two points of view.   For one thing, such reform was part
of the ideology of the white rulers; and second, the emerging
India of a "modern" age required to present itself as rational
and ethical, however it might in general prize tradition.

Third, the new ideology needed to be believable by the middle classes and (importantly) reasonably impressive to British educated people -- or at least to some of them; but vitally it needed to contain a bridge to the people. A new interpretation of the heritage which cut the middle classes off from the mass of Indians; and which cut a reformed religion from popular fervour -- such an interpretation would be religiously weak and could scarcely prove a means of mobilising national sentiment.

Fourth, because India was substantially Muslim, there were problems in any manner of interpreting Hinduism aggressively. It could be hoped that the new affirmation of indigenous values might incorporate something too of the Islamic heritage.

In brief, a new ideology for the late 19th and early 20th centuries in India needed to be deeply indigenous, reforming, modern and yet popular, and more than Hindu. Moreover, from the angle of Hindu pride, it required to have a genuine response to the seeming arrogance of Christianity. For the Indian might take the trains and the telegraphs, modern science and philosophy as elements in human progress: but the foreigners were bearers too of Christianity, and this was often insensitive to the Indian soul. If the greased cartridges sparked the Mutiny, that last unseeing upheaval on behalf of the older order that now was passing, the missionary tracts and the evangelical zeal of the missionaries were hard too, for the emerging middle classes to swallow.

The first major new religious movements were Ram Mohan Roy's Brahmo Samaj and Dayanand Sarasvati's Arya Samaj. The one was unitarian in spirit, ethical, modern; the other was reforming, but aggressively conservative, even fundamentalist (in the sense that the old Vedic hymns, as suitably interpreted, contained all knowledge, and were inerrant). But the Brahmo Samaj was only in rather a weak way indigenous. Resting on a theistic interpretation of the Upaniṣads it owed little to the Vedantic treatises of later times, and still less to the rich symbolic life of Hindu bhakti (devotionalism). Though strong in its efforts towards reform, it had little appeal for the masses, nor did it contain a bridge to them. It was outward-looking towards both Islam and Christianity, in that it could see the unitarian message running through these religions.

In rejecting polytheism, the Brahmo Samaj could appeal to the educated, but ultimately more fruitful was the new Hindu affirmation, based on some old motifs, that the many gods really are so many manifestations of the One. The Arya Samaj's rejection of polytheism -- of what was identified as

Puranic Hinduism -- could prove dynamic when combined with
its xenophobia, especially in the Punjab. For there, with the
Sikh tradition and other movements whose bhakti was not tied
to the cult of images, there was a popular basis for it as a
religious and political ideology. But ultimately it was bound
to fail among the new classes. Though Arya Samaj exponents
could claim that atomic theory, electricity, the germ theory
of disease, etc., were all there implicitly in the Vedas ("Anything you can do we did much earlier"), Vedic fundamentalism
was in no way modern in outlook. On the other hand its radical rejection of most popular religion was no basis for mass
support. Then again, its anti-Islamic character did not help
in the task of rallying the incipient forces of nationalism.
Nor did its anti-Christian stance help with the subtle task of
digesting the newly arrived modern forms of Christianity. In
brief, it was indigenous but not widely popular, reforming
without being genuinely modern, and Hindu without being syncretic.

What of the Brahmo Samaj? Ram Mohan Roy's wide learning and genuine concern for the scientific spirit, together with
the way in which the movement attracted some of the best
minds of the Bengal renaissance, meant that the Samaj could
claim real modernity, in alliance with a spirituality which owed much to the Christian ethic. But it was less strongly indigenous in character than even the Arya Samaj, bypassing the
Puranas and Vedanta in its plunge back to the Vedas. Ram
Mohan Roy could see theism in the Īśa Upaniṣad: but his
theism was too gently enlightened and perhaps too reminiscent
of Akbar, to have the dynamism of bhakti -- that fervid theism
so wrapped in the pulsing life of temple and ghat as to be
problematic for Roy's unitarian nature. His creed was more
than Hindu, and he owed much to the Christian and Islamic
traditions. But its lack of deep indigenous roots crippled it
as an engine of national revival.

The Zeitgeist supplied a brilliant solution in the twin
form of Ramakrishna and Vivekananda -- between them pioneers
of the new Hinduism. The saint and the philosopher were combined as the inspiration of a movement which has won wide
respect and helped vividly to incarnate the new ideology.
What is that ideology? It is something which in differing
forms one can see in the writing and thinking of so many
Hindus of the modern period, especially in Bhagavan Das,
Sarvepalli Radhakrishnan, and Mahatma Gandhi. (But I shall
treat Gandhi separately, as representing the explicitly political
phase of the new Hindu ideology.) Briefly the ideology is as
follows.

All religions point to the same Truth. That Truth is
best expressed through Vedanta and in particular a version
of Advaita Vedanta, in which the higher Godhead beyond God

is something to be realized inwardly in the human soul. The
testimony of Sufis,Christian mystics,Buddhist contemplatives and
others is brought to bear on this thesis. The genius of Hinduism is that it caters for different conditions and levels of religion. It is tolerant and embracing, not exclusive (like Christianity: Christ is no bogeyman, but the missionary is). In
particular, the many gods of Hinduism are so many faces of
the one God. Thus Hinduism is not polytheistic: all the gods
are One. Also, Hinduism in its emphasis on spirituality is
not hostile to modern science, but only to a shallow materialism. Though there are blemishes in Hindu society, they can
be corrected through reform, and through a new humanism
which sees the infinite worth of individuals as a consequence
of their inwardly and essentially divine nature. This ideology
can be supported by appeal to the ancient texts, and so is
not something new. All this is the essential Hinduism.

The ideology does many things. It is deeply indigenous
in its appeal to sources; it is popular for it defends "polytheism", i.e. the whole bhakti movement and temple cult; it
is modern, for it recognizes modern scholarship and science;
it has a strongly reforming edge; and it is eirenic towards
Muslims and Christians.

As J.N. Farquhar writes: "It was (Ramakrishna's) teaching on the religions that laid hold of his disciples. He im-
pressed all who came into contact with him as a most sincere
soul, a God-intoxicated man; but what distinguished his
teaching from the teaching of others was his defence
of everything Hindu and his theory that all religions are
true."[2] As vivid and charismatic pioneer of Hindu universalism, Ramakrishna was not to know how congenial his teaching
would be not merely to his follow-countrymen but a handful
of influential Westerners -- for instance,through Vivekananda's
dramatic appearance at the world Parliament of Religions at
Chicago in 1893. The support of the Theosophical Society to
Hinduism was a sign that the religion could plausibly be held
as a universalistic system. Here a point of living social logic
is worth making.

If a religion claiming universal validity comes into contact with a "tribal" religion, that is, one which is simply the
belief and practices of a group, the latter is at a disadvantage until it can claim some kind of universal validity -- even
if such a claim is part of a theory of chacun à sa foi. The
religion of India was "tribal" in the sense that it is rooted
strongly in the customs of the sub-continent, and religious duties were conceived as belonging to people in virtue of their
descent. But the new situation made a riposte to universalistic
Christianity inevitable. The telling response was chacun à
sa foi, and all faiths point to the one Truth so anciently perceived in the Hindu tradition.

More: India was able to throw up charismatic figures who could feel the new Hinduism in their bones. If in Rama- krishna we see the religious form of the new Hindu ideology, in Gandhi there appeared the incarnation of its political di- mension.   He was not really a religious teacher, though he was religious: much more vital was his translation of religion into a politics of nationalism uniquely adapted to the struggle. His appeal to village values and his simplicity of style gave Congress access to the masses; his alliance with Nehru gave Congress also a Westernized aspect.   His spiritual and ethical ecumenism brought the reforming spirit of modern Hinduism into the stream of political struggles.   If his teaching has had on- ly slight impact on the shape of post-independence India it is because he set his face against modernity.   Whether or not such modernity -- in the shape of industrial and technological development -- is well suited to Indian conditions may be a question.   But undoubtedly the whole thrust of the Indian renaissance to which Gandhi was in his own idiosyncratic way an heir was towards a blending of spiritual values with the new education and science.

Obviously, the new Hindu ideology owed much to the im- pact of the outside forces which flooded India in the 19th cent- ury.   Hinduism was born as a religion.   The question was pos- ed to Hindus: Can the old tradition supply materials for an outlook which justifies the tradition in the face of Christian criticism, while at the same time opening up possibilities of reform and modernization relevant to the new educated class and to the struggle for national independence?   The resources of the old tradition were indeed adequate to this task, and they formed a vital ingredient in the new religion that most of us know as Hinduism.

II

Despite the rich achievements of the Chinese religious and philosophical tradition they notably failed substantially to pro- vide dynamic ingredients for a modern Chinese outlook.   There is, it is true, a certain Chineseness about Mao's Marxism, but it is more in atmosphere than content.   Though Mao's thought is not orthodox, its unorthodoxies stem from the particularities of the Chinese situation under the threat of imperialism rather than from the absorption into it of Chinese religious and philo- sophical motifs.

The Chinese problem in the 19th century arose from the same source as did that of India: Western incursion. But the problem was stated in a different way. For one thing, China did not possess the adhesive anarchism of Indian society. It was long centralized and the centralization came from a bureaucratic system whose mind was Confucianism. Also, the foreign challenge was not that of the conqueror. Rather the European powers plus Japan and the United States were exploiters of China, underminers of its old fabric, economic forces opening up a hinterland. Without considerable social change and internal rearrangement, China would not be able to stand up to these outer forces. It was the collapse of the twenties and thirties of this century that precipitated the Communist advance.

As far as its ancient resources went, China was in some difficulty in attempting to cope with the new incursions. Confucianism as a set of ideas was woven into the study of the classics. How could the imperial bureaucracy sacrifice its soul in opening itself up to the quite different assumptions of modern Western knowledge? The situation was very different from that in India. There Western education could be used in parallel with and in some degree in the service of the indiginous intellectual tradition. In China, Confucianism was not just an ethico-religious system: it was incarnated in the traditional educational system itself. Destroy the latter and Confucianism withers. The abolition of the old system was, not surprisingly, the prelude to the revolution of 1911.

Taoism had three somewhat disparate characteristics. On the one hand, its roots lay in the ancient mystical anarchism of the book of Lao Tse. This had been rediscovered at different phases of Chinese history and had entered the bloodstream of Buddhism through Ch'an. Then later Taoism manifested itself as a complex hierarchical cult administering popular and magical rites. Third, Taoism had in some degree inspired the secret societies, thus re-expressing its ancient anarchism, but in more violent form. Taoism of the second kind, magical, scarcely had the power to reshape itself along lines relevant to the reconstruction of China, while the old anarchism was too quietistic. If the secret societies had relevance it was because the forces welling up through the peasant rebellion might one day cataclysmically alter China, and the secret societies kept alive the spirit of rebellion. Yet oddly it was a Christian impulse that gave rise to the greatest harnessing of that cataclysmic peasant force — through the Taipings: greatest that is, until Mao followed with a different head joined to the peasant body.

While institutionalized Taoism and Confucianism for different reasons found it difficult to cope with Western knowledge;
theoretically there was an easier rapprochement between science
and Buddhism. The considerable Buddhist reformer T'ai-hsü
(1890-1947) was able to perceive rightly that an intellectual
synthesis between modern science and Greater Vehicle metaphysics is feasible, but his call to China to adopt Mahayana
as its national religion was scarcely realistic. For one thing,
the religion was insufficiently militant. But also, though
T'ai-hsü involved himself movingly in social welfare, he had
no conception of a great reconstruction of society.

A similar criticism can be levelled at the evolutionary
Confucianism of K'ang Yu-wei, whose originality lay in making
the conception of a future harmony, the Great Harmony of older
historical speculation, into a future state of mankind. He saw
a new age of human peace and democracy dawning, and hoped
for the disappearance gradually of racial divisions and family
distinctions in a utopian communalism. But he disliked the
thought of strife, and found Darwinian evolutionism repellent
from that point of view. Mao remarked drily that K'ang did
not and would not find the way to the Great Harmony. [3]

Of all the movements in 19th and early 20th century
China which were a response to the impact of the West the most
vital and instructive was the Taiping rebellion (or as some
say, revolution). The stimulus for the events of 1851 and after
was undoubtedly the Opium War, for this drew attention to and
helped to deepen the problems of rural China in a period of
increasing dislocation. The time was ripe for another wave
of peasant rebellion such as constituted a recurrent pattern
in Chinese history. Both the Taipings and later the Communists created what may be called peasant rebellion with a
mind. The ideology of Hung Hsiu-ch'üan was religious --
intensely so, but it was also powerfully social. In a somewhat
blind and unsophisticated way Hung's visionary leadership
groped towards a solution of China's discontents. But oddly
his religion had a Christian content. His contact with Protestant missionaries gave his shamanistic visions a Christian core,
and out of the interplay between Protestant prophetism and old
Chinese thinking about a Heavenly Kingdom, the T'ai P'ing,
there was born a new and rigorous plan of social and spiritual
change. The revolution, however, was not overtly directed a-
gainst foreigners, but rather against the still somewhat alien
Manchu dynasty. Moreover, its Christian aspect was in part
expressed through the smashing of images -- in short a direct
attack on the popular cultus of the "Three Religions" of China.

Socially, the Taiping programme was most radical: col-
lectivism of property, land reform, equality for women, moral

changes (e.g. the giving up of opium and tobacco), a new calendar, linguistic reform. No wonder the Communists have looked back in wonderment at the Taipings: were they, for all
their religious obscurantism, genuine forerunners of the Marxist
revolution? But despite the great successes of the Taipings —
the capture of Nanking and the control of a great area of central and south China — their movement ended in disaster.Why?
There was a purely military side to this defeat: the Taipings
for all their ardour did not have the communications or the
strategic insight to overthrow the imperial power.   But there
was an ideological side to their defeat too.

First, the Taiping ideology was not intellectual enough.
It is not possible to promote a successful revolution without
an ideology which will help to direct the minds of the leadership and of the bureaucracy necessary in the new administration.   The fact that the old mandarinate's ideology was failing
did not mean that it would be possible to get by without an
alternative.   The Taiping beliefs were too remote both from
modern science and economic analysis to give more than temporary leadership to rural rebellion.   In picking up from the
West an aspect of the latter's Christian dynamism it was un-
aware of the fact, evident to a later generation of Chinese,
that there was a conflict within the European mind between
religion and the new natural and social sciences.   Moreover,
by being foreign-oriented the Taipings brought an ambiguity
to their movement.   The foreigners were the stimulus to a new
Chinese self-consciousness.   The problem was how to combine
learning from the West with a nationalist feeling that was
bound to contain xenophobia.

The problems of the Taipings were brilliantly solved in
Maoism as a new religion to replace the older traditions of the
Central Kingdom.   Thus social reconstruction was given a
systematic basis by the doctrines of Marxism, here adapted to
recognize the essential peasant basis both of revolutionary
struggle and the new economy.   The question of the relationship between ideology and science was apparently solved
through the scientific character of Marxism.   Older Confucian
ideas of praxis were replaced by a new synthesis of theory
and practice.   Moreover, the contradiction in the Taiping was
overcome.   The Taipings drew on the West,through Christianity,
and were not intrinsically hostile to the foreigner.   Marxism
had the advantage of drawing upon Western ideas while at the
same time giving a licence to a fierce struggle against imperialism.   Now the class struggle could be seen as part of the
national struggle.

One can perhaps understand Maoism's relationship to the
older Chinese religious and ideological values by seeing how

Maoism performs an analogy of function and a reversal of content in respect to the old trio of religions. The reversal of content was necessary because in different ways the trio was an obstacle to that kind of modernization of China which could restore China to independence of the outsider. But the analogy of function was important insofar as the feelings of both the masses and the educated classes could be mobilized upon behalf of a new programme. That mobilization required folk to go through bitter and dangerous trials, only half-justified by the perception of anarchic misery and humiliation which the crumbling China of the 20th century experienced.

Confucianism implied a theory of government and an ethos for the elite who administered government. That theory, politically, centred on the Emperor's capacity to mediate the will of Heaven; but such a theory was controlled by the ultimate recognition of the principle that the people may in some circumstances overthrow the ruler from whom the mandate of Heaven has been withdrawn. Marxism could fit this conception. It provided a new theory of government, and a mandate of the People. It provided an ethos for the substitute for the mandarinate, namely the Party and the cadres. In Maoist literature, the ethos is worked out vigorously, and the recurrent attacks on Confucianism are a reminder that the new ethos has a very different content from the old. At a local level the old clan system was replaced by the brigade and other collective groups.

Thus functionally Maoism supplies a new ethos to replace the old, and also a new learning -- not the old Classics now, but scientific socialism as expressed in the Marxist classics and Mao Tse-tung thought. But there remained a functional tension in the new system: the Communist Party and the cadres were necessary to the whole apparatus of administration, and functioned by analogy to the old imperial bureaucracy. But whereas the old ethos had been frankly elitist, Maoist ethics could not be. The Cultural Revolution and the democratization of learning by boiling the new classics down to the Little Red Book were attempts to resolve the tension.

Buddhism in Chinese society functioned as deliverer of personal hope, among other things. The devotionalism of the Pure Land was the context of an eschatology which fused with the Chinese quest for immortality. To some extent the next world functioned to redress the balance of this world. Marxism provided a collectivist version of hope, in which the future was brought in to redress the balance of the past. If Mao allowed his followers to create a cult of his personality, it latched on to motifs of the older Bodhisattva ideal. But while Buddhism served as a vital ingredient in the faith of the masses, it also had its intellectual dimension, nurtured some-

what archaically in the monasteries.   Its subtlety at this level
always represented a challenge to Confuciansim, and part of
the aim of Neo-Confuciansim was to provide a vital, Confucian,
alternative to the dialectics of Suchness in Buddhism.   Marxism
functioned both as practical philosophy and the bearer of a
new metaphysics.

Taoism at the grass roots was in part magic, in part
the tradition of the Secret Society.   Marxism supplied the alternative to magic.   Sometimes indeed it became magic, as is
testified by the compilation of The Miracles of Chairman Mao.
As for the turbulent anarchism of the Taoist tradition, the
Communist Party serves as a new Secret Society, and was a
creative harnessing of the fraternal and conspiratorial traditions of the old groups.

But the content-reversal was drastic.   The reverence for
the past was replaced by a gaze fixed on the future.   If anything, the young were to be prized against the old.   The new
ethos was no longer hierarchical but egalitarian, and the ty-
rannies of the old family system were to be uprooted. Practical
learning was more vital than book learning, and dirty hands
were to be preferred to the scholarly mind.   At its most intense this distrust of book-learning caused the closing of the
universities during the Cultural Revolution.   The mandate of
Heaven was replaced by the mandate of the People.   The techniques of classical study were no longer needed.

Reincarnation and karma, so vital to Buddhism, were replaced by the dialectic of history.   Meditation was rejected
in favour of practical action.   The ideal of the monk was as
obsolete as that of the Confucian gentleman, for the monk stood
aside from the process of social reconstruction.   Logically, the
Buddhist Sangha was an affront to the Marxist programme.
The old compassion must be changed to a new sense of class
solidarity.   The Pure Land was an illusion: the new China
was real.

If there was a quest for life beyond death it had to be
through the people; and if there were to be anarchism it could
really go no further than democratic centralism allowed.   For
the plethora of Taoist gods and magic, there was to be substi-
tuted the new and potent edifice of scientific socialism.

In brief Mao Tse-tung thought supplies a radical replacement of the old trio.   The Yin and the Yang are only
dimly to be seen in the new dialectical thinking.   In taking
up Marxism, China used the West against itself, but ultimately
the worth of the new synthesis of Marxist theories and Chinese
needs which found expression in Mao's thought is to be judged

by the test of whether it succeeded in solving China's national problem, namely how a decaying Empire which did not think of itself as a nation could be transformed into that typical and world-wide product of the 19th century, the modern nation state. By that test it succeeded brilliantly. It has become an effective national religion.

III

We may now reflect on the opposite and complementary experience of India and China. Effectively, both Hinduism and Maoism came to be ideologies relevant to the national struggle. Imperialism was a potent exporter of nationalism -- for a number of reasons. One was that European invasion and incursion confronted the two cultures in question, as well as every other culture outside Europe, with the fact of the Other. This was specially unnerving for two civilizations that had lived each at the centre of its own world. For the traditional Indian the overseas world only dimly existed, and the trans-Himalayan regions were only vague sources of aggression from afar. For the Chinese elite the foreigners they knew were either discreet tributaries or barbarians: the unwonted, unprecedented power of the Europeans forced a revision. Barbarous they might be, but they had science and other potent inventions, such as new political theories. Another reason for imperialist export of nationalism was precisely that nationalism was the growing ideology of Europe. The conception of the linguistic or cultural national state was itself given extra force by suffering and humiliation. As the peoples of Italy or the Hapsburg Empire had grown restive under foreign dominance, so too the peoples of Asia were destined to be given a new self-consciousness in an era when the nation state was fashionable. But the solutions to the national problem were, as we have seen, very different.

Essentially, the modern Hindu ideology was a redisposition of ancient resources. India's commitment to a spiritual view of life was mediated politically through the non-violent policy of Gandhi. By contrast China, unable effectively to draw upon its past, made use of a European ideology and adapted it to the Chinese situation. If there are analogies with small-scale societies, India's solution to the problem of its identity is neo-traditionalist, as among the Torajas of Sulawesi; while China's is akin to the solution offered by the independent forms of Christianity in Africa, such as Zulu Zionism.

But having achieved their major collective results both the new Hinduism and Maoism are losing direction somewhat. After more than a quarter of a century since independence and liberation, new agendas are forming. But both Maoism and the new Hindu ideology are experiments in the reshaping of identities. The polarities remain intriguing: one tolerant, the other non-tolerant; one spiritual in theory, the other materialist; one deeply indigenous, the other foreign; one non-violent in principle, the other born in a theory of warfare; one ahistorical in flavour, the other historically dialectical; the one concretized in the holy man, the other in the poetical revolutionary; the one reformist, the other socially cataclysmic; the one diffuse and multiple, the other disciplined and central-ized; the one full of archaisms, the other lusting for a brave new world -- indeed the one anchored in antiquity, the other aggressively eschatological. India, conquered, conceded far less of its old culture.

As new religions Hinduism and Maoism are in essence i-deologies designed to cope with a threat to cultural identity. Insofar as the modern nation-state is a means of giving a sense of identity, prestige and security to people under threat, the two ideologies can be compared to movements in smaller scale societies which have attempted to cope with the powerful impact of Western culture and colonialism. The problem is what psychic deal will prove best in the circumstances. In India, for various reasons, it was possible to sacrifice only a few elements of the past in the shaping of a new outlook -- partly because the circumstances of conquest left the national struggle basically in the hands of the new educated classes. In China most of past literary and religious culture was sacrificed. Under these circumstances the future which compensates has to be very real. Hence Maoist zeal.

IV

It may be that the contrary examples of modern India and China may have more relevance to new smaller-scale reli-gious movements than might at first appear. There is, as I have suggested, the question of how people can make differing psychic deals. Thus from some points of view official science and the apparatus of its applications can be perceived as threatening to traditional symbolic values, and in this con-frontation various moves are possible -- to adapt traditional values (but not much) and reduce cognitive distance, as with scientific humanism and liberal Christianity; to reaffirm tradi-tional values conservatively and reject parts of official science (as in diverse ways through Christian fundamentalism); to change values but retain adherence broadly to official science while sceptical of its applications (neo-Buddhism, etc.). There is, however, a complication which the case of China illustrates. Part of any modern ideology is that it should be "scientific": but science is in its nature critical, and this opens up a different gap between it and authoritarianism than merely the cognitive one. Often official science absorbs the "anti-science" with which it is challenged (so now yoga is investigated on a scientific bases, acupuncture is acknowledged, "small-is-beautiful" is respectable.) This methodological openness poses problems of a further order -- what might be called the methodological distance bwteen critical modernism and authoritarianisms, whether ancient, modern, large or small, political or private.

Finally, it seems appropriate to conclude with the thought that secular and religious ideologies need to be treated together. The line between them is itself an ideological one needing critical investigation.

NOTES

1.   Spear, 1965, 127.

2.   Farquhar, 1919: 199.

3.   Mao, SW: 4, 414.

4.   Urban, 1971.

FROM ACROSS THE BLACK WATER
TWO IMPORTED VARIETIES OF HINDUISM --
THE HARE KRISHNAS AND THE
RAMAKRISHNA VEDANTA SOCIETY

John Whitworth
Martin Shiels

In North America during the nineteen seventies, in the wake of the "counter culture" of the previous decade, many long established sectarian groups increased their membership, imported versions of oriental faiths attracted large numbers of predominantly youthful converts, Pentecostal and charismatic fellowships flourished and a wide range of therapies and "spiritual disciples" mushroomed into existence. This efflorescence of religious and quasi-religious groupings which, to hostile observers appeared to find its logical culmination in the tragic events at Jonestown, Guyana, has generated considerable private and public concern. In consequence, "deprogramming" is a flourishing minor industry and Federal, State and Provincial Governments throughout North America have established a wide range of investigatory committees and commissions into religious sects and cults.

Private individuals and governments are thus alike concerned to arrive at answers to the question "Why do exotic, unorthodox, religious groups attract adherents", and the authors of this article fully agree with Barker's recently expressed judgement that converts to the "new religions" are not necessarily (but certainly sometimes are) "inadequate", "mentally disturbed" or "victims of sophisticated brainwashing techniques."[1] We feel with Barker that such converts find,or hope to find, shelter, succor, temporary relief or additional strength to enable them to avoid or cope with the stresses, dilemmas and sheer deprivations to which they are exposed in the "mainstream" society which brands them as "deviants" or "cranks."

No fully satisfactory sociological analysis of these "new religions" has yet been presented, a fact largely attributable to their number, variety, often transient nature and the natural reluctance of most sociologists to give hostages to fortune, but probably most students of the field would roughly agree with the summary conclusions of the author of Modern Religious Cults and Movements who states of the new religions:

155

They are in general a quest for a new type of religious reality: they are largely due to certain
marked inadequacies of the more accepted religious
teachings . . . They are re-enforced by the restless
and unsettled temper of a time subject to great
changes of habit and outlook through the breaking
up of old industrial and social orders and the impact of new forces driving in from every direction. [2]

As the footnote to the above quotation reveals, this work
was published in the United States in 1923. At the beginning
of the decade which is conventionally understood as the high
water mark of American complacency and rampant materialism,
the author, Atkins, was concerned to analyze the appeal of
the many sects and cults (ranging from Christian Science
through New Thought to Bahaism and Vedanta) which purported
to transcend orthodox Christianity or which were derived from
religious traditions alien to the American population. The
above reference to Atkins' work is not simply an exercise in
"rescue archaeology" performed in the sociology of religion,
but rather is intended to serve two purposes. The first is to
some extent self-serving, as one of the two religious groups
discussed below -- the Ramakrishna Vedanta Society -- was
established in the United States in 1896 and so is not "new"
in the sense of being a recent growth in the pullulating jung-
les of American minority religions. However, the Vedantists'
teachings, values and (in some cases) life-styles are culturally aberrant in the American context and the group has continued to expand slowly in recent decades. The second purpose
is to indicate that the term "new religions", like most summary
titles, does rough justice to the complexity of the empirical
realities it embraces and perhaps tends to give an undue impression of novelty and historical discontinuity in the development of North American minority religions.

In a symposium devoted to the "new religions" it may
seem somewhat churlish or pedantic to question the very rubric
under which this article is written, but the fact remains that
the term, even if strictly applied to the religious sects and
cults which have flourished since the waning of the counter-
culture, is fraught with ambiguity. The adjective "new" may
imply religious groups which have arisen and developed within
the particular cultural context in question but which, at least
superficially, are markedly different from earlier groups in
the same context (the "Jesus Freaks" or the ill-fated members
of the People's Temple might serve as an example in the United
States). However, the same adjective "new", is also applied
to groups which represent importations of genuine strands of
alien religious traditions (Tibetan Buddhism) and to syncretistic, bastardized or spurious versions of such traditions which
are, consciously or unconsciously, adapted to western tastes

and expectations (The Moonies, Transcendental Meditation and the Happy, Healthy, Holy Society might fit within this category). Finally, as already indicated, not all of the non-Christian religious groups which have expanded in the last decade are of recent establishment.

Despite our reservations regarding the accuracy and possible ambiguities of the term "new religions", it remains true that in contemporary North America a greater proportion of the population than ever before is, or has recently been, involved with or influenced by, religious and quasi-religious groups which are not essentially derived from the Judaeo-Christian tradition. In a short paper we cannot hope to arrive at a satisfactory total explanation of this phenomenon; but in the sections which follow we will present an inevitably somewhat cursory discussion of two groups, the Hare Krishnas and the Ramakrishna Vedanta Society ("Vedanta" for the sake of brevity), in an attempt to assess the nature of the gratifications which their adherents receive from membership in them.

While we recognize that both groups are small and are likely to remain so, we also feel that study of such relatively miniscule religious groups may ultimately possess more than purely ethnographic interest. In other words, our conviction is that in sociological terms every "microcosm" has its "macrocosmic" implications. The very fact that sectarian groups arise and win adherents on the basis of denunciations of perceived evils should tell us something about the wider society from which they are concerned to separate themselves and about the tensions, frustrations and deprivations suffered by some members of those intra-societal groups (socio-economic and other) from which the members of a particular sect originate.

Superficially, the two sects discussed below, the Hare Krishnas and the Vedantists, appear very similar, but the ostensible similarities cover divergent belief systems, forms of social organization and attitudes to the world, which appeal to markedly different "sorts and conditions" of men. Both groups were founded by charismatic leaders and are infused with charismatic elements. Both are based on teachings which are "orthodox" strands of Hinduism.[3] Both regard the present age of the world as the corrupt Age of Kali Yuga and purport to bring the wisdom of the East to the especially benighted West which is embedded in the slough of spiritual ignorance and materialism. The Hare Krishnas have existed for little more than a decade but have attracted much sociological attention, while the Vedantists, who have been established in the West for upwards of eighty years, have been largely overlooked or neglected by sociologists.[4]

THE INTERNATIONAL SOCIETY FOR KRISHNA CONSCIOUSNESS --
THE HARE KRISHNAS

The Hare Krishnas believe that the present age is the Age of Kali Yuga -- a "demonic" era of especial corruption, materialism, sensuality and spiritual desolation. They feel that the misery of the world arises from ignorance of the nature of God and of the duties incumbent on men and that their founder, Bhaktivedanta -- the "spiritual master of this age" -- offered such knowledge. The world is in a fallen state and the prime task of the individual is to seek to free himself from misery and enslaving desires by practicing Bhakti-Yoga and so attaining permanent, ecstatic "Krishna Consciousness" which will lead ultimately to full salvation.

For the devotee who aims to attain Krishna Consciousness there are moral rules to be followed and sinful actions which must be avoided, for without these pre-conditions karma would make the attainment of salvation impossible. Such virtues as chastity, truthfulness, cleanliness, tolerance, gentleness and modesty are enjoined, and lust, deceitfulness, vanity, greed, arrogance, anger and pride must be striven against. As the devotee grows in knowledge he learns of many more offences to be avoided and virtues to be practiced, together with the means of doing so, all of which are set out in great detail in the various classical scriptures and Bhaktivedanta's commentaries on them.

All these injunctions have the aim of leading the devotee to Krishna Consciousness, but there is another aspect of service to Krishna which follows naturally from the first -- the spreading of Krishna Consciousness throughout the world. Krishna is the soul of every living entity, and service to Krishna therefore means service and love for all living beings. The form which this universal love and service takes, however, is different from that social welfare activism which has been characteristic of many of the liberal Christian denominations. The physical parts of the universe, including for example, the disease, starvation and poverty of the masses in India, are only temporary, and in any case are the result of maya and karma -- ignorance and sin.

The vital concern of the Hare Krishnas is to help the real, inner selves of people to attain the permanent good of Krishna Consciousness, rather than simply to ameliorate the temporary condition of bodies in one incarnation. For those deprived of the enlightenment which comes from Krishna Consciousness one physical incarnation, however miserable it may

be, is no more than the blink of an eyelid in the journey
through eternal time. To concentrate on alleviating the physical distress of one lifetime, (which may, in any case, be worse
in the next incarnation) is, quite literally, irrelevant. The
goal of the sect's teachings is to raise the consciousness of
people to a level where they might achieve liberation, or at
least be assured of rebirth in a form more likely ultimately
to achieve it. The task of the Hare Krishnas is thus two-fold.
First, and probably for most of the unsophisticated devotees
primarily, they must seek to achieve selflessness in this life
and salvation thereafter. Second, they must evangelize while
remaining aloof from the demonic world. In the terms of Wilson's typology of sectarian responses, they are a conversionist
sect but one with marked and, we maintain, growing, introversionist tendencies. [5]

The attainment of Krishna Consciousness is thought to require unremitting discipline and vigilance and the sect's organization is strictly authoritarian. During his lifetime Bhaktivedanta was revered as an avatar. He personally made all
important appointments to positions in the sect's hierarchy and
(like Mrs. Eddy, the foundress of Christian Science) had the
prescience to "bureaucratize" his charisma by appointing twelve
male devotees to a Governing Body Commission which now
superintends the widely scattered "temples" or societies. The
intellectuals of the sect are the "sannyasis", monk-like ascet-
ics, who have taken permanent vows of renunciation breaking
all earthly ties and attaching them to a life of pure spirituality. They are considered to be very advanced spiritually, and
practice special austerities. Their twin duties are the study
and preaching of sacred scripture, and they therefore travel
constantly, especially visiting newly founded temple communities.

Within the individual temples supreme authority rests with
the temple President, whom the rank and file are ordered to
treat with the respect and obedience due him as Bhaktivedanta's local representative. Every action of every member, fully
initiated, novice or "householder" (married persons who sometimes continue to live in the temple) is closely regulated and
privacy is non-existent. With the exception of some six hours
or less for sleep, the sectarians follow a tightly prescribed
routine of private and communal devotions, study sessions,
necessary chores and fund-raising activities, interspersed with
frequent minor and major festivals which are generally open
to the public. Service, unquestioning subordination and
egoless detachment are the qualities which this regime is designed to inculcate and the rewards for such manifestations
of true Krishna Consciousness are the approval of one's peers
and superiors; possible promotion in the sect's hierarchy;ulti-
mate salvation and, according to devotees' reports, a state
of permanent selfless ecstasy -- "blissing out on Krishna".

A taste of this bliss is sometimes achieved in the communal ecsta sy of the worship ceremony performed in the temples several times each day. Devotees call the ritual arati, literally "waving the lights" before an altar on which stand the temple deities –– most popularly Radha and Krishna. The pujari, the devotee whose privilege it is to care for the temple deities and make the ritual offerings, begins the ceremony by lighting lamps of incense, camphor, and ghee. These are waved gracefully before the altar, and then passed among the devotees, who purify themselves by passing their fingers through the flames. Meanwhile, flowers, food and water are offered, and the pujari reverently waves a yak's tail fan to keep the deities cool and free from insects. Soon a conch shell is sounded three times, and one devotee leads a chant, the others responding. A prayer of respectful obeisance to Bhaktivedanta and his Vaisnavite predecessors in the disciplic succession is always chanted first, followed by others to Radha, Krishna, and even sacred places or plants. Before the final, essential invocation a variety of chants are performed, their number, and the number of repetitions being at the discretion of the chant leader. Finally, the familiar Hare Krishna mantra –– the Mahamantra –– is chanted:

> Hare Krishna, Hare Krishna,
> Krishna Krishna, Hare Hare,
> Hare Rama, Hare Rama,
> Rama Rama, Hare Hare

It begins at a slow and measured tempo, the leader beating time with the mridanga, a drum suspended from his shoulders. The tempo gradually speeds up, and the drumming is joined by the sound of finger-cymbals (kirtalas), flutes, bells, hand-clapping, stamping feet and the occasional ecstatic yell. As the noise reaches a crescendo the devotees "bliss out", leaping high in the air and waving their arms, stamping their feet hard on the floor, and whirling like dervishes, carried away in communal, esctatic devotion to Krishna. The climax comes with three loud blasts on the conch shell, at which all the devotees prostrate themselves before the deities and murmur a quiet prayer in dramatic contrast to the commotion of a second before. The intense emotions generated by this ritual, the powerful feelings of joyful release and transcendental union with Krishna, are believed to be literally a foretaste of heaven, a confirmation in direct experience of the reality of the hoped for Vedic paradise.

Once fully established, each temple is expected to be financially independent and funds for the maintenance of the temple and the devotees are raised by collections at public meetings, soliciting gifts from well-wishers, selling literature, food or flowers to "karmis" (worldly persons) in return for offerings and by outright mendicancy. All funds raised in excess of immediate needs are sent to the central organization to subsidize the publications of Bhaktivedanta's translations of Vedic scriptures; the sect's periodical "Back to Godhead" and, recently, the construction of a temple-complex in India. In addition, the group owns an incense factory in California which, by using the unpaid labour of devotees and charging high prices for its products, makes an annual profit of upwards of two million dollars.

In terms of social composition, the majority of the Hare Krishnas are youthful (predominantly under thirty years of age), middle class, white, relatively well educated[6] and many, perhaps especially the older, long-standing members, report having been actively involved in the "counter-culture" and previously being "heavily into drugs". There are approximately twice as many males as females in the group, a fact which is undoubtedly attributable to the sect's Hindu theology. Women are regarded as being at once childlike and dangerous as it is in their nature to tempt men from the paths of virtue, and are felt to be less intelligent than men and hence less reliable. No positions of responsibility in the sect's administrative hierarchy are held by women and the Women's Liberation Movement is dismissed as a typical demonic manifestation of the Age of Kali Yuga. [7]

Within the temples men and women (including married couples) are strictly separated when sleeping and even working. Persons joining the sect without their spouses are encouraged to break off their attachments with "karmis" by divorce, but intra-sect marriages are elaborately celebrated and are regarded as indissoluble. Premarital sexual activity of any kind, or even special attachments and friendships are vehemently condemned and married couples are instructed that sexual intercourse should be performed for purposes of procreation only once a month on the day most auspicious for conception. The children of the sectarians are educated in sect-run private schools (the main one, with perhaps one hundred and fifty children, being in Texas) where the basic American curriculum plus sanskrit is taught by spiritually advanced sectarians and where the daily worship routines of the temples are also practiced. The sectarians have high hopes of their children who are being raised in full Krishna Consciousness and who, they devoutly expect will successfully convince large numbers of sinful, worldly persons of the error of their ways.

The attitude toward the external society expressed in the sect's publications can perhaps be best described as one of "compassionate antipathy" but many of the rank and file members speak of the "karmi-world" (when they can be induced to speak of it at all) with loathing and contempt. The sectarians regularly perform dramatic entertainments which, in format and sophistication, are like poor examples of medieval mystery plays, depicting the horror, folly and hypocrisy of life in the corrupt world. They despise all worldly governments (although they do not omit to register their temples as religious charities to avoid taxation) and condemn militarism and democracy alike as at once causes and symptoms of the moral and spiritual collapse of modern civilizations and as betokening total ignorance of the divine ordinances of Vedic law.

As indicated above, the initial recruits to the Hare Krishnas appear to have been primarily drawn from among the more "spaced out" victims of the late nineteen sixties counterculture and they still derive recruits from among youthful runaways and drug users. Nevertheless, as the sectarians themselves recognize, their original pool of recruits has almost run dry and the novelty of their doctrines, dress and public musical performances has waned. In consequence, the Hare Krishnas appear to be moving towards less demonstrative "doorstep evangelism"and also to be gradually adopting a more markedly introversionist position. In many of his writings, Bhaktivedanta eulogized the self-sufficient, vegetarian, Vedic village community and recently in North America the sectarians have purchased land in fairly remote areas where they insist (in tones which express gleeful anticipation of the fate of a world which has largely ignored their message) they and their children will be safe from nuclear holocaust or ecological breakdown.

THE RAMAKRISHNA VEDANTA SOCIETY

Vivekananda, who introduced Vedanta to the West, taught, and Vedantists believe that, while Vedanta provides the eternal principles for liberation in all ages, these principles must be interpreted and "adjusted" to suit particular cultures or individuals' capacities for spiritual development. India is regarded as the "guru of the world" and the inhabitants of materially corrupted western societies are not expected to emulate the ascetic feats or attain the same pinnacles of spiritual awareness as Indian adepts and swamis. Further, Vivekananda condemned "priestcraft" by which he apparently meant the proliferation of caste regulations and taboos and ritual which had degenerated into meaningless, but profitable, rites and ceremonies. He insisted that the life of the sanyasi -- the life of total renunciation -- was not for everyone.

The upshot of all this is that the virtues which Vedanta seeks to inculcate (in a degree appropriate to the spiritual capacity of the individual) are mildness, gentleness, tolerance, sympathy, and brotherliness. Unselfishness is, for the Vedantists, the key to spiritual advancement, but the quality of unselfishness and the capacity to renounce the world are not necessarily linked with material poverty, rather they are the product of a state of mind. Most lifestyles are therefore acceptable to the Vedantists provided they are not in flagrant contradiction to the above virtues. Finally, in conformity with the teachings of his mentor, Ramakrishna, Vivekananda insisted that the essential thrust of all religions was towards unselfishness -- persons of all creeds might attain salvation through motiveless service to others. Nonetheless it should be recognized that the universalism of the Vedantists is really only "ostensible" -- all religions point to the true path, but Hinduism marks the path most clearly -- among the world religions, it is primus inter pares.

In terms of their response to the world and sense of mission, the western Vedantists are difficult to pigeon-hole in the most generally accepted typologies of religious sects. They are not particularly interested in social reform nor do they expect a revolutionary overthrow of the world order, and they evangelize only in the mildest way by advertising their meetings discretely and routinely. They have been concerned to differentiate themselves from such "thaumaturgical" groups as the Theosophists and Spiritualists and do not, like "manipulationist" sects, claim that their philosophy promotes the attainment of material possessions. Rather, they seek the spiritual benefits which accrue from the altered perception of the world which Vedanta offers. The Vedantists' response to the world appears to approximate most closely to the "gnostic" type which Wilson described in an earlier, less elaborate typology. [8]

Each of the North American Vedanta societies has as its leader an Indian Swami appointed by the central governing body of the group in Bilur, India. The swami is primarily concerned with the spiritual governance of the society and considerable variations occur between societies in ritual and other matters as a result of the convictions and preoccupations of individual swamis. The more mundane affairs of the society are largely left to others. Each society is incorporated as a religious charity and each possesses a Board of Governors who are elected annually from the subscription-paying membership, who must be approved of by the swami prior to admittance to the Vedanta Society.

Discussion of social control in the Vedanta societies inevitably involves consideration of the varying degress of commitment of the different categories of members -- the monastics,

initiated lay members and those who are only loosely committed
to the sect.   The swami of each society is the ultimate locus
of all spiritual authority but his ability to exercise this
authority varies directly with the degree of commitment of the
individual members.

The true monastics, those men and women who live in
the societies and aspire to become "sanyasis" and attain full
enlightenment have, literally, placed their souls in the swami
or guru's keeping.   True to Hindu tradition, utter faith and
trust in the guru is understood to be a prerequisite for spiritual advancement, and the probationer is required to follow the
swami's instructions unquestioningly even if he does not understand the reason for them.   Such total trust takes time to develop and many swamis allow or tolerate considerable latitude
in their followers' behaviour.   Expulsion is the ultimate sanction, but is rarely employed as disaffected members usually
leave on their own accord.   The aspiring Vedanta monastic
spends a period of six months to a year as a probationer and
then is initiated into "Brahmacharya" which is the celibate
spiritual novitiate.   He takes formal vows of poverty, chastity
and obedience in a ceremony which varies greatly in elabor-
ateness and formality from one society to another.   The period
between initiation and the taking of final vows is usually from
nine to fifteen years, during which the initiate works, studies,
and meditates according to a schedule devised by the guru.

Within the monastic core of the society everything centers
on the guru; he is the man who has the answers that all are
seeking.   The stability and effectiveness of the monastic community, indeed its very existence, depends upon the Swami's
ability to create and maintain this guru-relationship with his
followers.   He must convince them of his true vision, his
discernment of their souls' needs and the means of meeting
those needs.   To the extent that he succeeds in doing so the
unity and integration of the group is assured.   On the other
hand, the death or departure of the swami may lead to dissension and even the dissolution of a society.

The process of becoming a sannyasa is long and difficult,
and obviously evidences deep commitment to Vedanta.   The same
is not true of all lay members.   Some do little more than pay
the fees, and perhaps attend a service occasionally.   Others
rearrange their whole way of life and commit themselves completely to Vedanta and the spiritual life.   The majority of
members on the fee-paying roll tend toward the first attitude.
For a householder member with a job and a family, the doctrines of Vedanta make few demands -- they require that such
a person fulfill the duties of his station in life honestly and
well, love and provide for his spouse and children and treat
others tolerantly and charitably.

Thus interpreted, Vedanta teachings provide a satisfactory rationale for a life of material prosperity and comfort, without instilling feelings of guilt or making outrageous demands. Such members maintain friendly relations with the Swami, and usually profess a deep admiration and respect for him. Often he is consulted on a wide variety of matters, from buying a new house, or moving to a new town, to adopting a child. This is as close as most lay members get to the guru-relationship: he is a wise man, a philosopher, a mystic -- therefore a dispenser of wisdom and comfort. To these members the Swami gives advice but not commands, and the society has little noticeable effect on their way of life. Visible commitment amounts to payments of not more than a few dollars a month, occasional attendance at lectures, and a friendly chat with the Swami and other members. These people are likely to have many friends who are not Vedantists, and their social life does not revolve around the Society and its affairs.

However, there are many members who are a great deal more committed than this. The principal criterion of wholehearted commitment for the lay membership is initiation. This is the formal establishment of the guru relationship; the soul is placed in his hands, he has a right to command, the devotee has a duty to obey. A few such members are householders and nearly all are women. These people pursue a spiritual path determined by the guru (with their co-operation, of course -- it is rarely arbitrary), spend part of every day in meditation, attend lectures and classes as often as possible, and usually have a shrine to Ramakrishna or even a meditation room in their homes. They are encouraged to participate in worship ceremeonies and to make offerings.

Not all centres equally favour ceremonial; it depends on the judgement of the Swami concerned. Nevertheless, virtually all initiated members will sometimes attend worship ceremonies, either public or private, which are valued as a means of concentrating the mind on God. They are celebrated in a shrine-room, usually a screened off part of the temple, with an altar and pictures of Ramakrishna and others such as Vivekananda, Jesus or Buddha. The basic pattern of the worship ceremony is simple enough, though it may reach bewildering elaboration if many traditional Hindu rituals are incorporated. Any appropriately trained member, male or female, may be pujari, while others sit in silent meditation. Symbolic hand gestures (mudras) are made; flowers are smeared with sandal paste and placed on the altar; water is poured repeatedly from one bronze jar to another, and some is sprinkled about the shrine and over the pujari himself. A little rice is scattered about; two or three candles or ghee lamps are lit and waved before the altar (arati) and the same is done with incense; for several minutes the pujari sits motionless in meditation, perhaps

with a flower balanced on his head; bells are rung -- it is
all very impressive and mysterious to the uninitiated visitor.

The details of the ceremony vary from time to time and
place to place,   but the underlying meaning is always the
same; it is a mixture of dualism and non-dualism.   Many of
the gestures mime the welcoming of Ramakrishna, who is ima-
gined to be physically present, and plied with food, flowers
and incense like a visiting lord.   This is extreme dualism.
At   another point in the ceremony the pujari meditates on the
fact that he is a Brahman worshipping Brahma even while he is
a devotee worshipping Ramakrishna;   the flower offered to the
deity is placed on his own head.   Thus the conception of dualism (seeking the personal God) is a stage on the way to
monism, and the link between bhakti and jnana, is expressed
in the ritual.   This much would be recognized by any initiate
whenever he happened to be present at a Vedanta centre worship ceremony.

A major discipline and stumbling block for the householder initiate in pursuit of spiritual realization is the need   to
sublimate and channel the sex urge.   Frequent sexual intercourse even with one's spouse is regarded as a barrier to
higher realization (with anyone else it is abhorrent -- the
worst Karma).   If spiritual advance is the serious goal of the
householder member then prolonged abstinence is a necessity
-- "for as long as he can".   Sexual abstinence is an   absolute
prerequisite for high spiritual achievement.   In consequence
most initiated lay members are unmarried, being either widows
or spinsters as a rule, and some have remained unmarried for
the express reason of maintaining a high level of spirituality. [9]
Clearly this represents a great deal of commitment to Vedanta,
and a deep trust in the guru.   For many such lay initiates
Vedanta becomes the central concern of their lives.   The core
members of the societies form tightly-knit groups, every aspect
of whose lives falls under the authority of the guru.   The
discipline of religious community life thus extends beyond the
monastics to encompass some of those who, although living outside the temple dwelling, remain within the spiritual communion
of the guru-relationship and the commitment to mystic enlightenment as life's only goal.

Financially, most of the societies, which receive no monetary support from India, appear to be extremely soundly
based.   Annual subscriptions, which vary considerably from
society to society and collections taken at the weekly "services"
of the group are important for   maintenance of the societies'
buildings and gardens (some of which, especially in the flourishing California societies, are extremely elaborate) and for
supporting the swami and the monastic "temple-dwelling" fully

committed members. However, most of the societies derive a considerable additional income from conservative investments which have been made possible by generous gifts from the typically affluent members and by legacies.

The wealth, or at least affluence of the longer establish-ed Vedanta societies is indicative of the group's social composition. The vast majority of the subscription-paying lay Vedantists are middle-aged or elderly members of the affluent, white middle class. Most of the male members are professionals or securely established businessmen. Many of the female members, who outnumber the males in a ratio of roughly two to one, are unmarried and have private means, while the married women members are typically also well-to-do.

The educational level of the Vedantists is generally high (university professors being over-represented), and the typical highly committed member will display a broad range of interest in, and considerable knowledge of, philosophy, history and science. The longer established societies possess well stocked libraries which cover a wide range of subjects and most of the swamis converse readily on topics which appear far removed from the Vedic scriptures. Such is the self-confidence of the Vedantists that they accede readily to sociological investigation as knowledge of virtually all sorts is prized and they see no real grounds of conflict between the rationality of science and the rationality of their "perennial religious philosophy".

Finally, the relations between the Vedantists and the external society are generally good. Their stance in regard to social issues, political concerns and potentially competitive religious bodies is quietist, non-interventionist and generally accommodative. As a result they have experienced no clashes with constituted authority throughout their entire history in North America. Although they deplore rampant materialism and the undue emphasis on sexuality in modern societies, they feel that little better can be expected in the Age of Kali Yuga and revelations of corruption in high places neither surprise or unduly perturb them. In the midst of the turmoil of modern society, the average committed lay Vedantist quietly goes about his self-appointed task of striving to attain an appropriate degree of spiritual enlightenment, while the monastics seek spiritual perfection in an ordered and usually beautiful environment amid an atmosphere of calm, even profound, spiritual peace.

CONCLUSIONS -- THE APPEAL OF "EXOTIC" SECTS

The Hare Krishnas and the Vedantists differ markedly in their religious teachings; associated paths to salvation; the structure of their communities; life-styles; social composition and attitude to the wider society. Many persons in "main-stream" society would be, and are, amazed and outraged if they were told that a young person they knew had, on joining the Hare Krishnas, renounced his former friends and possibly his wife; dressed in outlandish oriental garb and submitted himself to a spartan regime in which he was regimented and scrutinized with more than military vigilance. The same indi-viduals would probably display similar, if perhaps somewhat more muted reactions, if told that a highly educated person of their acquaintance had pledged himself to lifelong celibacy and to unquestioning obedience to an alien teacher and had embarked on an undemonstrative but yet extraordinarily de-manding quest to attain a state of egoless detachment and e-ventual "sainthood".

To put the matter more simply, the common reaction to members of the new and not so new "imported" religions is that they must be mad, deluded or in some sense sick. As we indi-cated at the beginning of this article, we are in complete a-greement with Barker that (in most instances) this is not the case and that in terms of their life experiences many adherents to the new religions are acting rationally. To seek refuge from the storms and stresses of life is not evidence of madness or delusion although it may be interpreted as indicating "weakness". To adhere to canons of rationality and concep-tions of the meaning of life which are, literally, alien to the values predominating in our society is not pathological nor necessarily symptomatic of delusion.

In the case of the Hare Krishnas it is undoubtedly true that, prior to their conversion, many of their members were, as a result of overindulgence in drugs, malnourishment and sometimes physical and emotional abuse, bordering on, or in a state of mental or physical collapse. The counter-culture of the nineteen sixties offered its members liberation -- freedom from inhibition and the shackles of convention -- but for many this rosy dream developed into a nightmare of drug depend-ency, exploitation in many forms and almost total psychic and social isolation. To such persons, whether they be regarded as the spoiled children of a permissive society or the victims of the co-optation of the counter-culture by repressive, hege-monic capitalism, groups such as the Hare Krishnas presented, and still present, definite attractions.

Thus the Hare Krishnas offer a sanctified world of meaning and a sense of purpose and special election combined with the promise of "easy" salvation through the performance of sacred duties, rituals and celebrations of the deity. To persons who were formerly isolated and possibly emotionally incapacitated, they offer a largely non-affective community in which the individual experiences "personalized" ecstasy at least periodically. Additionally, it seems likely that even some of the most severely injured of those wounded by the counter-culture still nourish deep-rooted antipathies to the values, lifestyles, and modes of behaviour of "straight" society. (Thus members of the sect sometimes refer to their begging as "ripping off the karmis for Krishna".) For the unimaginative, membership in the Hare Krishnas is about as "far out" as it is possible to get.

For young persons who, whether because of personal deficiencies of a multitude of forms or because of previous deeply disturbing experiences, suffer from feelings of inadequacy, worthlessness and despair, the Hare Krishnas offer (to plagiarize the title of a recent book on the institution of the family) a haven in a heartless world. Neither of the authors is attracted by the Hare Krishnas' beliefs or life-style, and in this case they accept Wilson's characterization of the new religions as offering refuges from culture rather than contributing to it. However, we recognize that in the vast impersonal ocean of modern societies havens of any sort are hard to find. For naive, inexperienced voyagers suffering from severe cases of psychic scurvy, the Hare Krishnas offer spiritual nourishment and a relatively safe temporary harbour, or for some a permanent anchorage in which they can be certain of obtaining at least the necessities of subsistence and can develop a sense of self-esteem which is bolstered by mutual reassurance.

The future development of the Hare Krishnas can only be a matter for conjecture. The sectarians insist that the recent death of Bhaktivedanta will make no difference to them -- he is with Krishna and they will ultimately rejoin him. Despite such optimistic statements it seems that the present governing body of twelve "regional commanders" will lack the unifying charismatic influence of the "Spiritual Master" and, given the geographic scattering of Hare Krishna communities in several continents -- some still expanding rapidly, others stagnating -- the movement seems fraught with the potential for schism.

In North America it is likely that the sectarians will move to an increasingly introversionist position in which they are likely to suffer from the stultifying process of accumulation of dependents which the senior author has discussed elsewhere[10] At present the sectarians in North America appear to be pin-

ning their hopes for future expansion on the children who have
largely been raised in full Krishna Consciousness, but the most
adventurous, innovative and mettlesome children are likely,
if they follow the same developmental pattern as their parents,
to leave the sect which, however bizarre it may be to persons
in the world, to the children will be the natural focus for a-
dolescent rebellion.

If the Hare Krishnas can be conceived of as inhabiting
a haven protected by a cordon sanitaire from the corruption
of the world, the Vedantist societies can perhaps be compared
to oases where the sectarians believe true spirituallity flourishes in the midst of a desert of materialism, sensuality, error
and lack of purpose. The population of these Vedantist oases
consists of three groups, two settled, one transient. The true
denizens and smallest population group of the oases are the
Vedantist monks and nuns, who despite their western upbringing have found only a lack of fulfillment and of true understanding of the Divine in the religiosity or a-religiosity of
North American middle class life. In full conformity with the
traditions of eastern religions they have authentically abandoned the world and embarked on a prolonged, arduous, demanding and disciplined quest intended to bring them to the
ultimate goal of Hinduism -- unity and merger with the Godhead.

The second class of settler, the intiates who do not a-
spire to achieve full spiritualization, have experienced life
in the outside world (usually in a relatively advantageous position) and have found it lacking in meaning, purpose and
spiritual quality. To such persons the Vedanta societies also
offer a refuge, but a refuge which is highly intellectualistic
and yet provides, through the charismatic swami-disciple relationship, channels for the expression of non-physical love, devotion and loyalty which they freely admit that they had lacked
or been deprived of in the outside world.

The swamis of the Vedanta societies acknowledge that for
the third population group (the majority of the members), their
oases function as temporary places for rest, relaxation and
spiritual victualling which fortify them for their journeys
through the desert. For some of the householders being "members" of Vedanta societies probably amounts to little more than
making perfunctory contributions to a good cause. Nevertheless, it seems likely that the majority of the lay members receive positive and, admittedly on a small scale, "culture serv-
ing" rewards from a group which insists that its members practice tolerance, sympathy, compassion and honesty towards others. The Vedanta Society will probably continue to expand

slowly in future years as, although their philosophy and the monastic life is "exotic", it is not the type of exotica which attracts excessive attention and then fades rapidly as the novelty wears off.

NOTES

1. Barker, 1978.

2. Atkins, 1971. (Reprint of original edition published in 1932). Given that imported "exotic" faiths have long been a feature of the American scene, it may be false to conclude that a qualitatively unique sense of disenchantment with denominational religion and American society is responsible for the upsurge of interest in the new religions. At the risk of sounding cynical, it may well be that, with more widespread affluence, popular education and the extension of social options some of the former spiritual as well as the material "luxuries" of the middle and upper classes -- anomie, disquiet of the soul, intellectual restlessness and existential despair -- are available to broader sections of the population.

3. The very concept of "orthodoxy" is scarcely applicable to Hinduism but we mean to indicate that both sects are genuinely based in existing variants of the Hindu tradition.

4. On the Hare Krishnas see, among others, Judah, 1974 and Francine J. Daner, "Conversion to Krishna Consciousness" in Wallis (ed), 1975. As indicated, little sociological information exists on the Vedantists. Vesey, 1973 contains an interesting chapter, but the author largely confines himself to the inner core of Vedantists and has little to say of developments in recent years. See also Damrell, 1977.

5. Wilson, 1963.

6. The adverb "relatively" should be stressed here; many converts report having "been at college for a year or two", which does not necessarily imply very much.

7. The male sectarians insist that the females are happy with their lot, but what scanty evidence there is indicates that women defect more frequently than men.

8. Wilson, 1959: 3-15.

9.   The Vedantas differ from the Hare Krishnas in that they do not denigrate women, but there has never been an officially recognized female swami.

10.   Whitworth, 1975: 236-238.

NEW RELIGIOUS MOVEMENTS IN SWEDEN

Ted A. Nordquist

The past few years have witnessed an increasing abundance of theories and explanations regarding the new religious movements (NRMs) in Western industrialized societies. Although the proliferation of, and interest in, NRMs has been greatest in the USA, many of the groups which became well known through the mass media have also established themselves in Europe and Scandinavia.[1] The purpose of this paper will be to focus on a number of the Swedish groups to see if research in this area can inform us about general social processes in the Swedish society.

NEW RELIGIONS IN SWEDEN

Compared to America and other European countries, NRMs have received little attention in Sweden. Only two monographs have been published on the subject, neither of which claims to be objective.[2] A thorough research project on Swedish NRMs has not been completed, and this in itself is a point of some significance.

While the mass media in America, Great Britain, and West Germany have paid particular attention to NRMs, the Swedish media have, relatively speaking, ignored them. On the whole, the mass media and the general public, as will be pointed out below, seem to be uninterested. Articles which have appeared have been heavily influenced by news from abroad (concerning the People's Temple and other cults in America in particular) while factual information about Swedish groups has been minimal.

What does the total field of NRMs look like in Sweden? Since little data is available, an answer to this question requires a number of sophisticated guesses, and can only give a rough idea of the movement as a whole. There are about thirty known groups which are sufficiently organized to advertize in two magazines, Sökaren and Nexus, and through the only "New Age" Book store in Sweden, Vattumannen in Stockholm. Sökaren and Nexus have less than three thousand sub-

173

scribers each.   This can be compared with 84,000 for Hälsa
which is a leading health food magazine.   Spiritual figure-
heads like Pir Vilayat Khan, leader of the Sufi Order who
draws hundreds of listeners in the USA and Europe is met
in Stockholm by a handful of interested persons.   One can
safely say that less than a fraction of one percent of the
Swedish population of eight million is directly involved in
NRMs, although a knowledge of and interest in the ideas these
movements represent is difficult to assess.

An effort to improve upon this meagre knowledge of Swedish NRMs was made during the summer of 1979.   Using a ques-
tionnaire containing eighty-four main items, the author visited
and interviewed representatives of six NRMs in the Stockholm-
Uppsala region.   The results of this study are tentative,
since the project calls for additional interviews of individual
members and participant observation which has yet to be carried out. [3]

The NRMs included Sri Chinmoy Center (SCC), Divine
Light Mission (DLM), Hare Krishna Movement (ISKCON), Ananda
Marga (AM), Unification Church (UC), and Siddha Yoga Dham
led by Swami Muktananda (SYD).   All of these NRMs are local
branches of large international organizations which have their
center in the USA, with the exception of AM whose main center
is in India. All six of the groups were founded in Sweden between 1970–73, and apart from some minor exceptions, they
have all experienced slow but steady growth.   Each group
has its major center near Stockholm except for SCC which
is in Uppsala.   They are small.   Their combined membership
does not exceed 450 persons in the whole of Sweden (see Table
1).

Table 1: Six New Religious Movements in Sweden. 1979

Group	Founded in Sweden	Member- ship	% Men	% Women	Age %		
					16–30	30–40	+40
SCC	1972	25	42	58	25	50	25
DLM	1973	250	70	30	47	33	20
ISKCON	1973	50	60	40	88	10	2
AM	1973	64	50	50	83	14	3
UC	1973	35	40	60	68	30	2
SYD	1970	25	46	54	33	40	27

SCC=Sri Chinmoy Center; DLM=Divine Light Mission; ISKCON=Interna-
tional Society for Krishna Consciousness; AM=Ananda Marga; UC=Uni-
fication Church; SYD=Siddha Yoga Dham.

Three of the groups, SCC, DLM, and SYD have a majority of members over the age of thirty, while ISKCON, AM, and UC seem to fit the poular conception of NRMs as "youth movements" (Table 1). The age of the Swedish center leadership is, however, between 30-40 years for all six groups. As the age of the local leadership increases it seems likely that new members may come increasingly from older age groups. However, it is important to note that the first three groups mentioned above (SCC, DLM and SYD) demand less commitment in the way of change in lifestyle than do ISKCON, AM and UC. ISKCON and UC are communal organizations which demand total commitment, and AM has very strict rules which lead to radical changes in lifestyle if one is to remain a member. Since individuals under thirty years of age are less bound to prior commitments such as family or work, demands of the group upon changes in their lifestyle may be an important factor regarding the age group of new recruits. Previous studies of NRMs in other countries have linked them to the counter-culture and youth protest movements of the late 1960's. The leadership of these groups does indicate that it consists of the 1960's generation. However, recruitment of new members is occurring outside the 1960 generation of youth. Thus, it is no longer viable to link NRMs directly with the counter-culture. Indeed, it seems doubtful that a "counter-culture" approximating that of the 1960's generation in America and Great Britain has ever existed in Sweden. SCC, DLM, and SYD members hold regular jobs and students are rare among the new recruits. Recruitment seems to be occurring from a broad spectrum of social groups and not, as has been claimed in studies in other countries, from drop-out college students and marginal groups (Judah, 1974). AM is the only group which seems to recruit most of its members from among the more marginal members of society.

It should be pointed out, however, that the above six groups were investigated on the grounds that they were empirically definable phenomena accessible to the investigator. Although more diffuse, two additional groups deserve a mention which is necessary for a more balanced perspective. The Anthroposophical Society, which came to Sweden in 1913, has approximately one thousand members. It owns land and has several industries in Järna, just outside Stockholm. The philosophy, particularly in education, natural medicine, and biodynamic gardening has had quite an influence on Swedish society, the full extent of which is extremely difficult to determine. A later group, Transcendental Meditation (1960), is probably the most successful movement, claiming over forty thousand initiates in Sweden to date. Since TM purposely attempts to integrate its Eastern ideology with modern science and secular interests, the boundaries of its influence as a group are even more difficult to delineate than those of the Anthroposophical Society. The influence of TM may, because

of this integrative process, be much greater than any of the
groups studied above. A common occurrence during the investigation of these NRMs was the discovery that many of the
members of the groups studied were formerly initiated into
TM.

HOW SWEDISH ARE SWEDISH NRM'S?

The founders of local NRMs in Sweden have either been
missionairies from other countries, usually the USA, or Swedes
who spent time in centres outside Sweden and then returned
to start a local branch. In all cases the operation of the
Swedish centers depends almost entirely upon continued contact
with leaders outside Sweden. This contact involves visits
by the leaders to the Swedish centers and/or repeated visits
of Swedish center leaders to leaders outside the country.
The main reason for this exchange is as a source of spiritual
inspiration rather than for organizational or economic reasons.
All of the local centers operate quite independently from the
main centers outside Sweden in terms of financing and local
decision-making concerning practical matters. On the other
hand, each of the groups has as its primary goal some form
of Self-Realization or contact with the Divine. The "impulse"
for this spiritual activity is derived primarily from a charismatic guru outside the country. In each case, the literature
used as the source of inspiration for members is derived from
outside Sweden. Literature in the Swedish language consists
usually of translations of works or lectures almost exclusively
from the English language, which in turn derive much of
their inspiration from Asia.

Each of the groups studied has at least two or more
members of non-Swedish origin. DLM claims that over 97%
of its members are Swedish citizens, while twenty of ISKCON's
fifty members are aliens. The regional leaders of ISKCON,
AM, and UC are aliens. Although the local leaders of DLM,
SCC, and SYD are Swedish, they visit their respective gurus
outside Sweden at least once a year. In the case of DLM
and SCC nearly all the members visit their gurus once or
twice a year. Thus, one can conclude that the groups studied
represent primarily a form of missionary activity focused towards turning the attention of Swedish citizens from materialism
to spirituality.

NRM'S AND SWEDISH SOCIETY

All of the groups agree that Sweden is the least "spiritual" country in the Western Hemisphere. They experience the Swedish people as having a general disinterest, if not mistrust, in anything that looks as though it might be associated with religion. On the other hand, they claim that Sweden is unique in that once a Swede makes the decision to join a group, s/he rarely leaves. Unlike the American and British centres, leaders of ISKCON and UC claim that only a small fraction of their members have left the movement. The typical statement is that "it takes a long time for a Swede to make a commitment, but once s/he does it tends to be a stable one."

Although Swedes seem to be difficult to convert, they show some signs of interest in what these groups have to offer. ISKCON, for example, relies almost entirely on the sale of books, literature, records, and incense for its income. During the Christmas holidays last year ISKCON sold 16,000 books over a period of two weeks. It is not unusual for their main center at Korsnäs Gård, outside Stockholm, to receive up to one hundred visitors during a week day, usually school classes studying "religion" at first hand.

Representatives of each of the six NRMs were asked if there was anything within the Swedish society that they, as a group, were critical about. The only point that all the groups agreed upon was that Swedish society was too materialistic and needed to develop spiritually. This spiritual development would in turn improve the society as a whole. SCC, DLM, and SYD are strongly guru oriented, and lack any kind of social ideology. They feel that spiritual disciplines will improve the morals, lifestyle, and social attitudes of their members, but this is always left up to the individual. Consumption of alcohol, drugs, tobacco, and meat is strongly discouraged, and anyone persisting in such habits would eventually leave the group. ISKCON, UC, and AM are more specific and tend to be more critical of politics, bureaucracy, urbanization, pollution, etc. However, all "social issues" are relatively unimportant to them since they feel that these issues are symptoms of a materialistic world view. To them, the only real enemy is egoism in the form of selfishness and greed. Egoism can only be overcome through a "change in consciousness". This change in consciousness involves spiritual disciplines and surrender to higher spiritual goals. Organized religion is criticized for its lack of commitment to personal spiritual development, which explains why these groups refuse to call themselves "religions".

The most common critique of society raised by these NRMs is the lack of goals. They see Swedish society as a directionless society offering no purpose in life other than the temporary satisfaction of instinctual desires. With no goal, the means -- work -- becomes meaningless beyond survival. Thus, it is not surprising that each group's primary function is to inform others of their specific world view, the goal of life, and how this goal can be attained.

The world view offered by these NRMs tends to be comprehensive and simple enough for the layman to understand. All aspects of life and death (frequently including some form of reincarnation) are integrated and related to "states of mind" in the here and now. Where science tends to project an extremely relative and highly complex view of reality, the NRMs offer views which cut through this complexity and place the responsibility of how each individual experiences the world within the scope of personal experience. A person's values, attitudes, actions, and inner fulfillment become, in the NRMs, subject to change according to the degree to which one follows the "spiritual path" or "principles" mapped out by the guru. Thus, all that the individual experiences now, and all that can be experienced in the future, is brought into focus and placed in the heart and mind of each individual.

Each group has some form of concrete example of what it has to offer. One is not asked to "believe" in something but rather to "participate" in something which the group claims will bring purpose and meaning into one's life. The example of someone who has "made it", the guru, the way to reach the goal (spiritual path or principles), and group cooperation, commitment, and "inner peace" are central to the message of the NRMs. The test of the fruits of one's lifestyle lies in personal experience, in "inner states of being", rather than in abstract reasoning or material success. Still, the number of participants in the NRMs is a very small minority of the total "religious" population which itself comprises less than perhaps fifteen per cent of Sweden's inhabitants.[5]

It seems unlikely that the NRMs like ISKCON, UC, or AM will attract large numbers of new members. They demand a level of commitment and offer forms of religiosity which are extremely "alien" to the Swedish society as a whole. However, despite the alien nature of the NRMs, the intrinsic problems and existential questions which they address can be seen as symptomatic of deep underlying problems within the Swedish society and in this respect they should be taken seriously.

Since most of the research on NRMs has linked their growth in the 1970's with youthful discontent over secularization and the bureaucratic state, the question arises as to why NRMs are so relatively "unsuccessful" in Sweden, which by most international standards is one of the world's most secularized countries.

HISTORICAL PERSPECTIVE

A preliminary clue to the answer to this question can be sought through an understanding of the way in which Swedes view "religion". This in turn will be closely related to the history of the Swedish Church.

Christianity established itself in Sweden during the middle of the 11th century in Sigtuna at Lake Mälaren, and later in Uppsala under the Roman Catholic Archbishop Stefan. The rule of the Catholic Church was strong until the Reformation of the 16th century, which witnessed the national uprising against the union with Denmark and Norway, led by a young Swedish nobelman, Gustaf Eriksson Vasa, who had been elected King of Sweden in 1523. In opposition to the danophile churchmen he favoured the Reformation, which was successively introduced in a rather conservative way. The National Lutheran Chruch was definitively established through a large church assembly at Uppsala in 1593. Roman Catholicism, Calvinism, and all other "grievous errors" were completely rejected. In 1617 strict religious practices were established in accordance with the principle laid down in the peace treaty of Augsburg in 1555: cuius regio ejus religio. Catholics from abroad were not allowed to enter the country, and apostates from the Church of Sweden were forced to leave their country. However, in time, revivalist movements during the 19th century, in and outside the Church, made it necessary to liberalize the ancient regulations. In 1860 "it became permissible for Swedish citizens to withdraw from the Church and either join some other approved Christian denomination or establish congregations of their own, the latter after obtaining the sanction of the Government" (Murray, 1961:68). From a practical point of view, religious freedom was silently becoming more and more recognized. It was judicially confirmed by law in 1951. But even today, a child born by parents of which one belongs to the Swedish Church, as well as adults who have not applied for withdrawal, are, statistically, Church members. Furthermore, those who have withdrawn still pay 60% of the Church tax as the Church performs a number of secular tasks.

The earliest establishment of an alternative to the Christian tradition came in the late 19th and early 20th century
in the form of such movements as the Theosophical Society
(H.P. Blavatsky and H.S. Olcott) and the Anthroposophical
Society (Rudolf Steiner). Strains of pietism had erupted
every now and again from the 18th century until the early
20th century in the form of a revival movement both within
and outside the Swedish Church. These led to the later organization of the Swedish Free Churches (Methodists, Baptists,
Pentecostal, etc.), which usually call for more intense religiosity and group worship within the Christian tradition. These
Free Churches, however, continue to represent a small minority
of the total population (less than 5%) and in most cases members of the Free Churches continue to remain members of   the
Swedish Church, which still claims 96.8% of all citizens.[6]

Contrasted with this very high membership in the Swedish
Church, however, studies of Swedish religiosity usually rate
Sweden as one of the most secularized countries in the Western
Hemisphere, a conclusion based upon such criteria as Church
attendance, publication of religious books, and orthodox Christian beliefs.[7]   R.F. Tomasson, writing in 1968, gave three
reasons for the relatively high degree of secularism prevailing
in Sweden:

1.   A long-term religious homogeneity which has
prevented religion from becoming a focal point of
social differentiation.

2.   The alignment of the Swedish Church with the
old order during the crucial period of early modernization, particularly the last two decades of the
19th century, alienated those segments of the society
oriented toward modern values.

3.   Empirical and positivist value orientations,
along with a pragmatic attitude toward norms and
values predominate in Sweden.   This is largely a
result of a relatively late, intense, and extraordinarily successful and rapid modernization which
thoroughly discredited the nineteenth century society
with its traditionalist and idealistic values.   Such
dominant value orientations as characterize contemporary Sweden would appear to be supportive of
agnosticism and nonbelief in terms of traditional
religion and pragmatism in terms of conventional
morality (Tomasson, 1968:496-497).

This situation can be compared with the USA where NRMs are more numerous. Drawing upon a large body of literature concerning "utopian communal movements" and religious cults or sects from Hellenistic culture to the present, Robert Ellwood in Religious and Spiritual Groups in Modern America (1973) describes a continuous tradition throughout Western history which he calls "an alternative view and experience of reality". According to him two distinct views of reality have existed side by side, one more dominant than the other. The first view is derived from among the ancient Hebrews and Greeks of the Homeric era, which assumes that men are separate entities living and acting in the stream of world history and dominant over nature. Here, man's task is to lead a life in harmony with the laws of a transcendent God (or Gods). The second view, according to Ellwood, is traceable to early contact with India and Asiatic shamanism, which is grounded in wonder and amazement at Being itself and man as part of nature in a monistic cosmos. "A man's task is to attain to individual initiatory expansions of consciousness and awareness until he becomes mentally one with the whole cosmos" (Ellwood, 1973:43). In Christianity, Ellwood sees these two views as having been reconciled to some degree, although the first usually predominates if conflict arises. But it is the second view of reality which Ellwood calls an "alternative reality tradition" which has always existed side by side with organized religion. According to him, NRMs can be understood as carriers of this tradition. In other words, the American culture contained within itself a latent symbology for the expression of discontent in alternative religious forms.

However, this was not the case in Sweden. Since the Swedish Church and the Crown united after the reformation to implement a strict form of Lutheran Protestantism where alternative forms of religiosity, including "folk religiosity" within the Christian framework were supressed, the availability of an alternative religious symbology was minimal. In addition, since the Swedish Church has been traditionally aligned with the State, opposition to the status quo has always been expressed in "political" terms, usually some form of socialism or communism. Thus, in the minds of most Swedes, "religion" is associated with the Church and the State, which in turn symbolize the established norms of the status quo, while "social change" is always thought of in "political" terms calling for rational criticism, analysis, and planning. This explains why members of the NRMs find it so difficult to explain to Swedes that their "religiosity" assumes social or structural change.

The members of NRMs believe that in order to improve society one must first focus upon changing individual values and personal relationships, which in turn center around "states of consciousness". To the Swede this is an alien concept. Social change is a matter for the politicians while one's values and, particularly, one's consciousness are private. It is of course a matter of degree, but it can be argued that this long tradition of "religion" being imposed upon the Swedish society by law and the unavailability of an alternative reality tradition, offering "religious symbology" for discontent, explains the relatively meagre response the NRMs have had in Sweden.

Another factor affecting the Swedish response to NRMs is the very intense "organizational structure" of Sweden. Since the implementation of social democracy, most of every Swede's activities concerning work and recreation tends to be organized along "planned" channels of communication. The welfare system seeks to guarantee opportunities for "everyone" based primarily upon material standards which are centralized and operate according to commonly accepted routines -- usually involving some form of "application" and "receipt" of services. This planned way of life has its roots in the long winter months where without these rational processes a person would either starve or freeze to death. Over forty years of social democracy have resulted in a highly organized social system in which social innovations are centralized. New ideas are fed into the bureaucratic matrix and only after extensive investigations, reports, discussions, new reports, and more discussion does the "new idea", now transformed, altered, and reformulated filter down from the institutional level to every day reality. The process is time-consuming and tends to discourage spontaneous social experimentation, but once accepted by the "experts" it is rapidly put into practice and readily integrated into the system.

Again, this system can be compared with the USA where social innovation often takes the form of individual initiative and grass level organization. After many mistakes and tests on a practical level, innovative ideas may later be adopted by the government and an attempt made to implement the idea on a national level. Briefly put, in Sweden new ideas take a long time to become accepted, but the process of implementation after acceptance is a rapid one, while in the USA new ideas have a good chance of being tested on a small scale but require more time and greater effort to implement on a national level. As far as NRMs are concerned, this means that unless their ideas are capable of being integrated into the Swedish way of thinking and living, they will remain marginal to the society as a whole. On the other hand, if the NRMs are expressing a need in the Swedish society which cannot be met by traditional institutions or belief systems, it may be too early to dismiss them as unimportant. The principles of spiritual discipline, a unified world view, the divine quality of the individual, a simple yet meaningful lifestyle, etc., may, stripped of religious jargon, indirectly attract the attention of the Swedish people, particularly the youth. In fact, there are signs that although these movements appear to be alien to Swedish society, the problems they address are not.

GENERATIONS AND CULTURE

In Sweden, as in other highly industrialized countries, secularization and modernization were accompanied by urbanization, an increase in the general standard of living, more liberal and pluralistic attitudes in almost all aspects of life, and the proliferation of a scientific world view within an expanded university milieu. In addition, the striving for a high standard of living in a welfare state brought new problems such as increased consumption and abuse of alcohol, narcotics, and drugs, and, in the early 1970's, a sharp increase in unemployment among the youth.[8] It is no secret that there is widespread dissatisfaction, particularly among the younger generation, with the modern, bureaucratic system. Sweden has a number of communes, environmental groups, left wing political groups, a growing human potentials movement and a "back to the land" movement all of which in their different ways represent alternative values, attitudes, and opportunities for individual commitment within the society at large.

A 1974 survey of the attitudes of Swedish youth between 15-18 years of age (N=2208) indicated that although not interested in "religion" in traditional terms, over half were positive towards meditation and telepathy. Over thirty per cent were positive towards reincarnation and nearly twenty per cent were positive towards Buddhism.[9] Preliminary results obtained from a 1979 survey conducted among four hundred high school students in two small Swedish towns indicated very low concern with religious questions while concern for the environment and the future was very high. Indeed, although not interested in "God" there was a high concern for questions involving love, personal worth, and aid to the dying. Results of this survey concerning an interest in meditation, telepathy, and reincarnation were similar to the above-mentioned 1974 study, although knowledge of or association with any of the NRMs was minimal.[10]

Perhaps more significant, however, is the widespread confusion and hopelessness reflected in the attitudes of many Swedish youth concerning the future, which was indicated in the 1979 survey (above) and recent debates in the mass media. The Swedish school system has promoted an unbiased and neutral presentation of history, religion and science, resulting in some normative confusion regarding the individual in relation to society and the cosmos. While social responsibility and the importance of "work" are highly stressed, this quasi-scientific world view (primarily as presented in the social sciences) seems to have undermined traditional imageries about "god" and the nature of man (see Glock, 1972). Since a "scientific" world view offers no clear alternative formula either for organizing society or for living one's life" (ibid: 362) the meaning and purpose of participating in society has become problematic.

Karl Mannheim (1952) observed that in every society there is a continuous flow of "new generations" into the social process. For him, in a relatively stable society marked by steady social change, the transmission of cultural possessions (norms, values, selective approaches, etc.) continues primarily unconsciously and with little difficulty. In other words, socialization takes place quietly as the social norms of the dominant society are internalized by advancing generations. However, during times of rapid social change or historical events of an unusual nature, this process becomes problematic, causing rational elucidation and reflectiveness over norms and values among the younger generations. The young are the most sensitive to this problematic precisely because they lack experience. In youth, where life is new, formative forces are just coming into being, and basic attitudes in the process of development can take advantage of the moulding power of new situations (Mannheim, 1952:295-296). He goes on to say that "the possibility of really questioning and reflecting on things only emerges at the point where personal experimentation with life begins -- round about the age of 17, sometimes a little earlier, and sometimes a little later. . . The "up-to-dateness" of youth therefore consists in their being closer to the "present" problems (. . . as a result of their "fresh contact" with the cultural heritage), and in the fact that they are dramatically aware of a process of destabilization and take sides in it. All this while the older generation clings to the re-orientation that had been the drama of their youth" (ibid:301).

Since research on the American counter-culture of the 1960's and NRMs of the 1970's revealed that participants were largely middle class youth between 18-25 years of age, Wuthnow (1976b) Starr (1970), and Balswick (1974) utilized Mannheim's theory to demonstrate the idea that when a significant body of the younger generation experiences the need for "rational elucidation and reflectiveness" over what is normally a smooth process of socialization, then overt or underlying inconsistencies exist in the society.   But while this explanation may have some validity in the USA since it could be argued that the number of cults and sects there reflects this problematic, it has to be acknowledged that the youth of Sweden has not so easily adopted "religious" forms of expression.   Thus, although the "problem" may be similar in both the USA and Sweden, the language and style of "rational elucidation and reflectiveness" seems to be quite different.

This observation suggests that the growing number of NRMs during the 1970's may primarily represent problems of modernization in societies in which the value of the individual in relation to the whole has become confusing, particularly for the young.   Since, for historical reasons, the Swedish youth has not as readily as American youth sought solutions in religious terms (either within or without the Christian tradition), the question then arises, if neither the Church nor "science" is able to provide meaning and direction in life, from where will meaningful values emerge?   Or, put another way, are "religious" beliefs and values necessary in a modern state?   It seems too early to answer this question. What is important to understand is the indication that although not numerous, NRMs in addition to the many alternative groups in Sweden, reflect the normative breakdown of traditional beliefs which in turn has caused some confusion regarding the individual's purpose and meaning in life.

CONCLUSION

The Swedish NRMs are primarily concerned with alternative forms of religiosity and commitment.   They are local branches of international organizations which appeared at a time when strains in the social structure of a modern industrialized country were apparent, coupled with a large and mobile youth population.[11]   Social factors, which may have influenced NRM-participants such as urbanization, unemployment and the breakdown of the family, are typical of Sweden as well as of other Western countries.   The Swedish groups seem to reflect, primarily, a growing mistrust in the future of the modern bureaucratic state, and the need of a comprehensive world view providing a meaningful goal in life.   However, the number of NRMs and the response of the Swedish society to them indicate that thus far they have not been very influential.   This was explained as being rooted in historical factors concerning the domination of the Swedish Church and the symbolic associations Swedes attach to religious terms.

The Swedish Church, which had dominated as the only legitimate form of religious organization since the Reformation, has experienced during the last decade a slow but steady decline in religious participation. The Free Churches, which formed at the turn of the century, have witnessed a slight polarization: the older Churches such as the Methodists and Baptists, which tend to be more liberal and ecumenical, have declined, while the younger Churches, such as the Pentecostal Movement and Örebro Mission, which call for more intense individual religiosity and commitment, have grown in member-ship.[12] It seems valid to assume that the NRMs studied here are part of a movement which is a reaction to both organized religion and secular values in the Swedish society.

On the other hand, the relatively meagre success of the Swedish NRMs brings to question the validity of many of the theories presented by researchers in the USA and Great Britain where NRMs are more numerous. Although Sweden is one of the most secularized countries in the world, there is every indication that Swedes are not reacting to problems of modernization, if indeed this is a major cause of NRMs, in terms of "religious" symbols or associations. Although the problem of meaning and purpose in the modern bureaucratic state seems to be apparent among the youth, a general state of confusion and a feeling of helplessness concerning the future appears to predominate, while interest in "religious" solutions to world views appears to be negligible.

Some reservation is required regarding the influence of NRMs on Swedish society. Although the groups referred to in this study appear to be too alien to the Swedish way of life to be very influential, it may be too early to write off the possible influence of "alternative views of reality" which are more suited to the Swedish culture. There does seem to be a deep feeling of dissatisfaction or alienation among a sizable proportion of the Swedish population, particu-larly the youth. Since the highly organized nature of Swedish society makes rapid innovative change difficult in the begin-ning but rapid in potential implementation, it remains to be seen what the next decade will hold for alternative views of reality in Sweden.

NOTES

* Special thanks to Professor Emeritus C.M. Edsman, Department of the History of Religions, Uppsala University, for his comments and recommendations concerning the section on Swedish Church history.

1. See Robbins, Anthony and Richardson, 1978 for an overview of theory and research on NRMs and Romarheim, 1979 for a brief review of research on NRMs in Europe and Scandinavia. Romarheim, 1977 is the only available outline yet published on NRMs in Scandinavia.

2. Wikström, 1977 and Sundström, 1979 describe and analyse NRMs from a strongly Christian point of view. Both see these movements as a threat and a challenge to the Swedish Church.

3. This research was carried out in cooperation with Britta Jönsson, Department of Sociology, Uppsala University.

4. See Nordquist, 1978 and Wuthnow, 1976a for an overview of this literature.

5. See note 7. Figures on Swedish "religiosity" range from 5 to over 40% depending upon the variable and methods. This 15% figure is a rough estimate based on available data.

6. Aktuellt: informationsblad fran Svenska Kyrkans Centralrad (2) 1979.

7. See Gustafsson, 1972 for trends in Swedish religiosity from 1955-1970; Wuthnow, 1977 on the publication of religious books; and Sigelman, 1977 on international comparisons.

8. For a general overview see Ung 1979: Promemorior från SCB (6) 1979; on alcohol see Hibell, 1977 and SIFO's Ungdomsundersökningar 1971 - 1975; on alcohol and drugs, including narcotics, see Report 1979: on the alcohol and drug situation in Sweden, CAN, The Swedish Council for Information on Alcohol and Other Drugs, Stockholm, 1979; and on unemployment among the youth see Ahlqvist, 1979.

9. See Ungdomens fritid och samhällssyn, sammanfattning av en undersökning gjord inom statens ungdomsrad av Rune Persson och Anita Dahlgren. Stockholm: Prisma, 1975: 106-112.

10. "En undersökning gjord bland nagra elever i Bollnäs" av Lena Netterstedt och "Undersökning vid Falu gymnasium höstterminen 1979 an elevers uppfattning om sig själva och

10.   (cont.) sin situation" av Margareta Nybelius   in   Nutida
Religiösa   Rörelser,   mimiographed   study,   Religions historiska
Institutionen (hum. avd.), Uppsala Universitet, 1980.

11.   See Ung 1979, op cit, page 7.

12.   See "Smärre meddelanden: antalet medlemmar i valda
samfund i Sverige 1960–1978.   Kommentarer och internationella
jämförelser." Religionssociologiska Institutet (4) 1979.

IV

NEW RELIGIOUS MOVEMENTS:
SOCIAL RESOURCES, INDICATORS OR REFLECTIONS

COMING-AGAIN
HOW SOCIETY FUNCTIONS THROUGH ITS NEW RELIGIONS[1]

Warren Lewis

"You have noticed," wrote Mark Twain, "that the human being is a curiosity. In times past he has had (and worn out and flung away) hundreds and hundreds of religions; today," Twain continued, speaking from the midst of the religiously fecund nineteenth century, "he has hundreds and hundreds of religions, and launches not fewer than three new ones every year. I could enlarge that number and still be within the facts." (Satan, Letter III, Letters from the Earth)

New religions in the history of the American people have served at least one particular function: they have allowed the nation to focus upon, explore, work out, and relieve deep cultural needs. American society functions through its new religions to solve within the laboratory of those religions some more general cultural problem. At times, the new religions supplied the cultural demand abundantly, yielding a crop of operable social options for future generations, new ideologies to guide the larger society and even shelves full of marketable hardgoods. Other times, the new religions failed to help society solve its problems immediately: in these cases, society suffered an intensification of the problem itself. Both times, society frequently responded with persecution of the new religions, reacting out of a paradoxical fear of having to face and resolve its own complex needs.

The whole of American history can, in fact, be written from the perspective of the successive waves of religious excitement which have passed through the "nation with the soul of a church" at increasingly frequent intervals over the three hundred fifty years of its existence. One speaks of the Four Great Awakenings (McLoughlin, 1978), reads the history of the nineteenth century in terms of "dispersing ultraism" (Cross, 1950) and charts the entire historical flow in terms of the ebb and flow of the needs of affiliation and power, achievement and warfare (McClelland, 1975a). The regular pattern is observable through empirical analysis of popular literature and in the historical correlation between religious revival and social spasm. Whenever America has produced new religious movements, she was calling herself to new spiritual inspiration and religious intensity, whether through simple revival or to

the millennial dream which is the tap root of her theological
myth of Manifest Destiny and the creedal conviction of the
"American Civil Religion." Every major war has been fought
under a sacred canopy; every major wave of social reform has
been borne on the tide of moral righteousness. Inspirations of
religious fervor have often sought a social, secular expression: institutionalization   of Christian love in the public sector, which, therefore, somehow ran contrary to the other major, Enlightenment myth: separation of church and state.

The final stage of this pattern of religious zeal and
righteous reformism was often the eruption of carnal warfare
waged against external enemies of ourselves and of God. In
the nineteenth century, however, the religious and moral issues were weighed to the uttermost in the balance of the society itself and a holy war between the states. Allowing for
slight variation, the general pattern is remarkably persuasive: With historical, chartable regularity, once the frame of
mind had been reached in which religious vision inspired a
drive to implement those social reforms for which adequate socialized means of achievement were lacking, the kinesis of
piety and morality energized the nation for war against the
enemies of rightness and righteousness.

CHREOD: LIFE AND DEATH, BURIAL AND RESURRECTION,
AND COMING-AGAIN —
THEOLOGICAL HOMEORHESIS OF NEW RELIGIONS

A few researchers have attempted to elaborate a language of "stages" with which to explain the development of American new religions: Pritchard describes a four-stage theory;
A.F.C. Wallace, a five-stage; and Burridge, a three-phase, in
his description of Pacific religions.[2] Untried as the hypothesis
may be, I suggest one can combine the concept of processive
stages in the new religions with two neologisms, borrowed
from the life sciences, to define the organic qualities of the
"religious factor" within the new religions as an empirically
observable, sociologically predictable quantum of human experience (however divine it may also be). C.H. Waddington[3] defines a "chreod," that most important feature of developing biological systems, as a stabilized time trajectory which, if something happens to alter the flow, is brought back by its control mechanism not to where it was at the time the alteration
occurred but to where it would normally have got to at some
later time. "Homeorhesis," similarly, is the time-oriented equivalent of homeostasis and describes a system which keeps a
particular course of change stable as time passes. For example, when a stream flowing down the mountainside is interrupt-
ed, its path diverted by a landslide, gravity, nevertheless,

predetermines that the stream shall ultimately reach the valley below. From hill to vale, the stream follows its chreod,
that is, its inevitable descent, no matter what. Or, a young
plant set out in my garden in the springtime — whether there
is too much rain or sun, too little of both, the soil was of
proper or improper quality for the kind of plant, or my neighbor's dog decides at some point to make his bed in my flower
garden — shall blossom at the chreodically fated time, even
if the stem is stunted or the bloom tarnished by the intervening events. Some plants, if the dog cannot be dissuaded, may
even have to come back from the roots, if there is to be a
harvest.

The chreod of a new religion is as organically natural
to it as is the homeorhesis through which a growing plant
must pass. Adequately to describe the functioning of society
in its new religions and the functioning of new religions in
their society, one must understand the nature of the organic
life of the religion itself — what it means for it to be ger-
minated, to grow, to suffer persecution from the neighbor's
dog, to fructify, to die, and to green again in another form.
The paradigm is a multiphasic chreod of life and death, burial and resurrection, and coming-again in any of a variety of
ways. These metaphors are familiar not only to Christians but
belong also to the history and comparison of religions in
broader ways.

The language seems both connotative enough to evoke the
vitalistic aspects of the chreodic surge but also sufficiently
denotative to serve as explicit signposts of the chreodic turn-
ings to which new religions inevitably return, no matter how
far they may be forced off their own ideological or doctrinal
agendas. But whatever these detours prove to be, despite what
the new religion considers its own appropriate theological
agenda to be, the inevitabilities of its chreodic life will take
it through the homeorhesis of death, burial, and possibly several kinds of multiply-determined comings-again. Suffering and
death are understood in most religions somehow to be redemptive; of resurrection, E. Becker would call it the religious "denial of death"; and W.G. McLoughlin speaks of "revitalization
movements," by which "regeneration takes place both individ-
ually and en masse."[4] And if Dr. Freud were with us, he
would take my part in asserting that getting it up, and coming again, and again, and as many times as we possibly
can, is a well-nigh universal human preoccupation, theologi-
gal commitments aside. It is not only because I am a Christian that language native to Christianity seems best to me to
describe the homeorhesis of new religions, but because Christianity itself was once a new religion (and, from the Jewish,
Hindu, and Buddhist perspective, still is) and thus manifests
the same chreodic stages common to all new religions.

The chreodic paradigm of the new religions seems to function more or less as follows: Society herself is their virgin mother who, inseminated by religious inspiration from beyond, bears her progeny of new religious movements from the dark womb of her deepest social needs. By "beyond" and "virgin" I mean to say that the language of sociology thus far remains inadequate to explain and describe the origin and emergence in society of the religions, theological novelty, and social holiness. Society is also the great devouring mother, Babylon the Bitch, drunk on the blood of her own offspring, who persecutes those religions, martyrizes their leaders, and drives the new communties into the wilderness.

Society herself is also, moreover, the new religions themselves. Just because someone converts to become a member of a new religion, it does not mean they have ceased to be a citizen, even if irate parents and unconstitutional deprogrammers with their sympathetic police officials and judges persist in treating the devotees as though they had forfeited their civil rights by becoming religious. Every person is a member of some sect or other and is, therefore, manifestly sectarian to some degree. No one can be a member of society-at-large apart from a sub-societal identification with, perhaps, a religious minority, a labor union, an intellectual community, a political party, a sexual orientation, or some other individuating yet socializing condition not shared by the generality of society. The struggle of the new religions seems to be an essential part of the chreodic process by which society fructifies through its sectarian manifestations. Mother society holds her hapless children in her hands, wanting to love them, hating them because they look so much like herself, and swaying between the urge to hug them and feel loved and the urge to bite them and consume their blood. But where there is no death and burial, there can be no resurrection; and without resurrection, there is no coming-again. To propose, even theoretically, abolition of the ambiguity would be an attempt to negate the homeorhetic dynamic which is essential to the organic life of a new religion within society and, thus, in turn, a denial of the productive good for society which the painful functioning of the new religions implies. To stop the homeorhetic process would also mean to deprive the religions of the social shaping and forming which befalls them along the path of their chreod.

The pattern of death-burial-resurrection seems to replicate itself in three phases, and in a succession of stages as numerous as the innate vitality of the new religion can bear. The first phase is at the level of the paradigmatic life, charismatic deeds, and possibly martyrial death of the founder-hero ("hero" in the sense of Campbell, Eliade, and the anthropologists of shamanism). The second phase follows after the founder-hero (whether he/she is a native child or an immigrant is immaterial) has thus exemplarily suffered the gospel. Either during or after his/her lifetime, the original community founded by the hero recapitulates that gospel of death, burial, and resurrection through the parallel social course of being persecuted, suffering dismay and loss of faith, taking flight, and regrouping and enjoying second-founding. It is typically in the experience of second-founding, under the leadership of the second founder, that the founder-hero achieves his or her coming-again. Thirdly, after the gospel has been suffered both by the founder-hero and the original community, the movement itself may experience its own coming-again in history through its mutual exchange with the surrounding society. The new religions, to whatever degree they prove to be socially viable options answering to the genuine requirements of society for new direction, rise chreodically and homeorhetically, coming again within society in ways as diverse as the religions themselves.

At this point in the inevitable current, even if the community has been forced off its founder(s)' and its own proposed agenda, a substantiation within society, often in highly concrete, tangible forms, occurs. The religious movement begins to have its greatest impact on society — an impact which, indeed, the religion itself may neither have desired nor foreseen, but which, through the interaction of the religion and its society and the focusing of society's needs through the new religion, serves as society's experimental means towards solution of its problems. For the religion itself, a multidimensional configuration of forces in this moment of societal impact can mean the final proof of the hero's original religious inspiration, the test of effectiveness of the communities as the vehicle for the hero's coming-again, and the expansion of the communities' own viability as a social form. The coming-again of the whole new religion is its ultimate social test, namely, whether the genius of the founder-hero, mediated through the communities, can be adequately substantialized in society, whether through the on-going life of the religion or in some transubstantiated, secularized form.

A NINETEENTH-CENTURY SAMPLER

Some historical examples taken from the nineteenth century will make the matter clearer.

Joseph Smith, as a young lad, like many other shamans before him, suffered soul-loss in his agony over which of the many contending religious parties was the right one. The spirit world accomodated his struggle with revelations and visions, made him a master of spirits, and elevated him through his first experience of spiritual death and resurrection to the new

life of seer and revelator. On this foundation of his own heroic
experience, he founded his community, the Church of Jesus
Christ of Latter-Day Saints, in upstate New York in 1830. Many
of the original community, following their leader, also became
doers of deeds; four attempts were made at building model Mormon cities. But when the founder-hero was lynched (crucified)
in 1844, and the original community itself was persecuted unto
death and burial in the winter of 1846, they fled the burning
temple at Nauvoo to be led by Brigham Young, the second
founder and thus the one through whom Joseph Smith came-
again. Driven literally out of the country by the agents of
the American people's free republic, the Mormons trekked to
Utah, littering their chreodic path with a host of splinter
spin-off second foundings and organizational comings-again.
At home in the Western Zion, the original community implemented divinely-revealed architectural and irrigational designs
and enjoyed its resurrection. This growth stage has lasted a
hundred years. The Mormon commonwealth in history is now
reveling in a new burst of missionary zeal, political domination in Utah and other Western states, and the "rest of the
saints in Zion," where "all is well." In giving us the State
of Utah, the Mormon Tabernacle Choir, Donnie and Marie, and
a style of moral political leadership, which commands the respect of its liberal opposition, the Church of Jesus Christ of
Latter-Day Saints thrives in the perfection stage of its coming-
again in history within a society which has now expanded to
embrace it.

A comparison of the Mormon experience with that of the
less-well-known Perfectionists of Putney, Vermont, and, later,
Oneida, New York, shows a sociological variation on the basic
chreodic theme, and by contrast at the points where different
circumstances alter the case, demonstrates the patterned persistence of the homeorhesis of a new religion, despite its psy-
cho-sociological variations and the impact of neighboring
dogs.

Phase One: John Humphrey Noyes, the founder-hero of
Oneida, experienced his shamanic calling (termed by him his
"inspiration" or "afflatus") during the 1831 revival of Charles
Grandison Finney.[5] Noyes' conversion moved him towards Yale
and a version of theological perfectionism: "As Noyes wrote
later in his Confession of Religious Experience, 'Within a few
hours the word passed through the college and city. "Noyes
says he is perfect" and on the heels of this went the report:
"Noyes is crazy".'"[6]

Phase Two: The original community was gathered from
1840 to 1847, and experienced its first death and resurrection,
precipitated by publication of the infamous "Battle Axe Letter,"
by being driven from Putney to Oneida. There, once they had

regrouped, Noyes' ideals enjoyed their coming-again in the elaboration of his perfectionist communism (made functional on
the basis of home industry rather than the agriculture so often attempted by communitarians), complex marriage (including
sexual communism, experimentation with eugenics, and the discovery of contraception), mutual criticism, and "ascending fellowship."[7] In the words of granddaughter Constance: "The Kingdom of God was established and in business."[8]

Phase Three: The original community died in 1879, crucified at the hands of public opinion incensed at the rumours
about complex marriage, however beneficial their steel traps,
patent safes, and other products of Perfectionist ingenuity.
The coming-again in history of the community took place after
the second founding in form of a joint stock company in the
smithing of lustrous silverware. The coming-again in history
of John Humphrey Noyes took place through his family and community, of course, but also continues to take place through
the rediscovery in contemporary American life of his inspiration regarding sexuality: only now do we begin to appreciate
the equality of the sexes, the sexual freedom, and the human
ecological responsibility implicit in Noyes' teaching and practice of complex marriage.

The chreodic trajectory for both Perfectionists and Mormons, running through different psycho-social contexts, deflect-
ed by a variety of social forces at differing points along the
homeorhetic canal of the life of the respective religious organ-
isms, is essentially the same. In one case, an on-going church
perpetuated the gains of the original community into the twentieth century, whereas in the other case, the coming-again of
the founder-hero and his original community is manifest in a
transubstantiated social structure and in the resurrection of
insights in markedly different ideational forms. And, although
the two movements justified their claims along drastically divergent theological lines (the Mormons, with a myth of America and Christ's appearing and second coming here; the Perfectionists, with a totally realized eschatology of Christ's second coming having already transpired in A.D. 70), the homeorhesis of the two movements is the religious constant common
to both. After death, burial, and resurrection, the founder-
hero, the original community, and the community in history
all, and each at their own homeorhetically eschatological
kairos, come-again. The variety of forms in which the coming-
again of new religions manifests itself, and by which they ultimately respond in a creative and positive way to their usually antipathetic, persecuting society, is the litmus test of
authentic religiosity of the new religions and the ultimate
proof of their concrete human productivity, as well as the final indicator of how they function in society.

The sweep of nineteenth-century American religious culture itself provides an example of the chreodic paradigm. From Finney's born-again revivalists to Oneida's Perfectionists of sexuality and home industry; whether under the inspiration of Joseph Smith's latter-day revelation or Alexander Campbell's supernatural rationalism and frontier ecumenism, the Second Great Awakening promised, in a miscellany of prophetic voices, the coming of the Kingdom of Heaven to earth. According to Whitney Cross, the revelatory passions of intense "religious ultraism" peaked about 1836, after which it began to disperse. It enjoyed a potent resurrection in 1843/1844, when even the orthodox, become enthusiastic, were "laying out our plans upon this basis: THE MILLENNIUM IS AT HAND."[9] One hundred years before, Jonathan Edwards had prophecied that the latter-day glory was likely to begin in America. A generation after him, Mother Ann Lee and her Shakers had "opened the gospel of Christ's second appearing according to the female line" in America. A generation after that Revivalists were whipping expectations into the lather of the mourner's bench; Mormons had proclaimed America to be uniquely and surprisingly eschatological real estate prepared by Providence to receive the coming Kingdom; Perfectionists assured the masses that quintessential moral change in the present tense needed for Kingdom living is possible in a variety of ways; and Adventists said they could see it coming on the clouds: the moment was now!

It was William Miller who focused eschatological expectation for the greatest number with his prediction of the Parousia for 1843, and again, when the Lord tarried, for 1844. After the final date was missed, Miller reasonably retired from the field. But the religious momentum, which had begun to mount since at least 1801 across the spectrum of American new religions until yet this next frustration of the Kingdom which could not come in 1844, was not to be so easily dispersed. An initial response of a segment of society which had not believed Miller's predictions was to punish the Adventists with destructive attacks upon their presses and other property. Ellen G. White, prophetess of health and second foundress of Millerite Adventism, adjusted Miller's version of God's timetable and led the Seventh-Day Adventists into one of several comings-again of the new religion, Adventism. The religious backwaters would shortly eddy and team with a variety of one-idea, religious ultraisms of biblical fundamentalism, millennialism, and pietistic moralism. The Campbellite vision of reunited Christendom and the cultural supremacy of the English-speaking races came to little more than the Ecumenical Movement and its opposite, a handful of jangling, fissiparating sects. The Shakers went into steady decline. Some of the energy of the ever-and-never-coming Kingdom dissipated into Masonry; some of it filigreed into Transcendentalism, Christian Science,

Theosophy, and other styles of gnosticism; and very many aspects of it yielded the crop of marketable hardgoods, which are so often the spin-off products of religious fervor, the tangible contributions of the religions to their society.

Oneida gave us silver plate, steel traps, contraception, and sexual mutuality. The Mormons gave us Utah, the Tabernacle Choir, and Republican politics. The Shakers gave us many simple gifts: anti-Victorian furniture, packaged seeds, condensed milk (by allowing Mr. Borden to experiment in their workshops), and the flatbroom. Adventism cum vegetarianism gave us the cornflake and the Graham cracker. Millennialism gave us abolition and the Civil War.

Society, while rejecting the new religions per se and their specific sets of theological jargon, consumed the moral and marketable products of the religions and was changed as a result. As a result of Mrs. White's health crusade for vegetarian breakfasts, America gave up English greasy fried breakfasts. Similarly, as a result of abolitionist moral crusading, fired by the fuel of religious revivals, America gave up Black slavery. The chreod of the culture was intersected by the chreod of the dominant nineteenth-century new religious movements at a moment of homeorhetic readiness for which the society had been prepared by these new religions. The inspiration of the Kingdom Coming, transubstantiated into moral righteousness, came-again in American history, power implementing love, just at the moment when the nation could reap both benefit and blight from her abortive new religions in a kairos of pervasive social readjustment. The adventist-revivalist-perfectionist religious drive transmogrified into a variety of moral crusades and righteous causes, from opposition to Demon Rum to women's suffrage, and the greatest of these was abolition. The entire society became engaged in working out the balance of needs, affiliation and power (McClelland), and in realizing eschatology, if not at the anagogical level, then at the moral. Even though the whole nation had not believed the millennialist prophecy, much of the society had been re-enchanted by its own religious myth: the promise of an American millennium — whether sacred or secular, certainly civil. When the New Jerusalem did not alight as the religious seers said it would, then it had to be the eyes of the entire nation which saw the "glory of the coming of the Lord," but only as He "trampled out the vintage where the grapes of wrath are stored." Fifteen years after the failure of Christ's coming kingdom, the American people, split asunder in civil war, fought, among other reasons, over enactment of the religiously motivated cause of moral righteousness, abolition of Black slavery. The moral issue was further complicated by a divergence of theologies in support of mutually exclusive Northern and Southern civil religions, known in political history as "federal unionism" and "states' rights." [10]

Not only McClelland's thesis, then, but other sociologists of religion as well lend support to the homeorhetic theory of how society functions through its new religions.[11] Both at the level of the individual founder-hero and at the limited level of the original community as well as the level of the social-cultural broad base, the new religions of society die, are buried, rise, and come-again in transformed bodies resembling the earlier religious and reformist phases of the chreod. Society itself goes to war to implement the religious insight and the reformist cause, religiously reforming itself and, at the same time, provides the natural habitat for the chreodic coming-again of the new religion. Whatever the new religions may have intended, it is society which goes to war, makes communal love, and eats cornflakes in resonance to the chreodic results of society's religions.

The Second Great Awakening awakened homo religiosus americanus to the expectation of a righteous and heavenly Kingdom on the American continent. That same religiously-awakened American, together with his evangelized converts, was raised up abolitionist in his moral outrage to advance the cause of the coming Kingdom by freeing the slaves. Those same human components and their children in the field of nineteenth-century American religion finally took arms to enforce with power what their religiously inspired sense of affiliation demanded, all other social means having failed; thus the chreod reached its inevitable conclusion in a field of war. Society's needs, having been explored and tested in the sectarian enclaves of its new religions, were resolved in the clash of arms as a total, pan-social undertaking. In retrospect, the majority of that society judges the chreodic results to have been worth the costs, and acknowledges its debt to the homeorhetic functioning of the new religions in its midst. A strong minority points out, however, that similar results might have been reached rationally and technologically without resorting to the religiously-inspired, reformist blood-letting. The proponents of sweet reasonableness, however, are talking against the social-historical "law" of religious homeorhesis. Dame Society in the delivery room of her new religions, surrounded by rational doctors and the latest technology of the social scientists, still groans in travail to be delivered of her needs. When God impregnates the nation through religious revival to righteousness and fills her with a fullness of expectation of the Coming Kingdom, the moral-ethical response to this heavenly visitation is social activism, whether to prepare the way of the Lord and make His paths straight, or to cooperate with Him in setting up the Kingdom by synergistic human hands. (Differing theologies of grace would require this aspect to be described in a variety of ways; the net social result, nevertheless, is approximately the same for all — except Quietists — namely, heavenly labor.) But then, when the Kingdom delays

and the Lord tarries, the chreodic flow, which has now brok-
en its water in coming-again, spills over upon the unconvert-
ed and extends the mercies and the judgements of the Lord to
all in the society, but at the point of a sword or down a gun
barrel. Whether in Israelite landgrabbing (both ancient and
modern), Constantinian politics, Islamic submission, Muntzer-
ian haste, Calvinist self-righteousness, Cromwellian frustration, American manifest destiny, or Guyanan disillusionment,
the experience of religion is the experience of divine power
generating human power, which will be expressed.

Just as America suffered the chreodic fate of its new religions' coming-again in the nineteenth century, so it will
again, I suggest, in the twentieth century. McClelland ginger-
ly tenders his own prognosis for the immediate future:

> If the Vietnam War is not the true outcome of the
> reformist zeal of the 1960's, then we are faced
> with the awesome probability that it has yet to ex-
> press itself in some morally justified way in the
> 1970's. (McClelland, 1975:355)

The most likely candidate for this war, he surmises, is a ji-
had against the Arabs to protect, in one fell blow, the oppressed Israelis and "our" oil. We would thus reap the harvest of the Fundamentalist-Evangelical love-affair with the
Holy Land, assert our moral righteousness in avenging the
Jews again, and serve our national self-interest in the essential matter of energy resources.[12] In view of Afganistan and
the Iraq-Iran war taking place in the oil fields themselves,
McClelland — if, in tried-and-true millenialist fashion, we
reset his date from the seventies to the eighties — begins to
look like a true prophet. There are, however, other factors;
a wider perspective; and another, representative twentieth-
century new religion which need to be considered.

CHREODIC WAR AGAINST COMMUNISM
AND A TWENTIETH-CENTURY NEW RELIGION

The Fourth Great Awakening has taken place in the Consciousness Revolution of the 60s. Oriental influences, psychological self-help technologies, and archaizing Christian charis-
manias — all of which had their nineteenth-century counterparts — throb in the veins of American society, the hot blood
of religious inspiration. Prophetic types attuned to the dawning of the Age of Aquarius and its opposite, ecological apoll-
yon, forecast doom and glory anytime from 1975 to 2054. Moral
reformism has accompanied and followed closely on the heels
of religious revival. Small groups dynamically work out personal problems; civil rights, women's rights, gay rights, and
children's rights are among the available causes. A president

was dethroned for a kind of social-political immorality particularly offensive to Americans (however familiar to Europeans)
— the failure to be "open." The war, in Vietnam, fought during this period does not seem, however, to correspond to the
War between the States in terms of homeorhetically dispersing
the intense energy of righteous religious reformism. America,
accustomed to winning wars, lost this one, and thus added military frustration and lack of achievement to the failure of religion and the apathy of morals which characterized the 70s.
It is unlikely that the net effect of this mounting social tension will be a national decision to desist from the historic
paradigm of religion-reform-war.

Contrary to secularist interpreters, the American public
has never been more religious than it is now. New religions
are proliferating to an incalculable degree, there now being
reported upwards of 1300 separate religious bodies.[13] In 1976,
fifty million and more born-again Evangelicals elected their
own "New-Testament" President: Carter, an avowed born-again
Baptist, distinguished himself as an "agent of reconciliation"
between Jew and Arab, did works of charity in becoming the
"savior" of the Social Security system, proclaimed the good
news of the Equal Rights Amendment, and consistently turned
the other cheek to the Russians and Iranians in his non-use
of military power at a number of points of potential confrontation. In 1980, those same religionists, now identifiable as the
"Moral Majority," took credit for electing an "Old-Testament"
President for equally religious reasons, however different the
political motivations had become during the intervening four
years: Reagan, a spokesman for the American Civil Religion
tradition, promises a neo-orthodoxy of hardline recovery of
American strength and image in the face of aggressive Russians and wayward Arabs, wants to do away with the social
welfare system, programmatically and patriarchally opposes
the Equal Rights Amendment, and appoints a Vietnam War general as Secretary of State to lead the new cold and holy war.
Both Presidents are religiously motivated, as are the people
who elected them, though specific political policies differ.

Similarly, the issues of morality are more numerous now
than they were in the 60s, though polarization over the war
and civil rights then made the nation appear to be preoccupied with morality. Righteous causes now critical include
whales, no-nukes, inner-city blight, the roster of personal
rights mentioned above, alternative forms of energy, pornography, "law and order" in the streets, disarmament and self-
defense, and a good many more. But the greatest issue remains the agony of national identity, social self-definition.
Manifest Destiny has reached its greatest geographic extent
possible on the American continent, reaching out even to the

islands of the sea. Some voices now urge detente, arms limitation, and sweet reasonableness in dealing with the rest of the
world. Other voices, stronger since the recent election, argue
for a massive defense effort and readiness to manifest America's destiny on a global scale, to "keep the world safe for
democracy," as we are thought to have done in opposing the
Kaiser, the Führer and the Komissar. On the day following Mr.
Reagan's election, the stock market broke all kinds of previous
records, and defense-related issues sold like gold. The military-industrial complex is presumably the most powerful single
element within American society, certainly the most patriotic,
and therefore the most religious in an American civil sense.
The proper question, then, is, who is the unrighteous enemy
against whom to hurl this power and might?

American economics is essentially anti-communist and
American politics is usually opposed to foreign totalitarianism. American military and insurgency forces have already
done battle with communist powers in numerous countries. Were
America's constant need to define national identity to be cata-
lyzed in the presence of international economic collapse, a
race for the oil fields, a nuclear stand-off, or stimulation of
the American penchant for protecting underdog nations like
Korea and Israel (or the self-protective need to intervene
in our Latin-American backyard), America's ears would be
tuned to pick out from the preachments on international righteousness a frequency of martial response to the perceived
threat. Legion voices now address those ears, speaking directly to the issues of national identity, foreign policy, and America's spiritual, economic, and military responsibility to the
rest of the world. Among those voices is the Unification
Church of the Rev. Sun Myung Moon, a new religious movement
which assays to become influential in the coming decade.

From a certain sociological perspective, one may say
that Korean Unificationism is a new American religion, bred
in America's western-most state during the 1950s, sired by
American Presbyterian moralistic missionizing and syncretized
in the womb of Korean culture with oriental popular philosophies and autochthonous Korean messianism.[14] America has saved Korea at least three times: once from sin, once from Japan,
and once from the communists. The Unification Church is the
new religious group which celebrates that salvation, and seeks
to reciprocate it by providing a focal point through which
American society might function to solve some of its own deep
needs: the fragility of American marriage, recovery of a sense
of divine destiny in the heavenly kingdom on earth, and opposition to, and abolition of, the slavery of totalitarian communism.[15]

Not that the Rev. Moon intends to lead America on an aggressive, bloody crusade against the communists. His gospel, like that of the abolitionist Quakers and reformist Methodists of a former era, is ordered to peace and love and the abundance of a coming utopia. Rev. Moon offers God's "absolutely perfect ideology," revealed in Korea, to satisfy everyperson's "original desire" and provide the foil for God's current number-one enemy: Marxist-Leninist-Maoist-Kim il Sungist communist ideology. In God's name, the Rev. Moon calls upon America as a chosen nation to serve the world, preach the new ideology, and safeguard Korea — and all the "free world" — from the horror in the North. Unificationists, well within the bounds of the Presbyterian tradition, preach the religious myths of America's manifest destiny, constitutional freedom, and the providential intervention of New England's never-failing God. Every Unificationist with whom I have discussed these issues, however, has insisted upon making perfectly clear that neither the Rev. Moon nor the Unification Church wants to start a shooting war with the communists. Most Unificationists, like most Americans, would argue for the concept of a "just war" and believe in military self-defense. Nevertheless, one occasion of Moon's difficulty with the authorities in South Korea involved his own alleged evasion of the draft, holding his religious mission to be of greater value than his service in the army to his nation. In answer to an American youth, who sought Moon's advice in the event of war, he said:

> No true religion in the last days would advocate a violent showdown with the satanic world, encouraging anyone to harm or kill his opponent. That method could never represent the true religion of God.... I will never tell you to fight or confront anyone in a violent way.[16]

Unificationists foresee God's "Victory Over Communism" as an ideological one, a victory of love over greed and of the God-centered spiritual world descending to overcome spirit-negating materialism.

> The Heavenly side will never be able to escape from the attack of Satan's theory, unless the democratic world can set forth the truth which will subjugate his ideology. Here lies the historical ground in the providence of restoration that the Heavenly side must proclaim the perfect and absolute truth. The Third World War is going to be that in which God intends to restore, as the final measure since He began the providence of restoration, the ideal world by having the democratic world subjugate the communist world.[17]

The third world war, Divine Principle teaches, is inevitable and must be fought, one way or the other. If the internal, ideological warfare fails and the communists attack, then
a war of weapons shall have to be fought first. In this case,
the Satanic side will then be subjugated externally, after
which the enemy can be subjugated internally and united with
through love and reason. I suggest the Rev. Moon has in
mind America's external defeat of Imperial Japan and its internal, post-war subjugation by MacArthur, as an example of
how it might work. A multi-million dollar, Unification-financed
cinematic production, not released, Inchon, lionizes Mac-
Arthur's liberation of South Korea from the communists.

> ...Korea, where the Lord will come, should become
> the front line of God's immense love and, at the
> same time, that of Satan's growing hatred; in other
> words, where the two powers of democracy and com-
> munism should conflict with each other. The 38th
> parallel of Korea was formed according to this
> providence of restoration. [18]

Should the spiritual revolution delay, however, and the communists attack in all-out war, defense of South Korea and the
rest of the non-communist world would be, most Unificationist
leaders affirm, an act of providential holiness, to which the
United States in particular is called.

Ideologically, both the American public and the Rev.
Moon agree with the American New Left that institutionalized
communism, as it is practiced by North Korea and its supporting superpowers, is retrograde and anti-human.[19] Both Americans and the Rev. Moon have suffered at the hands of the communists: he, in North Korean jails and a concentration camp;
we, in North Korea, South Vietnam, and in a growing list of
Bay-of-Pigs-type embarrassing skirmishes. He, like us in Afganistan and in Latin America, is involved in a permanent ideological standoff with the communists. He, then, the
founder-hero of a vital new religion, offers himself as a
world savior to the American society as a world savior in the
ideological, cosmic, third world war against "Satanic" communism. The "third world war," says the Rev. Moon, is now being fought ideologically, but may have to be fought militar-
ily, if America fails in its God-appointed mission.[20]

It seems unlikely that increasingly pluralistic America,
however religious, would follow the tune of any one theological Pied Piper into yet another ephemeral heavenly kingdom.
Much less would racist Americans care to imagine that the returned Christ might be an Oriental, and many are too secular
to care. Other religious and moralist elements within the society, however, sufficiently resemble the Rev. Moon's anti-
communist stance in their social-political orientation, even

though they might want to distance themselves from his particular theological jargon or utopian vision. The conservative
religious, educational, medical, and psychological establishments, now energetically opposed to Unificationism as a theo-
logical-social option, even to the point of unconstitutional
skullduggery in the form of deprogramming and related evils,[21]
would co-opt Unification's religious momentum to oppose the
foreign threat. The military-industrial backbone of the economy, middle-of-the-road suburbanites, Protestant and Catholic
churches and Jewish synagogues, the patriotic New Right in
politics and religion, indeed, the entire middle class of the
not-so-silent Moral Majority, agree with the Rev. Moon and
his sociologically middle-class church that loving God, revi-
talizing capitalism, and America's manifest destiny to keep
the world safe for democracy are all within the divine plan.

Similar to its nineteenth-century counterparts, Unification already manifests its viability as an American new religion through its cultural impact (e.g., the annual International Conference on the Unity of the Sciences), social relevance
(e.g., emphasis on staunchly monogamous and interracial marriage), and production of consumer goods (e.g., ginseng tea,
fish, and, of late, a new idea in delicatessen fast food:
Korean barbeque steak sandwiches). But the significant impact
on American society might come for the Unificationists as it
did in the nineteenth century for the peaceable Quakers and
the reform-minded abolitionists. America is liable to hear the
Rev. Moon's ideological opposition to the communists and transform his appeal for spiritual revolution and American generos-
ity abroad into a providential justification for military triumph over God's and our enemies. Were this to happen, American society would have functioned both religiously and morally through one of its new religions, as it often has before,
to resolve a perennial cultural need through reaffirmation of
the national identity. If the cultural patterning of American
society is functional in the present as it has been in the
past, the chreodically inevitable outcome would then appear
to be a third world war against the communists fought within
the next decade in the name of God and morality.

SUMMARY

The "law" of the relationship between society and its
new religions is that society functions through the religions
by expressing itself in them. The religions are society seeking the resolution of its own cultural needs. This interaction
proceeds according to a homeorhetic trajectory running in parallels through both the organic life of the religions and the
history of the nation itself. The chreod provides for the initial spawning of the new religions from the matrix of society,

the rejection and adaptation of the religions within society, and the historical coming-again of the religions through their impaction of society. The nineteenth-century paradigm, seen in terms of the leaven of millennialist religion, the fermentation of moral reformism, and the fomentation of a War between the States, promises a replication of the pattern in the twentieth century. A wide variety of social forces presently at work, among them the new Unification religion, which offers itself as the ideology to overcome threatening communism, now bid well to focus the pervasive myths of American religious culture in support of an all-out, defensive war of righteousness.

EPILOGUE

The original form of this paper was prepared for the International Conference of the Sociology of Religion (Venice, 1979), three years before it was published. During those three years, international events and developments within the Unification movement have given me additional supportive material with which to argue the case for the current working out of America's religious chreod. During this time, both Unificationist and non-Unificationist critics of the paper have offered many helpful comments.

It was never my intention to suggest either that the Unificationists are warmongers seeking to foment hostilities with the communists or that Korea is the most likely place where the conflagration will ignite. Kim Il Sung is, after all, in his dodderage and Mao is no more in China. South Korean politics, never stable, seem to require constant American attention sufficient to keep a permanent warning flag hoisted toward the North. Who can say when or why any communist power might decide to initiate a conflict? This is not a paper about international politics nor does the chreodic theory of the functioning of new religions within society offer to explain what the communists might do.

Not even the Unificationists are willing to say of themselves that they have sufficient political clout on the American scene successfully to lobby for a declaration of war — defensive or offensive — against the communists. Their public image is already too "political" for comfort within an organization which prefers to think of itself as a church. The time will providentially come, most Unificationists hope, when direct political influence on the American government will be possible; but, they acknowledge, that time is not yet.

What has taken place, however, is a noticeable shift to the Right in overall American affairs. Carter is out, Reagan

is in. Unificationists in great numbers walked the streets of
New York City in long hours of electioneering for Reagan. The
Unificationist daily News World (and its Spanish-language sis-
ter-paper Noticias del Mundo) was the only newspaper to headline, on Election Day morning, a "landslide" for Reagan —
a headline which was dictated personally by the Rev. Moon
himself in New York and which was duly noted and appreciat-
ed by President-elect Reagan that afternoon in California. The
News World headline on the following morning: "Thank God!
We were right" was not a bit of cheap New York cussing, but
a theological comment. It is no stretch of the political imagination at all to suggest that Unification, most active in New
York — a state crucial for the election — contributed materially to the defeat of Carter and the victory of Reagan. Unificationists are more modest in their claims than are the Moral
Majority people; but Col. Bo Hi Pak, publisher of the News
World and special advisor to the Rev. Moon, speaking before
an audience of more than 600 international scientists at the
9th Annual International Conference on the Unity of the
Sciences in Miami Beach following the election, took as much
of the credit for the election as he thought appropriate, giving all the glory to God and Rev. Moon.

All this merely illustrates the chreodic confluence of the
dynamics of American new religions (in this case, chiefly Unification and the Moral Majority) with the on-going need of the
society to define itself internally in terms of its moral stance
and externally in terms of its political posture. The chreodic
theory of the function of new religions in society is not a sim-
plistic attempt either to predict warfare or to argue a cause-
effect nexus between any particular religion and any particular political result. It is, however, a sociologically ordered,
theoretical formulation which explains the relationship between
society and society's new religions in their mutual functioning
to define the nature of social existence. I am neither a date-
setting millennialist nor a prophet of the Battle of Armageddon; although, if McClelland's and others' theories continue
to be borne out in conformity to the chreodic pattern described herein, one hardly needs to be a prophet to foresee a major military conflict well within the decade of the 80s.

If that war comes, it shall be incorrect to say that the
Unificationists either caused it or led America into it. It shall
be correct to say, however, that Unification provided a service for the American society which new religions typically
provide their mother culture in supplying a theological-moral
rationale for both the providential inevitability and ethical
rightness of fighting a war. This service, which the shaman
has ever provided the tribal chieftain is an emotional necessity in wartime. Humans going to war must believe in "God
with us," or they lack the morale to fight to win (Vietnam).

Both America and communism existed in mutual opposition before Unification came along; therefore, it would be nonsense
to say that the new Unification religion "caused" the third
world war in any formal way, and it is unlikely that Unification, now numerically shrinking and socially ostracized, shall
be able even in ten years time to afford the ideological occasion for broad-base American opposition to a foreign enemy.
Nevertheless, as a new American religion, however small,
along with others of its political ilk — Neo-Evanglicalism, the
New Right, the Moral Majority — Unification shall have afforded the society a religious means through which the society
can express its need to formulate a theo-rational justification
for the social necessity of military opposition to an alien aggressor, and that, in terms consistent with historical, national myths and a projected national millennium. In turn, Unification shall enjoy its chreodic coming-again within a society
in which its religious ideology shall seem to have been vindi-
cated by history. Whatever becomes of the Rev. Sun Myung
Moon as Messiah-designate or the Unification Church as God's
True Family, the Unification new religion will experience a social coming-again in concrete, historical terms, wherever we go
to wars against the communists, whether in the Middle East,
Latin America, or Korea.

NOTES

1. The theological interpretations in this paper are not claiming to represent the official teaching of the Unification Church but are the views of the author.

2. Linda K. Pritchard, "Religious Change in Nineteenth Century America" in Glock and Bellah, 1976: 298, has developed a similar series of "stages of religious transformation,1820-1860" which describes the same religious chreod (see note 3 below). She speaks of Stage One: established religion in crisis (death); Stage Two: catalysts (burial); Stage Three: development of new sects (resurrection), and Stage Four: creation of a new established religion (coming-again). At her third stage, however, she categorizes in terms of regenerative sects, schismatic sects, cultic (non-Christian) sects, and quasi-religious (secular) sects thus leaving the impression that the categories might not also be applied equally meaningfully at other stages and that any of the given new religions to which the categories might be applied could demonstrate regenerative, schismatic, cultic, or secular qualities, depending upon the homoerhetic point at which one transects the religious chreod with a given category. The inadequacies of this kind of categorizing lead her, for example, inaccurately to categorize Noyes' Oneida foundation of 1847 as a "quasi-religious sect." (p.322) Whereas one might rightly transect the Oneida chreod at the coming-again stage with the chreodic stages, "regenerative" and "schismatic" are equally fair descriptions. Further, if one theologically-ethically (and incorrectly) judges complex marriage to be non-Christian, then one might also apply "cultic" as a category for the period between 1840 and 1879, though probably not much before and not at all afterwards.

McLoughlin, 1978:9-22, appeals to the work of Anthony F.C. Wallace, especially his "Revitalization Movements", 1956: 264-231. McLoughlin defines religious revival in American culture as "periods of fundamental ideological transformation necessary to the dynamic growth of the nation in adapting to basic social, ecological, psychological, and economic changes. The conversion of great numbers of people from an old to a new world view (a new ideological or religious understanding of their place in the cosmos) is a natural and necessary aspect of social change. It constitutes the awakening of a people caught in an outmoded, dysfunctional world view to the necessity of converting their mindset, their behavior, and their institutions to more relevant or more functionally useful ways of understanding and coping with the changes in the world they live in." (p.8) There have been five such major functionings of new religious outburst in the history of American society: the Puritan Awakening, 1610–1640; the First Great Awakening, 1730–1760; The Second Great Awakening, 1800–1830; the Third Awakening, 1890–1920; and the Fourth Great Awakening, 1960–1990(?). These religious movements have proceeded through a five-stage pattern: (1) during a societal crisis of legitimacy in traditional norms, the revitalization begins in a stage of the "period of individual stress," followed by (2) the "period of cultural distortion" (death and burial); after which comes (3) the period of building new "mazeways" (resurrection)and (4) social experimentation (usually by the prophets among the youth) and (5) winning over the older, less enthusiastic to the new way (coming-again). Burridge, 1969:170.

3. C.H. Waddington, "The Theory of Evolution Today" in Koestler and Smythies (eds.) 1969:366: "Systems usually exhibit a kind of stability. I have used the words canalization or homeorhesis to describe this. The latter is a new word. It is related to the well-known expression homeostasis, which is used in connection with systems which keep some variable at a stable value as time passes. . . We use the word homeorhesis when what is stabilized is not a constant value but is a particular course of change in time. If something happens to alter a homeorhetic system, the control mechanisms do not bring it back to where it was at the time the alteration occurred, but bring it back to where it would normally have got to at some later time. The "rhesis" part of the word is derived from the Greek word "rheo", to flow, and one can think of a homeorhetic system as rather like a stream running down the bottom of a valley, if a landslide occurs and pushes the stream off the valley bottom, it does not come back to the stream bed at the place where the diversion occurred, but some way farther down the slope. There seems to be no recognized word for a stabilized time trajectory of this kind. Since they are the most important features of developing biological systems, I have invented a name for them -- the word "chreod", derived from the Greek chre, it is fated or necessary, and hodos, a path."

4. McLoughlin: 1978:21.

5. "Light gleamed upon my soul in a different way from what I had expected. It was dim and almost imperceptible at first but in the course of the day it attained meridian splendor. Ere the day was done I had concluded to devote myself to the service and ministry of God," from Robertson, 1977:1. Nor should we overlook the theological potential in in Noyes' sexual-personal crisis when his heart's true love, Abigail Merwin, refused to marry him. The Battle-Axe Letter appears to be not only the theoretical foundation of the Oneida

order and its rejection of sexual jealousy, possessiveness, and exclusivity as un-Christian but also Noyes' personal justification of how he might have retained the affections of both Abigail and his devoted and dearly loved wife, Harriet Holton Noyes; see Carden, 1969, 1969:8.

6.   Noyes, 1977:2.

7.   DeMaria, 1978 provides the most thorough and sensitive appreciation of "complex marriage" available, and draws together the relevant but elusive evidence from the thousands of pages of primary source material.

8.   Noyes, 1977: 15.

9.   Cross,   1950: 201. Modified Millerism was as widespread then as the Late-Great-Planet-Earth mentality is now.   Heated debate over pre-, post-, and a-millenial points of view were the theological order of the day.   American millenialism (that is, Christian eschatology with an American component) was a preoccupation inherited in the 19th century directly from the 18th, and before that, the 17th; and before that, the 16th. John Winthrope preached to the covenanters on board the Arrabella, 1630, that they were to become a "cittie set upon a hill" in the New World, God's commonwealth in the wilderness. Jonathan Edwards, 1742, mused that New England was most probably the place where the "latter-day glory" might begin and God would "renew the habitable world of mankind."   Following in   the   footsteps   of   these   greatest   preachers   of   the   Great Awakenings before him, Charles Grandison Finney, the greatest preacher of the 1820's and 30's, predicted in 1835 that, if Americans   and   their churches   would simply "do   their duty, the   millennium can come in three years." (in McLoughlin, 1978 130) Cf. Davidson, 1977, passim.

10.   McClelland, 1975a passim; partial results of his study were reported in McClelland, 1975b: 44-48.   McClelland observes and documents the patterns of chreodic connections between religious revival, subsequent moral reformist zeal, and warfare in terms of the interplay among the motivational need for power and need for affiliation (or love), as these drives are balanced and modified by need for achievement   and the ability to achieve power in a socialized way. McClelland supplies compelling proof of his thesis as it has worked in British society from 1500 to 1825 and in America from 1785 to 1975.   Independent, critical analysis of literary themes of affiliation and power in the children's stories, hymns, and best-selling novels of the periods under scrutiny forms the empirical basis of his judgement.

For our purposes, McClelland's thesis can be summarized
as follows: When the rise and fall of the need for affiliation
and the need for power reach a state of balance, an "imperial
frame of mind" is produced. Although McClelland says he does
not know how a "collective motivational state sets in motion
a chain of events eventuating. . . in warfare," approximately
fifteen years of "lead time" following this imperialistic condition in the nation, religious revival motivates a drive for social reform. If the need for power is fairly strong, the need
for affiliation tends to drop, thus producing a situation in
which a strong, socialized power-drive, reflective of the zeal
for reform, will seek to achieve its political and other social
ends. When the opportunity for a socialized satisfaction of
these needs is lacking and the need for achievement is high,
approximately another fifteen years of "lead time" will bring
America (and England, on a somewhat similar pattern) to warfare. The experiences of war, then, cause the need for affiliation to rise (as the need for power has been gratified during
the carnage), thus re-establishing the balance of need for affiliation and need for power, the imperial frame of mind, and
thereby starting the cycle over again. McClelland, similar
to Cross' notion of "dispersing ultraism," sees this pattern
having eventuated in two 19th-century wars: the religious fervour of the Second Great Awakening, ca. 1820, eventuated in
Jacksonian Populism, ca. 1835, which together produced the war
with Mexico, in 1850. The recrudescent Awakening at its millennial peak, ca. 1843/44, eventuated in fifteen years' worth
of abolitionist righteousness and ultimately produced the War
between the States, ca. 1860. McClelland makes specific the
connection betwen religious revival, reformist zeal, and war
in these words:

> . . . The link between the imperial motive pattern
> and war is reformist zeal. Religious revival in the
> two instances studied in English history (the Puri-
> tan reformation, which produced the Civil War; and
> the Wesleyan revival, which presaged the war with
> the colonies) was connected with social reform, as
> it is in several instances in American history.
> Usually, in fact, religious revival precedes a con-
> cern for social justice. . .

> The paradox of the reform movements is that they
> have an unintended consequence: they seem to cre-
> ate an action orientation that makes war possible.
> Before, and more recently during, reformist periods,
> the need for Power is high, the need for Affiliation
> is low, and a martial spirit leads to zealous
> actions to right wrongs on behalf of the oppressed
> . . .the poor, the blacks, or the women. . .The
> irony, of course, is that the reformers have no in-
> tention of starting wars. They are, in fact, often

pacifists, since pacifism is one other form of protest against traditional right-wing male militarism.
. . . We need to understand the possible intrinsic,
though paradoxical, linkage between increased devotion, moralistic reform, and later violence. When
people repeat the slogan, "Make love not war," they
should realize that love for others often sets the
process in motion that ends in war. . .In other
words,. . .there is an intrinsic connection between
Christian devotion and violence. (especially pp.341-
359, charts, pp. 341, 347).

McClelland underestimates the chreodic impact of the Great
Awakening on the American Revolution, (p. 349) which clearly
fits his theory and literary evidence which he could probably find. The Great Awakening from 1740 to 1760 resurrected
in revolutionary republicanism in the 1770's and chreodically
came-again in the War of Independence in 1776 -- fifteen years
following the religious and subsequent moral revival and therefore right on schedule to fit McClelland's fifteen-year lead-time
pattern.   A major defect in McClelland's presentation is his
use of out-dated secondary resources in American religious history, and his lack of use of primary resources or current periodical literature.

McClelland (p.351) wobbles a bit in setting forth his
theory when he says: "The religious revivals, however, do not
seem to precede or follow motive shifts in any regular way,
and occasionally they seem to follow a wave of social reform,
as when the Second Great Awakening occurred after Jacksonian
populism." By simply dating the Second Great Awakening earlier
than he does, the basic pattern of shift from religion to reformism to war remains intact. Cross (1950:9) dates the beginnings of the Second Great Awakening no later than 1799, with
the Great Revival in western New York and the Cane Ridge
stirrings in Kentucky; Andrew Jackson was president from 1829
to 1837.

11.   A religious interpretation of these data comes with a
built-in clue as to how religion and reform occasion war. Warfare, in terms of the homeorhetic logic of the religious chreod,
is a "natural" consequence of an equation of the religious experience and the experience of power.   Martin, 1969a:37: "How
does the church operate in society? The church itself embodies
a dialectic, between love and power. . .". Burridge, 1969:107:
"What the heart and stomach cannot passively accept, the
mind's desire leaps forward to command. Aware of what might
be, impotence swells with what might become potent. Yet this
impulse to join the mainstream of power, to find a new integrity, does not necessarily imply being at the centre of the interactions of social life. For though the sectarian elect necessarily stand aside from the hub of established social life, they

believe themselves to be more at one with that source of all power which the members of the wider society are also taken to acknowledge. What matters is that power, once recognized, should be ordered and rendered intelligible and that integrity should derive from this ordering." McLoughlin, 1978: 23: "More often than not this reunited sense of national millenarian purpose has led Americans into war in the effort to speed up the fulfillment of their manifest destiny. It might be more accurately said that our periods of great awakening have produced wars rather than resulted from them."

12.   McClelland (1975b:355, 357-359) is moved to a pacifist-Quaker conclusion by his research (as, indeed, his religious perspective may have controlled his research): ". . .the only safe Christian (or religious devotee of any kind) is a pacifist." Remembering, however, the unintentional linkage between religious revivalism and social reformism and war (which McClelland himself points out), and that many a pacifist Quaker worked alongside the Methodists both in England and America for the abolition of slavery and in other social reform causes, one wonders just how "safe" Quakers are.

13.   Melton, 1978.

14.   Warren Lewis, "Hero with the Thousand-and-First Face" in Bryant and Richardson (eds), 1978: 275-289.

15.   Moon, 1973: 491, 493, 494, 523-525.

16.   Moon, 1976 passim, especially pp 32-34; for the Rev. Moon on war and peaceableness, see "The Master Speaks on the Restoration and Judgement" in Moon, 1967: 11-14; ibid, MS-4:6; "Parents' Day" (8 April 1978) in Moon, 1978:4. See also Sontag 1977: 149-154.

17.   Moon, 1973, 493.

18.   Ibid: 491, 493, 494, 524.

19.   McLoughlin, 1978: 211.

20.   Unificationist attitudes towards communism are expressed in Moon, 1976 and Moon, 1973: 449-496; and by the Freedom Leadership Foundation, publishers of The Rising Tide, an anti-communist fortnightly, and see Freedom Leadership Foundation: 1973 and 1975.

21.   Bromley and Shupe, 1979; Shupe and Bromley, 1980; Richardson, H., 1977.

THE NEW RELIGIONS AS SOCIAL INDICATORS

Roy Wallis

In this paper I propose to examine the new religions of the 1960's, synthesizing extant empirical information and theoretical formulations to create a typology of new religions which can then be employed as the basis of a theory of their origins and an account of their major features.[1] Such a theory should also provide an explanation of recent developments in the new religions and permit some predictions of the likely future direction of change.

I shall suggest that the new religions are not simply of intrinsic interest, but that they provide a source of insight into the nature of the society within which they emerge. We can see this in two ways. First, in the beliefs and mode of social organization which they espouse, new religious movements either react against, or celebrate, major features of their society. Second, their emergence can be traced to a particular range of social factors which are conducive to their development and which also help us to account for the differences that can be found to exist in the movements under consideration.

In order to demonstrate these points I shall distinguish new religious movements into two types: (1) world-rejecting, and (2) world-affirming. That is to say I shall argue that new religious movements can usefully be classified precisely in respect of the perspective which they take upon society, and indeed that their social organization is a direct consequence of the perspective which they take.

THE WORLD-REJECTING MOVEMENT

The world-rejecting movement views the prevailing social order as having departed far from God's prescription and plan. Mankind has lost touch with God and spiritual things, and, in the pursuit of purely material interests, has succeeded in creating a polluted environment; a vice-ridden society in which individuals treat each other purely as means rather than as ends; a world filled with conflict, greed, insincerity and despair. The belief system of the world-rejecting movement

216

condemns the wider society and its values, particularly that of individual success as measured by wealth or consumption patterns. It rejects the materialism of the advanced industrial world, calling for a return to spiritual values and guiding principles, and often calling for a return to a more rural way of life. It anticipates an imminent and major transformation of the world. The millennium will shortly commence or the movement will sweep the world, and when all have become members or when they are in a majority, or when they have become guides and counsellors to kings and presidents, then a new world-order will begin, a simpler, more loving, more humane and more spiritual order in which the old evils and mistakes will be eradicated, and utopia will have begun.

Meanwhile, the faithful have come out of the world, set themselves apart from it, living characteristically a communal life whereby they can keep themselves separated, uncontaminated by the worldly order, able to cultivate their collective spiritual state unmolested. The religious involvement of members is thus a full-time activity. The committed adherent will need to break completely with the worldly life in order to fulfill the movement's expectations. It is a "total institution", regulating all his activities, programming all of his day but for the briefest periods of recreation or private time. Not only will he live in the community, normally he will also work for it. Although this may sometimes mean taking a job "in the world", the risks of this are quite high for a movement that so heartily condemns the prevailing social order. Usually an economic base for the movement will be devised which limits involvement in the world. Often this can be combined with proselytising, as in the case of the Krishna Consciousness devotees who offer copies of their magazine, books, or flowers, or the Children of God who offer copies of their leader's letters printed in pamphlet form, in return for a donation. Contact with non-members can then be highly routinised and ritualised. It is anyway transient. It provides the opportunity for contact with people who show some interest or sympathy, and thus occasions for conversion, but even hostile responses merely serve to confirm the evil nature of the world and thus the virtues of the movement. Most movements tend to have multiple economic bases often also deriving income from the possessions of new members handed over to the collective fund on joining; donations from sympathetic or unwary businessmen; and remittances from parents of members; as well as street sales and manufacturing enterprises.

Although sexual activity may be severely restricted, as in the Unification Church and Krishna Consciousness, the communal units of the world-rejecting movements tend to display

a high level of diffuse affectivity in contrast to the formality
and unemotionality of the wider bureaucratic society. Members
will often kiss or hold hands with other members, hug them
in greeting, and make constant verbal affirmation of affection.
In contrast to the individualism of the wider society, the
communal life tends to require considerable subordination
of self-interest, individual will, and personal autonomy in
order to maximize communal solidarity. Such movements, regarding their leaders as Messiah, or prophet, or guru, also
tend to be highly authoritarian.[2] The constraints of the
communal life and an authoritarian leadership provide the
grounds for claims by hostile outsiders that the youthful members have lost their identity, personality and even "free will"
in joining.[3]

THE WORLD-AFFIRMING MOVEMENT

The world-affirming movement on the other hand views the
prevailing social order less contemptuously, seeing it as possessing many highly desirable characteristics. Mankind contains within itself enormous potential power which, until now,
only a very few individuals have learned effectively to utilize,
and even then normally only by withdrawing from the world.
Movements approximating this type claim to possess the means
to enable people to unlock their physical, mental and spiritual
potential, without the need to withdraw from the world --
means which are readily available to virtually everyone who
learns the technique or principle provided. No arduous prior
period of preparation is necessary, no rigorous system of
taboos enjoined. No extensive mortification of the flesh nor
forceful control of the mind. At most, a brief period of
abstention from drugs or alcohol may be requested, without
any requirement of continued abstention after the completion
of a training or therapy period. No extensive doctrinal commitment is entailed. There may even be no insistence that
the adherent believe the theory or doctrine, as long as he
is willing to try the technique and see if it works. While
followers of such movements may object to some limited aspects
of the present social order, the values and goals which prevail within it are normally accepted. They have joined such
a movement not to escape or withdraw from the world and
its values, but to acquire the means to achieve them more
easily and to experience the world's benefits more fully.
The social order is not viewed as unjust nor society as having
departed from God. The beliefs of these movements are essentially individualistic. The source of suffering, of disability,
of unhappiness, lies within oneself rather than in the social

structure. The spiritual dimension in particular is a matter
of individual experience and individual subjective reality
rather than social reality or even social concern. Moreover,
God is not perceived as a personal deity imposing a set of
ethical prescriptions upon human society. If God is referred
to, it is primarily as a diffuse, amorphous and immanent
force in the universe, but present most particularly within
oneself. For many of these groups and movements, the self
is the only God there is, or at least the only one that matters.

It follows from this individualistic ethos that collective
activities have no sacred quality and indeed are likely to
have only a small place in the enterprise unless it is particularly centered upon some group-based or interpersonal technique such as encounter groups, and even here the group
is of importance only as means to self-liberation.

As the movement does not reject the world and its organization, it will quite happily model itself upon those aspects
of the world which are useful to the movement's purpose.
The salvational commodity includes a set of ideas, skills
and techniques which can be marketed like any other commodity
since no sense of the sacred renders such marketing practice
inappropriate (as it would be for example in, say, the idea
of marketing the Mass, or Holy Communion). The logic of
the market is wholly compatible with the ethos of such movements. Thus the product will be tailored for mass-production,
standardizing content, instructional method, and price, distributing it through a bureaucratic apparatus which establishes
or leases agencies, just as in the distribution of Kentucky
Fried Chicken or Ford motor cars. The methods of mass instruction employed in universities or mail-order colleges are
drawn upon for pedagogic technique. The outlets are situated
in large cities where the market exists, rather than reflecting
an aspiration for a return to the rural idyll. As with the
sale of any commercial service or commodity, the normal round
of life of the customer is interfered with as little possible.
Courses of instruction or practice are offered at weekends
or in the evenings, or during periods of vacation. Full-time
involvement and complete commitment are not normally required.
Membership is a leisure activity, one of the multiple role-
differentiated pursuits of the urban dweller. His involvement
will be partial and segmentary rather than total.

Such movements tend to employ quite normal, commercial
means for generating income. Their followers are mostly in
orthodox employment, and the movement simply sells them a
service or commodity for an established price plus local taxes,
sometimes even with facilities for time-payment or discounts
for cash! Only for the staff of full-time professionals employed

by the organization will life normally approximate to any
degree the "total institution" setting of the contemporary
world-rejecting religions.

It is evident, then, that in the context of a Christian
culture the world-rejecting movements appear mluch more conventionally religious than the world-affirming movements.
Christianity has tended to exhibit a tension between the
church and the world, based in part on the institutional
differentiation of Christianity from society, which leads us
to expect religious institutions to be distinct in form. This
differentiation is much less evident in Hindu and Buddhist
culture, where, too, the more immanent conception of God,
the idea of each individual as a "divine spark", and that
of the existence of hidden wisdom which will lead to salvation
are also familiar. Many of the world-affirming movements
have been to some extent influenced by Hindu and Buddhist
idealist philosophies. But they have also drawn substantially
upon developments in modern science and psychology for their
beliefs and practices, and, marketing a soteriological commodity in quite highly secularised surroundings, the tendency
has been to emphasise the scientific character of their ideas
and techniques, and to suppress the more overtly religious
aspects, although an attitude of pragmatism has informed
their practice in this regard. Transcendental Meditation,
for example, was first presented in the West in much more
explicitly religious terms than it is today, the religious rhetoric being dropped on largely marketing grounds.[5] Scientology,
on the other hand was made more explicitly religious when
it seemed this would be a useful public-relations device in
the face of government hostility and intervention.[6]

The world-affirming movements could perhaps more com-
fortably be called "quasi-religious" in recognition of the fact
that, although they pursue transcendental goals by largely
metaphysical means, they lay little or no stress on the idea
of God nor do they engage in worship, and they therefore
straddle a vague boundary between religion and psychology.
Which side they are held to fall upon will depend entirely
on the nature of the definition of religion employed.

Having offered a characterization of the two types of
new religion, I should now like to consider whether we can
identify any social factors conducive to their emergence, and
any which might help us to account for the differences between
them.

SOCIAL CHANGE AND THE NEW RELIGIONS [7]

Undoubtedly the major long-term trend underlying the emergence of the new religions, and indeed underlying most features of the world as we know it in the industrial West, is, as Max Weber recognized, that of rationalization. Rationalization is the process whereby life has increasingly become organized in terms of instrumental and causal considerations, a concern with technical efficiency, and the maximizing of calculability and predictability, and the subordination of nature to human purposes. Rationalization thus tends to bring secularization in its wake, since transcendental values and absolute moral principles find it hard to survive this increasing preoccupation with causal efficacy and utilitarianism. Rationalization thus tends to produce what Max Weber has called the "disenchantment of the world", a loss of our sense of magic, mystery, prophecy, and the sacred.

Rationalization also produces major changes in the relationship of individuals to social institutions. In particular as Peter Berger has noted, it produces a differentiation and pluralization of life-worlds or institutional domains. For example, industrialization created a separation between work and the family. In contemporary Western societies there is a high degree of differentiation between institutional arenas in which individuals live out their lives: where they live is separate from where they work, which is separate from where they play, etc.

Unlike his forebears, then, modern man cannot so readily identify himself with his public institutional roles because their very variety may make it impossible to gain more than a fragmented conception of self from them. Moreover, as rationalization has led to ever greater routinization and mechanization of work, to an ever greater division of labour in the interest of efficiency, so a major focus of identification for earlier generations, the occupational role, has tended to become less attractive for all but a privileged few in prestigeous or intrinsically satisfying occupations. Identity for the majority becomes de-institutionalized and individuals begin "to assign priority to their private selves, that is, to locate the 'real me' in the private sphere of life". [8] The public institutions of education, the state, and the economy tend to be viewed by many as agents of a baleful and dehumanizing constraint on the realization of the "authentic self" and the "good society".

Rationalization of production has the further effect of creating a shift from ascription to achievement (not who you are, but what you can do) as the basis for selection into adult occuptional roles. Status and a sense of worth thus come to rest on the level of achievement which has been attained in the course of one's life. But where achievement is viewed as an end in itself, such a sense of worth and of status is inevitably precarious since there are no clear guides as to when enough has been achieved, and the chances are that comparison with others will lead the individual always to feel a relative failure.

De-institutionalization of identity has been accompanied and enhanced by another consequence of rationalization and industrialization, that is by the attentuation of community. Industrialization destroys traditional forms of community and inhibits the creation of new forms due to the levels of mobility both geographical and social which become characteristic, and due to the differentiation among people which tends to follow from an increasing division of labour and a consequent divergence of life-styles. This attentuation of community is experienced as a lack of close ties with a group of persons outside the family with whom the individual has a relationship of more than a role-oriented kind; of a group of persons with whom he can "be himself", who will accept him as, and for what, he is rather than as the producer of a particular performance. In practice most interactions are with individuals with whom lack of prolonged acquaintance has not permitted an easy, growing intimacy and which are inevitably therefore somewhat fragile and threatening.

The new religious movements have developed in response to, and as attempts to grapple with the consequences of, rationalization. But having identified two polar types it is clearly important to distinguish the more specific factors which have led to their distinctive forms of salvational message and of organization.

THE SOURCES OF SUPPORT FOR THE WORLD-REJECTING NEW RELIGIONS

The world-rejecting new religions of the past have characteristically been composed of the poor and the oppressed. In the form of millennialist movements anticipating the imminent total transformation of the world and the supernatural establishment of a heaven on earth, new religions have often formed in circumstances of great adversity. Defeat in war, colonization, natural disaster or economic collapse have often been heralds of millennialist movements. Supernatural forces, or even God himself, will come down to earth, transforming and purging it, banishing pain, evil and indignity, and ousting the op-

pressor. Introversionism, the pursuit of salvation by gather-
ing in a tight community of the elect, withdrawn from the
taint of the world" to preserve and cultivate their own holiness"[9]has often been a further development from millennialism.
Continued oppression, repeated defeat, or failure of the millennial prophecy may lead to the postponement of hope, tran-
scendentalizing it and projecting it into the distant rather
than the immediate future.

Millennialism and introversionism represent respectively
the active and the passive response to a world seen as beyond
reform. Both indicate the failure of, or the perceived unavailability of, secular solutions to the problems by which various
individuals and groups see the world or themselves beset.
Some of the contemporary new religions have an explicitly
millennialist character, for example the Children of God who
anticipate Christ's return in 1993 and the Unification Church
which foresees the onset of the millennium in the 1980's.
Others, such as Krishna Consciousness, are more introversionist
in their form.

The new groups and movements which fall into the world-
rejecting category sometimes pre-dated, but scarcely flourished,
before the late 1960's. The Unification Chuch, for example,
had a tiny following in California in 1960, but the miserable
failure of its efforts to recruit any substantial following until
late in the 1960's are well documented.[10] The Jesus People
did not make an appearance until about 1968. Krishna Consciousness, although established in America from 1965, only
rather gradually built a following, and the Divine Light Mission was not established in the West until 1969.

The principal early following of each of these movements
was drawn from among the hippies, drop-outs, surfers, LSD
and marijuana users among the American and European young,
and many more from those who sympathised with, and shared
aspects of, the same sub-culture as these groups. Often the
conversion of these young people was so sudden, the transition
so abrupt and dramatic, that parents and friends would argue
that only brainwashing or hypnosis could account for it.

This conclusion followed readily enough if one reasoned
that the convert had had insufficient time and contact prior
to joining to gain any clear grasp of the movement's beliefs.
But this was entirely to misunderstand the nature of the conversion. What led these young people to abandon their
friends, family, education or career in this impulsive way
was not the promise of some future spiritual reward, nor any
extensive initial doctrinal comprehension, but the actuality
of the way of life which they observed and its immediate
consequences for the follower. What attracted them to the

movement characteristically was the warmth and affection with which they were treated, the sense of purpose and meaningfulness exhibited by the adherents, their openness and apparent sincerity, their joy or serenity.[11] Salvation for the convert to the world-rejecting religions was principally salvation from the loneliness and impersonality of the world. Salvation lay primarily in community, in the existence of a group which would provide a warm, supportive environment in which the individual would be treated as a person rather than a role-player and in which his or her idealism would be mobilized and given concrete meaning in terms of spreading the salvational message to the world.[12]

In many ways the almost exclusive appeal of the world-rejecting movements to the young at that point in time is readily understandable. The 1960's represented a peak in the history of youth culture. This phenomenon of a youth culture is itself of recent provenance, requiring the development of an industrial technology to free the young from productive activity, and establishing the need for extensive and often specialized education covering an increasing period of the life-cycle. Youth thus became the ambiguous status between childhood and the adult world or work, a status without any clear social place which nevertheless became the repository of ever larger sections of the population, many of whom were segregated into separate youth "ghettoes", such as advanced educational institutions . There they possessed much freedom and few responsibilities, but at the same time little power and few immediate rewards in terms of income or status.

Some measure of the scale of this development can be secured through statistics on higher education. Between the academic years commencing 1962 and 1967, the number of students in full-time higher education in Britain grew from 217,000 to 376,000, an increase of 73%.[13] In the USA between 1960 and 1970 "the number of people in college more than doubled."[14] Thousands and thousands of young people, most of them middle-class in social origin, were flooding into institutions where they had relatively little contact with anyone other than their age-peers. The affluence of the period provided not only resources for the emergence of industries directed towards the construction and sale of symbols of youth, such as the popular music recording industry, but also a sense of the imminence, and indeed the necessity, of progress. Technology it was believed, had resolved the problem of scarcity, and hence peace, plenty and social justice could now prevail for all, were it not for the reactionary forces or structures preventing them. Affluence encouraged idealism, and it also created a sense of security that entry into the world of work could wait, that something would turn up, that one would be provided for, if only by welfare, assistance from home, and petty or illicit trading, as in craft work or drugs.

Wider political and social events conspired to give this new social category an identity and a solidarity as persons of a distinctive type. The Civil Rights Campaign in America and the Campaign for Nuclear Disarmament in Britan began to create that solidarity which was symbolised and enhanced in new styles of music and dress 'promoted by industries eager to exploit this new market. The Viet Nam war, particularly among American youth where the draft created a heightened sense of urgency, was the major phenomenon leading to the alienation of the young from the structure and culture of adult society. Its impersonality, bureaucratization, and de-humanizing division of labour were already rejected in prefer-ence to a way of life closer to the warmth, intimacy and integration of childhood. This rejection was celebrated in the hippie life-style, the norms and values of which embodied an opposition to the Protestant Ethic dominating the world of work and adult responsibility. Hippie values comprised an emphasis on spontaneity against restraint, hedonism against deferred gratification, ego-expressivity against conformity to bureaucratic rules, and a disdain for work against its elevation as a virtue.[15] The hostility which this rejection of dominant values, life-styles, and career-patterns provoked against them, helped to weld this new social category into a social group in opposition to the structure and culture of the environing society, into a counter-culture. They "dropped out" of that wider society in varying degrees, seeking to find a better way of life in its interstices or at its margins, in Haight-Ashbury or the rural commune.

At the same time, the young had begun to develop a political consciousness, opposed, as one might expect, to the prevailing social order. In student political movements, and anti-war protest movements, through sit-ins and demonstrations, the young sought to transform aspects of their society.

But these attempts to recreate the world by secular means largely foundered. The hippie vision of love, peace, com-munity, and everyone "doing his own thing" had been found to lead to disorganization, entropy, mental illness, exploita-tion, and the victory not of the meek, but of the most insensi-tive. Youthful political activism resulted in bloody confronta-tions on the campuses; in Chicago at the 1968 Democratic Convention; in Grosvenor Square, London; in Paris; and else-where. The utopian vision had become a rather sordid reality

In was in this context that many of the world-rejecting new religions began to find their converts. Proclaiming that they offered a "high that never lets you down", or claiming to be "spiritual revolutionaries" or the "revolution for Jesus"; displaying their opposition to prevailing social institutions and playing rock music, they possessed many cultural continui-

ties with the counter-culture. Since secular change efforts
had failed, many young people were open at this point to
the idea, encouraged by the drug experience, that a supernatural realm existed, and that salvation could now come
from it alone. Robert Ellwood, in his discussion of the Jesus
People, argues that at this point in time, "what was needed
was a religion for a situation of failure".[16] But equally significant was the fact that the youth culture vision of creating
a functioning, meaningful, loving, sharing society appeared
to have been realized in the communalism of the Children
of God or the Unification Church, and other such movements.
Since the way of life seemed so successful, many young people
were prepared to take the movement's beliefs on trust. It
seemed to offer much that the drop-outs and hippies had been
trying to achieve: a stable, warm community; a rejection
of worldly materialism, competition and achievement; a structured setting for the experience of ecstasy or mystical insight.
Since individualism and voluntarism had proven unsuccessful
in attaining any of these things for long, they were often
willing to subordinate their autonomy for the benefits of this
new way of life when it was offered. Not all who joined,
of course, had experienced the hippie culture, but all identified with its aspirations for a more idealistic, spiritual,
and caring way of life, in the context of more personal and
loving social relationships.

THE SOURCES OF SUPPORT FOR THE NEW WORLD-AFFIRMING RELIGIONS

The world-affirming religions also gained members from
the failure and disintegration of the counter-culture. Many
young people faced by their inability to change the world
decided to accommodate to it to a greater or lesser extent.
For some the world-affirming movements were to provide the
recipe or the anodyne for this accommodation. Nonetheless,
these movements did not owe their development to so transient
a phenomenon as the counter culture of the 1960's. Rather,
they have their origins in pervasive features of advanced
capitalist societies.

One source undoubtedly lies in the unequal distribution
of various scarce resources in society: power, status, self-
confidence, personal attractiveness, interpersonal competence,
etc. But rather than transforming the world or creating an
alternative to it, these movements offer recipes, techniques
and knowledge to ensure their possessor an improvement in
his access to these resources. Their main attraction lies
in their provision of facilities for exploring and cultivating
the self within a social structure which is largely taken for
granted. [17]

Movements approximating to this type form part of a progressively unfolding tradition in American culture where individualistic instrumentalism has been a major ideological theme. As a study of best-selling religious literature in America has shown,[18]popular religion over the last hundred years has increasingly stressed the this-worldly, instrumental benefits of religion, for the relief of anxiety, the increase of self-esteem and self-confidence, the improvement of health and welfare. Organized movements offering access to these goals have been a constantly renewed accompaniment to the development of industrial America. In the late 19th century, Christian Science and New Thought focussed prarticularly on the instrumental goals of providing physical healing at a time when medicine had made only limited progress in achieving routine efficacy. But to these traditional magical elements of religion have been added new concerns deriving rather more from the problems produced by an advanced industrial society than from the universal concern for physical health.

North America has tended to lead the world in its support for self-improvement movements, providing a home more conducive to the growth of psychoanalysis, for example, than even its native Europe, and, since then, exporting to the rest of the world a varied range of therapeutic cults and self-exploration and self-improvement systems: primal therapy; Scientology; Pelmanism; encounter groups; Gestalt therapy; sensitivity training; and biofeedback, plus dozens of lesser-known systems and practices. Many of them began to develop soon after the end of the Second World War, and their following until the late 1960's was characteristically middle-aged and even then continued to draw from this age group, in contrast to the world-rejecting movements which were all but exclusively youthful.

Their techniques include massage, marathon group interaction sessions, meditation, physical and mental exercises, and individual confrontation. Their belief systems tend to stress the notion of liberation. The individual will be released from constraints on his thought and behaviour; from conventional ritual; habitual modes of speech or interaction; inhibitions acquired in childhood; repressions of instinctual life; or from a learned reserve.[19] Such movements and their practitioners stress the right of each individual to enjoy life, to experience pleasure,to open him or herself to a broader range of experience, while also offering respite from strain and tension through calming the nervous system, eradicating trauma and pain, and leading the neophyte to bliss, serenity and peace of mind. En route to these desirable states, limitations on his or her human potential will be removed; greater intelligence, personal power and competence, and more effective modes of relating to others, will be released. By casting off constraints and restrictions on his physical, mental and spiritual functioning the individual will not only discover who and what he really is beneath the habits and neuroses, but also more readily achieve all those things which should be possible for one who really is as he now discovers himself to be beneath it all. As a catalogue for the Esalen Institute, a major centre of the human potential movement in California puts it: "Each of us carries within him, buried beneath layers of psychic and physical tensions, the fertile seeds of a new self"[20] Kurt Back, who has studied "sensitivity training" and "encounter" groups, puts it as follows: "The ethos of the groups . . . promotes belief in a new or real identity where the restricting and varying norms of society are less important and the authentic self, that is, what a person would like to believe himself to be, is the only important fact to consider."[21]

While the world-rejecting religions offer an alternative to the anonymity, impersonality, achievement-orientation, individualism, and segmentalization of modern life, the world-affirming religions and their secular counterparts take these things for granted. They offer salvation for those who already have firm attachments to the modern industrial world, or those who, like former American youth radical, Jerry Rubin, now a Human Potential teacher, had decided that there were not viable alternatives to it.[22]

The paradox of the world-rejecting new religions is that, like the radical movements which preceded them, they drew their support primarily from those who had apparently most to gain from the world as it was currently structured. The paradox of the world-affirming new religions is that they offer means of coping with a sense of inadequacy among social groups which are, by the more obvious indicators, among the world's most successful and highly rewarded people.

Support for the world-affirming new religions is thus generated by central characteristics of an advanced capitalist society. In a society where the allocation of rewards depends upon achievement rather than upon inheritance for most of the population, success in terms of status and income and upward social mobility are still highly sought after. But the opportunity for such successes inevitably falls short of aspiration for many, who may therefore be in the market for some assistance in their endeavours, even if the techniques offered have some metaphysical or supernatural overtone.[23] Even the few who are fortunate enough to fulfill their mobility aspirations may be disappointed to discover that rationalization has denuded public institutions of the power to provide most

of those engaged in them with a completely satisfactory identity, forcing them to seek personal meaning and a sense of
worth in their private rather than public lives.

        And here lies a major contradiction of modern Western
life. Success in a rationalized public arena often rests in
large part on behaviour and attitudes derived from the Protestant Ethic and its stress on deferred gratification, the virtue
of hard work, conformity to rules, repression of instinctual
desires, and the reduction of activities to a routine. The
worlds of leisure, play and the private sphere of life generally
tend to rest on behaviour and attitudes quite antithetical
to the Protestant Ethic, this is, on short-run hedonism, the
virtue of pleasure, spontaneity, and the pursuit of excitement.[24] Hence, at the same time as the emergence of a market
for recipes for worldly success, there has emerged a need
for methods of escaping the constraints and inhibitions usually
required in order to achieve that success. Methods are sought
for overcoming the effects of a lengthy socialization into the
Protestant Ethic, in order to explore the private self, to but-
tress a deinstitutionalized identity, and to indulge hedonistic
impulses in an affluent, advanced industrial society in which
consumption has become as much an imperative as production.
A relatively secure and comfortable middle-class now sees
itself as possessing a right to some measure of indulgence
and enjoyment,[25] but faces the problem that the self-control
and repression which enabled it to achieve or to maintain
its secure and comfortable position have often destroyed its
capacity for guilt-free relaxation and pleasure. Hence a
range of movements, some religious and some secular, have
arisen to meet this complex of demands.

                              CONCLUSION

        In this paper I have sought to show that the new reli-
gions provide a source of insight into the wider society both
in terms of the beliefs and practices which they espouse,
and in terms of the social factors which we can identify as
playing a causal role in their emergence and development.

NOTES

1. This paper originally formed part of an Inaugural Lecture delivered by the author at The Queen's University of Belfast on May 3, 1978 under the title "The Rebirth of the Gods?".

2. Robbins, Anthony, Doucas and Curtis, 1976; Judah, 1974; Daner, 1974.

3. See for example, Patrick (with Dulack), 1976; Shupe, Spielmann and Stigall, 1977.

4. Donald Stone, "The Human Potential Movement" in Glock and Bellah (eds), 1976; Maharishi Mahesh Yogi, 1962.

5. Woodrum, 1977.

6. Wallis, 1976.

7. This section draws heavily upon the ideas of Bryan Wilson and Peter Berger, for example: Wilson, 1976 and 1970b; Berger and Berger, 1976; Berger, Berger and Kellner, 1974.

8. Berger, 1965.

9. Wilson, 1970a: 39.

10. Lofland, 1977.

11. Taylor, 1977; Judah, 1974: 165.

12. Robbins, Anthony, Doucas and Curtis, 1976: 122. Colin Campbell, in the following paper, perhaps misunderstands what I am arguing here when he reconceptualizes it as a functionalist argument dependent upon the identification of various needs. My argument is that a set of structural and cultural circumstances created an environment and attitudes which made certain new movements and life-styles particularly attractive. There was no universal need here and there were plenty of functional alternatives. However, within this changed environment movements which offered something that people wanted (not needed) attracted some who were prepared to see a religious movement as meeting those wants.

13. Richard Layard and John King, "Expansion since Robbins" in Martin (ed.) 1969:13.

14. Howard, 1974: 163.

15.   Young, 1971.

16.   Ellwood, 1973:18.

17.   Edward J. Moody, "Magical therapy, an anthropological investigation of contemporary Satanism" in Zaretsky and Leone (eds), 1974: Wallis, 1976; Randall H. Alfred, "The Church of Satan" in Glock and Bellah (eds), 1976.

18.   Schneider and Dornbusch, 1958.

19.   Back, 1972; Wallis, 1976; Stone, op cit; Schur, 1976.

20.   Howard, 1974: 189.

21.   Back, 1972: 34.

22.   Rubin, 1976.

23.   Berger, 1964.

24.   Young, 1974.

25.   Wilson, 1976: 100.

SOME COMMENTS ON THE NEW RELIGIOUS MOVEMENTS, THE NEW SPIRITUALITY AND POST-INDUSTRIAL SOCIETY

Colin Campbell

It is largely by means of functionalist arguments that the rise of the new religious movements is presented as revealing something significant about the nature of contemporary society. Their initial appearance and, in many cases, subsequent rapid growth, is taken as evidence of the deficiency of the prevailing culture and in particular, of the widespread existence of unsatisfied needs; even, in the more ambitious form of this argument, of the universal and ineradicable need for religion itself. At the same time, the most common approach to the problem of explaining these movements is via a framework of assumptions that are nearly always either explicitly or implicitly functionalist. This is to say that the origin or growth of the movements are usually accounted for by pointing to some individual or collective need which they can be said to satisfy. Almost all the main studies refer to such needs as that for community, identity, shelter, release from the pressures of a competitive work ethic and the like in the course of "explaining" the phenomenon. It is therefore important to recognise the deficiencies which are inherent in this form of functionalist statement, a necessary ingredient though it is in any overall explanation, and of the dangers in using such a perspective to deduce something of the character of modern society. In particular, such a perspective has the major disadvantage, by focusing on the functions of membership, of deflecting attention away from the larger cultural context in which these movements flourish and from the specific cultural trends which can be identified as conducive to their growth.

One obvious difficulty with the functionalist perspective surrounds the concept of need itself. To take one example, it is commonly argued that the progressive industrialization and urbanization which has marked modern society has eroded and attenuated traditional forms of community (while also inhibiting the creation of new ones). Consequently, one can account for the appeal of some of the new religious movements to the extent to which they supply a traditional style community with its warm, supportive environment. Briefly, the "need" for community was not being met and these movements provided for it. However, many problems are glossed over in this account. What is this "need for community"? How is it nor-

mally manifest?   What   alternative   expressions can it take?
Since not everyone appears   to have   such a need what determines its existence?   Clearly,   an   explanation   in terms of
the "need" for community raises as many questions as it answers,   and   pushes   the   problem   of   explanation   back   to the
prior question;   what determines the existence of a need for
community, and why was such a need not as prominent in the
fifties as in the sixties?

To   identify a social or cultural item — in this case
a religious movement — as functioning to satisfy a given
need is, in the absence of any consideration of functional
alternatives,   not an explanation of that item's persistence
or growth.   Only if comparative judgements are made and
the superiority of the item's ability to satisfy the need demonstrated could this be true. ² Thus, Wallis, in his discussion
of world-affirming and world-denying movements, identifies
some of the needs which they fulfill as related to the problems
of marginality and the pressure to succeed in a capitalist
society. ³ But such needs do not necessarily lead to the creation of religious or quasi-religious movements, for there are
secular alternatives in both cases.   That there are secular
alternatives to the world-affirming movements is obvious enough
for the line between the religious and the secular is very
hard to draw for this kind of movement, but there are also
alternatives to the world-rejecting movements.   Political religions like communism and nationalism can be regarded in
this light, while there is a form of secular privatization which
parallels the path of religious introversionism.   Thus, to
relate the growth of new religious movements to the creation
of widespread needs such as these, consequent upon the progressive rationalization deemed characteristic of capitalist
society, is to omit a crucial stage in the explanatory process.

It is not difficult to point to useful and valuable functions performed for individuals or groups by a new religious
movement and then posit these functions as in some way
"explanations" of its success.   However, the same exercise
can also be done for the established churches which perform
similarly useful functions for their members as indeed do
many secular organizations.   The crucial point which must
be established is the feature or features of the new movement
which gives it a distinct advantage over its conventionally
religious and secular rivals in the satisfaction of this need,
and this can only be established by means of the kind of
comparative study of old and new movements which is rarely
undertaken.

Most of the functional explanations which have been
presented to account for the growth of the new religious move-

ments are those which have long been proffered with respect
to the established churches and sects and indeed for social
movements in general. These are the theories of relative
deprivation, of compensation or consolation for failure or
alternatively the facilitation of success, together with the
need for identity and community. [4] Such theories are indeed
applicable for they do help to explain why people join organizations, but they are largely non-discriminatory and, in
particular do not explain why people should join new religious organizations. The question, which is most likely
to lead to a better understanding of modern society as a whole
via an examination of the new religious movements, is not
so much why people join as why they find their meaning-
systems plausible. For only when this is the case can such
movements actually be "available" to recruits and yet for
this to be true such recruits must already be attuned to the
particular movements' beliefs and values.

Daniel Bell has written "when religion declines, cults
appear."[5] The logic underlying this claim would appear to
be functionalist; that is, cults are seen as arising to satisfy
those individual and social needs which the decline of religion
has left unsatisfied. This "nature abhors a vacuum" thesis
is widely adopted. Needleman, for example, regards the
growth of the new religions as "arising to satisfy the lack
in our society of a place where young people can be exposed
to transcendent ideas in a way that allows them time and
space for pondering and critical reflection."[6] However, arguments which present the new religious movements as direct
functional alternatives to established religion do pose problems.
In the first place, if the experience of Britain and America
is considered the two processes could not be said to have
proceeded in parallel with a decline in orthodox religiosity
being matched by a rise in cults or cult-like movements.
Instead while there has been a steady decline in support
for orthodox religion throughout the twentieth century, the
rise of the cults has only really dated from the 1960's. Secondly, it follows from this that the defectors from the established churches are not the same people as those who have
moved to join the cults, even though some of them may have
had similar social backgrounds: the distance of a generation
would appear to separate them. [8] Thirdly, the number of
people involved are not equal in that the extent to which
there has been a growth of cults does not match the degree
to which disaffiliation from orthodox religion has progressed.
While the Roman Catholic Church and the main Protestant
denominations, not to mention the Church of England, have
all estimated their memberships in the hundreds of thousands
even the most successful cults and quasi-religious movements
rarely estimate their numbers in much more than tens of thou-

sands. Thus, even when allowance is made for the difficulties involved in estimating membership and support for these movements it would seem that the growth of new religions does not approximate to the shortfall in membership of the established churches. Finally the very difference between the cults and the churches seem to argue against the functional alternatives thesis. After all, if the cults are fulfilling the same needs the churches formerly fulfilled why are the cults so different in their organization, beliefs and practices? Indeed, if they are fulfilling the same needs why have the churches declined? Clearly the rise of the cults can only be explained if one assumes that they are satisfying needs not met by established religion. Alternatively, one can assume that the churches have long since ceased to satisfy these needs and that the new religions have arisen in consequence. This argument, however, requires that there should have been an inter-regnum when needs were left unsatisfied, an assumption which appears equally destructive to the functionalist thesis.

Such considerations point to the rejection of the view that cults arise to meet a general unfulfilled religious need and are hence direct functional alternatives to the churches. That some of the cults fulfill needs for their members which are similar to those which the churches have traditionally satisfied is very probable but this is not to say that the decline in the churches and the growth of cults is to be understood in these terms. The decline of the churches may, however, be seen as a necessary rather than a sufficient condition for the growth of the cults. On this view the decline of established religion helped to remove a major constraint against cult growth so that there was no longer any obstacle to the spread of heterodoxy or alternatively in the sense that the decay of coherent theologies made fresh material available for the construction of syncretic cultic teachings. This perspective would seem to fit the known facts a little better as the time-lag between the decline of religion and the rise of cults ceases to be a problem. However, it does mean that other factors have to be introduced to account for the growth of cults, ones which are identified as the necessary conditions.

THE NEW SPIRITUALITY

Studies of new religious movements have typically focused upon their teachings, practices and patterns of authority and recruitment. Such a focus naturally leads to a better

understanding of the movements themselves but it is doubtful
if it is capable, by itself, of generating a satisfactory explanation of their origin and growth.   This can only be a-
chieved if attention is directed away from internal features
and towards the wider social and cultural environment.
Although this fact is generally recognised and most studies
of these movements include some reference to such postulated
societal characteristics as secularization, alienation,or anomie,
the link between these and the growth of the movements is
either left unspecified or is sketched in the vaguest terms.
Indeed, the brief comments made concerning the external
factors contributing to the growth of the new religious movements usually contrast very sharply with the extended and
detailed discussion accorded to the internal ones.

One of the principal reasons for this would appear to
be the lack of a pertinent level of analysis intermediate between that of the movement itself (clearly the most convenient
unit of study) and society at large.   One necessary step in
bridging this gap is to recognize that specific religious movements are themselves merely part of a larger and more diffuse
phenomenon; one which can in turn be related to general
social or cultural conditions.   This more diffuse phenomenon
is predominantly cultural and is best considered as an ethos
or cluster of values and beliefs which accords a general place
to spirituality.   The evidence for the existence of such an
ethos is found in the varied manifestations of the new religiosity which have appeared in recent years.   This greater
preparedness to positively evaluate the spiritual, mystic
and occult has occurred among a much larger section of the
population than can be counted as members of the new religious
movements proper.   Whereas the latter constitute only a tiny
minority of the population, the former are a sizeable proportion.

The contrast between the figures for attendance at places
of worship and participation in religious activity on the one
hand, and the figures for general religious and spiritual belief
on the other, suggests a sizeable number of people sympathetic-
ally disposed towards some form of spirituality but not participating members of any particular church.   It is the emergence
of this population which is the critical and necessary condition
for the creation of the new religious movements.   They might
perhaps be best envisaged as a population of incipient seekers.
Certainly there is little evidence that these non-church-goers
accept orthodox religious doctrines to any degree; they are
not, in that sense, "believers".   On the other hand, there
is evidence of high levels of unorthodox religious and metaphysical beliefs and of interest in spiritual matters, although
little evidence of the acceptance of coherent belief-systems.

An explanation consonant with these observations would be
that there has been a major shift in recent decades, not so
much from belief to unbelief as from belief to seekership[9].
That is, away from any commitment to doctrine and dogma
towards a high valuation of individual intellectual growth
and the pursuit for truth coupled with a preparedness to
believe in almost any alternative or occult teaching. Wuthnow's
research in America seems to endorse this view and his survey
of readers of Psychology Today, in particular, indicated how
extensive was the phenomenon of people interested in "religious questions" but not actively involved with or committed
to any religious organization.[10] These people Wuthnow names
"experimentalists" and provides evidence of their sympathetic
attitude towards the new religious movements. Here, then,
is the factor which is taken for granted in most explanations
of the new religious movements, the existence of a sympathetic
population who already hold beliefs and attitudes which pre-
dispose them towards acceptance of the distinctive teachings
of the individual sects or cults.

The evidence for such a population in Britain is less
clear-cut, but if the two beliefs which Wuthnow identifies
as most characteristic of experimentalists are considered --
belief in God as an impersonal force, a "something more",
and belief in reincarnation -- there is data which suggests
that a similar trend is discernible here. Over the past
two decades opinion polls have consistently revealed that
a declining proportion of the British population adhere to
such conventional items of the Christian creed as belief in
the devil, hell, life after death or that Jesus Christ was
the Son of God. However, in contrast, belief in an impersonal
God and reincarnation has actually become more widespread.
The number of people who give a positive answer to the
simple question "Do you believe in God?" has only declined
slightly in recent years (from 77% to 72% between 1968 and
1975 according to Gallup) yet when this belief is sub-divided
into belief in a personal God and belief in "some sort of
spirit, a life force" it can be seen that there has been a
rise in the latter at the expense of the former. Between 1957
and 1979 belief in a personal God fell from 41% of the population to 35% while belief in some sort of spirit has risen from
37% to 41%. At the same time, belief in reincarnation has
been growing steadily, from 18% of the population in 1968
to 22% in 1978 and 28% in 1979.[11]

Further evidence that there are high levels of non-
natural belief in the population despite the continuing decline
of Christian beliefs can be found in a national survey of religious attitudes of young people carried out in 1978.[12] While
this showed that 25% of fourteen to eighteen year olds believed

that God was merely a "force for good" compared with 18%
who believed in a "personal God who can be known", it also
showed that 25% believed in reincarnation, 41% in ghosts and
and spirits, and 50% in UFO's. These results confirm those
of an earlier and less structured inquiry into young people's
beliefs carried out by Bernice Martin and Ronald Pluck on
behalf of the Church of England General Synod Board of Education.[13] In their interviews they also found that while there
was much rejection of Bible literalism and orthodox doctrine
there was a widespread belief in survival and considerable
acceptance of superstition and psychic and occult beliefs.
Insofar as there was any discernible pattern to these it
was that they were associated with an "emphasis upon open-
mindedness, individuality and the private nature of belief". [20]
When this observation is linked with the fact that many of
the young people also seemed to believe in the polymorphous
nature of religious truth,[15] it can be seen that there are
grounds for claiming that Troeltsch's Spiritual and Mystical
religion is finding favour in contemporary society. [16]

STUDENTS, SPIRITUALITY AND POST-INDUSTRIAL SOCIETY

    Little is known about this growing population of seekers
except that they are generally young (under thirty-five),
not fully settled into either marriage or a career, predominantly middle-class and frequently have been or still are involved
in some form of higher education.[17] This latter point is perhaps
the most important, for it has long been assumed that education
was one of the main channels of rationalization and hence
indirectly of secularization. Certainly the educated young
of the thirties, forties and fifties were more, rather than
less, secular in their outlook than their parents. Bryan
Wilson has attempted to explain this new anomaly by suggesting that students are insulated from the larger society and
thus less exposed to the forces of secularization.[18] This, however, only applies if secularization is taken to refer to social
processes such as the increasing specialization of labour or
bureaucratization rather than cultural ones. Even here, of
course, the proponents of the multiversity thesis would wish
to take issue with Wilson's claim. [19]

    It is true, of course, that students are, if not "insulated"
from the larger society, at least freer than most people from
the constraints and obligations of everyday life. Usually
newly broken from the primary ties of family and community,
the student is at that stage of life of greatest independence
before the pressures of a family of procreation, a work-place
and neighbourhood become experienced. At the same time,

the role of student carries with it the obligation of inquiry and the expectation of personal intellectual growth and under-standing. It is easy to see how this fits with the concept of seekership. Nonetheless, it has largely been assumed that although the role of student involves an emphasis upon ideal-ism, personal inquiry and intellectual growth, their exposure would be to intellectual systems which stressed rationality and empiricism. Thus it is that the growth of theoretical knowledge in general and the extension of further education to larger sections of the population has been taken to favour the process of rationalization and hence of secularization. But, though this may well be true of the natural sciences, it is doubtful if it applies to the arts, humanities or social sciences in the same way.

It is necessary to distinguish between two different senses of the term "rationalization", the one referring to the process whereby any set of cultural symbols is rendered more coherent, systematic and subsumed under a higher order princi-pal; the other, the process whereby the values of rationality, technical efficiency and calculability are introduced into areas formerly governed by traditional or intuitive values. Rational-ization in this second sense clearly favours secularization since both traditional and revealed sources of legitimation are forced to give way but rationalization in the first sense máy occur in relation to systems of thought such as surrealism or existentialism which enthrone feeling, will, or imagination, thus having the effect of making non-rational criteria more rather than less powerful cultural forces. Indeed, the one form of rationalization may actually promote the other as for example, in the film industry where the rationalization of production and distribution has proceeded hand-in-hand with the further exploitation of sex, horror and fantasy. A similar trend can be said to have occurred in higher educa-tion in the sixties where the institutions and procedures were rationalized but where the content of the syllabi came more and more to include material from intellectual traditions (such as neo-Freudianism and romanticism) which do not enthrone rationality and efficiency. It is for this reason that it cannot simply be assumed that rationalization will bring secularization in its wake. It may do so, but then it may also serve to strengthen the superstitious, esoteric, spiritual and mystical tendencies in modern culture.

This is, in fact, all the more likely given the shifting focus of economic and commercial concern in contemporary society from the satisfaction of physical wants through consum-er goods to the fulfilment of expressive needs via cultural goods and personal services. Although the satisfaction of these needs will no doubt become ever more rationalized, our culture may gradually become more and more dominated by products which reflect an expressive rather than a cognitive logic.[20]

Examination of the new religious movements has helped to demonstrate how mistaken it is to assume, as so many nineteenth-century intellectuals did, that a secular culture that was independent of religion would automatically be hostile towards it, or that the freeing of areas of culture from religious dominance would necessarily mean their submission to rational criteria. That view was based on a particular model of the relationship betwen the two, in which church religion was opposed by an especially materialistic science. But neither religion nor secular culture is all of a piece, and the range of relationships is therefore much wider than this single, over-emphasised, example. In particular, secular culture is much broader than merely the natural sciences and includes spheres, such as aesthetics and metaphysics where emotion and intuition may receive a greater emphasis than reason. The currency of the term the "Two Cultures" is testimony to the general recognition of this fact. As long as the prestige of science remained high and could easily be associated with idealistic longings for a better world, the non-scientific or "literary" culture (to use C.P. Snow's term) was overshadowed and on the defensive. But when doubts and suspicions over the anti-life possibilities of scientific advance became more widespread in the late nineteen-fifties and early sixties, the other culture was able to come into its own. This intuitive and artistic culture is deeply embedded in our civilization and is by no means diminishing in power and influence. It is strongly entrenched in both the commercial and the fine arts and in education, and in the more humanistic social and behavioral sciences, sectors which expand in periods of consumer boom such as the sixties and which seem likely to be prominent in the personal-service dominated economy of the post-industrial society. Secularization will no doubt continue as a general social process with the churches continuing to lose members as well as power and influence. But culturally the future may well witness a conflict between the secular, scientific world-view and a generalised spiritual-mystical religion, with the latter continuing to spawn new religious movements.

NOTES

1. See, for examples, the summary review of work on the new religions in Robbins, Anthony and Richardson, 1978, together with the several contributions to this volume, especially those of Nordquist, Wallis and Whitworth.

2. For an elaboration of this point and an elucidation of the conditions which have to be met before a functionalist account can become an explanation, see C. Hempel, "The Logic of Functional Analysis" in Gross, 1959: 271-307.

3. Roy Wallis, "The New Religions as Social Indicators" in this volume.

4. For an examination of some of these theories in relation to both secular and religious movements, see Wallis, 1979.

5. Bell, 1971.

6. Needleman, 1971.

7. For data on the decline of the churches in Britain see Currie, Gilbert and Horsley, 1977.

8. Wuthnow, 1976a.

9. On the social role of the seeker and the concept of seekership see Lofland and Stark, 1965; Campbell, Colin " The Cult, the Cultic Milieu and Secularization" in Hill (ed), 1972: 119-136; and Balch and Taylor, 1977.

10. Wuthnow and Glock, 1974; and Wuthnow, 1978.

11. These figures are from Gallup, 1976, with the exception of the figures for 1979 which were kindly supplied by Social Surveys (Gallup Poll) Ltd.

12. Bible Society, 1978.

13. Martin and Pluck, 1977.

14. Ibid. p.49.

15. Ibid. p.21.

16. Campbell, 1978.

17. It is interesting to note in this respect that the highest rates of reported religious experience are found among graduate students. See Hay and Morisy, 1978: 263.

18.   Wilson, 1976:39ff.

19.   See, for example, the hypothesis adopted by Scott and El-Assal, 1969.

20.   This view is one advanced forcefully in Bell, 1976.

CONTEMPORARY RELIGIOUS FERMENT
AND MORAL AMBIGUITY

Dick Anthony
Thomas Robbins

ABSTRACT

The current American religious ferment reflects the increasingly problematic nature of moral meanings in American
society. Today's religious movements bifurcate sharply into
"eastern" mystical movements and evangelical Christian(and qua-
si-Christian) groups, which embody different strategies in dealing
with a morally ambiguous milieu.The core concepts of popular "eastern" movements and quasi-religious therapeutic systems acknowledge
the problematic nature of moral evaluations. Assumptions concerning the oneness of the universe, the illusory nature of the
phenomenal world, and the "law of karma" imply the relativity
of all moral distinctions and the impossibility of judging actions by fixed and absolute rules. Evangelical and "Jesus
movement" groups, on the other hand, resurrect traditional
moral absolutism. Core concepts such as a transcendent God,
unconditioned free will, and moral rules, which unambiguously
divided humanity into sinners and the saved are elaborated
into a viewpoint which regards the surrounding morally corrupt
milieu as on the brink of apocalypse. The current resurgence
of fundamentalism and evangelicism is viewed as a traditionalist response to moral ambiguity which attempts to re-constitute
unambiguous moral meanings as a normative context for daily
living.

INTRODUCTION

The emergence of deviant religious movements has been
analyzed in terms of a crisis of moral meanings in which a
society's "moral boundaries" are becoming indistinct (Erikson,
1966; Tiryakian, 1967; Rossel, 1970).[1] We contend that this
analysis can be fruitfully applied to the current proliferation
of religious movements, with particular attention to "eastern"
cults (e.g., Guru Maharaj-ji, Meher Baba) and to the sharply
contrasting "Jesus movement" and evangelical groups. Both
types of groups are responding to a situation in which moral
meanings are increasingly problematic. The "monistic" theodicies of current "eastern" movements contain clearly relativistic

elements which implicitly acknowledge the problematic nature of situated moral meanings. Resurgent evangelicism and fundamentalism can be viewed as a counterreaction to recent relativistic tendencies and a response to the deepening moral ambiguity in terms of a strident reaffirmation of traditional dualistic moral absolutism.

THE TRADITION OF DUALISTIC MORAL ABSOLUTISM

Traditional biblical morality has been a negativistic morality expressed in fixed negative injunctions prohibiting specified acts. Such injunctions, however, have a latent "permissive" dimension; they indirectly legitimate "residual" acts not expressly prohibited, which now become "good" qua not proscribed. But such residual legitimating processes presuppose fixed and absolute rules to clarify the "boundaries" between prohibited ("bad") and "not bad" behaviour; rules must be unambiguous and prohibited acts must be clearly and restrictively defined. Thus, if "theft" is narrowly and clearly defined, then "residual" social inequality, exploitation, profiteering, price-fixing, etc., are "good" qua not-proscribed.

Negativistic morality has been tied traditionally to absolutistic morality; "Western societies became firmly committed to an absolutist world view, and. . .an absolutistic conception of morality," which "has always remained dominant and has been very strong in certain societies since its great resurgence in the Protestant Reformation" (Douglas, 1970A:20). Social actions have been viewed as objectively either conforming or deviant (Douglas, 1971). The spiritually grounded assumption of "free will" and the individual's presumed ability to control his actions has enabled moral evaluation of others to be made with exclusive reference to putatively absolute rules.

The Americanized protestant ethic or American success ethic of competitive individualism represents a variant of traditional dualistic moral absolutism. As Douglas has noted, the concepts of "success" and "failure" are morally meaningful categories to middle class Americans (Douglas, 1970A:6-7) from which holistic evaluations of human worth can be inferred (Williams, 1970: 454-455). What is crucial here is that intentionality is being inferred from external actions or consequences (e.g. material wealth). The assumption of "equal opportunity", a secular socioeconomic counterpart of "free will", precludes the subtleties of consciousness and motivation as well as variations in "external" circumstances from presenting "extenuating" circumstances for "failure". Moral absolutism is voluntaristic; its theistic (fundamentalist) and secular (competitive individualist) forms both presuppose assumptions of "free will" and "equal opportunity", which have operated as legitimating premises for American capitalism (Glock, 1972).

DECLINE OF MORAL ABSOLUTISM

Today, however, consensual moral absolutism is visibly declining as moral meanings become increasingly problematic in an ideologically pluralistic society (Douglas, 1970A; 1971). Moral meanings and rules are increasingly "situationally problematic" in the sense that the situated application of deviant labels is increasingly problematic, i.e. the classification of events as "crime", "drug use", "racism", "terrorism", "sex perversion", etc., is becoming increasingly subject to debate and controversy.

While deviant labels may have always been "situationally problematic" in terms of their concrete applications, their problematic and arguable quality has now become increasingly self-evident. As individuals become increasingly aware of pervading moral pluralism, many are compelled to recognize that "in the current morality, one man's crime is another man's worthy cause" (Royster, 1974:257). The dominant theoretical frameworks in the sociology of "deviance" (labeling theory, ethnomethodology, the "new criminology") reflect pervasive relativism by highlighting "the political and historical relativity of the general concept of crime" (Taylor and Taylor, 1973:8).[2]

Moral meanings may be said to be increasingly problematic with respect to imputing blame and guilt. Intentionality is becoming an increasingly problematic property of human experience. The emergence of the concepts of sociological and psychological determinism has led to "the abandonment of the traditional concept of responsibility in American law" such that "increasingly, however, in American courtrooms, judges and juries are experiencing difficulty in assigning responsibility to those who either acknowledge and/or have been found guilty of committing a crime" (Glock, 1972:14). In the context of a bureaucratic and impersonal society, the "free will" assumption loses its "plausibility structure"; people do not feel "autonomous" and masterful (Glock and Piazza, 1978; Wuthnow, 1976b). The erosion of "free will" orientations, however, undermines the basis of dualistic moral absolutism. Without being able to assume that "it might have been otherwise", there is no psychological basis for evaluating actions by absolute rules (Douglas, 1970A). Moral judgements are thus increasingly viewed as relative to the factors which constrain social action. The decline of a priori absolutist voluntarism thus enhances moral ambiguity and contributes to contemporary spiritual flux (Glock, 1976).

The growth of moral ambiguity and pluralism is not entirely a matter of expanding "permissiveness". Many formerly legitimate arrangements now come under moral scrutiny. When negative injunctions are relativized by the multiplication of

"extenuating circumstances" and cease to be absolute, the
implicit legitimation of "residual" behavior falling clearly outside the scope of fixed taboos breaks down. As the "boundaries" of rules become uncertain, what is clearly legitimate
as well as what is clearly "wrong" becomes harder to specify,
and any act becomes a potential recipient of deviant stigma.
Military and police violence, "brainwashing", social inequality,
"institutional racism", sexual discrimination in athletic programs or in hiring airline stewardesses, corporate pricing
practices. . .all enter the population of potentially deviant
acts. Moral judgements are increasingly "up for grabs."

A number of factors have contributed to the erosion of
dualistic moral absolutism in America. The emergence of a mass
consumption of economy and complementary hedonistic and "permissive" milieu encourages the violation of traditional moral
absolutes regarding sex, drugs, alcohol, and frugality. The
development of bureaucratic regulation of the economy entails
a complex web of rules and hierarchical authority relations
which violate the fate control assumptions integral to the traditional ethic. The diffusion of scientific and social scientific
perspectives "effectively deny that human destiny is entirely
either in man's or God's control" (Glock, 1976:361). Finally,
the post-Vietnam undermining of the manichean "cold war"
meaning system, which contributed to post-World War II moral
solidarity in America (Vidich, 1975), has helped create a climate of politico-moral ambiguity to which certain anti-communist millenarian sects are making a direct and vehement response (Anthony and Robbins, 1978; Robbins, et al, 1976).

In our view, the disintegration of traditional dualistic
moral absolutism and the associated ethos of personal responsibility and fate control underlies much of the spiritual flux of
the past decade. We will argue that "monistic" mystical world-
views and "dualistic" evangelical outlooks embody contrasting
responses to deepening moral ambiguity.

MONISTIC MYSTICISM AND MORAL RULES

"Eastern" mystical movements have been prominent in
America for over a decade (Needleman, 1970; Cox, 1977; King,
1970; Robbins and Anthony, 1972). These movements have a
generally "monistic" conceptual apparatus stressing the illusory
nature of conventional perception (maya) which veils the latent
oneness of the universe. Robert Bellah writes:

A central belief shared by oriental religions and
diffused widely outside them is important because
of how sharply it contrasts with established American. views. This is the belief in the unity of all

being. Our separate selves, according to Buddhism,
Hinduism and their offshoots, are not ultimately
real. Philosophical Hinduism and Mahayana Buddhism reject dualism. For them ultimately, there is
no difference between myself and yourself and this
river and that mountain. We are all one and the
conflict between us is therefore illusory. (Bellah,
1976:347). [3]

Most devotees of eastern movements also affirm reincarnation and the associated notion of karma in which "the world
is viewed as a completely connected and self-contained cosmos
of ethical retribution. Guilt and merit within this world are
unfailingly compensated by fate in the successive lives of the
soul" (Weber, 1964:145). The goal of spiritual endeavor is to
realize one's true self as an emanation of universal spiritual
consciousness. Maya, or the veil of illusion, "prevents man
from nearing the Lord, i.e. realizing his own self. By working
out one's karma alone, according to the law of one's own being, this veil can be rent and the end accomplished" (Prabhavanda, 1965:107).

While monistic systems are most fully elaborated in some
oriental mystical sects, monistic elements are implicit in many
therapeutic movements such as EST, Arica, Scientology and human potential grops (Robbins, et al., 1978) which stress the
primacy of inner realization and self-actualization. The quasi-
monistic "subjectivism" of such groups has contributed to the
application to them of the label "narcissist" (Schur, 1976;
Marin, 1975) which has also been applied to oriental mystical
groups (Cox, 1977).

Karma and the associated ideas of maya, the oneness of
reality, the immanence of the Godhead, the eventual attainment
of union with "reality" and a consequent escape from the
wheel of rebirths, comprise a viewpoint which Weber considers
one of the two rational theodicies (Weber, 1964:138-150). The
other fundamental rational theodicy is the Judaeo-Christian-
Islamic conception of a radically transcendent deity who is
fundamentally separate from the world, which he confronts as
his creation and to which he "legislates" by revealing his divine commandments. [4] This latter response to the problem of
meaning embodies a basis for moral absolutism inhering in the
universal absolute validity of God's commandments. The monistic theodicy, we will argue below, implies a qualified moral
relativism and is thus increasingly relevant to increasing
moral ambiguity in America.

If "all is oneness", all distinctions and dualities are
relative; "good" and "bad" valuations, like pleasure/pain or

self/other distinctions lack ultimate metaphysical reality. These distinctions must be transcended in the process of spiritual awakening. This perspective is illustrated by the following excerpt from Yogananda's Autobiography of a Yogi, the popularity of which is itself part of the oriental mystical vogue. Yogananda is relating a discourse on the true meaning of "eating the forbidden fruit" in Genesis as a descent into distorted dualistic perception:

> The knowledge of "good and evil", promised Eve by the "serpent", refers to the dualistic and oppositional experiences that mortals under maya must undergo. . .Falling into delusion through misuse of his feeling and reason. . .man relinquishes his right to enter the heavenly garden of divine self-sufficiency. The personal responsibility of every human being is to restore his. . .dual nature to a unified harmony or Eden (Yogananda, 1973:198).

Absolutistic distinctions between "good" and "evil" are thus viewed as qualities of illusion which characterize the dualistic consciousness of the non-enlightened. There is, thus, a sense in which "one is not essentially an ethical being:ethics belong to the world in which one is momentarily lodged; it does not penetrate to the soul" (Danto, 1972:39). Meher Baba, who has a substantial American following (Anthony and Robbins, 1974) has written:

> Like other opposites of experience, good and evil are also in a sense opposites which have to be withstood and transcended. One has to rise above the duality of good and evil and accept life in its totality, in which they appear as abstractions. Life is to be seen and lived in its indivisible integrity (Meher Baba, 1971:74).

It is not our intention to imply that current eastern mystical movements are totally "amoral" in the sense of lacking rule for guidance in everyday life. The Hare Krishna movement, for example, imposes numerous rules on followers, whose lives are stringently disciplined and regimented (Snelling and Whitley, 1972). However, in a monistic context rules are not usually articulated in terms of moral obligation (e.g. of God's creations to the creator); rather rules in a monistic context have an essentially instrumental significance in attaining the spiritual goals which embody the moral consensus of the group. The monistic conception of rules as instrumental and non-absolute is clearly indicated by the following resumé of a talk given by Dr. Allen Cohen at Meher Baba House in New York City in the fall of 1972:[5]

There is no inherent moral order based on fixed
codes. It is not what one does which is important
but why one does it. The ultimate implications of
an act are difficult to discern in the immediate
situation. Conventional rules cannot be applied to
those who are in obedience to a spiritual master.
The role of the master is to be able to be specifically relevant to each individual's life. What is
"good" is what helps to liberate one. "Evil" is what
holds one down, what holds one's identity to that
which is more limited. One can "get imprisoned in
the good". Meher Baba says taking refuge in "the
prison of the good" is easier than really following
God. Baba is not looking for you to make a little
bulletin board with gold stars. Nevertheless, since
one doesn't really know the ultimate spiritual significance of one's actions, one is better off following
the rules pertaining to self-control and selfless behaviour and practical wisdom based on conscience
and Baba's teachings.[6]

Moral rules in a monistic context are thus viewed as relative: relative to unique situations, relative to the inner development of consciousness, and relative to the accumulated
karma of past actions. According to Swami Prabhavananda,
"The fortunes that await a man after death depend upon his
moral quality, and that in turn depends upon his deeds; yet
the 'deeds' referred to are not wholly the deeds done in the
present life, but also the deeds done in all past lives." (Prabhavananda, 1964:59). Each "deed" perpetrated by an actor "is
not a product merely of the action that precedes it; rather it
is the product of a state of moral character which itself is
the cumulative product of all past deeds" (Prabhavananda,
1964:59). The moral significance of a given act is relative to
the accumulated karma of past life-times. The same act may
thus have different moral meanings for individuals with different karmic backgrounds. Fixed rules cannot be applied to
specific acts in a given life-time because present actions continue the commitments of past incarnations. Actions which may
appear deviant in the context of the immediate situation or
life-time may nevertheless reflect "karmic necessity". A follower
of Meher Baba, interviewed by one of the authors, stated:

There are certain things that people have to work
out, and irregardless of social codes, or things
that you and I may accept as being moral or im-
moral or whatever, Baba's going to have somebody
work out that karma. They're going to work it out
regardless of what people think about it. And this
is why I can't get into a condemnation trip, because
I really believe that karma exists.

The "deeds" which produce karma do not refer exclusively to external physical action, "but also every thought, feeling, impulse, imagination" (Prabhavananda, 1964:59). Salvation in a monistic context is usually conceived in terms of "realization" or "enlightenment" because, "bad karma arises from ignorance, not perversity. . .one remains a prisoner in the net of illusion because one has not been thinking the right thoughts -- has not gained the proper knowledge. . . ." (Braden, 1967:67). The emphasis thus shifts from external action to inner consciousness. From a monistic standpoint, "experiences are determined by one's underlying state of consciousness and moral judgements must be relative to the actor's state of consciousness" (Anthony et al., 1977:882).

As one "Baba-Lover" told one of the authors:

I don't believe that any act is good or bad in itself. It's what's behind the act, the consciousness behind the act. . .a conscious being does nothing "right" or "wrong", a conscious being just does.[7]

In a published account of the attitudes of followers of Guru Maharaji, a devotee (Messer, 1976) notes the disintegration of commitment to fixed absolute rules, which is replaced by a generalized "loving" impulse; "a fixed moral code becomes a desire to respond to the internal cues without reference to any existing standard. . .there is no pool of guilt which is evoked by wrongdoing" (Messer, 1976:7). Fixed notions of right and wrong "are simply replaced by a minute-to-minute sense that one is being instructed constantly and the notion of an unchanging code of behaviour fades into the background. The only fixed reference becomes the meditation itself" (Messer, 1974:10).

Eastern groups' lack of emphasis on fixed moral rules is also indicated in a recent study of ritual patterns among "new" youth cultures religious groups (Bird, 1975). In a study of a number of primarily eastern religious groups (e.g., Sri Chinmoy, Nicheren Shoshu, Integral Yoga) the researcher observed "with one notable exception (a Catholic Pentecostal group), almost all of these groups lack any kind of rites for confession, penance, or atonement" (Bird, 1975:6).[8] In western religions, confessional rites have functioned "as a means of reinforcing commitment to specific moral conceptions by which adherents acknowledged their moral accountability and responsibility for transforming their lives and world in relation to a moral code or covenants" (Bird, 1975:7). The conspicuous absence of confessional rituals in Bird's sample of (primarily eastern) groups indicated that "these movements generally place very little emphasis on any kind of established moral code or covenant" (Bird, 1975:6).[9]

In our view, elaborated monistic meaning systems represent systematizations of pervasive relativistic and subjectivistic elements in cultural modernism and a conversion of these elements into rational theodicies.

THE TRADITIONALIST REACTION

At present monistic movements appear in some respects to be less dynamic and influential than radically contrasting dualistic groups. The "Jesus movement" of the 1970's, the growing conservative churches, pentecostal and charismatic movements, evangelical revivals, and the controversial "moonies" all embody spiritual ideologies characterized by sharp ethical dualism and moral absolutism. These groups are becoming increasingly strident and politicized in part as a reaction against modernist relativist, secularist and "permissive" tendencies (Lorentzen, 1980; Dabney, 1980).[10]

Relativistic tendencies in modern moral culture run clearly counter to the dominant tradition of moral absolutism in America (Douglas, 1970A). The conflict of present relativistic tendencies with traditional moral absolutism poses a problem for many persons who find it increasingly difficult to "make moral sense" out of an increasingly pluralistic moral universe. This problem may be particularly acute among young people whose familial socialization may have been more absolutistic and definitely "principled" with respect to moral norms being urged than the "tolerant", relativistic and accommodative public morality encountered in adolescence and young adulthood.

There is some evidence that neo-fundamental "Jesus" movements appeal to young people from different social backgrounds and with different social attitudes than those attracted to relativistic eastern movements. Several studies have indicated that young persons from rural and conservative christian backgrounds are disproportionately represented among "Jesus freaks" (Harder and Richardson, 1972; Robbins, 1973; Gordon, 1974).[11] Recent survey findings indicate that persons involved in "eastern" groups in the San Francisco Bay area tend to come from more educated, culturally sophisticated and socially privileged backgrounds than persons involved in neo-christian groups (Wuthnow, 1976a; 1978). Persons involved in eastern groups also tend to be more politically liberal and more sympathetic to "counter-cultural values" regarding drugs, sexual experimentation and other matters than persons involved in christian groups (Wuthnow, 1976a). In contrast, persons experimenting in neo-christian groups tend to be relatively conservative and opposed to non-conventional life-styles; they are less socially privileged and educated than persons involved in eastern groups.

Miller and Swanson (1958) have demonstrated that children
from contemporary lower middle and upper lower class families
are socialized in a traditional manner which emphasizes invariant moral principles and strict control of sensual impulses.
On the other hand, children from middle and upper middle
class families are socialized in ways which inculcate a qualified moral relativism. Their parents emphasize sensitivity to
shifting moral absolutes as a moral guide. A traditional emphasis upon the training of children in invariant moral absolutes has also persisted in rural entrepreneurial families. Urban families and families whose breadwinners work in bureaucratic settings, however, tend to emphasize relativistic, other-
directed patterns of impulse control. It seems likely, then,
that some people who enter the neo-evangelical groups are re-
solving an adolescent crisis of moral ambiguity by resurrecting
moral patterns emphasized in childhood. Young persons entering
eastern groups and "consciousness", on the other hand, may
be embracing meaning systems which extend and elaborate into
a rational theodicy the relativistic moral emphasis of their
childhoods.

It is our contention that the current resurgence of fundamentalism, including the "Jesus movement" (Adams and Fox,
1972; Enroth, et al., 1972; Ellwood, 1973; Balswick, 1974), the
Catholic Pentecostal or Charismatic Renewal movement (Harrison, 1974; McGuire, 1975) and the current growth of established fundamentalist groups (Kelly, 1972; Bibby and Brinker-
hoff, 1973), represents in part a neo-traditionalist solution to
the problem of moral transition facing individuals who must
crystallize or sustain personal identities in a morally ambiguous milieu. As Adams and Fox have argued, with regard to
"Jesus freaks":

> Not only does commitment to Jesus preserve childhood
> morality with its absolutistic definitions of right
> and wrong, but it provides an ideology based on
> personal, internal and, for the most part, unex-
> plainable experience rather than on critical, ra-
> tional, or realistic analysis. Indeed, the ideology
> is unchallengeable and thereby not available for
> analysis by the uninitiated (Adams and Fox, 1972:
> 53).

The ideology of the Jesus movement thus not only stridently affirms moral absolutism, but also provides legitimating
mystiques which are not susceptible to rational inquiry and
criticism. The Bible is viewed by Jesus converts as the "inerrant Word of God" and thus "becomes a means of great security
for the young Jesus person"; moreover, "since the believer has

reached his conclusions about Biblical authority through a subjective experience with Jesus, no amount of rational attack upon the authenticity of scripture is going to shake his confidence in its authority" (Balswick, 1974:364).

Although situated interpretations of scripture may be constructed through social interaction such that Biblical meanings
may still be viewed as "situationally problematic" from the
standpoint of the observer, these meanings are viewed as absolute by converts and interpretations are assumed to be objectively correct derivations from absolute biblical norms. This
is very different from the interpretive context of the Meher
Baba movement (Robbins, 1973) in which situated moral meanings are explicitly identified as problematic and relative, and
absolutistic judgements for specific situations are rejected. In
a study of California Jesus followers in the early seventies,
Robbins (1973) identifies Berkeley Jesus followers' "apparent
fixation on the literal word of the Bible, i.e., for each personal opinion ventured by a convert, the convert was expected
to produce explicit scriptural support. If he was unable to
produce this, he tended to disavow or downgrade the opinion"
(Robbins, 1973:323).

It is our contention that the current evangelical explosion
represents a strident traditionalist response to deepening moral
ambiguity in America and a counterreaction to conspicuous
relativistic tendencies in modern culture (Lorentzen, 1980).
Oriental gurus and "cults" are perceived by many evangelicals
and pentecostals as a key aspect of contemporary moral de-
gradation (McGuire, 1975; Robbins, 1973).[12]

The "puritanical" tendencies of the "Jesus movement" of
the early seventies have been widely noted as have devotees'
traditionalist attitudes regarding sex, drugs, contraception,
abortion, and the role of women (Harder, et al., 1972; Adams
and Fox, 1972; Balswick, 1974). In the opinion of one writer,
"The Jesus people, in adhering to a rigorous Biblical view of
authority, may be reacting against a very permissive hippie
morality in favour of a nebulous ideal of love, and in the process have seen and experienced sexual exploitation. They have
thrown off societal tradition, rules, regulations, and restraint
in pursuit of liberty, and in the process have seen and experienced disillusioning chaos and disorder" (Balswick, 1974:364).
As indicated above, some studies of youthful Jesus groups indicate that young converts tend to come disproportionately from
rural and fundamentalist backgrounds (Harder and Richardson,
1971; Gordon, 1974; Richardson, Harder and Simmonds, 1972;
Robbins, 1972). For these "returning fundamentalists", conversion to the Jesus movement represents a reaffirmation of an
earlier world view, whose "betrayal" during a phase of revolt

and hedonism had engendered intense guilt (Richardson, et al.,
1972). The rigid fundamentalist dichotomy of the elite of
"saved" juxtaposed against the vast legions of condemned "sinners" may be psychologically rewarding for guilt-ridden and
disoriented young persons or confused or outraged adults who
feel displaced and deprived of status in a bureaucratized urban society. Robbins (1973) quotes one Berkeley "Jesus convert",
". . .so I'm gonna be up there in Heaven with Jesus Christ
and the rest of the saints that are taken from the earth to
judge the world by the Word of God" (Robbins, 1973:290).[13]

The current conservative Christian revival represents not
only a resurgence of traditional puritanical moral absolutism
but also a resurgence of manichean orientations in which dis-
approved social phenomena are attributed to the influence of
Satan and the Anti-Christ. This development is illustrated in
a recent study of the Catholic Pentecostal movement (McGuire,
1975) in which Catholic Pentecostals were seen as manifesting
"a renewed interest in dualistic interpretations of events. The
forces of order are seen as contending with the forces of disorder, the good and the evil, God's side versus Satan's side"
(McGuire, 1975:98). The influence of Satan was viewed by
Pentecostals as manifesting in the spread of pornography,
"false religions" (e.g. eastern gurus), T.V. violence, etc.
"Practices such as exorcisms and prayers against the influence
of evil were common in the Pentecostal groups studied. The
forces of evil were sometimes identified and personified in
movements, issues or personages that threatened the values of
members (e.g., 'my sister who brings Satan's influence into
our house', pro-abortionists, or 'those who want to take religion out of the schools')" (McGuire, 1975:98).

The relationship between manichean resurgence and a
cultural climate of moral ambiguity is indicated by the tendency of evangelicals and pentecostals to choose phenomena a-
bout which there is moral dissensus (e.g. pornography and
abortion) as manifestations of satanic influence rather than
indisputably condemned phenomena such as mugging or geno-
cide.

McGuire (1978) sees the crystallization of a distinctly dualistic theodicy as a common element linking resurgent evangelical, pentecostal and fundamentalist movements. This symbolic
framework is functional in terms of assisting devotees in coping
with anomie in the context of contemporary cultural flux. A
dualistic theodicy derives both the sources and "solutions" of
social and personal problems from the transcendent realm. Adherents are able to locate their problems and strivings within
a quasi-military cosmic framework in which their daily struggle
against "evil", even in trivial contexts, takes on a heroic significance (McGuire, 1978; 1981).

Finally, today's resurgent evangelicism represents a reaffirmation of traditional voluntarism and the sovereignty of "free will". According to one scholar, the emphasis on human choice in the west coast Jesus movement "serves the ideological needs of the movement by reducing social problems to individual choice, making the mission of the church a simple re-affirmation of salvation" (McPherson, 1975:12). In the Jesus movement, "The Christian belief in salvation is transformed into a social belief in voluntarism: individual choices make all the difference between good and evil in the world" (McPherson, 1975: 12-13).

We propose that the early Jesus movement and the present resurgence of fundamentalism and evangelicism represent a strident reaffirmation of traditional absolutism in the context of an increasingly pluralistic and relativisitic moral milieu. However, moral absolutism necessarily resurrects the legitimation of "residual behavior"; theft and other "deviant" acts are once more narrowly and restrictively defined such that "residual" socioeconomic inequality which falls beyond the fixed boundaries of specifically proscribed acts escapes moral scrutiny. It is partly for this reason that religious and political fundamentalism often converge and evangelicals are often political conservatives (Grupp and Newman, 1974; Dreidger, 1974). Several studies have documented developing right-wing political tendencies in "Jesus movement" groups (Adams and Fox, 1972; Robbins, 1973; Mauss and Peterson, 1973).

Fundamentalist absolutism represents a moral orientation which is in some ways incongruent in the context of modern cultural pluralism. The apocalypticism of the Jesus movement, which has been widely noted (Adams and Fox, 1972; Enroth et al.; Ellwood, 1973; Robbins, 1973), represents a symbolic resolution of the problem posed by the seeming obsolescence of moral absolutism by means of a vision of the imminent destruction of the impersonal bureaucratic society and its relativistic standards. The relativistic and "permissive" society will perish before the righteous wrath of the Lord, and only the "Saints" who have obeyed the absolutistic codes will be saved.

Millenarianism is integral to the meaning system of Catholic charismatics and is closely interlinked with dominant dualistic themes (McGuire, 1978; 1981). According to McGuire (1978:17) "The belief in the coming of the millenium relativizes the problems and oppositions of the present by the knowledge that all of these will be overcome in a glorious future. They can feel that "things" are really bad now and probably will get worse, but that they are not personally threatened by the disorder and ambiguity, since they know that they are allied in the present with the source of order and will have a privileged position in the unknown glorious future."

TABLE 1

ISSUE	"JESUS FREAKS"	"BABA-LOVERS"
Is salvation a dichotomy	Sharply distinguish between "saved" and "damned" persons. This duality is an eternal feature of God's universe.	There is no qualitative distinction between saved and not-saved. Some develop their consciousness more than others, but all will eventually be "God-realized", not necessarily in present incarnation.
Exclusivity	View own spiritual involvement as exclusive "one way" to God and truth. Other involvements are "false religions" inspired by Anti-Christ. Only "true Christians" can really be good, loving persons.	Believe in a universal religion underlying apparent spiritual diversity. Buddha, Christ, Krishna, etc., are prior incarnations of Baba and embody valid spiritual paths. Those who do not overtly follow Baba may sometimes be inwardly closer to Baba than overt followers.
Possibility of judging others in terms of dichotomous moral categories.	Confidently judge selves and others dualistically. Certain feelings, impulses are attributed to Satan. Converts reject old selves upon being "born again". Biblical literalism provides "objective" standard for all ethical judgments.	Eschew judging others in spiritual terms. Spiritual significance of any feeling or action is problematic. Seemingly "bad" actions may represent karma one needs to work off, may be spiritually necessary. Continuity in spiritual growth is stressed.
Orientation toward American "success" ethic of competitive individualism.	Project competitive individualism into sacred cosmos. Duality of success-failure applies to salvation — some people fail: are damned. Competition of Lord and Devil for souls reflected in competition of Jesus movement with "false prophets."	Believe that "we are all one" and one can really only compete with oneself. Since all souls will ultimately be reunited with the "over-soul", there is no "failure" in spiritual terms. "Karmic determinism mitigates apparent worldly 'failure'."
Dualistic "armageddon" style apocalypse.	Predict imminent reign of Anti-Christ followed by Second Coming. True Christians will be removed to heaven before reign of Anti-Christ.	Envision a gradual evolution of a new spiritual culture of "new humanity."

Table 1 compares the ideologies of the Meher Baba movement and the Berkeley-Oakland Christian World Liberation Front (CWLF) as they were studied by the authors during a three year period from 1969 to 1972 (Robbins, 1973; Robbins, Anthony and Curtis, 1973; Anthony and Robbins, 1974).[14] Our comparison involves five issues of spiritual orientation which have monistic or dualistic-absolutistic alternatives.

The meaning systems of the "Baba-Lovers" and "Jesus freaks" represent the poles of relativistic monism and absolutistic dualism around which most of today's dynamic spiritual movements cluster. Most of the "eastern" cults (e.g. Hare Krishna, Divine Light Mission, Integral Yoga) exemplify a oneness-maya-karma theodicy, while other movements, most notably the evangelical and "Jesus movement" groups, exemplify a strident ethical dualism. The passage below is quoted from an interview with a member of the Unification Church of Reverend Sun Myung Moon. The passage highlights the issue of moral absolutism vs. moral relativism, which is quite salient to church members. The respondent is discussing the movement's emphasis on "absolute value" and an absolutistic standard for morally coding actions.

> Well, in the Bible Jesus said, "I don't come to bring peace on earth, I come to bring a sword." And what that means is that what he is trying to bring us is a sort of symbolic sword to divide good and evil. You know, because the whole world is sort of wishy-washy and the whole world is sort of in between. You know, sort of with one foot in the boat and the other foot on the deck. So for God to create an ideal world is for God to completely separate good and evil. . .so that, so that people can, you know, completely see the difference (quoted in Anthony and Robbins, 1978:88).

CONCLUSION

The period from the middle sixties through the present has been characterized by normative flux and institutional breakdown in American society. Indices of this crisis include rising crime rates, falling rates of voter participation, rising indices of family disorganization, and various survey results revealing a loss of confidence in American political and economic institutions. More overt manifestations of dissidence include the campus/ghetto eruptions of the late sixties and early seventies and the "taxpayers' revolt" of the late seventies. A final indicator of the normative ambiguity and dissensus of the present period is the remarkable religious ferment of the past fifteen years. This development includes a luxuriant growth of unconventional "new religions" and quasi-religious psychotherapies, a powerful resurgence of "conservative" evangelical Christianity and neo-orthodox Judaism, and dissensus and defections within Roman Catholicism and the major "liberal" denominations of Protestantism.

A linkage between the contemporary spiritual ferment and a broader crisis of values in American culture has been widely noted. Several writers have related the current upsurge of unconventional spiritual movements to discontinuities in American "civil religion". American civil religion, according to Robert Bellah and others, involves a complex of shared national purpose which rationalizes the needs and purposes of the broader community. However, as Bellah (1975:145) argues in The Broken Covenant, "Today the American civil religion is an empty and broken shell." In Bellah's view, the present spiritual ferment attempts a "birth of new American myths" as a response to the decay of civil religion.

We have argued that moral meanings in American society are becoming increasingly problematic and non-consensual (Douglas, 1971; Roof, 1978). The moral milieu of America is increasingly pluralistic and moral relativism is widespread. It is in this context that the monistic and quasi-monistic meaning systems of many mystical, guru, and therapeutic groups has a growing appeal to many persons including some young persons making a transition from personalized familial milieux to impersonal adult institutions and relativistic public morality. Other young persons (and many older persons), however, embrace evangelical and pentecostal groups which recreate a milieu of moral absolutism and moral solidarity among their members and provide a rationale for the rejection of relativistic public morality and the perceived corruption of morally confusing bureaucratic institutions. They utilize the traditional core concepts of a transcendent God, ethical dualism, and free will to denounce the corrupt and relativistic secular environments, most of whose members are expected to go to Hell in an imminent apocalypse. Monistic-relativistic and dualistic-absolutistic ideologies represent alternative strategies for consolidating psycho-social identity in a cultural climate of moral ambiguity and grounding the transition from childhood to adulthood in broader social values. In this connection, there is some indication that the choice of monistic or dualistic outlook is influenced by strictness of religious upbringing and childhood socialization and by education and general cultural sophistication. More comparative analyses of "monists" and "dualists" are called for as well as longitudinal studies aimed at investigating whether involvements with religious and therapeutic movements are transitional in nature or become permanent contexts for adult identities.

In his recent essay on "Religion and the Legitimation of the American Republic", Robert Bellah (1978) argues that American political thought has entailed a dialogue between two conflicting ideals: the virtuous republic which actively supervises the moral life of the citizenry, and the laissez-faire liberal constitutional state which merely provides a minimal framework of public order within which citizens' pursuit of private gain will putatively be harmonized to produce the public good. Federalism provided one basis of compromise between these ideals as did the assumption that the churches qua powerful social forces would maintain a moral consensus such that the formal state apparatus and constitutional settlement could be patterned in terms of the laissez-faire liberal ideal. "We artfully used religion as a way of evading the incompatibilities in our political life. For as long as the religious bodies remained vital and central in our public life the evasion was (at least partially) successful. Today when religion, more even than our other institutions, is uncertain about itself, the evasion is no longer tenable" (Bellah, 1978:18).

In effect, the decline of moral consensus and the diminished vitality of the churches as moral agents[15] has discredited the liberal constitutional state and revitalized, among certain groups and individuals, the vision of the virtuous republic in obedience to a politically enforced "covenant". The deepening moral ambiguity has produced a resurgence of strident moral absolutism and ethical dualism, which is "spilling over" into the political realm and generating movements aimed at driving toward the crystallization of a "godly state" which will enforce obedience to divine law. Yet the collapse of moral consensus has also produced the opposite response — embodied in explicitly relativistic and subjectivistic spiritual ideologies with implications for enhancing religious privatism and "narcissistic" concern with self-realization at the expense of explicit civic concerns. These latter groups are derogated, perhaps a bit unfairly, by Bellah (1978:23) as "privatistic and self-centered" groups which "approach the consumer cafeteria model of Thomas Luckmann" and are thus incapable of renewing a sense of national ethical purpose. Yet the religious spectrum is increasingly polarized between such "privatized" groups and resurgent and politicized evangelical-fundamentalist movements seeking a biblical covenant.

NOTES

1.   See also the formulation of Eister (1972) who relates the current upsurge of religious "cults" to a "culture crisis" involving "dislocations in the orientational and communicational institutions of contemporary societies — and especially in the norms and elements of communications of 'meaning'" (Eister, 1972:327).

2.   The contemporary general tendency toward the politicization of deviance is discussed by Horowitz and Liebowitz, who note "the breakdown in the distinction between crime and marginal politics" (Horowitz and Liebowitz, 1968:291). The increasing "politicizing of crime, the criminal, and the criminologist" is discussed by Reasons (1974). See also Taylor and Taylor (1974) and Sykes (1974).

3.   Monistic philosophies thus imply a goal of self-annihilation or extinction of the illusory separative ego-self, which must merge with the infinite universal self or universal consciousness or energy. Since the distinction between the illusory separative self and the exclusively real universal self is relatively intangible, monistic philosophies of self-annihilation will appear to external observers to be philosophies of self-deification (as Weber characterized mysticism), thus making possible a charge of amoral selfishness and neglect of social responsibilities in favour of a "naval gazing" preoccupation with internal consciousness expansion (Marin, 1975). What is important is the degree to which "monistic" assumptions of the illusory or non-objective nature of apparent phenomenal reality and the derivative premium on inner development have diffused into a number of cultural currents, most notably the "Human Potential Movement", which has been strongly influenced by eastern mysticism (Braden, 1967; Marin, 1975).

4.   Weber contrasts karmic monism with "the bifurcation of the world which is found in ethical dualistic religions of providence". In monistic karmic theodicy, "the dualism of a sacred, omnipotent, and majestic God confronting the ethical inadequacy of all his creatures is altogether lacking"; moreover, "strictly speaking there is no sin, but only offenses against one's own clear interest in escaping from this endless wheel, or at least in not exposing oneself to a rebirth under even more painful circumstances" (Weber, 1964:146-147).

5.   One of the authors was present as a participant observer and took notes on Dr. Cohen's talk.

6.   On another occasion, the author was present at Meher Baba House when an informal quasi-T group session was emerging in which the participants interpreted their experiences in

terms of Meher Baba's hidden manipulative influence in compelling them to confront themselves. The conversation eventually
generalized to a discussion of morality and the problem of
judging others. The consensus seemed to be that one should
"follow one's inner voice" but be cautious in condemning others, since the spiritual significance of another's actions is
not immediately discernible to the observer, who does not know
how Baba is working with and manipulating the individual.

7.   Use of the karma concept can have the consequence of
annihilating guilt. A follower of Guru Maharaj-ji has stated:
"I don't experience guilt any more. . .if I do something in-
consistent with knowledge. . .I know it's my karma. And probably there's something I'm learning from it" (quoted in
Anthony et al., 1977:868). Deviant acts can thus be interpreted
in terms of their heuristic value for the development of spiritual consciousness. This transcendence or evasion of guilt has
led some critics to link the spread of eastern religion in
America to the growth of a milieu of "narcissistic" hedonism
and social irresponsibility (Cox, 1977; Schur, 1976; Marin,
1975).

8.   Significantly, the one group which did prominently feature confessional rites was the only clearly "western" group
-- a Charismatic Renewal group. Other groups studied were
Integral Yoga, Transcendental Meditation, Hare Krishna,
Shakti, and Subud.

9.   The relativistic dimension of monistic meaning systems
is illustrated by a journalistic account (Kelley, 1973:40) of responses of followers of Guru Maharaj-ji to criticisms of a violent act perpetrated by devotees, "Ranhan Chadha. . .elaborat-
ed further: "There are no hard and fast rules being holy. In
India, there have been gurus who have led their followers into
full scale wars. The perfect master does whatever the best
thing is for that time and space." The point here is that the
relativistic nature of monistic ideology does not provide a conceptual framework and a rhetoric for absolute condemnation of
deviant acts. This is not to imply that monistic movements encourage such acts.

10.   It is important to realize that from the standpoint of
evangelical christianity, monistic pantheism and "secular humanism", the bête-noir of many evangelicals (Dabney, 1980),
appear convergent. There are subtle differences between believing that God doesn't exist and thus "man is the measure of all
things" and believing that universal force immanent within human consciousness as a depth of self is the ultimate reality,
yet both perspectives deny traditional theistic perspectives and
appear to say, "man is God." Cf. a recent sociological analysis

of modern mystical and quasi-mystical therapeutic movements as representing the "cult of man" (Westley, 1978).

11.   Judah (1977) reports a significantly higher proportion of Catholics in the Unification Church compared to the Hare Krishna sect.

12.   A follower of Meher Baba reported, at a meeting attended by one of the authors, being denounced by a "Jesus freak" for telling persons "they're good. You didn't even tell them they were sinners!" The same observer later attended a three-day Unification Church workshop in which the chief lecturer criticized Guru Maharaj-ji for moral relativism.

13.   Lorentzen has recently (1980) utilized the concept of status politics to explain the increasing conservative political activism of evangelicals, who are involved in a symbolic crusade to defend and legitimate their traditionalist values and life-style in the face of dominant liberal secular culture. See Gusfield (1963) and Schwartz (1970) for earlier analyses of the relationship between fundamentalism and "status politics".

14.   Our study was conducted by means of participant observation supplemented with clinical interviews. See Robbins (1973); Robbins, Anthony and Curtis (1973); Anthony and Robbins (1974) and Anthony et al. (1977) for documentation of most of the assertions in this table. It should be noted, however, that the orientations ascribed to CWLF members pertain specifically to the period, 1969-1972. On the early CWLF, see also Streiker (1971:90-107). The attitudes and symbolic meanings of today's evangelical and pentecostal groups seem similar in many respects to those of the early CWLF.

15.   According to Bellah (1980:23), the decline of moral consensus and the crisis of national identity presently impinge most heavily on local institutions which are responsible for conveying moral ideologies. The "soft structures" which deal with human motivation -- such as the churches, the schools, and the family -- have been undermined more than other institutions in recent American upheavals. They have been especially weakened with respect to "their capacity to transmit patterns of conscience and ethical values." In this connection, Roof (1978) has analyzed survey data on religious defection in the early and middle seventies. According to Roof, defection from established churches has reached "staggering proportions." These defections plus the upsurge of new movements are part of "a larger climate of unrest in the religious realm" involving numerous Americans "breaking with their institutional commitments." Defectors are more likely than non-defectors to be committed to the permissive "new morality" and to have liberal

attitudes on issues such as homosexuality and abortion. Protestant and Catholic faiths are internally split over such issues and over the conflict of "counter-cultural" values and the conservative reaction.

V

SOCIAL PERCEPTIONS OF NEW RELIGIOUS MOVEMENTS:
REVELATION AND CONTROL

SOME SOCIAL FACTORS AFFECTING THE
REJECTION OF NEW BELIEF SYSTEMS

Bert Hardin
Günter Kehrer

Because modern Western societies claim to guarantee freedom of thought and religion, and to accept the idea of cultural pluralism, we have come to expect tolerance even when the society is confronted by new and strange ideas and beliefs. At the same time we do not expect any widespread adherence to the new beliefs. Yet, with regard to the new religious movements we find a third response to be quite common. This third response is rejection. Rejection is used here to mean that the rejecting person or group actively seeks support from other individuals or groups to ensure that the new beliefs will not be accepted and/or will cease to exist. The concept of belief systems used in the paper is defined as a system of related ideas to which the adherents exibit some commitment.[1]

As is the case with almost any phenomenon with which one is concerned, there is a multitude of aspects to be considered. We have limited our discussion to those factors which we believe to be most important. We think that these factors will be involved in a rejection process occuring in any modern society. The extent to which rejection occurs and the focus of the rejection will vary among societies.

CHARACTERISTICS OF BELIEF SYSTEMS

In every society there are shared perceptions about certain characteristics of belief systems. The kind of differentiation of the types of belief systems is dependent upon specific historical conditions. We wish to consider four of the possible characteristics which might be used in a specific society to determine the legitimacy of a belief system. These four characteristics are (1) the content of the beliefs, (2) the amount of commitment which a belief system requires of its members, (3) the social action which is related to the belief system which includes a) the type of action and b) the area in which the action takes place, and 4) the nature of the carrier of the belief system. It would seem that the members of any given society have an idea of the general boundaries of each of these characteristics even if there is not always a clear conception of every item which may fall within the boundaries.

For example, even though individual perceptions of these characteristics will vary, the normative system will be sufficiently shared to allow one to speak of a general conception of the legitimate attributes which a carrier of a particular type of belief system may (or must) have. While it is allowed that there is no single religious or single political belief system in any of the Western societies, all possible variations will not be considered legitimate.

TABLE 1

Characteristics of Political and Religious Belief Systems

Political Belief System	Religious Belief System
Content	**Content**
Statements about the order, economics, and foreign relations of a society. Statements about the evaluation of the changeable conditions.	Statements about the nature of good and evil in a substantive sense. Statements about the meaning of life. Statements about the "eternal" destiny or fate of man.
Amount of Required Commitment	**Amount of Required Commitment**
The amount of time, money, and emotional involvement required (these differ according to the position – e.g. one time voter or professional politician – of the believer.	Same as for the political belief system. The position may vary between a nominal member and a professional clergyman.
Related Social Action	**Related Social Action**
Where? e.g. at work, in school, or in private.	Where? e.g. at work, in the church, on the street.
What? e.g. demonstrate, boycott, strike.	What? e.g. pray, meditate, beg, solicit.
Carrier	**Carrier**
The amount and form of organization. "Respectability" and training of individual representatives.	The same as for the political belief system.

Just as there is an overlapping of conceptions which provide a common basis for decision making among individuals, there is also a portion of the conceptions which has much less sharedness. It is this grey area of partial sharedness which allows for variation. In fact, if this variation did not exist, new belief systems would pose no threat because they would not be able to recruit new members. Some of the individuals or groups will view belief systems having characteristics in the grey area as being acceptable while others may want to reject them. Characteristics which fall completely outside this grey zone are most likely to give cause for rejection.

Thus it is not just the simple case of those belief systems which have nonconformist characteristics being automatically rejected. Despite all of the sharedness there are still the variations in perceptions and there are variations in the value of the separate characteristics. For example, some individuals or groups may consider the content criteria extremely important while considering the attributes of the carrier to be of little or no importance. Further, those individuals or groups wishing to reject a belief system possess different amounts of power.

REJECTORS

For present purposes we shall consider four types of power holders hereafter referred to as "rejectors". Each of the types may or may not be involved in rejecting a new belief system, but all of them must be involved if there is to be a successful rejection. The first type of rejector is the individual citizen who has had some form of direct contact with the new belief system. He/she has little chance of bringing about a successful rejection by him/herself. The second type consists of organizations which represent a similar type of belief system to the new one. They become involved because of their vested interest. Their chances of success in rejecting are greater because of their organiztion, but they are also limited just because they have a vested interest. The third type is the mass media. They are less likely to be involved in a rejection process because their rights and privileges are based on concepts such as the protection of general societal interests, respect of pluralism, and some form of objectivity. Just because of this basis, if they do become involved the chances of total rejection are greatly increased. The stigmatization which is necessary to accomplish total rejection is dependent upon the aid of the mass media. The fourth type is that of governmental institutions. In many respects they are the least likely to be involved because of constitutional guarantees which forbid the rejection of religious belief systems. However, they can still become involved in one way or another through decisions about tax statuses or through activities of the department of justice.

It is understandable that the extent of rejection will depend upon which types of rejectors are involved. Simply stated, the more cooperation involved among the types, the greater the chance of successful rejection. Cooperation will depend upon the amount of motivation for rejection and the motivation will vary according to the value the rejector places on the separate properties. The motivation for rejecting at the individual level depends upon the extent to which the individual views his identity as being jeopardized by the new belief system. On the organizational level, the motivations will be more dependent on defending rights and privileges on the one hand, and the obligation to "defend the faith" on the other. Once confronted with a new belief system the mass media may decide to reject because one of their major functions is to represent the beliefs of the dominant culture. The motivation for the governmental institutions is twofold. First of all they share a similar function with the mass media; secondly, they must ensure the legality of the behavior associated with a belief system.

In deciding to reject a new belief system it is not necessary for the rejector to base the decision on all of the characteristics. It is possible for the individual to use only the amount of commitment which a belief system requires as a criterion for rejecting the whole belief system. However, a religious organization does have to consider the content of the new belief system because of its obligation to "defend the faith". In addition, it is likely that it will use other properties, e.g. the characteristics of the carrier of the new system. The mass media will place emphasis on the behavioral aspects of the properties, but it is the most likely among the four types of rejectors to consider all characteristics. On the level of governmental institutions, it is virtually impossible, in any legitimate way, to base the decision on the content of a belief system; because of the relationship between the state and religion only behavioral aspects of a new belief system can be considered.

Our primary interest is concerned with that form of rejection which includes cooperation among all the different types of rejectors in the attempt to achieve total societal rejection. Cooperation necessitates combining the differing motivations of separate rejectors and making the varying conceptions of properties compatible with each other in order to arrive at a common strategy. This is difficult when one rejector uses criteria which are "forbidden" to other rejectors. For example, one could think here of the church organizations and the mass media where both reject a religious belief system. The church organizations may use content legitimately, but it is "forbidden" for the mass media to use content as a basis for rejecting. In the same case, the mass media may reject the area of social action whereas the church organizations will hardly be able to do so because within their own belief system it is thought that if one really believes, the effect will be felt in all areas of life. The example refers only to properties which may be used legitimately and ignores the possibility that a rejector, having support from other types of rejectors, may directly or indirectly come to use non-legitimate arguements. Because of the range of power and the limitations of legitimacy it is necessary that all four types of rejectors cooperate if total societal rejection is to be achieved. The effectiveness of the rejection will also increase with the number of different characteristics used in common as a basis for rejection. Thus if there is agreement among all types regarding the content of the new religious belief system an effective campaign against heresy will be possible. If the reasons for rejection are all different the effectiveness of the rejection will depend much more on the intensity of the rejection at the various levels.

Althcugh we use the data from a single case to exemplify the rejection process, we have legitimate reasons for assuming that the one case is typical because the history of rejection of the Unification Church (UC) in Germany is a part of the total history of rejection of new religious groups in Germany. The following three tables provide an overview of the development of the UC in Germany and the reaction to this development. Table II begins with the first UC missionaries in 1963. These were Germans who had become UC members in California. Only major events are included in the table. (The information comes from interviews and analyses of material by and about the UC) Tables III and IV present the activities of the rejectors and the properties used in the rejection process. Even a very short glance at tables III and IV shows firstly that the genuine process of the rejection on a societal scale did not start before 1975, and, secondly that the stress laid on the various characteristics has changed in this process. It is evident that the events which have led to something approaching total rejection did not occur in a way that fits all relevant points in our general discussion. However, we can find all the important steps that are necessary for a total rejection. Although we have no documents about the first reactions of individuals we can conclude from the complaints of parents which date back to 1971 that in most cases it was the type and area of social action which led to rejection. It is often the case that apocalyptic belief systems require members to deny "this worldly" things, e.g. leave family and jobs, which in terms of the belief system is logical. To reject a belief system because of this requirement would seem to be a rejection because of its content. However, since individuals lack fitting religious categories they do not have the possibility of checking the content of such a belief system. Instead of rejecting the content, they deny the right to exist to a religious group whose members do not live in accordance with the dominant values.

Table II: A Partial History of the Unification Church in Germany

1963: Peter Koch and Ursula Schumann return from USA to Germany as first missionaries. First center in Frankfurt. Contacts through work, other religious groups, evening schools. UC totals 2 members plus an American soldier in Giessen.

1964: Barbara Koch returns to Germany, then Paul and Christel Werner with Elke Klawiter return. First German convert. First organization founded as legal body (eingetragener Verein). Seven members (six from the USA).

1965: Germans established centers in Spain, Austria, and France. Number of members unknown.

1966: Centers in Essen and Hamburg established.

1969: Rev. Moon comes to Essen. Wedding of 8 couples (first convert weds old member Barbara Koch). Sixty members from all of Europe come to Essen for meeting. Paul Werner becomes German leader, Peter Koch goes to Austria to replace Werner. Change in methods to include street mission. Fifteen members.

1970: First success in Essen. Twelve members go to other cities in Germany. Number of members unknown.

1971: First mobile mission teams (caravans) of 12 members in 21 cities. Street mission in cities where centers exist are supported by mobile mission team.

1972: Rev.Moon comes to Essen again and gives his first "public" speech in Germany. Centers now in 30 cities. Beginning of fund raising by selling literature. German translation of the Divine Principle in final form is first available. (Hand typed translation from Peter Koch available to this point.) 120 members.

1973: Purchase of main training center in Camberg (Taunus). Rev.Moon becomes established in USA, and USA becomes the country of reference for the German Unification Church. Mobile mission teams are stopped, and 110 German members go to the USA. Number of members unknown.

1975: The German UC initiates activities with the parents of young members partly as a reaction to the foundation of the parent organizations which are anti-UC.

1978: Mr. Vincenz, first German convert, becomes leader of UC in Germany. Paul Werner goes to the USA. House missionizing is added to the street mission. A public relations officer is added to the staff. 700 active members, plus 1,300 marginal members.

Table III: Activities of the Rejectors

YEAR 1969	INDIVIDUAL ?	CHURCHES ---	MASS MEDIA ---	GOVERNMENT BODIES ---
1969	?	First theologically "scientific" description of new group.		
1971	Involved persons (parents etc.) combat the UC.	Further "scientific" description of new group.	First polemical report in a popular magazine (one case).	First inquiries regarding unlawful detention.
1972	"	"	Polemical report in Trade Union paper (one case).	Inquiries suspended.
1973	"	Description becomes more polemical. Some clergy became involved in combatting the UC.	Polemical reports in serious regional papers and magazines. (one case).	Inquiries without results.
1974	"	First purely polemical booklet by a church official.	Polemical reports (case study) in various newspapers.	Inquiries without results.
1975	Parents' organization founded to combat new "cults".	More polemical articles and booklets. Clergy and theologians involved with parents.	Start of campaign by many newspapers against UC. More cases used for illustration.	Inquiries without results.
1976	Parents' organization very active — letters to president and political leaders.	Continuation of polemics against the new religions.	Continuation of campaign with radio and TV.	Political parties involved as UC takes part in general election campaign. Federal Government says it cannot be active against new groups.
1977	Continuation of activity in all public areas.	Continuation of polemics, now in church-sponsored papers.	"	Officials of Fed.Gov. take part in congress re: new religions. Governmental sponsored research. Attempts to bring together all rejectors.
1979	"	Activities on all levels of church organizations.	Continuation of above. Popular books (2 by major magazines.)	Special funds and staff to deal with the new religions.

Table IV: Assessment of the Characteristics Used by the Rejectors

YEAR	CONTENT	AMOUNT OF REQUIRED COMMITMENT	TYPE AND AREA OF SOCIAL ACTION	CARRIER
1969	Used in the first theological description.	?	Unknown but was likely used by the individuals.	?
1971	Used in the description by the church institutions.	Used in first report of a popular magazine.	Used in the first report by a magazine and by parents of the girl whose case was reported.	Parents attempt to disqualify Paul Werner as a religious leader of supposed illegal activity.
1973	Only one church institution continues to describe UC belief system content.	Used in polemical reports in the popular press.	Used by popular press. Also used by some of the clergy.	"
1974	Slowly ceases to be used by serious church institutions.	"	Same as above. Now used by some church organizations.	Parents attempt to disqualify Werner and Moon because of above and economic activities.
1975	Hardly used; if used only single aspects, often false.	Used sparingly and always with other characteristics.	Becomes focus in campaign of parents, churches, mass media.	"
1977	"	"	Used for first time by political or quasi-political institutions. Other rejectors continue to use this property.	Issues of illegality and economics are dropped. All religious qualities are nihilated by parents and churches.
1978	Use comes to an end.	"	Becomes almost sole argument used by all rejectors. Reinforced by events in Jonestown.	Same as 1977. Reinforced by events in Jonestown.
1979	Seems to continue as in 1978.			

The information   about the UC has been presented in tab-
ular form to save space and to facilitate following our argument.   However, since the situation in Germany regarding the
rejection of the new groups is unique, we think it necessary
to outline additional general information about the form and
amount of rejection which has taken place before we attempt
to draw any conclusions about the German society. To begin
with, all the major magazines and some of the minor ones have
carried a series of articles about the various new religious
groups. Without exception the accounts are polemical and full
of both fact and fiction. All three of the television networks
have carried "documentaries" about the "youth sects" as they
are referred to in Germany. In addition, television plays have
been written and shown using one or more of the groups as
a motif. Even though the names of the groups have been
changed, e.g. the "Sing Sect" from Taiwan, they are readily
recognizable -- in this case Moon from Korea. These plays,
often of poor quality, are used to "enlighten" the public about
the threat posed by these groups by stressing themes such as
suicide, mental breakdowns, isolation from the family, and
(maybe for the Germans the most important factor) the quitting
of jobs and school.

Furthermore, various institutions have been mobilized to
"combat" this threat. Almost all social work agencies having
to do with youth are involved with programs, conferences, and
publications. Non-profit organizations, e.g. Aktion Jugend-
schutz" (action for the protection of youth), are involved.
The established churches, or agencies thereof, are very much
involved. For example, there are several positions which have
been created where the person, most often a theologian, is
paid by the church to study the "sects" and, in one form or
another, to help in work against them. These positions are
in addition to long established church positions which have
the task of keeping tabs on all forms of new religious behavior
and ideologies. Even higher levels of German government are
involved to some extent. The ministry of Youth, Family, and
Health commissioned preliminary studies in 1978 concerning the
legal and medical-psychological aspects of the new groups as
well as a review of the literature available by and about the
groups. In 1979, a sum of approximately DM 500,000 was set
aside by this ministry for research in this sector. A last area
which should be mentioned is that of the parents' organizations. These organizations exist in other countries, but they
do not seem to have the cohesiveness and political visibility
there which they have in Germany.

The process of the rejection of the new religions, including the Unification Church, was rather difficult to establish
because of the problems involved in finding common properties

to use for rejection.   In fact it would seem that the guarantee
of religious freedom would prevent any efficient rejection.   As
the churches must be interested in the maintenance of religious
liberty, there was only one way to take part in the rejection
process: the denial of the religious quality of the so-called
"Jugendreligionen".   The new cults were stigmatized in order
to handle them as dangerous.   We think that even the expression "youth religion" serves as such a stigma.   Although there
are only a few members of such groups who are under 18 years
of age, it seems possible to evoke the impression that these
new religious groups attract young people who are not in a
position to decide what they want to do.   It is for this reason
that a lot of governmental or quasi-governmental institutions
that specialize in questions of youth and protection of youth
can take part in the rejection process.   It is the protection
quality that enables these agencies to view the new religions
as dangerous, because these religions are against some of the
goals of education in Germany.   Even in 1976, "the Federal
Government has been observing the development of the new
youth religions to which the Moon sect belongs.   The efforts
of these groups are not in accordance with the goals of the
youth policy of the government . . . (e.g. the absolute authority of the leaders, the complete obedience. . .)"[2]   However,
the same declaration also states that despite this fact, the
mentioned groups are within the frame of reference of the constitution.   Two years later the state secretary of the ministry
for Youth, Family and Health declared, "Wir sagen den Kampf
an" ("We are declaring the battle against the sects").

It seems typical of the German value system that the first
attempts to reject the new belief systems and groups which carry them were made by looking for assistance from authorities
of the state.   These attempts did not have the desired results
at least not at first.   Considering this situation, one has to
ask the question why is the rejection of the new religions so
wide-spread?   Are they viewed as being a threat to society?
When one looks closely at the information which has been disseminated one readily notices an over-representation of certain
groups, whereas other groups get no mention at all.   One could
postulate that the amount of reaction is somehow related to the
subjectively felt or objectively seen threat which a group
poses, the objective threat either being related to the absolute
numbers of members and growth rate, or to practices or teachings which are held to be more damaging or threatening than
one would find in other groups.   This assumption proves difficult to maintain however, since the two groups most often covered in the information are the Unification Church and the
Children of God (Family of Love).   One might argue that the
UC has become comparatively large, but it is by no means the
only large group in Germany. (Using the latest "official" report

provided by the Minister of Work, Health, and Social Welfare in the state of North Rhein-Westphalia, the UC has 2,000 active members and T.M. some 60,000.) ³

In the case of the Children of God we are talking about one of the smallest groups. (From our own research, the Children of God seems to have around 100 members today although the above-mentioned report places the membership at 800.) With regard to the practices of these two groups, the same charges of programming and "brainwashing" are applied to all of the groups. On the point of teachings one finds differences of course, yet the actual teachings are not part of the information disseminated to promote rejection. Rather, the idea is often transmitted that all of the groups are the same, with little attempt being made to differentiate their respective teachings. This allows the same stigma to be attached to all of the groups.

All of the questions which are raised when one views the rejection which has taken place cannot be answered satisfactorily with our data. For example, one can only speculate about the reasons for some groups receiving more attention than others. Yet we think that rejection of groups and/or belief systems reflect the dominant values of a society. Thus in the remaining space our effort is to relate the rejection process to certain assumptions about German society by utilizing the four characteristics which determine the legitimacy of a belief system.

CONTENT

We stated earlier that members of a society have a conception about the boundaries within which the content of a new religious belief system would have to exist. These boundaries refer to their own concept of religion, i.e. in the German case some forms of the Christian belief systems. In modern times, there is also an awareness that there are "legitimate" non-Christian belief systems which exist outside the boundary of content. The recognized world religions, including Islam, Hinduism, Buddhism, etc. are accepted, to an extent, as being legitimate in their own right. The reference systems used to judge the legitimacy of content for such a new belief system are different and only "experts" are able to apply these criteria. However, new ʳeligious belief systems which fall within the Christian tradition are judged according to the reference system of what is "legitimately" Christian. The characteristic of content is only used by the normal "powerholder" when confronted with belief systems which seem to fall within this Christian tradition. (In other words, a Xenophobic reaction to exotic belief systems does not occur because of the exotic content. In fact more tolerance seems to exist toward such

groups than toward the Unification Church and the Children of God.
Rejection of the exotic groups seems to occur through the lumping
of all groups together). Yet there are further limitations on the
practicality of this criterion. The "power-holder" or rejector must
have certain fundamental beliefs or "truths" which will conflict
with the new beliefs. It is understandable that the churches hold
such "truths"; however, the opinion polls tell us something different about the individual. Although the majority of individuals belong to one of the major churches, they do not believe the fundamental "truths" of the churches. Even the belief in a personal God
is not very widespread in German society. The mass media very
rarely discuss problems of religious content. At first glance, one
can see a number of religiously oriented programs on radio and television. However, these programs result from privileges granted
to the major churches after 1945, and they should not be interpreted as fulfilling a religious need.[5] An example of what is meant
can be seen from the results of a study done in Munich related to a
Saturday night program "With Regard to Sunday" (Das Wort zum Sonn-
tag). This is a presentation by a member of the clergy of approximately 10 minutes' duration which comes between the drawing
of the winning number of the weekly lottery and the late evening program. During this short period, the Munich water supply and sewage system experience one of their peak periods
of use.

The political parties seek to maintain good relations with
the major churches, yet the church creeds play no role in the
political understanding of the parties or the governmental
authorities. Even in the case of the Christian Union (CDU and
CSU) it is declared that adherence to the Christian belief system in a religious sense is not a necessary condition to becoming a member. The holders of political authority in all of the
parties espouse the ethical values which are a part of the
modern, Christian belief system although they need no support
from the churches in order to be accepted in the German culture. It is possible to have a major political figure who does
not belong to any church. Thus it was not suprising to find
that the content of the belief system was not an important criterion in deciding to reject the Unification Church. Only the
churches were in a position to do so, but they could not easily
find support from other types of "power-holders" when the decision to reject was based only on content. This interpretation
can be supported by the history of the struggle of churches
against the other religious belief systems in the 'fifties. These
"sects", as they were seen then, (e.g. Mormons, Church of
Christ) did not become the object of a total rejection process
despite the efforts of the crusaders.

AMOUNT OF COMMITMENT

It is difficult to separate the amount of commitment from the third characteristic (area and type of social action). If we limit the argument to those activities usually connected with religious commitment, such as church-going and praying, we can say that despite the theoretically high amount of commitment required by the Christian churches, the members of the churches feel obligated to a very small amount of commitment. They expect the religious professionals to exhibit greater amounts of commitment, but even this obligation is of no great consequence. The mass media and the governmental institutions are not in the position to discuss "proper" amounts of commitment. In general we can maintain that the small amount of shown commitment correlates with rather diffuse conceptions about the "proper" amount of required commitment. A religious belief system requiring a high amount of commitment of its members (e.g. the UC) is rather suspect. However, this in itself does not lead to a virulent rejection.

TYPE AND AREA OF SOCIAL ACTION

Once again, referring only to overt religious behavior and not to the influence of general moral and religious beliefs, one can say that the area where social action related to religion can take place is severely limited. For the non-cleric this type of behavior can only take place in the church. It is reduced to very infrequent church attendance and the paying of church taxes.[6] Visits to church occur on the major religious holidays and on the occasions of a baptism, a wedding, or a funeral.[7] This limit on religious behavior even extends to the point that religion is not a legitimate topic of discussion. There is an expression in German which states that one should not ask this type of "Gretchenfrage" (as Gretchen asks Faust: How do you feel about religion?). The religious status quo between the two major churches which has come about in the second half of this century is based, at least to some extent, on mutual agreement of non-competitive behavior. This means that proselytizing is very low key and theological polemics are virtually non-existent.[8] Thus, if members of religious groups exhibit aggressive behavior they pose a threat to the status quo. In general, one can say that religion does not play an important role in the every-day life of the individual in any direct sense. One does not expect religion to prescribe aspects of every-day behavior or to require commitment much beyond nominal membership. To a certain extent the idea is that "I pay my church taxes, therefore I have certain rights and no obligations." Thus direct contribution to the parish or fundraising for a church as an expression of religiously motivated behavior is very unusual in Germany. On the contrary, the combination of religion and money, though as old as religion

and money, seems for most Germans highly scandalous because
both established churches were never forced to live by fund-
raising.   A fund-raising small religious group seems to do
this only out of selfish motivation.

A serious problem arises for the German in the case
where religious groups require that their members give up their
occupations or abandon their schooling.   This goes against a
most strongly held value in the society.   There is no concept
of a drop-out and little chance for re-integration of such individuals.   The concept of social security is so important, and
affects so many areas, that it is difficult to explain it to non-
Germans.   To give a simple idea of what we mean, we maintain
that a main raison d'état in the "post economic miracle" period
is found in the social security system. [9] With few exceptions,
any person who does not work (and pay into the social security system) is seen to be useless for the society and, to some
extent, worthless as an individual.   Since the entrance to most
of the occupations requires schooling and apprenticeship, young
persons who break off their training are demonstrating behavior which is seen as being beyond the irrational (either
crazy or under evil influence).   This behavior presents a common ground for all types of "power-holder" upon which they
may base their rejection.

Indeed, it is easy to see that all of the rejectors concentrate on these issues.   The average German is not very
tolerant when a religious group interferes too much in the affairs of daily life.   This is even more the case when economic
issues are involved.   It is not readily understandable for such
individuals that religion can be taken so seriously that it can
affect the life and labour of the believer.   A prominent German
sociologist once stated: "Churches are insurance companies a-
gainst the risks of too much religion." [10]

CARRIERS

The "power-holders" most likely to reject because of the
qualities of the carrier are the vested interest organizations
since they are also carriers of competing belief systems.   The
more institutionalized and professionalized they are, the more
likely the rejection of a carrier which does not meet the same
standards.   In the case of the new religions the two established churches are most concerned.   The lesser denominations
or "sects" are less involved.

Since there is no written law which states that theologians must be academically trained, the governmental institutions could not discriminate because of the carrier.   However,
in fact, only those religious organizations whose representatives have state university training are considered "serious"

partners of the State.   This is reflected in many special relationships, e.g. the collection of church taxes.   The same special relationship exists with the mass media, e.g. appointments
to the board of advisors of the television networks, the presentation of religious programs.

To some extent, this problem is related to the German
philosophy that qualities achieved in a process of formal training are necessary and sufficient for permanent location in the
social structure.   However, even if this opinion is very strong
it did not lead to violent rejection by the various "power-
holders" because it is not important enough.   Control of the
privileged positions is so firmly in the hands of the two established churches that rejection along these lines is not necessary.   Instead, omission or exclusion suffice.   Furthermore,
the belief systems of the established churches contain no reason
for insisting that all carriers of religious belief systems be
academically trained.

CONCLUDING REMARKS

The question posed earlier as to whether the new religious groups constitute a threat to German society can be
answered in the affirmative when one considers the relevant
"power-holders".   Many of them believed and are still convinced that the central values of the society are jeopardized
by these groups.   The arguments and polemics are most often
focused on factors related to work, social security and the
family, whereby a great amount of stress is placed on the fact
that becoming a sect member may entail the loss of social security.   The loss of this is not only not understandable, it
also means that such individuals will someday become a burden
on society.   We can deduce from our observations that religious
heresy is not the point of contention.   It is also not the fact
that some people hold strange ideas about God and the world.
Instead, it seems to be the fact that some people take their
religious beliefs so seriously that they are willing to act in
accordance with their beliefs.   Some strange behavior in
modern societies which is related to religious fervor is tolerated for example, when a young woman joins a cloister, because
the belief system can be related to legitimate carriers.   In
the case of the UC there are no legitimate carriers.   Despite
the guarantee of freedom of religion given in Article IV of the
constitution of the Federal Republic, we think that only "neu-
tralized religion" will be considered legitimate in Germany.[11]

SUMMARY

We have presented a model for viewing how a society
goes about rejecting a new belief system.   The Unification

Church in Germany was used as a basis for our model. We
isolated four characteristics of a belief system which apply
to any belief system. These characteristics are: content,
amount of required commitment, type and area of social action,
and carrier. They can be used by the four types of potential
rejectors: the individual citizen, established churches, the
mass media, and governmental institutions. Societal rejection
can only take place by having all potential rejectors cooperate. The criteria which a potential rejector can legitimately
use differ. Thus to have a successful rejection a common strategy must be found. In the case of Germany this was the type
and area of social action. This characteristic is the one
which is the most amenable to comparisons with the normative
system of the society. This allows a propaganda which is
understandable for everyone. Thus the arguments used against
the new groups reflect some of the basic values of the society.
In Germany, the new groups are seen as posing a threat to
economic stability and the social welfare system.

NOTES

1.   This usage is borrowed in part from Borhek and Curtis,
1975. However, in certain respects, we use the concept quite
differently.

2.   Antwort der Bundersregierung auf eine Kleine Anfrage vom
26. Oktober 1976.

3.   Sachstandsbericht des Ministers für Arbeit, 1979:2-4.

4.   In 1967, 68% of the German population believed in God,
48% in a life after death. Harenberg (ed.), 1968:62.

5.   The situtation of television and radio in the Federal Republic of Germany is unique in the Western World. After 1945,
the allies changed the status of what was formerly the state-
radio to a "pluralistic" institution. All important societal
groups (trade unions, political parties, churches, etc.) shared
control over the radio and later on television. Because of this
power the so-called important groups can influence the programs.

6.   The fact that more than 90% of the population actually
pay their church taxes does not mean that the Germans are
very willing to financially support the churches. These church
taxes are collected by the state's tax bureau, and are in fact
a part of the general income tax system.

7.   In 1967, 25% of the German population declared that they
visit the church every Sunday.   Harenberg (ed.), 1968:59.
This percentage is very high, probably higher than the actual
church attendance.   After 1970 church attendance declined in
the two major churches.   Further information about the religious situation can be obtained from: Günter Kehrer:"Germany:
Federal Republic", in: Mol (ed.), 1972:189-212, and Hild, 1974.

8.   Religious peace between Protestants and Catholics dates
from the end of the second world war.   In part, it is a result
of the threat of the Nazi ideology to the churches, and partly,
it resulted out of the loss of importance of religious questions.
That religious peace could not be taken for granted before 1945
can be seen by an article of Max Scheler from 1920:"Der Friede
unter den Konfessionen" (The Peace Among the Confessions),
in Scheler, 1963: 227-258.

9.   This assumption is based on the political culture of the
German society after 1945.   The national identity of the German
population is orientated around economic categories.   Thirty-
three per cent of the German population declared that they
were very proud of their economic system (including the social
security system), whereas even in the USA, the comparable percentage is only 23%.   Almond and Verba, 1963.   The stability
of the German political system is a function of her economic
stability.

10.   Mühlmann, 1961:373.

11.   Adorno, Frenkel-Brunswik et al., 1950:727-743.

BEYOND THE PALE:
CULTS, CULTURE AND CONFLICT

James A. Beckford

POPULAR SENTIMENT AND UNPOPULAR CULTS

Even the most introverted and retreatist of the new religious cults which are currently at the centre of so much controversy can hardly fail to provoke some hostile responses from society at large. The very fact of their desire to withdraw from participation in the conventional order of things is sufficient to make them an object of sometimes intense suspicion. Not surprisingly, those cults which do attempt to evangelize and proselytize in public are even more likely to come under criticism for what is perceived as their open disregard for some taken-for-granted aspects of "conventional" social life. For feelings of hostility and suspicion are partly aroused by the belief, which is widespread in many sectors of societies in the West, that new religious cults amount to an organized attack on some of the very foundations of civilized society. These feelings may not necessarily find expression in active opposition to new cults[1] but they undoubtedly contribute strongly towards unease about them, and their members' experiences often confirm the view that the general public is reluctant to accept them as "normal".

Now, there are very good reasons for trying to be precise and discriminating in any discussion of new religious cults, but it is essential for my purpose not to lose sight of the popular view that such groups are uniform and uniformly distasteful. This deliberate obtuseness on my part is necessary because I intend to analyse the kinds of concern which lie behind popular feelings toward new religious movements. In other words, the state of popular feeling, as interpreted by me and as expressed through the media of popular newspapers, television programmes, personal conversations and structured interviews with people personally involved in various ways with a particular new religion in Britain, will serve as the topic of analysis. It would not, then, be appropriate for me to repair popular usage.

The main aim of the paper is to expose the deep-rooted sources of popular sentiment[2] concerning what are commonly

284

called "the cults". In this way it is hoped to explain why "the cults" are regarded as problematic in so many different spheres of society and, thereby to contribute towards an understanding of British society's response to challenging innovations in ideology, religion and life-style.

The paper will consider in turn each of eight different points at which popular sentiment in British society reacts in a hostile (and perhaps defensive) fashion against what are culturally defined as limits to the normal and acceptable range of options for individual action, thought, emotion and social relations. The operations of various new religious movements in this country can thereby serve to throw into sharp relief some important, but usually unrecognized, features of this society's cultural and social structures. My plan is, therefore, to use new religious movements as a way of exploring some aspects of one of the societies in which they are now active. Incidentally, of course, the process of exploration may also reveal something about the new religious movements themselves, but I should emphasize that the primary resources on which the present analysis is based are drawn from expressions of popular sentiment and cannot be taken as accurate or reliable accounts of the movements.

BOUNDARY DISPUTES

In their differing ways, each of the following hostile responses to new religious movements centres on the crucial, but shifting, boundary between "normal" and "abnormal", or (in a practical sense) "acceptable" and "unacceptable". The responses are far from being disinterested assessments of the relative weight of attributes on each side. They are in fact highly charged and potentially political judgments which reflect deep-rooted assumptions about what is normally taken for granted and what is, therefore, considered problematic. Much of the private argument and public debate about the "cult problem" therefore takes the form of a dispute about the location of certain boundaries.

One of the circumstances which aggravates and complicates the boundary disputes is the widespread reluctance to consider the matter in relativistic terms. The disputants are not content to assess the relative normality or abnormality of particular features of new religious movements. On the contrary, the argument is frequently couched in terms of absolute, black-and-white, mutually exclusive categories which admit of no search for middle ground. One of the reasons for this high degree of intolerance is that the issues at stake cannot, except for analytical purposes, be disentangled. Rather, they are each experienced by all concerned as integral parts of a whole world-view which may not be articulated as such but which nevertheless has a constraining effect on judgments concerning each separate boundary dispute. In other words, the location of each boundary is not in the least arbitrary but actually conforms to a pattern or profile which, in turn, derives from interrelated values and assumptions.

Furthermore, the patterns of values and assumptions are not entirely a result of personal preference but are partly conditioned by patterns of thought predominating in the culture to which the individual is exposed. Just as one must acknowledge variety among new religious movements therefore, one must also recognize diversity among cultural communities. This point has been made neatly by Ellwood in connection with the distinction which he has drawn between the "temple" and "cave" paradigms of religious styles in the United States:

> For every community has an idealized image, supported more by symbols and styles than concepts, of what an ideal personality is, and knows quite well what "fits" and what does not. (Ellwood, 1979: 8)

To complete the task of identifying the scope of this paper, I should add that cultural systems are inseparable in their implementation from such social arrangements as the legal and educational systems. The main implication of this is that an understanding of public responses to new religious movements must draw on material extending far beyond the personal motives of individuals and the programmes of anti-cult movements, for these phenomena only make sense in the context of wider cultural values and social arrangements.

THE PERSON

At the centre of most of the controversies surrounding new religious movements in the West lies a complicated and multi-faceted set of views about the individual person's ideal state of mind and social condition. These ideals are commonly contrasted with characteristics allegedly describing cult-members. I shall present these contrasts as a series of discrete conflicts, but in practice they are all interrelated. Indeed, they all express in different ways a unitary fundamental division between models of man as either autonomous or plastic.

(See Hollis, 1977.) On the one hand is a set of views about man's basic rationality and freedom, while on the other is an opposed set of views about cult members' basically reactive and dependent nature. Few people seriously believe that the polar types are ever fully realized in reality, but that is not the point: the point is that polarization forms an integral part of the rhetoric whereby criticism of new religious cults is tactically deployed by its advocates. In other words, it is politically expedient for the critics of cults to emphasize contrasts in the struggle to promote and to defend their particular point of view.

The following list of oppositions is a schematic abstraction from the subtle and sometimes confusing material presented in the mass media, everyday conversations and structured interviews:

Fig. 1

The Person in a Cult

Allegedly	Normally
Brainwashed	Free thinking
Harmful to self	Self-concerned
Controlled	Autonomous
Infantile	Adult
Drifting	Purposeful
Fanatical	Balanced
Artificially committed	Genuinely committed
Family-indifferent	Family-minded

In what follows I shall illustrate the force of each of these oppositions as they occur in popular sentiment against religious cults. However, let me again emphasize that I have separated out what I feel to be the main categories of anti-cult sentiment for solely analytical purposes. In reality, of course, the sentiment is naturally expressed as a constantly changing, but relatively coherent and even unitary, view. It is convenient to take most of the illustrations from interviews conducted by me with the relatives of practising and former members of the Unification Church (U.C.) in Britain,

but confirmation of the wider social location of the dominant
themes in anti-cult sentiment could, if space allowed, be provided from journalism, fiction and everyday conversation.

1. BRAINWASHING

The most common popular guises in which these oppositions occur are variants on the theme that some cults "brainwash" their recruits either at the time of recruitment or during
the subsequent period of socialization and induction. "Brainwashing" in its popular usage has been used to imply loss of
free will, fanaticism, psychological dependence on others, ir-
rationality and other kinds of conditions, all of which are allegedly in sharp contrast to the typical cult recruit's previous
state of mind and patterns of action.

Newspaper headlines such as "Vicar saves 'prisoner' of
the Moonie zombies" (News of the World, 23.10.1977), "My Judy
and the strange spell of the Moon people" (Daily Mail
25.6.1978), "Fight to bring Moon children back to earth" (The
Observer, 20.2.1977), "Mr Moon woos the brains of Britain",
(The Sun 20.11.1976) or more straightforwardly, "U.S. cult leaders on brainwashing charge" (Daily Telegraph, 15.10.1976) all
play on the mysterious and potentially threatening character
of cultic campaigns to recruit members in Britain. Perhaps
a certain degree of poetic licence and fantasy is allowed to
headline writers, but the same kind of sentiment is also found
in the statements made by the close relatives of some of the
cults' members and ex-members. The theme of mental enslave-
ment is frequently inseparable in their statements from quite
explicit claims about the before-and-after differences in recruits' state of mind. The father of a young woman who was
effectively "talked out" of the U.C. by her parents, for example, claimed that:

> I realized very quickly that she was brainwashed
> . . . She had this sort of glazed look . .
> I realized that she was not with us. . . She
> was no more my Marilyn, she was quite a different
> person.

The brother of a practising member of the cult was adamant
in an interview that the proof of his brother's brainwashing
was plain to see in his incapacity to fill in routine administrative forms competently, to conduct a coherent telephone
conversation and to make his own travel arrangements. In

the words of another member's mother, her son ". . . has thrown away a promising career, but the worst aspect of it is that he has been turned into a human computer, spouting the loony beliefs of this man Moon". In these and other cases my informants were at great pains to emphasize that it was partly the sharpness of the before-and-after contrasts in states of mind which convinced them that the cult member's mind had been tampered with.

This is not the place to illustrate in full my point that the accusation of brainwashing is at the centre of most people's disquiet about the U.C.,³ but it serves as an organizing principle for many expressions of popular sentiment against cults. Some people organize all their thinking about cults in terms of it and can thereby articulate a complete theory of the effects of cultic recruitment strategy. But since the theory is not universally supported, I have chosen to keep separate the various arguments which, in some people's opinion, definitely amount to a unitary explanation. I shall therefore concentrate on the close, but usually implicit, connections which exist between use of the brainwashing accusation and various other charges made about the abnormality of cult recruits.

2. SELF-HARM

One of the prominent charges made against cults and which is more often than not linked to notions of brainwashing is that their members have somehow been induced to abandon responsibility for themselves to such an extent that they are actually in danger of harming themselves and/or other people. This may take the form of a claim that physical and/or mental damage has been sustained as a direct result of the involvement in the cult. Evidence of health problems, for example, was prominent in the argument of one parent that when his daughter was in the cult:

> She looked like a zombie; she was an absolute fright. She had a nervous twitch and her face had erupted. Her ear was sore, and we were so worried about her.

A very similar account was given in an interview by the mother of a member who had spent several years working for the cult abroad before being brought home unexpectedly suffering from a variety of mental illnesses which have required intermittent treatment in hospital over the past few years:

> When he came in he didn't recognize anybody.
> He was absolutely drained physically and mentally
> . . . He was incapable of doing anything,
> and he didn't have anything to eat or drink.
> Of course, I rang the doctor first thing the
> next morning, and they got him into hospital
> that night, and he was in there for about
> a month, I think. Maybe a little longer.

Not surprisingly, this kind of claim about physical and mental harm is a common feature of mass media accounts of religious cults, although the headline "Moonie link in death riddle" (Daily Express, 25.8.1979) is untypically extreme in its suggestiveness. More typical of the general unease felt by some close relatives of cult members is an anxiety about the physically demanding conditions of life in the U.C. and about the locus of "offical" responsibility for members' health and welfare. Thus, the father of two members of the cult was quite explicit in saying that:

> . . . . my fight with the Church wasn't on
> religious grounds. No, it was about people.
> First of all, the stopping of the education
> of two young people; and now, secondly, the
> mishandling of the health of one of their members,
> i.e. my daughter, who had suffered for about
> a year in America, not having proper medical
> treatment or being properly examined, and
> then coming over here, again not being properly
> examined, and then being dumped on us here.
> When she was finally sent to the local hospital,
> it was very quickly diagnosed that she had
> a tumour of the brain. This had been going
> on for a year and should have been diagnosed
> beforehand.

3. EXTERNAL CONTROL

A variant on the claim that cults may be harmful is the view that the member's fundamental sense of selfhood is eroded and replaced with a pathologically heightened sense of the self's immersion in the collectivity. Another way of putting this is to say that the normal boundary between the public and private presentation of self has been destroyed and that all manner of normally private aspects of life are acted out

in public in the cult.   As in the case of the brainwashing accusation, the intended effect is to suggest that the locus of
self-control has shifted from an inner to an outer area and
that the self's normal defenses   against outside forces have
thereby been weakened.

Some complaints under this heading were of the rather
trivial kind which interpreted the practice among the rank-
and-file U.C. members of pooling their clothes and other personal effects as evidence of defective individual identity.   In
fact, some relatives were so shocked to discover that a member's prized possessions had been given to the cult,or at least
shared with other members, that they could only infer that
brainwashing had been employed.   It was as if the member's
pre-cult identity   had resided in his or her possessions: do-
nating a treasured guitar or record-player to the cult could
only be taken as evidence of severe mental disturbance.

Other complaints had to do with the fact that religious
experiences, beliefs and practices were expressed publicly in
many cults, while popular sentiment seemed to categorize such
things as essentially private.   Some people are offended and,
in many cases, shocked that public displays of what they feel
to be intensely personal matters are normal for cult members.
Their   relatives, for example, sometimes find it disturbing
and embarrassing that questions of religious faith, commitment
and feeling are raised in conversation at home or in correspondence, and this is often seen as evidence of inappropriate
behaviour or incongruous emotion.   The sound in their own
homes of fervent prayer, devotional songs or reading aloud
from sacred texts is deeply disturbing to people who   confine
"normal" religion to either private devotions or public ritual.

More worrying still to many people was the suspicion
that gifted cult members were being prevented from expressing
or developing their capacity to enjoy such interests as music,
fiction or photography.   From the point of view of members'
relatives the loss of opportunities to pursue interests which
had previously been satisfying and challenging was felt to be
a further loss of self-hood and a capitulation to an imposed,
rather than a freely chosen, course of development.   Significantly, in the eyes of the cult's critics, it is the basically
private and inner-directed interests in arts and hobbies whose
abandonment by its members was most strongly criticized.   The
mother of a female member of one year's standing, for example,
thought that the waste of talent was tragic:

I   think that sort of shut-off, closed-in, blinkered
life -- well, it's just like being a nun, which
I also think is a waste of time for somebody

who's   bright   and   enthusiastically   interested
in   everything,   to   turn   everything   inside   out,
particularly   when   you   haven't   been   that   sort
of person.

This   kind   of   criticism   is   often   linked   with   the   further   complaint   that   the   solitude   and   privacy   which   might   provide   for
resistance   to   externally-imposed   ideas   are   denied   cult   members.
In   the   words   of   the   younger   brother   of   a   U.C.   member   who   had
spent   only   a   few   weekends   in   the   cult's   centres:

They   wouldn't let   me   do   anything   on   my   own.
They   always   had   group   activities,   like   playing
games,   or   even   if   you're   drawing   pictures
and   writing   poems   you're   in   a   group   doing
that.   They   don't   like   you   being   on   your   own
at all.

While   some   critics   of   the   U.C.   see   in   this   a   sinister,
custodial   function,   others   merely   complain   about   the   highly   dependent   relationships   which   are   thereby   generated   and   sustained   among   the   members.

4.   INFANTILIZATON

It   is   a   short   step   from   this   complaint   to   the   charge   that
s ome   cults   deliberately   reduce   their   members   to   a   state   of
mental   immaturity   akin   to   infantilization.   This   is   a   common
complaint   among   close   relatives   of   members   and   is   usually
documented   with   extensive   "evidence"   of   childish   and   child-like
behaviours   which   allegedly   conflict   sharply   with   behaviour   pri-
or   to   recruitment.   Indeed,this   is   the   most   prominent   theme   in
one   of   the   most   widely   read   exposés   of   the   U.C.   written   by
an   apostate   (Edwards,   1979),   and   it   has   elicited   the   support
of   very   many   parents   of   cult   members   who   have   echoed   in   various   ways   the   observation   of   a   former   cult   member's   mother
that:

One   of   the   things   that   they   did   that   I   found
very   significant   --   it   makes   me   think   that
it's   some   type   of   hypnosis   --   they   were   always
saying   "let's   have   a   choo-choo".   And   when
they   said   this,   everybody   grabbed   hands,   and
Thomas   said   they   were   fierce   in   grabbing,
they   were   frightened   in   case   they   were   left
out   of   the   circles.   They   had   to   grab   somebody
and   hold   somebody's   arm   or   hand   and   they
sang   a   little   childish   rhyme.

Interestingly, this is precisely the rationale for some acts of "deprogramming" in which infantilization is attributed to definite procedures for undermining adult self-responsibility by social, psychological or dietary means.

5.   DRIFT

A further extension of the idea that cult members are deprived of their free will and that they cannot be presumed to be responsible for themselves is the fear that they are unable to control their own future development.   In the case of some members' relatives this fear takes the form of a specific anxiety that the cult-member has abandoned a career or an ideal, for example, which had formerly meant a great deal to him or her.   Thus the father of a former veterinary student felt that:

> At the beginning [of his daughter's involvement with the U.C.] we were absolutely horrified.   We just felt that it wasn't Susan at all.   Partly, I think, because her attitutde towards animals changed and we were used to her being vegetarian.

Like many other parents, this father inferred that his daughter must have abandoned control over her self-development in order to become absorbed in a movement which departed in so many ways from her former ideals and interests.   Other relatives were less specific in their anxieties, voicing instead a general unwillingness to accept that a life-long commitment to the U.C. could ever be taken as a satisfactory career.   This is sometimes coupled with a strong suspicion that development of intellectual skills, personality strengths and emotional stability is arrested by the abandonment of self-responsibility.   It is often specifically denied that experience of life in a cult can be rewarding in any other ways because the direction of any such development would have been dictated by other people.

6.   FANATICISM

If it is objected, in defence of cults, that their members do enjoy some beneficial changes in their personality, their skills in interpersonal relations or their practical experience

of the world, the usual reply is that these things are gained
only at the cost of an unhealthy fanaticism. It is claimed
that the narrow focus of cult life on a highly restricted range
of emotions and activities in the exclusive company of like-
minded people produces an imbalance in interests and feelings.
The former wife of a U.C. member, for example, recalled that:

> Seeing him always reading the Divine Principle
> drove me mad. Listening to the prayers and
> the fact that he had no conversation but about the
> U.C. He didn't want to talk about anything else
> and he's still the same today apparently. He visits
> his parents occasionally and that's all he talks
> about . . . He ends up crying because he just
> can't get through to them at all about the U.C..

A mother of a strongly committed member had no doubts that,
since her daughter had "decided that this was it so far as
she was concerned, it really wouldn't matter within reason
what they did". For the single-minded pursuit of goals which,
to make matters worse, have allegedly been imposed by other
people is considered damaging to self-development and positively inimical to the idea of a well-rounded person with multiple
interests in different social spheres.

Another aspect of the concern with fanaticism is the
suspicion that what is seen as an intensely one-sided focus
of all the cult member's energies on a single project or theme
only amounts to a passing fad or phase. Part of the resistance strategy of anti-cultists is, therefore, to draw attention
to the unexpectedness of most members' conversion and recruitment in order to diminish their significance in the individual's
whole life. Thus, the mother of a young man who had been
in the U.C. for four years still felt that his membership was
a passing fad. In fact, she likened him to his elder brother
who had dabbled in the Divine Light Mission of the Guru
Maharaj Ji and the "Flower People" before becoming an atheist.
Similarly, the mother of two U.C. members admitted that:

> When we heard about this fantastic new thing that
> our son had joined we think "Ah, it'll pass." When
> you hear that his sister has joined too, you think,
> "Oh well, she always follows Henry and they'll both
> come out soon". . . You think "Oh well, they won't
> be there long.

This particular style of reasoning is also strongly supportive
of the brainwashing argument through the implication that a
"normal" conversion would not be achieved so quickly and so
unexpectedly. It is also closely connected with the charge

that underhand tactics must have been employed and that the whole appearance of a genuinely religious conversion is nothing but an artificially induced illusion.

7. INSTABILITY

In this context the testimony of <u>ex-members</u> takes on a special significance, " since they appear to demonstrate by their very existence the "artificiality" and fragility of cultic conversion. Of course, the details of their accounts are highly prized for what they allegedly reveal about misdeeds and malpractices within cults, but the mere fact that some people can be shown to have passed through them within quite a short period of time is often taken by itself as evidence for the short-lived and phase-specific nature of cultic conversion and commitment. Ex-members become living proof for some people that cultism is unstable and therefore illegitimate. This argument is also extended to include the charge that, in view of the allegedly short-lived and artificially induced or imposed nature of cultic commitment, the period of membership represents nothing more than a temporary and in itself worthless interruption of the normal course of personal development or life-history. This is part of the refusal to take seriously the cults' claims to authenticity and part of the catalogue of criticisms directed at their hold over many young people. It reinforces the claim that cult-members are merely drifting or marking time, while the highly esteemed tasks of constructing a career and forming a family are supposedly neglected.

In cases where cult-members of long-standing have actually married, produced children and apparently developed a career within the cult, the argument has to be modified. But the relatives whom I have interviewed have shown no consequent willingness to grant the normality or acceptability of cults in these cases; they simply switch to a different method of attack. They complain, for example, that the children are not cared for properly or that they are artificially alienated from "outside" relatives, that the marriage has an unstable basis and that the prospects for ever living an adequate life outside the cult diminish with increasing length of membership.

8.   FAMILY INDIFFERENCE

In this respect it is important to consider the objections
which are loudly voiced by many close relatives of cult members against any suggestion that life in a cult might itself
be part of a new career and might result in some kind of marriage or family-making.   For this suggestion usually provokes
violent ripostes to the effect that a life-time of imposed drudg-
ery in subjection to others could not possibly qualify as a
career and that in no sense could anything approximating to
a stable human family flourish within cultic confines.   In both
cases the objection is based on the assumption that personal
authenticity cannot be expressed in conditions in which the
individual actor is not, theoretically, at least, free to choose
the path of his or her development.   To the extent that decisions about careers, marriages and parenthood within the cult
and relations with the family of orientation are felt to be ex-
cessively influenced by other people they are considered inval-
id.   A   source of great annoyance   to many relatives of cult
members,   for example,   is the claim that association with parents and/or siblings is denied to members on the grounds that
it might undermine their commitment.   One father went so far
as to say that his whole opposition to the U.C. would cease
if his son were allowed home occasionally for a holiday.   Another cult member's mother who has suffered serious ill health
during her son's membership was most bitter about what she
saw as the U.C.'s failure to allow him home to visit her.   She
compared the cult very unfavourably in this respect with the
practices of other religious groups with which she was familiar.
A more measured response came from the father of a long-serv-
ing member who said:

> I   suppose, as I have made it clear to Paul, why
> we fuss is because its so sad to us that we never
> see him and therefore he never takes part in some
> of the things which have been essentially, are
> essentially, family things.   And we have been a
> closely-knit family -- that's the sad thing.

This particular family is very wealthy, and the son's
failure to settle down in a career with a stable future was
not a major concern of his parents.   Others, however, were
adamant that it was the cult's apparent reluctance to encourage its members to complete courses of education and training
which was most disturbing and vexing.   As one mother put it,
when describing how her son broke the news that he had
abandoned higher education to enter the U.C.:

> Well, I burst into tears.   I was shattered, abso-
> lutely couldn't believe it.   You cannot believe that

all the sacrifice in years is just tossed lightly on
one side, and nobody's the slightest bit concerned
that here are two parents, and many like us, that
have done without to give their children a good
start in life, and it's tossed on one side, and they
are told that colleges and universities are satanic.
It's nonsense and very wrong.

Finally, it must be added that, even when cult members
spend time at home, there is often friction and embarrassment as a result of the failure of each side to comprehend the
other's point of view. Close relatives lose patience, for example, with members who dress incongruously, persist with attempts to preach to the family or show no interest in their siblings other than trying to recruit them to the cult.

The other side of the coin, as far as the popular unease
about cults' attitudes towards members' families is concerned,
is that the domestic relationships prevailing within cults are
the object of intense suspicion and derision.[5] The grounds for
this attitude relate directly to the point made earlier about
public/private boundaries. The idea that marriage might be
contracted between cult members on the advice or orders of a
leader is profoundly shocking to many outsiders because it
flouts some major assumptions in modern Western cultures about
the essentially personal and intimate nature of marital relationships. To act on such advice is widely regarded as an
abdication of self-hood and a capitulation to forces having no
proper relevance to what is nowadays seen increasingly as a
free contractual relationship between two free, isolated individuals. The opinions of many relatives were summed up in the
words of a mother of two cult members:

It frightens me really, I mean, the idea of anybody
choosing a partner for anybody else I think is fantastic. Quite fantastic. . .I mean, the thought
of marriage with someone who someone else thinks
is fine for you is beyond comprehension, quite beyond my comprehension.

There is also a particularly strong sense of revulsion
in the popular feeling against the associated idea that marriage partners in cults might spend long periods of their lives
in separation or might not enjoy any right to domestic privacy
within a cult's residential centres. Again, the basis of such
revulsion is the extremely deep-rooted conviction that marriage
is nowadays a largely private matter, subject only to the conditions imposed freely on it by the two partners alone.

But feelings of outrage probably reach a peak in connection with the collective child-rearing practices of some cults.
This is a particularly sore point for those people whose close

relatives in a cult have produced children whose upbringing
has become largely the responsibility of the cult as a collectivity. Many grandparents, for example, are profoundly disturbed by the thought that their grandchildren in a cult may
be separated from their mother for long periods of time and
may be effectively reared by a succession of short-term, inexperienced child-minders recruited among the cult's newest and
therefore youngest members. This is widely felt to be an unhealthy and potentially damaging practice[6] which, again, represents for some people an illicit invasion of the private
sphere of life by a public agency. This kind of argument follows on quite naturally from the charge of brainwashing which
can also be translated into the terms of an illegitimate transgression of the "normal" boundary separating the private area
of mind from the public area of cult indoctrination processes.

CONCLUSIONS

      I wish to draw three conclusions from the above analysis
of popular sentiment against unpopular cults. Firstly, the
analysis has shown the high degree of coherence among the
varied strands of critical sentiment. They are far from being
a random collection of disparate grievances. On the contrary,
they evince an underlying logic (in the loosest sense of the
term) which ties them all together and binds them into a coherent position. The key element in this logic is a sharp
and pervasive contrast between, on the one hand, the supposedly normal states of the person as an autonomous rational and
free being, and, on the other, the allegedly characteristic
states of the person in a cult as a dependent, irrational and
controlled being.

      The analysis has shown, secondly, that critics of cults do
not merely voice irrational fears or prejudices: they can provide "evidence" for their accusations which is selected quite
rationally in the light of complex cultural assumptions about
normality. Anti-cult sentiment may be encountered in scattered
fragments in casual conversation as well as in more carefully
constructed responses to interviewers' questions or lawyers'
cross-examination; and the degree of rational inference from
"evidence" to "accusation" to "theory" is correspondingly variable. What remains fairly constant, however, is the implicit
reference back to cultural assumptions about normal people or
normal religious groups. This is the (usually) unstated bed-
rock of anti-cult sentiment and it amounts to an eloquent testimony concerning the taken-for-granted values of British society. Unwittingly, the cults expose the limits of normality al-

lowed in this society to religious feelings, actions and institutions.

My third conclusion is that, in the light of what the analysis has revealed about, on the one hand, the very real and rationally grounded fears of cult critics about cults' alleged transgression of many critical cultural boundaries between normal and abnormal, and, on the other, the rigid and sometimes ill-examined assumptions of cult critics about the normal states of the person, it is not helpful either to dismiss anti-cultism as a witch-hunt or to dismiss the cults as irremediably evil. At present, unfortunately, the two sides to the dispute are polarized in their thinking and each is largely unreceptive to the other's point of view. The result is that conflict has moved on to the level of mutual abuse: brainwashing extremists vs. reactionary McCarthyites. I am not naive enough to believe the dispute could be resolved simply by dialogue and reasoned argument. But I do believe that a retreat from the continued practice of mutual abuse would go some way towards a clearer understanding of the issues at stake.

Understanding the nature of anti-cult sentiment is a small step in the right direction. As I have tried to explain, this step involves an examination of the taken-for-granted assumptions popularly made in British society about the nature of the person in the "normal" and "abnormal" states. In other words, the response to so-called cults reflects some critical features of the cultural classifications, categories and boundaries with which people make sense of their everyday experience. If space had permitted, this analysis could have been profitably extended backwards in time to have included earlier instances of public hostility to new relegous movements, for I lean towards the view that there are some remarkable continuities in the social pre-conditions and phenomenal forms of anti-cultism. New religious movements cannot, in my view, be understood in isolation from their socio-cultural contexts, and other chapters in this book reinforce this view with regard to particular movements in various places.

NOTES

1.   In popular usage this term refers, in an often pejorative way, to those religious movements which have succeeded in recruiting thousands of young members in many countries in the past two decades. Some, like the Unification Church, Transcendental Meditation, the Divine Light Mission and Krishna

1. cont.   Consciousness, have brought Eastern ideas of spirituality to the West, while others, such as the Family of Love (formerly Children of God), assorted Jesus Freak groups and Scientology, have embroidered on elements already available in Western cultures. The term "new religious movements" is probably a suitable and less offensive synonym for most purposes, but in this paper I shall conserve the use of "cults" because it conveys the nuances of unfavourable meanings intended by most (but not all) cricis of these groups. This is central to the paper's interests.

2.   "Popular sentiment" as I have chosen to refer to the vague and fragmentary impressions conveyed through the mass media and personal conversations as well as structured interviews, is by no means unitary. For a more "finely tuned" analysis of responses to cults in various spheres of society, see Beckford, 1979.

3.   For a more detailed analysis of the rhetoric of brainwashing accusations, see Beckford " 'Brainwashing' and 'deprogramming' in Britain: the social sources of anti-cult ment" in Richardson, J. 1981.

4.   For an enlightening investigation of this point in connection with anti-Mormonism in the nineteenth century, see Davis, 1971 and Hampshire, 1979b.

5.   Not all outsiders agree, however, that the influence of the Unification Church on personal relationships is baneful. See, for example, the view of Elizabeth Clark:

> "Unification Church members have told me that there are at present husbands and wives living apart, and children in the community being raised by adults other than their natural parents. In addition, the nuclear family is not the projected goal for personal relationships they claim; rather, it is envisaged that trinities of couples may live and raise their children together in a variation on the extended family system. All of these developments are encouraging, since they could be more liberating for women than the nuclear family arrangement sanctioned by our culture. I hope in general that Unification Church members will courageously attempt to live by these positive aspects of their vision and not relapse into the traditional patterns of relationship which are proving themselves to be increasingly unsatisfactory for young women.

(Elizabeth Clark, "Women in the Theology of the Unification Church", in Hodges and Bryant (eds). 1978.

6.   One measure of the perceived importance of this topic is
the growing number of enquiries conducted in several countries
into the effects of "cultism" on children and youths.   See
Bundesregierung, 1980; Conférence Episcopale, 1975; Dymally,
1974; Dole, 1979; New York State Assembly, 1979 and Newsweek,
1979.

THE UNIFICATION CHURCH AND THE AMERICAN FAMILY:
STRAIN, CONFLICT, AND CONTROL

David G. Bromley
Bruce C. Busching
Anson D. Shupe, Jr.

In this paper we shall explore from one perspective what the new religions reveal about the larger society in which they emerge, by attempting to delineate answers to two interrelated questions: 1) what social conditions provoked strain between the new religions and the larger society, and 2) how did this strain eventuate in the repression of certain new religious groups. The data that will be presented here are based on our several year study of the Unification Church (hereafter UC) and the loose coalition of groups opposed to the new religions which we have referred to as the anti-cult movement.[2] However, we would contend that the generalizations and arguments put forward in this paper are not necessarily limited to the American case of the Unification Church.

Numerous allegations have been lodged against the behavior of UC members and leaders: 1) that members are brainwashed, 2) that deceptive techniques are employed in both fundraising and recruitment activities, 3) that members' labor is exploited in order to accumulate vast sums of money for the church or Reverend Moon personally, 4) that church leaders are ruthless authoritarians on a manic quest for power, and 5) that the UC is engaged in illicit political activity on behalf of the South Korean government.[3] These charges, many of which are strikingly similar to those made against earlier "new religions"[4] lead to the conclusion that it is specific UC behaviors and activities themselves which have evoked strain, conflict and repression. However, we shall argue that it is not content but rather the social context of any behavior which determines the social definition of it and the social reaction to it. Behavior which is represented as illicit and manic in one context may be defined as religious rebirth in another.

SOURCES OF STRAIN

Behavior is likely to be regarded as deviant when it is expressed in a context which poses a challenge either to the power structure or goals of powerful groups. The conflict be-

302

tween the UC and parents of UC members originated from a
challenge to the goals and power structure of the families of
recruits. The first major source of strain between the UC and
the familial institutions developed   from the threat posed to
the family's goal of preparing offspring for participation in
the economic order, the cornerstone upon which individual's
careers, lifestyles and class mobility rested.   Parents directed
much of their socialization activity toward creating individuals
capable of playing highly specialized roles, who possessed
self-interested motivation, who were free of ideological cons-
straint and who held instrumental (as opposed to affective)
role orientations.   Toward this end, for example, parents typically sought to maximize their offsprings' educational opportunities; encourage their development of individual skills,
initiative and interests; reward them for conceiving of themselves as autonomous and independent individuals; support personal interest as the basis for major decisions (e.g. career,
marriage); and develop role playing abilities which allowed
them to adapt flexibly to various social settings and foster
decision-making on a calculating, rational basis.

The UC, in contrast, constructed a diffuse, member role
which required few, if any, specialized skills.   Nor was any
emphasis given to gaining the kinds of skill requisite for conventional careers, as maintenance of communal solidarity was
the pre-eminent concern.   Indeed, the communal structure of
the UC deliberately fostered suppression of self-interested
motivation by prohibiting accumulation of personal possessions
or wealth and even discouraging clothing and grooming practices which might reinforce individual distinctiveness. Members
expended a great deal of time and energy attempting to shed
ego, decisions were made for the good of the group rather than
the individual,   and goals were spiritual rather than materialistic.   Further, virtually all activities and aspects of individual role performance within the communal organization were
directly or indirectly linked to and legitimated by UC ideology.
Finally, individuals were expected to relate to one another
"heartistically" (i.e. in affective terms with an emphasis on
love) as "brothers" and "sisters" (i.e. on the basis of ascription rather than achievement).   Whatever else may be said a-
bout it, UC socialization does not prepare one for integration
into the current American economic system.

Therefore, when offspring radically re-oriented their life-
styles and values and concomitantly   rejected those career/
domestic aspirations which until that time they had shared in
common with their parents, the latter were predictably dis-
traught.   The following two statements made by parents of UC
members illustrate these feelings:

Our twenty-two year old daughter Anne was a de-
vout practising Catholic who dreamed for years of
being a public health nurse in Appalachia. She
even visited the town in which she would be trained
after her graduation. Her dreams and ours were
shattered suddenly last January, 1974 when Anne
came home unexpectedly and announced she was
quitting nursing college and joining the Unification
Church. (CEFM, 1976 V. II: 30)

Richard was three days into his senior semester
as a Pre-Med student , University of Texas, Austin.
He had a 3.989 grade-point average. The cult got
him almost on the spot. At this time he had no
ambition, no aims. This is the young man who was
to be an MD and President of the United States by
the age of fourty (sic). (CEFM, 1976, V. II. 18)

The other major source of strain within the family emanated
from the implicit power structure within family units.[5] While
socialization was devoted in large measure to transforming a
child into an autonomous adult, offspring were expected to tac-
itly acknowledge the titular leadership status of parents and
to maintain membership within the family unit. However, membership in the UC involved joining a fictive kinship system
in which all members were designated as brothers and sisters
and Moon and his wife were designated as "True Parents" (as
opposed to biological parents). Moon's charistmatic status as
a messianic figure accorded him moral authority over UC
"Family members" superior to that of biological parents. By
recognizing Moon's superior moral status, UC members ceded to
Moon the authority to make extraordinary claims upon them
personally, and they in turn assumed the status of disciples,
open and submissive to Moon's moral leadership.

This allocation of moral superiority to Moon by UC members had profound implications for their familial relationships.
On one level it was simply galling to parents that their sons
and daughters would unquestionably abandon alcohol, drugs,
cigarettes, profanity, long hair, and sexual freedom for Moon
when even parental advice on such matters evoked hositility.
However, there was a more significant implication of Moon's
moral authority. U.C. membership involved a series of activities and commitments -- giving up virtually all personal possessions, moving into a UC center, taking on a new identity,
abandoning previous career and marital plans, attenuating
relationships with outsiders, and devoting full time and energy
to the movement. At some later point even more permanent and
fundamental commitments were made as members were required
to marry within the movement, mates were approved or selected

by Church elders, and children were raised within the movement. Parents essentially were forced to acknowledge the
superiority of Moon's claims to their children's time, energy,
and loyalty -- either directly by supporting their activity or
indirectly by not opposing their involvement. Acceptance of
UC membership meant that parents had to reduce their own
claims on their children's time, energy, and loyalty. They felt
unable to demand, for example, that their children come home
for the holidays, in the event of illness or death in the family
or even that regular contact be maintained. Complaints containing these themes of rupturing of family ties abounded in
anti-cult literature and testimonies:

> After the few letters, our only contacts with her
> were collect phone calls from scattered areas. In
> almost three years she has been allowed to come
> home twice. . . (CEFM, 1976, V.I: 35)

> She has given up her freedom and is willing to
> go wherever Moon sends her, to marry whomever
> he chooses, to do whatever he asks. . . (CEFM,
> 1976, V. II: 35)

> She didn't even send her father a birthday card
> . . . She said she didn't even consider us her
> real parents, only her physical parents. Moon and
> his wife were her real parents. (The Rome News,
> New Brunswick, N.J., 10/12/75)

DYNAMICS OF STRAIN

For the families of UC members, of course, the "crisis"
of a "loss" of a child they experienced occurred at a particularly awkward time. Not only had parents deliberately attempted to move their sons and daughters toward autonomy and a-
dulthood in the mainstream of society but also their sources
of leverage over their offspring declined directly as they did
so. It was, therefore, particularly upsetting that just as what
families perceived of as years of preparation and sacrifice
were about to reach fruition their offspring abruptly "threw
away" these often hard-earned opportunities.

Parents' initial response to their offspring's announce-
ment of UC membership was often a mixture of disbelief, horror
and panic. Since a substantial proportion of UC members joined the UC while travelling or away from home working, or
studying at college, family discussion of these choices was difficult and frequently limited to long distance phone calls or
exchanges of letters. The latter form of communication, of

course, provided much opportunity for delays and breaks in contact. Parental expressions of concern and pleas to reconsider hastily made decisions were countered by their children's reassurances that the UC was the most wonderful and fulfilling group which they had ever encountered. In large measure these parental reactions were shaped by the overwhelmingly hostile, negative media coverage accorded the UC after 1973[6] while UC members' reactions were shaped by the intense, liberating, confirmatory experiences which typify initial entry into a communal group.[7]

Strain was likely to increase as parents gained additional "information" about the UC through the media or through initial contacts with anti-cult groups (themselves frequently suppliers of much of the media reports), on the one hand, and as new UC members developed deeper commitments and involvement in the UC, on the other. In a frequently repeated sequence novitiates to the UC would first attend workshops or retreats lasting anywhere from a week-end to several weeks, then take up residence with the UC in a fundraising or witnessing team, and (once a full-time UC member) disavow indefinitely their previous career plans, romantic attachments, and virtually all other social relationships outside the UC.[8]

Once it became apparent to parents that UC membership was not a transitory or ephemeral phase, they began attempting to apply greater pressure on what they now perceived to be their errant, misguided offspring. These attempts included such measures as refusing to send money, recalling credit cards, calling on other family members (e.g. siblings, grandparents) to dissuade the offspring, occasionally travelling to where the offspring was actively involved in UC activities to confront him or her, and even the threat of disowning the latter. However, parents quickly found that most formerly effective mechanisms of social control now proved ineffective. Much of parents' remaining control over post-adolescent sons and daughters had been based on common (economic) interest in emerging careers, continuing economic dependency during college years, and of course affective family bonds. The former career plans had now been disavowed and the emotional bonds considerably diminished with parental resistance. Indeed exclusion from biological parents' affective support simply accentuated the importance of the UC's communal/familial relationships. Further, UC ideology, in anticipation of such resistance, interpreted all non-UC members as Satanically motivated and part of a "fallen" world. Therefore, parental resistance had a ready ideological interpretation within the movement which confirmed a number of assumptions about the "outside world" and the importance of the UC's mission, and which legitimated further disassociation from biological families. Offspring's progressive withdrawal from larger society into the UC sub-culture in mirror fashion, likewise convinced parents that their progeny were literally captives of an alien force or diabolical will that threatened the very concept of the American family and placed sons and daughters in grave psycho-physical jeopardy.

This process of mutual disaffection could span a number of months or even longer as each side sought to convince the other of the errors of its perception of the situation. Usually after numerous emotional exchanges that grew in intensity and frustration, a point was reached where one or both sides finally ran out of patience with the other. At this juncture attempts at further negotiation were dropped and the irresolvability of differences was squarely confronted. As one UC member, who had literally spent years in an ongoing dialogue with her family to coax them at least to a position of neutrality, finally wrote home in exasperation:

> I met very few Christians in the U.S. who were living the life they preached. But I see Unification Church members giving everything they've got . . . it grieves me that I cannot share my idealism or my faith with you at this time. . . You claim that you and Mom would not try to stop me from participating in the movement, although you personally don't want to join in. That's actually not quite honest, is it? Two years ago you thought it was a good idea to kidnap me and even "debrainwash" me. . . Have you changed your tune? (Finally locating the source of family conflict in her parents' own selfish desires, she concluded:) What a comedown it was for me to abandon my scholarship without asking your permission. "My daughter the distinguished student. My daughter the AP correspondent. My daughter the world traveller." But could you admit, "My daughter the brainwashed cult follower?" Wouldn't your friends feel sorry for you?

ANTI-CULT IDEOLOGY

At some point in the process of emerging conflict, families often concluded that their offspring were unable to respond to them in an appropriate manner (i.e., as the parents themselves might respond) and therefore there was no basis for sustaining a mutually acceptable relationship. In seeking to cope with this situation parents often became aware of and made contact with other parents confronting the same circumstances. Such parents formed interest groups which we have termed anti-cult associations to seek solidarity, a united front, and a solution to their common problems. These anti-cult associations sought to construct a symbolic interpretation for their offspring's behaviour which offered an explanation for their "incapacity" to respond "normally" and legitimated implementation of social control mechanisms which would return their sons or daughters to "normalcy". The metaphor around which anti-cult associations[9] constructed their ideology was that of "brainwashing". To assert that an individual was "brainwashed" implied a radical, unnatural personality transformation achieved by manipulative, coercive means. Brainwashed individuals were thought to have lost their free will and to have been directly controlled by malevolent agents.[10] The individual under such "mind control" was considered changed in virtually every respect and reduced to a zombie, that is, to a lifeless, unemotional robot-like being, controlled by pernicious cult leaders. The following newspaper headlines indicate the extent to which this imagery was disseminated through the media:

> He Was a Walking Zombie. [11]

> 'I Was Slave . . .Zombie' Returned Son Relates. [12]

> I Was Moon's Programmed Robot. [13]

> Members Are 'Slaves' [14]

Such "brainwashed" individuals could be dangerous to themselves and to others. Indeed, the power by which they had been "possessed" was allegedly so coercive and overwhelming that virtually everyone was thought to be vulnerable to it. UC members were credited with powers of "spot hypnosis" that could render strangers on the streeet immediately compliant within a few seconds. As one ex-UC member, who later joined the anti-cult movement, portrayed his experience:

> I think I was hypnotized at first. Basically by
> the girl that met me because she kept staring into
> my eyes and I kept being attracted to her eyes.
> Then, during the meal, it's very possible for some
> sort of drug to make me more susceptible to the lec-
> ture. Then after that it was brainwashing because
> I was hooked. I wanted to stay there; I wanted
> to learn what they had to say. There was repetition
> all the time. Very appealing. [15]

Even physical signs of such possession (e.g. UC members were thought to be identifiable by glassy eyes, vacant stares, gaunt appearances, a peculiar body odour, facial skin rash resulting from Vitamin A deficiency, monotone speech patterns, and a fixed permanent smile "with the mouth only")[16] purportedly existed, according to this anti-cult folklore.

REPRESSION OF THE UC

The anti-cult movement pursued two distinct but inter-related strategies against the UC. First, they authorized and financially supported individuals within their movement who would assume the task and risks of deprogramming. While not all parents were willing to go this far, enough were to sustain a lively business for moral entrepreneurs such as the notorious Ted Patrick.[17] When successful, deprogrammings of course a-chieved parents' pre-eminent goal of "recovering" their "brainwashed" offspring, reaffirmed the "brainwashing" ideology and simultaneously served as a technique for symbolic degrada-tion of the UC by virtue of the relatively lenient sanctions levied against it. Second, anti-cult associations, portraying themselves as coalitions of aggrieved families, sought alliances with other institutions which possessed greater sanctioning capacity.

Largely based on anti-cult movement initiatives, a number of other institutions undertook actions which symbolically or instrumentally excluded the UC from conventional social net-works. For example, numerous communities enacted municipal ordinances designed to impede UC fundraising, the New York State Board of Regents denied academic accreditation to the UC seminary in Barrytown, New York, the UC was denied member-ship in the New York Council of Churches, and the UC was not allowed by many colleges and universities to establish campus affiliate organizations. Further, a significant number of states held hearings and introduced legislation designed to dis-tinguish "cults" from legitimate churches. While these bills stood virtually no chance of passing constitutional muster, the hearings accompanying them served as an occasion for symbolic support and reaffirmation of the ideology underpinning the anti-cult movement. Thus, although the UC was not completely suppressed by the anti-cult movement's campaign, repressive activities nevertheless served to reassert the content of public morality and clearly placed the UC outside of its domain.

CONCLUSIONS

The study of the new religions is of sociological interest precisely because they are revealing of basic social structures and processes. In this paper we have attempted to elucidate one generic social process, the implementation of social control in response to a challenge to the power structures or goals of established institutions. We have argued that it is not the content but the context of behavior which determines the social response to it. Behaviors emitted which threaten institutional goals or power structures create strain.

Conflict increases as each side attempts, and fails, to formulate acceptable symbolic definitions of the new behavioral patterns, so that a basis for mutually voluntary exchanges is not re-established. At some point in this sequence one or both parties come to perceive that no such basis for sustaining mutually voluntary exchanges exists. If the threat and power differential are sufficiently great, the more powerful side (presumably the party representing institutionalized interests) attempts to move the other (the social movement organization and/or its members) into a deviant status. Successful designations of deviance involve both exclusionary activity and symbolic constructions (e.g. "brainwashing) which legitimate the kind of social control the established institution feels compelled to exert.

In the case discussed here the family was primarily concerned with "recovering" an errant member, and hence the ideology which was formulated focused on legitimating unilateral action (i.e. deprogramning) against the individual (although the UC was also discredited in the process). Because no formal legal procedure was available by which to undertake the kind of social measures families felt necessary (in large measure due to constitutional separation of church and state), informal vigilante-style deprogramming organizations arose to provide such "services" to families. Deprogrammers continued to operate through the 1970's because the legitimacy of the families in performing their roles as agents of socialization and preparation for economic careers allowed mobilization of support from numerous other institutions. Though deprogramming continued to remain a risky and marginal venture throughout that decade, there was sufficient ambiguity as to its scientific and moral bases to prevent the application of heavy legal penalties against deprogrammers. As a result, the new religions in general, and the UC in particular, experienced considerable social repression. Although not sufficient to destroy them, anti-cult activities did result in definitions of public morality which clearly located groups such as the UC outside the latter morality's bounds and which generated sufficient harassment to create, on the UC's part at least, a defensive embattled posture toward the larger society. This resulting "siege mentality" in turn rendered the kinds of social relationships they sought to establish within the movement much more difficult to sustain. Thus viewed from our perspective, the cult/anti-cult controversy is an example of deviance as an emergent process in which those challenging the interests and power structure of a system meet with a control response; the nature and extent of the threat experienced as well as the relative power of the two sides determine the outcome of the ensuing challenges over how behavior will be defined and treated.

NOTES

1.   This paper is the product of a combined effort. The order of authorship is alphabetical and does not imply any difference in the importance of contributions.

2.   Bromley and Shupe, 1979; Shupe and Bromley, 1980.

3.   See e.g. Bromley, David G., Shupe, Anson D. Jr., and Ventimiglia, Joseph C. "The Role of Anecdotal Atrocities in the Social Construction of Evil". Paper presented at the annual meeting of the American Sociological Association, Boston, 1979.

4.   Cox, Harvey "Deep Structures in the Study of New Religions" in Needleman and Baker (eds), 1978:122-130; Miller, Donald E. "Deprogramming in Historical Perspective" in Richardson, J. (ed), 1981; and Hampshire, 1979a.

5.   See eg. Lemert, 1962.

6.   See Bromley, Shupe and Ventimiglia op.cit. (note 3)

7.   Kanter, 1972.

8.   See Bromley, David G. and Shupe, Anson D. Jr. " 'Just a Few Years Seem Like a Lifetime': A role Theory Approach to Participation in Religious Movements", in Kriesberg (ed) 1979.

9.   See Shupe and Bromley, 1980.

10.   See Conway and Seigelman, 1978; Patrick and Dulack, 1976.

11.   The Knickerbocker News, New York, N.Y.: May 16, 1976.

12.   The Sun Press, Cleveland Heights, Ohio: October 16, 1975.

13.   The Dallas Morning News, Dallas, Texas: October 19, 1975.

14.   The Intelligencer, Coyleston, Pennsylvania: January 24, 1977.

15.   The Sun Press, Cleveland Heights, Ohio: October 16, 1975.

16.   See Shupe, Anson D. Jr. and Bromley, David G. "Witches, Moonies, and Evil" in Robbins and Anthony (eds), 1981.

17.   Patrick and Dulack, 1976.

THE ETHICS AND PSYCHOLOGY OF MEDIA CONSUMPTION

George Baker

This paper seeks to look at the way individuals and so-cieties consume media. We will look at this phenomenon through the eye of the holocaust at Jonestown, Guyana, in November of 1978. Our thesis is that Jonestown and its aftermath high-light in bold letters processes of conversion that take place in our ordinary lives. We will argue for a distinction between religious conversion and media conversion; and we will argue that Jonestown itself, its rise, destruction and after-shock, were instances of media conversion and its more potent form, brainwashing.

THE MEDIA AS A THEOLOGICAL MEDIUM

In the library of the **Graduate Theological Union** in Berkeley there is a major collection of books, periodicals and fugitive materials issued by new religious movements in America and elsewhere. Considered as media products, these materials are significant in two respects:

1.   They are marketed not as secular products but as items of a revelatory-like character having, therefore, a quasi-sacred status which sacramentalizes the time and effort spent in reading them.

2.   They are, in many cases, marketed as works of art in their own right; countless Buddhist groups, for example, adorn their writings with samples of Asian calligraphic and literary art.

A conclusion to be drawn is that, for participants, life as a converted Buddhist is both a gnostic and an aesthetic experience. A second conclusion is that converts to new reli-gions constitute a viable consumer market for media products. A third conclusion is that in these two respects the "spiritual economy" of new religious movements replicates that of mainline religions -- the Vatican is as much an aesthetic experience as a gnostic one, and there is no shortage of products and services for sale. Our general thesis is that the "secular media" seek to replicate the spiritual psychology of religion, and that life as a media-consumer is therefore intended to be both a gnostic-like and an aesthetic experience.

THE RISE OF THE SECULAR MEDIA

In addition to having a material culture and a social structure, societies possess informational cultures. In the tribal society information-flow mirrors social structures, but in the industrializing society technology intervenes to create both a commercial sub-culture of information handlers and an intellectual sub-culture of information consumers who respond to the content, technological medium and timing of reported events. As the industrialization and commercialization of information occurs, two important side-effects may be observed: the modernization of the tribal intellect takes place as a process of desacralization. An individual's outlook is as modern as his attitude toward public information is agnostic.

For this reason, we see media-reported events as devoid of inherent theological significance. God may have acted in history in earlier epochs, but in the modern outlook no public information is available. This means that our only data on God's activities in history is scriptural in character. Since printed and electronic media do not have the status of scripture, it follows that the news itself and the process of media consumption are secular affairs.

The other side-effect of industrializing information is ethical and moral in character. News is not only secular, but it comes down upon us at faster and faster rates. We may speak of the rising velocity of public information. Since the invention of the printing press the velocity has approached simultaneity by increments. The lag time between the occurrence of an event and its public-information marketing has been reduced through the application of successive generations of communications technology.

The psychological reciprocal of this reduction in lag time is experienced as an increased demand for rapid decision-making. Because these rapid, artificially-forced decisions are capable of being implemented with the same speed and technological means as mature decisions, a hidden, double standard of public morality is created. Some decisions to act stem from a maturely rooted sense of values and commitment, but others come from artificially heated information environments. The profound qualitative difference between these two orders of energy and intelligence is registered neither in the public media nor in public documents. Moreover, in the modern person, there is a secret willingness, one inherited from earlier centuries, to take a passive, peasant-like stance toward the affairs of Church and State, and this permits a predisposition to view public events as if they had been sanctioned or fore-ordained by tradition, precedent, or divine right. This means that the observer, the citizen with his coffee and morning paper no less than the historian with his note cards and archival documents, is caught in a moral and epistemological quandary. He is under pressure to evaluate a public event as if it arose from a reasoned commitment to long-term values, but he also knows that many of the events reported are of the order of knee-jerk reactions to high-velocity inform- ation. The observer, trained to weigh events according to their seriousness, suffers cognitive dissonance for being unable to identify the few real events in a crowd of artificial, media events.

The Jonestown holocaust was a case in point: The observer was under pressure from the media to consider the subject as a serious matter, but with each new wave of disclo- sures, it became apparent that on several levels the event and its simultaneous news coverage had been artificially heated -- manipulated -- by media tricksters who wanted to "go down in history." The post-Jonestown commentary in the media and academia arose from a desire for information about the events in Guyana that had been artificially induced. That desire had not grown out of any long-term commitment to researching the People's Temple and certainly not out of any commitment to studying religious communes in rural Guyana. That desire arose from the way in which one was affected by the news media reporting.

What deserves study and reflection, therefore, is the character of that desire for information and the process by which one was influenced by information that was presented in a certain way. To carry out such a study some definitions and additional distinctions are called for.

A PHENOMENOLOGICAL LANGUAGE OF REFERENCE

Because our general argument is that the processes of conversion take place in our ordinary lives, as well as in the lives of "converts," in the usual meaning of the term, a terminology suited to both autobiographical and sociological descriptions has been adopted.

"Media" should be thought of as a psychic process as well as a national industry. There are headlines in the mind and feelings as well as in the printed and electronic media.

"Religious conversion" is an ontological and psychological process opening a return to conscience in its autochtonal state. Religious conversion is a momentary state, an inner target of opportunity. One deepens, not changes, one's religion in such moments.

"Media conversion" is that process of absorption, self-accommodation and self-identification that takes place when the mind enters into the cognitive space of publicly-reported events. Examples abound in one's personal life as well as in the data of history and social science. I am on vacation in Yosemite Valley. In the morning I wake up to the smell of pines and the sight of towering granite walls. I feel close to these impressions of my body. Some unidentified inner movement takes place and, like Peter Sellers in the film, **Being There,** I turn on the television news. Quickly I become not only an observer of distant events but a pseudo-participant as well. I am bored or excited by, and pass judgment upon, the reported actions of others as if I were there beside them. I become a convert to this reported reality. This shift in my inner state I may call entertainment, civic duty, business, lifestyle, or, simply, habit. Admittedly, this mini- or micro-conversion to myself-as-an-extension-of-a-media-event will probably be over with, like an infatuation, quickly.

"Brainwashing." Unlike media conversion, which is a state in which my involvement with reported events remains passive, in instances of brainwashing I am put under pressure to act. But before I can be called on to act, my prospective role in events has to be defined or, at least, my own importance has to fit the event intuitively. As a modern buyer of ideas and information I am put under pressure to convert to a new, characteristically inflated, view of myself. I take on a new historical significance, and my beliefs about myself and my world take on an aura of transcendence, wisdom, and necessity. I feel forced, obligated, to act, as if decisively. My conversion, in other words, is to a new, emotionalized understanding of my own importance in the world. I am now ready to polarize my conception of issues in such a way that I come out either courageously "for" or "against" a dramatic action or cause.[1]

"Deprogramming." This is a term that was coined, I understand, by the recently convicted Ted Patrick, the Robin Hood of anti-cult movements in America.[2] Deprogramming has been used as a term to describe the forced abduction and counter-brainwashing of members of religious groups. Here I wish to use the term to mean the natural, as well as the forced, abandonment of a given activist stance. Natural deprogramming comes with the awareness that my earlier state of conversion or brainwashing had been media-induced.

These processes of conversion, brainwashing and de-programming take place in response to the headlines of the mind as well as in response to the headlines of the morning paper. In most cases the process is unnoticed. It is most likely to be noticed in information settings in which the ego experiences a seemingly irrestible pull to identify itself as a protagonist in the headlines. It is this temptation to give into this "pull" that is the pathological condition. The neurotic desire for "more information" only occurs after having abandoned a normal ego-identiy as observer and after having taken on a new identity as protagonist.

To introduce terms like "pathological" and "neurotic" is to make way for the entire vocabulary of psychoanalysis and psychotherapy; yet this process may be described equally well in the langugages of reference of a number of other disciplines: information theory, sociology of knowledge, cognitive anthropology, process theology, and international relations (to name but five.) It follows that to choose any particular set of descriptors is to slant the analysis toward the parent field of discipline from which the terms come. With this caveat in mind, a given language of reference may be artificially introduced for the sake of thought and discussion. Because of my early training in the sociology of religion under Weston La Barre, I am predisposed to choose a Freudian-style, medical model and to introduce terms like "media-induced hypnosis," "stage," "process," "introjection," and so forth. It is important to remember that the term "media" is being used both as a psychological metaphor and as a technological and social fact. Because this process is observable in institutions and larger social populations as well as in individuals, a number of illustrations from an outside field, American diplomatic history, will be brought up in passing, as examples of a potentially extended scope of inquiry.

MEDIA-INDUCED HYPNOSIS

Media-induced hypnosis may be observed as a recurrent process that unfolds in a number of stages. The first stage may be called "news shock," or "intelligence shock." An unexpected discontinuity is reported on a scale that captures the attention of a defined media-audience. The report must be world-specific, that is, the event must be located in historical time and space. The report must run counter to common sense or established expectations. The reported discovery of Russian intercontinental missiles in Cuba in 1962 was a news shock of immense magnitude to the foreign affairs community of the United States.

The second stage is one of a media-induced, identity confusion. The magnitude of discontinuity is such that the normal expectations of ego performance are suspended. In some instances a cognitive paralysis may be observed or experienced. In other cases there is a separation from ego performance patterns: the ego continues in its routine functioning but there is a separate process of watching taking place at the same time. This watching arises from a level of intelligence distinct from that required by the demands of routine tasks. This watching may continue even while the props of ego-identity are removed; otherwise a sense of falling is register-ed. The initial silence of the Eisenhower administration fol-lowing the report that an American U-2 spy plane had been shot down over Soviet territory exemplifies on the institutional level the catatonic-like behavior that is characteristic of some populations.

The third stage may be called, somewhat awkwardly, that of "media histrionics," or "artificial doing." The dichotomy between the ego and the media-event is in a state of maximum tension. The ego takes on a negative identify: it is what the media event is not.   The "doing" in this stage is charac-teristically histrionic and melodramatic.   What counts is the media-effectiveness of the reaction, not the cost-effectiveness of the probable results.   The reaction of the Truman admini-stration to the report of armed conflict in Korea in June of 1950 exemplified the behavior characteristics of this third stage: with the most fragmentary and inconclusive evidence at hand, it insisted on a theory of international, communist conspiracy and simultaneously demanded that an armed, counter-invasion be carried out under the flag of the United Nations.   The Truman administration succeeded in its bid for collective action by the United Nations, but in the process killed whatever chances the fledgling organization might have had for inter-national status as a morally and intellectually independent force.

The fourth stage may be called that of assimilation.   The media-event is either expelled from, or incorporated into, the ego of the media- or intelligence-consumer.   There are several patterns of media-event disposal: 1) disavowal, 2) anomaliza-tion, 3) typologicalization, 4) caricaturization, 5) moralization, 6) contextualization.   The result is the same: the psychic over-load is discharged, and the demand for "artificial doing" is quieted.   The diverse interpretations given to the phenom-enon of Jonestown were attempts to answer the question, How best to "dispose" of the mass suicides and murders?

1) Disavowal.   On November 22, 1978, the national office of the Disciples of Christ issued a statement stating that the Guyana colony of the People's Temple, a Disciples of Christ ministry, was "totally unrelated to the overseas ministries of the Disci-ples", and that Pastor Jim Jones' ministerial standing had been "under review" by the Northern California-Nevada regional office.

2) Anomalization. For other commentators the event was an anomaly, a unique, nonrecurrent event isolated in space, time and context from the main stream of new religious movements in America.

3) Typologicalization. For critics of the new religions the event was characteristic of the kind of behavior that could be expected of persons or groups of a certain description. The congregation at Jonestown was, said these critics, obviously brainwashed, on drugs, coerced, and/or fanatical. An out-pouring of scholarly activity was also in this vein. "It's all in my book" said one anthropologist of religion. Scholars sympathetic to the new religions characterized the People's Temple as a sub-type, nonrepresentative of the spiritual thrust of the new religions of the contemplative sort.

4) Caricaturization. One person, commenting on the sensational picture on the cover of Time showing the corpses surrounding the half-barrel of cyanide, said the caption would have been more telling had it read, simply, "Plutonium."

5) Moralization. Moralization was the characteristic response of black religious spokesmen. "How has the Black Church fail-ed to feed the Black People?" was a central question asked in the wake of Jonestown. "What was the moral significance of the event for the pastoral care ministry of the Black Church?" was another question.

6) Contextualization. Some commentators tried to put the event in cultural, historical or philosophical context: the event was a cross-section of American life, one that could be understood as a unique, but not particularly significant, expression of the potential history of the American people.

Media-events may also be assimilated by incorporation or introjection. A number of persons virtually changed their careers on account of Jonestown. In the San Francisco Bay Area several people formerly associated with the People's Tem-ple became public speakers, writers, and counsellors in matters relating to dangerous cults, brainwashing, and religious free-dom. In Berkeley, the Human Freedom Center was founded by ex-members of the People's Temple for the purpose of helping people make the transition from the cult world to normal life, and also for the purpose of alerting the American public in general, and law enforcement agencies in particular, as to the illegal activities of other cults that were deemed to be poten-tially dangerous.[3]

At least two of the journalists on the fateful trip to Guyana wrote books that were published within weeks of their return to the States. Several scholars in the field of religion

called for, or embarked on, major investigations of the events
leading to the apocalypse at Jonestown. Attorney Charles
Garry, who, with his colleague, Mark Lane, vowed to "write
the history" of Jonestown, declared his intention to proceed
with his own investigation. The FBI, of course, quietly went
about, following enigmatic leads, hoping to conjure evidence
bearing on the violation of the only federal law that was broken, namely, the one that prohibits the assault of a federal
officer. U.S. Senator Robert Dole, meanwhile, held an unprecedented congressional hearing on cults. All of these diverse
media-responses may be seen as ways to "identify with the
aggressor," as Freud said, in order to neutralize the aggres-
sion.⁴

     The fifth stage in the process of media-induced hypnosis
is recovery. One media victim realizes that, taken together,
Jim Jones, the People's Temple, and the news of the murders
at Jonestown, form a Rorschach test: what is "seen" tells
more about the psyche of the viewer than about what is "out
there in the real world." Another media victim realizes that
all attempts to "explain" Jonestown may be plotted on a single
anthropocentric scale located, in turn, in a one-story universe.
The scale extends from the world-specific to the world-generic:
at one end there are biographical and historical readings --
of Jones' biography and the church history of the People's
Temple -- and at the other end there are macro-system
readings, the Great Conspiracy, the Decline of this or that,
the Rise of something else. He sees that all of these historical
and social scientific explanations are interdependent, and that
their validity rests on the assumption that human intelligence
is self-sufficient and that the universe exists on a single ontological plane. A third media victim discovers that man-on-man
hermeneutics has a limited theological vision, and that the Joy
of which the Scriptures speak comes from neither good works
nor from good explanations but from the Holy Spirit. A fourth
media victim remembers the real point of the new, contemplative
religions in California: a more subtle order of intelligence
and moral effort may be learned through the quiet study of
the religious roots of human biology and consciousness. A
member of one of the new Tibetan Buddhist groups sees the
boldface type of the MORNING HEADLINES as a pseudo-mandala,
and he decides to return to his study of the authentic manda-
las of Tradition. A member of one of the Zen groups asks:
"Who, or what, is asking, 'Why Jonestown?'?" A member of
a Sufi group rediscovers the truth that his own wish to understand is not really "his"; it is the way that the pull of God's
love is experienced. In San Francisco, meanwhile, an ecumenical group arose spontaneously: the Guyana Emergency Relief
Committee conceived its aims in practical terms -- to bury the
dead, for example. In these and other ways the scientific and
religious health of media victims is restored.

Recovery is problematic. The case of the late Michael
Prokes illustrates the difficulty of, and the need for, media
disassociation. On Monday, March 12, 1979, Prokes, a former
senior Temple officer at Jonestown, called the Modesto Bee and
and asked if he could use its office for a general press briefing. When the Bee declined, Prokes arranged for a briefing
for a half dozen television newspeople and a reporter-photo-
grapher team from the Bee to take place the following evening
in a Modesto Motel. "I can't disassociate myself," he said,
referring to his fellow Temple members who had died in Guyana.
Unable to disassociate himself, and unable to expel or incorporate
the Jonestown deaths, Prokes, tragically caught in the stage of
media histrionics, staged his own press release suicide: he excused
himself from the group, went to the washroom and shot himself.

Knowing that explanations of Jonestown are going to be
packaged either by reference to notions of personal need and
motivation (the rationalistic approach to cultural criticism   and
social science) or by reference to impersonal,empirical observations and material conditions (the behavioristic approach), the
observer can predict the arrival of explanation-vendors of two
sorts: the one sort bearing evidence on Jones' "megalomania,"
the other sort bearing evidence on the "underlying conditions
that give rise to a Jonestown." The observer has scientific
reasons for not trusting the explanations of either sort.   He
has been told that the controversy in physics over "wave" and
"particle" explanations for the emission of light was settled
by an argument showing the logical complementarity of the
two theories. If so, the discussion in the social sciences over
the relative value of motive-theories and type-theories has yet
to be settled by an analogous argument showing the logical
interdependence and equivalence of the two explanatory strategies.[5] Pending such a rapprochement in the social sciences
the observer is right to suspend judgment.

Because of this bottleneck in social theory, and because
the research of scholars is far from completion, it is too soon
to write either the church history of the People's Temple or
the social history of its utopian settlement in Guyana. Some
matters, however, may be given immediate attention by the disinterested observer.

METROPOLITAN ETHICS AND THE MEDIA

The case could be made that the original cause of the
rise and destruction of the People's Temple was the failure of
communication between San Francisco media and religious
organizations. Jones had all but muzzled any negative press,
and informed persons, journalists and others, were afraid, or

not permitted to speak out. For years, no media organization wanted to be isolated as a critic of the People's Temple. So at this level, the lesson of Jonestown is that "criteria discuss-ions" need to take place among institutional competitors in the media industry.

What is not needed is another "Media Lamentation Society" criticizing the media for this or that. The problem is a deep-er one that affects many professions and industries. It is the enclave psychology which surrounds organizations that functions to protect an organization from unwanted, outside scrutiny but that also serves to debilitate its capacity to meet its public interest responsibilities. But what is public? It is true that there is no single public hermeneutic, no monolithic standard of the public good. It is also true that the new religious sensitivities are sources of radical insight in the quiet inner space of the individual, the self-observer. Because such a quietistic hermeneutic abhors single-cause lobbying and other forms of rock-throwing, no new political movement, in the ordi-nary sense of the term, can emerge. What can emerge is a quest for community and metropolitan ethics in matters of public information and programming.

This requires that the existing structure of religious com-munication in modern society be re-examined. The problem is one that has its visible and invisible sides. On one side are explicit information and communication theory questions such as: What needs to be communicated? To whom? On the other side are implicit ethical questions having to do with values and attitudes. This other side is as much a matter of the psychology and sociology of public information as it is a mat-ter of information content. Behind every San Francisco head-line on the latest gay outrage is a decision, one perhaps unconsciously made, that the reader is to be drawn into a state of mind in which the story of that outrage is significant and worthy of the reader's attention and quarter. That deci-sion arises out of attitudes, values, and criteria which are justified in part by the sales of the newspaper in the market-place but in part by the federal requirement (in the United States) to be responsive to the public weal. To the extent that such attitudes, values, and criteria are business matters, they may properly be considered under the heading of proprietary information, but to the extent that they fall under the heading of fulfilling the mission of public responsibility, they require responsible public discussion.

Such a quest could take many forms. There could be forums or workshops for public affairs officials from industry, government, academia, the media, and religion, or there could be small private meetings between top leadership people from these five sectors. A third form could be an Advisory Council on the Quality of Life of a given metropolitan area, one which might be established under the aegis of a local governmental office. Such a council would be composed of leaders from these sectors and would serve as a forum for positive discussions offering opportunities for building communication bridges between corporate criteria-enclaves. Such discussions, in turn, could enhance public information values in several ways: provide input into the media by way of articles, reports, interviews, and commentary; stimulate innovative programs, especially those of an inter-sector (and, therefore, inter-constituency) character; attract the insights, suggestions, and criticism of citizens and organizations addressing quality-of-life issues; and, possibly, serve as a proto-type or model of metropolitan value-focusing that might lend itself to the needs of other communities elsewhere. What is essential is that programatic efforts in the direction of building a metropolitan forum for the discussion of quality-of-life issues include follow-through mechanisms that foster a community-rooted sense of inter-sector and inter-criteria responsibility -- what used to be called civic pride.

TOWARD A PERSONAL HERMENEUTIC

I admit that my reaction to the media is ambivalent. I am attracted, desire information and entertainment, but fear pollution. I have seen only a few movies more than once, but "Meetings with Remarkable Men," the story of Gurdjieff's early years, I have seen five times. I ask myself, "Why?". The answer, I think, goes back to what was said at the beginning about the media as a theological medium. I want to approach what Gurdjieff called objective art, and I want the process sacralized. My intention is toward religious conversion, and my approach to the media might, in rare moments, be understandable in this context.

NOTES

1. "Brainwashing" and "advertising" are not synonyms. Admittedly, advertising, especially with consumer products, tries to sell, by the logic of contagious magic, the aura of the person behind the product; so that I become like the cowboy in the advertisement by smoking his brand of cigarette. But advertising becomes brainwashing only when the product or services are promoted as matters of historical necessity or moral obligation.

2. Here I do not wish to discuss the unconscionable acts on either side of the "religious liberty" argument going on in the United States and elsewhere.

3. Two of the founders of this center, Jeanie and Al Mills, were shot to death in their home in Berkeley on February 26, 1980. They were both defectors from the People's Temple and outspoken critics. Jeanie's exposé, My Six Years with God, had recently been published.

4. When a media-event is incorporated in this way it constitutes a "second-generation" reaction. The media victim is now a protagonist in the search for the authors of the "conspiracy" against the People's Temple. In this capacity he is an aggressor on a par with the original instigators of the conspiracy. Black comedian-activist Dick Gregory announced in December of 1978 that he would remain on a hunger strike "until the truth about Jonestown comes out." Gregory believed that the deaths at Jonestown had been planned and carried out by U.S. government and military authorities. Interviews with directors and actors involved in shooting the commerical motion picture on the "Guyana Massacre" would probably yield a rich cross-section of psychological data -- keeping in mind that the actors were paid to identify with and portray the lives of Jim Jones and his followers.

5. Several years ago, in Korea, I concluded that motive theories (the Rationalistic, great man, teleological or emic approach) is in the social sciences the epistemological residue of the "Mind" position in the mind-body dualism of ancient philosophy. Behavioristic theories (the empirical, quantitative approach) correspond to the "Body" position. Because any measurement implies units and purpose, the empirical and the rationalistic approaches jointly form the constitutional basis for social science inquiry. I called this interdependent complementary relationship the "B-R Loop."

APPENDIX

Characteristics which can be compared between new religious movements or the same movement in different times or societies

(This list makes no claims to be exhaustive and some characteristics can be duplicated under different headings.)

A) <u>Composition of Membership</u> (individual)

    1. Demographic Distribution (i) sex
                                            (ii) age (a) present distribution
                                                       (b) age of joining and
                                                           % "born into"
                                          (iii) marital status
                                          (iv) ethnic groupings

    2. Social characteristics   (i) class
                                            (ii) nationality
                                          (iii) religious, political, rural/urban background
                                          (iv) occupational type
                                          (v) educational level
                                        (vi) friendship patterns
                                        (vii) home/family background

    3. Predispositions for appeal   (i) seekership (conscious or potential for a) self
                                                         b) community
                                               by a) cognitive knowledge
                                                            b) experience
                                      (ii) health (psychic & physical)

B) <u>Structures and Organization</u> (group)

    1. Size   (i) absolute numbers
                                          (ii) numbers relative to other populations
                                          (iii) rate of change (growth/decrease)
                                        (iv) rate of turnover of membership
                                        (v) geographical spread/density

    2. Economic base   (i) income
                                        (ii) wealth

(iii) means of acquiring income and wealth
(iv) distribution - who spends
                 - what spent on
(v) changes in (i)-(iv) over time

3. Organizational Structure

(i) power/authority structure
    a) single/multiple hierarchy (eg. secular & spiritual)
    b) legitimation of control
    c) areas of control
    d) degrees of flexibility/ negotiation of control
(ii) communication structure
(iii) patterns of relationships (eg. between sexes; lay and priests)
(iv) bases of ascription/achievement (eg. sex, age, membership length, holiness)
(v) rigidity/fluidity of structures
(vi) strong/loose boundaries of membership
(vii) where live (eg. in community or nuclear family)
(viii) mobility (social and geographical)
(ix) work done, by whom

C. Beliefs and Practices

1. Theology/Religious Beliefs

a) composition (cosmology/theodicy/Christology/nature of man/of God/eschatology/soteriology, etc.)
b) type (eg. this/other worldly, active/passive, messianic, millennial).
c) how articulated, transmitted and held (oral/written).
d) source (revelation/interpretation/syncretism).
e) relationship with other beliefs (Christianity/Eastern)
f) degrees of permissible deviation
g) extent of esoteric knowledge (differential gnoses, personal interpretation of individual revelation)
h) use of symbolism
i) theological implications for action
j) sociological importance of beliefs as independent variable
k) balance between dogma/ritual/spiritual experience/ at individual and group levels

2. Secular Beliefs and Attitudes

    a)   Political
    b)   Social
    c)   Temporal (ie. attitudes to past, present and future)
    d)   Sexual
    e)   Economic
    f)   Racial
    g)   Aesthetic
    h)   Variation in these between members and over time

3. Rites and Ritual

    a)   type (formal/spontaneous)
    b)   performed by whom (elite/congregation)
    c)   frequency
    d)   importance and functions

4. Degree of Commitment

    a) total/partial (i) horizontal (areas)
                   (ii) vertical (intensity)

       eg. endogamy? work? community living? economic? Sundays only? variations between members and over time

    b) formal/informal (legal contract?)

D) Processes

1. History of the Movement
    (i) when, where, by whom founded
    (ii) changes in all other variables over time

2. Life Style
    (i) ordered/antinomian
    (ii) puritan/permissive
    (iii) areas & frequency of contact with others (internal and external relationships).
    (iv) material conditions, living arrangements, nutritional adequacy (vegetarian?), smoking, drugs, alcohol
    (v) hours of work, leisure, sleep
    (vi) commensality
    (vii) bases for division of labour
    (viii) variations and changes

3. Conversion
    (i) how, where, who first contacts
    (ii) methods of proselytising
          active/passive
          lectures, lovebombing, sex
          stimulation/deprivation techniques

(iii) stages of conversion
       speed (snapping/long periods)
       intensity of contact (whether breaks)
       follow ups
(iv) success/failure rates (at different stages)

4. Apostasy
    (i) numbers, rates
    (ii) differential propensity of types of members (sex, age, time, member, position in movement)
    (iii) reasons (given by apostates, remaining members, sociologist)
    (iv) whether institutionalised means for leaving
    (v) extent of outside intervention (deprogramming)
    (vi) numbers and rates of return to movement (why, after how long?)

5. Maintenance and Disruptive Functions
    (i) processes conducive to continued individual membership or withdrawal
    (ii) processes contributing to persistence or change in
      a) organizational
      b) plausibility structures

E) External Relations

    (i) strength and compostion of boundary between members and outsiders, how this experienced
    (ii) perception of members/non-members of each other
      factual knowledge/ignorance
      attitude (apathy, amusement, curiosity, antagonism)
      evaluation (good, bad, Satanic, neutral, mixed)
    (iii) how perceptions formed, selected, maintained, changed, disseminated
    (iv) foci of interest
      from NRM (economic, recruitment, acceptance)
      from outside (theology, finances, mind control, family breakup, policy, example, life-style).
    (v) contact initiated by NRM
      type/area (focus)
      by whom - PRO, leaders, rank and file
      intensity
    (vi) contact initiated from outside
      type/area (discussion, deprogramming)
      by whom: parents, Church leaders, politicians, the media, law, police, the public
    (vii) existence of anti-cult movement and interest in particular NRM

(viii) dynamics of external relations
deviance amplification, accommodation, assimilation, rejection, polarisation, symbiosis,
parasitism, tolerance, admiration, imitation

(ix) factors promoting and militating against (viii)
1. structural (NRM & society) eg. economic
dependency
2. cultural (NRM & society) eg. degree of
ideological exclusiveness

GLOSSARY OF NEW RELIGIOUS MOVEMENTS

Only those religious movements mentioned in the text are listed. The initials after the entry indicate the chief contributor to the entry. Movements which are in bold type have their own entry in the glossary.

ADVENTISM

Adventism was a transnational, interdenominational rage of millennial expectation which moved through the nineteenth century as the religious expression of the same sentiment expressed in secular ways as "progress," "evolution," and other varieties of social optimism. The Irvingites (also known as the Catholic Apostolic Church) and Plymouth Brethren were organized products of the movement in England, and the **Campbellites** or Restoration Movement, Christadelphians, **Mormons**, Millerites or **Seventh-Day Adventists,** and **Jevovah's Witnesses** arose in America and rapidly spread to Europe and elsewhere. William Miller (1782-1849), an upstate New York farmer, interpreted Daniel and the Apocalypse to set the date for Christ's return on March 21, 1843. A large number of pan-Protestant groups took up Miller's Adventist expectations. When the day passed, Miller adjusted the timetable and predicted March 21, 1844, and again, October 22, 1844. Disappointment at the failed eschaton led to persecution and disillusionment. Others regrouped, notably the Seventh-Day Adventists, under the leadership of Ellen G. White, whose followers considered her an inspired prophetess and a reformer of personal morals and health habits. (W.L.)

Numbers, 1976; Tuveson, 1968.

ANANDA MARGA

Ananda Marga (registered as Ananda Marga Pracaraka Samgha with the following branch organizations: Renaissance Universal; Progressive Utilization Theory or PROUT; Seva Dharma Mission; Education, Relief, and Welfare Section or ERAWS; and Voluntary Social Service or Vishwa Shanti Sena) was founded in 1955 in India by Shrii Shrii Anandamurti (born Prahbat Ranjan Sarkar in Jamalpur, West Bengal, 1921).

331

According to Anandamurti, the aim of the organization is "Self Realization and Service to Humanity." The spiritual practices, developed from Tantra Yoga, seek to help superior individuals unite to establish a world government based upon their moral superiority and enlightened judgement. Each member is given detailed instructions as to how to live and gain spiritual strength through daily meditations, chanting, rituals, diet, personal habits, etc. Followers are encouraged to "mercilessly fight sin" wherever it is found, including the use of arms where necessary.

The stories surrounding Anandamurti have been conflicting and confusing. Imprisoned for murder in 1971 he was later released when Indira Gandhi lost power. Ananda Marga gained the attention of the mass media in 1978 when Lynnette Philips burned herself to death in front of the UN building in Geneva and in 1979 when a Swedish group attempted to hijack an SAS plane en route to the USSR.

The organization is extremely hierarchical, authoritarian and missionary in character. Members are encouraged to place the needs and purpose of the organization above all personal desires. Ananda Marga claims millions of followers, the majority around thirty years of age, and hundreds of centers world-wide, although the true figures are probably more modest.

The main source of income seems to be through donations of members and voluntary work at odd jobs by devotees who live a simple, often mobile life-style. (T.N.)

Sarkar, 1978

ANTHROPOSOPHY

The Anthroposophical Society was founded in Berlin, Germany by Rudolph Steiner (1861-1925) in 1913. He served as head of the Theosophical Society's German branch from 1902-1909, but felt uneasy with Theosophy's orientalism and occultism. He stressed the scientific study of the spiritual world, man's reactions to it, and the superiority of Christ over Eastern Masters.

In Europe, Anthroposophy is known for its contributions in alternative forms of education (Waldorf Schools) and agriculture (biodynamic method).

Total membership is unknown, although several thousand people of all ages participate in their many activities in Germany, England, the U.S.A. and Scandinavia. (T.N.)

Shepherd, 1954; Steiner, 1969.

ANTI-CULT MOVEMENT

The term anti-cult movement covers numerous groups and individuals constituting a backlash to the new religious movements (generically referred to as 'cults') which swept across North America and Europe in the 1970s. The membership of the movement consists largely of relatives of converts to the new religions, but there are also strong components of ex-cultists, 'concerned persons,' and adherents of more established religious movements (particularly Evangelical Christians who are anxious to expose theological error as well as the allegedly harmful aspects of the cults). Many of these allegations are similar to those historically made about religions now generally considered socially respectable (e.g., Early Christianity, Roman Catholicism, Methodism, the Quaker movement and Judaism). Criticisms most frequently levelled at the contemporary cults include brainwashing, the splitting up of families, bizarre sexual practices, the amassing of large fortunes for leaders by exploited followers, tax evasion, and political intrigue. The mass suicide in 1978 of members of the People's Temple has provided a particularly potent cause for anxiety for the movement.

Groups in the movement disseminate anti-cult propaganda through newsletters and the media. They can also employ various degrees of persuasion to remove persons from the cults. These range from informal counselling to illegal kidnapping and the "deprogramming" of "victims". In America there have been several attempts (some of which have been successful) to institute legal proceedings which allow cult members to be held against their expressed wishes (by, for example, conservatorship orders).

Main targets for attack have included the **Unification Church, Children of God, Hare Krishna, Scientology,** and **Transcendental Meditation** but almost all religions have been critically examined by the anti-cultists and deprogramming attempts have extended to converts to Catholic, Baptist, and Episcopal churches.

Since the late 1970s there has been a further development, particularly in the U.S.A., in the rise of an anti-anti-cult movement. The membership of this is composed of some members of the cults themselves and of various bodies and persons concerned with civil liberties and/or religious freedom. (E.B.)

Shupe and Bromley, 1980; Richardson, H. (ed.), 1977; Richardson, J. (ed.), 1982.

ARYA SAMAJ

Arya Samaj was founded in 1875 by Dayanand Saravati (1824-1883), a Brahmin from Kathiawar in Western India. It holds that there is one God, that Sanskrit is the fountainhead of all languages, and that the Vedas contain, implicitly, all modern knowledge. It rejects popular Hinduism (images, temple worship, Puranic mythology), which it designates "Puranic" religion. Aggressively anti-Western and critical of Christianity and Islam, its chief successes were in the Punjab. Its cult involves Sunday worship and has followed missionary practice in setting up the Young Man's Arya Samaj and other such organizations. (N.S.)

BRAHMO SAMAJ

Brahmo Samaj was founded in 1828 by Ram Mohan Roy (1772-1883). The Brahmo (or Barahma) Samaj preached monotheism and the reformation of Hindu society: modern Hinduism was seen as a degeneration from an original monotheism, and a purified religion could also express the essentials of Christianity and Islam. In effect the Brahmo Samaj was predominately a Western educated Unitarianism with a Hindu background. The movement split three ways after Roy's death. The most vigorous has been the Sadharan or General Brahmo Samaj. Although never a popular movement, nonetheless, the Brahmo Samaj placed strongly on the agenda how Hinduism was to cope with Western knowledge and institutions. Its worship is modeled after the Unitarian pattern. (N.S.)

CAMPBELLITES

Alexander Campbell (1788-1866), with his father, Thomas (1763-1854), and later associates, notably Barton Warren Stone (1772-1844), led the "Restoration Movement," the first, indigenous American ecumenical movement. Campbell taught that a simple belief in Jesus as the Son of God, without reference to traditional creeds, and adult immersion was the biblical definition of Christian initiation. Weekly observance of the Lord's Supper, offered to any who wished to commune, was the true act of the Church of Christ, which, by definition of these elements of Christian primitivism, is organically and constitutionally one. Campbell opposed Calvinist predestinationism, emotional Revivalism and millennial Adventism arguing instead, in the spirit of John Locke, for a reasonable Christianity. A number of mottos characterized the frontier movement: "Where the Bible speaks, we speak; where the Bible is silent we are silent."

"In matters of faith, unity; in matters of opinion, liberty; in all things, charity." Differences over interpretation of Scripture, exacerbated by North/South and other, sociological differences, divided the movement towards unity into three main elements: the Disciples of Christ (now The Christian Church), the independent Christian churches, and the churches of Christ. There are numerous smaller factions. (W.L.)

Beazley, 1973; Harrell, 1966

CATHOLIC APOSTOLIC CHURCH (IRVINGITES)

See **Adventism; New Apostolic Church**

CHILDREN OF GOD

The Children of God was the name acquired by a movement founded by David Brandt Berg in 1968 in Huntington Beach, California. In its early years it differed little from the myriad groups generically called the **Jesus People**. It combined fundamentalism and countercultural hostility to the materialism and impersonality of American society. It was highly millenarian in character and proselytized mainly among alienated youth, requiring the converted to abandon the world, career, education, family, friends, "forsaking all," and giving their possessions to the common fund. Members lived communally, soliciting support from neighboring businesses and markets, or offering the letters of their leader and prophet—now called Moses David—on the city streets, for a donation. Over the course of time the movement's beliefs changed considerably as a consequence of the prophet's new revelations. Moses David found himself aided by various spirit helpers and gradually encouraged his followers to adopt a more sexually permissive style of life, even to the extent of using sex as a technique of conversion. The name Family of Love was adopted in 1978.

Although many more have participated in the Children of God for some period, its full-time, "live-in" membership never exceeded around 6,000. (R.Wa.)

Wallis, 1979; Wallis in Wilson (ed.), 1981

CHRISTADELPHIANS

See **Adventism**

THE CHRISTIAN CHURCH
See Campbellites

CHRISTIAN SCIENCE

The Church of Christ, Scientist, was founded in Boston in 1879 by Mary Baker Eddy (1821-1910).A distinctive feature of Christian Science is reliance on prayer alone for healing, although it is not primarily a health-system. Christian Science is generally dated from 1866, being the year in which Mrs. Eddy claimed to have been healed following a serious fall, through reading the Bible account of one of Jesus' healings. The full statement of its teachings is outlined in Science and Health with Key to the Scriptures, which Mrs. Eddy first published in 1875.

Christian Scientists see in the life and work of Jesus Christ a reversal of the accepted criteria of reality, and a breaking through into the senses' world of appearances, of primal spiritual law, which is evidenced in healing. Christian Science practitioners engaged in the full-time practice of healing are accredited by the church. Membership is predominantly from the educated middle-class with a preponderance of middle-aged or elderly.

The Mother Church of the denomination is situated in Boston. There are 3,000 branches in some 60 countries, with some 260 branches in the U.K. Detailed membership statistics are not made available. The church is not missionary and teaching is spread by individual contact and literature. Each church maintains a public Reading Room.

The Christian Science Monitor, which is distributed in 120 countries, is generally acclaimed as an excellent newspaper, having a readership which reaches far beyond the confines of Christian Scientists themselves. (C.K., W.L.)

Eggenberger, 1978; Gottschalk, 1973; Peel, 1966 and 1971.

CHURCH OF JESUS CHRIST OF LATTER DAY SAINTS
See Mormons

CHURCH OF SCIENTOLOGY
See Scientology

CHURCHES OF CHRIST
See Campbellites

CIVIL RELIGION, AMERICAN

American Civil Religion is a churchless, American sentiment which expresses itself on public holidays, in public school classrooms, and the Boy Scouts, in times of national distress and rejoicing. It combines the New England Puritan theology of America as the new world of the millennial dawn, whither the Children of Israel had escaped across the Red Sea of the North Atlantic from Egyptian bondage in England and Europe, with the notion of manifest destiny--the original idea of the nineteenth century that America was divinely destined to stretch from coast to coast--and reinterprets each American presidency and each American war as one more stage in God's salvation history to keep the world safe for democracy by means of a Pax Americana. (W.L.)

Bellah, 1975; Richey and Jones, 1974;
Robbins, Anthony, Doucas & Curtis, 1976

DIANETICS

See Scientology

DISCIPLES OF CHRIST

See Campbellites

DIVINE LIGHT MISSION

The Divine Light Mission is headed by Guru Mahara) Ji (born Prem Pal Singh Rawat, India, 1957), succeeding his father Shri Hans Ji Mahara) Ji of the Prem Nagar Ashram. Guru Mahara) Ji was elevated to his father's position as Perfect Master at the age of eight. In 1971 a few American Premies (followers) invited him to the U.S.A. acclaiming him as the boy satguru, Father, and Lord. He passed on "Knowledge" (a meditative method of experiencing an inner "Divine Light"), through his Mahatmas (close devotees of high rank). By summer of 1973 there were an estimated 1.2 million members worldwide, 50,000 in the U.S.A. with 24 ashrams in 24 cities. Membership declined, however, after an ideological and financial fiasco held at the Houston Astrodome--"Millennium 1973." Today the total number of Premies is an organization secret, but there are centers in most major Western cities, in parts of Asia, particularly India, and some other countries. At the "satsang" festival in England in 1979 about 25,000 Premies gathered from around the world to see and hear their Lord. Premies tend to be in their twenties or thirties, with men in the majority.

The organization appears to be informal, having few rules or disciplines, but the authority structure is highly selective. Song, spontaneity, divine love, and joy are characteristics held dear by Premies--as well as a fascination for the remarkable. Long hours of meditation at odd hours leading to mystical experiences and altered interpretations of reality are common. The world and society are seen as an unfortunate illusion. Only the experience of Divine Light is real. Guru Maharaj Ji stands in the center of the Light. (T.N.)

Downton, 1979

ENCOUNTER GROUPS

See **Human Potential Movement**, and T.C. Oden's and P.Heelas' papers in this volume.
Oden, 1972

ESALEN INSTITUTE

See **Human Potential Movement**

EST (ERHARD SEMINAR TRAINING)

See **Human Potential Movement**, and Encounter Groups and Sidda Yoga Dham

EVANGELICALS

Evangelicals are the most inclusive Protestant group in contemporary American religious life, comprising standard Reformation types, Fundamentalists, both classical and neo-Pentecostals, and a host of new groups dedicated to a variety of revivalist missionary undertakings. One charismatic evangelical group owns its own television network. Other groups, e.g., Campus Crusade for Christ and Intervarsity, specialize in witnessing to high school and college youth. The election to the presidency of Jimmy Carter was claimed by evangelicals as a moral and spiritual victory for the country. (W.L.)

Quebedeaux, 1978; Wells & Woodbridge, 1977

See also **Jesus People**

FAMILY OF LOVE

See **Children of God**

THE FARM

In 1970 acid guru Stephen Gaskin left San Francisco and his weekly meetings and took with him 65 vehicles to settle on 1,750 acres near Summertown, Tennessee. The Farm had approximately 2,500 members in 1978, including some in Guatemala, who are unified via taped Sunday sermons from Gaskin. Embedded in the counterculture, The Farm's communal living combines an emphasis on immediacy of experience, helping others (including midwifery), and collective social experience. Holding back (repressed) feelings is especially frowned upon, and a puritan naturalist ethic (no smoking, no drugs, no birth control, no divorce, no cutting of hair, etc.) also aids the establishment of being oneself in a markedly collective setting: "The idea of getting straight is to reach a collective point in which no subconsciously held viewpoints interfere with the simultaneity of consciousness." (P.H.)

Hall, 1978.

FIRST CHURCH OF CHRIST SCIENTIST

See **Christian Science**

HARE KRISHNA

In 1965 the International Society for Krishna Consciousness (ISKCON) was founded in America by His Divine Grace A.C. Bhaktivedanta Swami Prabhupada (1896-1977). It was to become one of the most visible of the new religious movements that came from the East. Bands of devotees became a familiar sight on the streets as they sang and danced their way through many of the larger cities, selling their own records, books, and incense or the magazine "Back to Godhead" in their saffron robes. ISKCON received additional publicity (and financial support) through the interest of the Beatle, George Harrison.

The Hare Krishnas are theologically Vaisnavite Bhaktas (devotional dualists) which, in more accessible terminology, implies that they reject the idea of ascriptive caste position and believe that ultimate salvation, or at least more favorable future incarnation, can be achieved through Bhakti-Yoga. This involves loving service to Krishna, which is expressed in a state of permanent, active devotion to Krishna, in which the mind of the believer never wavers in its contemplation of the name, form, and "pastimes" of Krishna. Life in the sect's temples is designed to inculcate this condition in the devotees and every action or thought is, or should be, a form of worship. For example, Krishna devotees repeat the Mahamantra 1728 times a day, refrain from meat, fish, stimulants, and sensuality in all forms. The young men shave their heads apart from a topknot (with which, they believe, Krishna will pluck them up when he rescues them at the time of the deliverance of the world). Only married couples engage in sex and then only for the purpose of procreation.

Since Swami Prahupada's death the Movement has been organized under 24 Governing Board Committee Members (11 American Acharyas or Gurus plus 13 additional Board Members). Under the Acharyas are Regional Secretaries covering geographical zones each containing a Hare Krishna temple and a Temple leader. There are about 100 centers worldwide and a total membership of approximately 20,000, about two thirds of whom are in the U.S. or Canada. The original membership was drawn largely from the hippie counterculture of the late 1960s. Now most members are in their late teens, twenties, or early thirties. A growing number of children are being born into the Movement which has its own special schools. Men are in the majority.

The typical temple is open to the public on Indian holidays and each Sunday when food, first offered to Krishna, is then served free of charge to guests.
(E.B., T.N., R.Wa, and W. & S.)

For further ethnographic detail see Whitworth and Shiels' paper in this book; also Judah, 1974.

HEALTHY-HAPPY-HOLY ORGANIZATION (3HO)

The Healthy-Holy-Happy Organization (or 3HO) was founded in California in 1969 by an Indian Sikh, Harbhajan Singh (Yoga Bhajan). The Movement has subsequently set up ashrams throughout the States and in Europe and Japan. The followers, who practice kundalini yoga, believe that they must work for important changes in personality and society—from material to spiritual concerns and from individual to group and God consciousness. These changes are seen as necessary as the world moves (after two thousand years of the "Piscean Age") into the Aquarian Age which will be of a radically different nature. (E.B.)

Tobey, Alan in Glock & Bellah, 1976: 5-30

HOLY SPIRIT ASSOCIATION FOR THE UNIFICATION OF WORLD CHRISTIANITY

See **Unification Church**

HUMAN POTENTIAL MOVEMENT

The Human Potential Movement is an umbrella term which covers a wide range of groups whose beliefs and practices are designed to promote 'wholeness', self-awareness, self-development or self-realization for the enlightened individual. Its roots go back as far as Gurdjieff but during the 1960s and 1970s the Movement expanded rapidly throughout the West—particularly in California—to encompass a multitude of techniques: ancient (such as various types of yoga), esoteric (such as some meditation mantra), or entirely novel (such as biofeedback). Included under the umbrella one can find massage, dance, the martial arts, dietary rules, psychodrama, humanistic psychology, gestalt therapy, and the more mystical forms of psychoanalysis. Encounter groups have been particularly prominent since the late 1960s—one of the most notable being the Esalen Institute in California. In these groups people are meant to release repressed emotions and talk about problems with each other. There is considerable variation in the methods used to achieve such goals. Thousands of Americans and Europeans have 'graduated' from est (Erhard Seminars Training), after being shut up for a weekend with abuse hurled at them in order to achieve personal growth; thousands of dollars have been paid out for individuals to release pent-up emotions by re-experiencing their own births in a deep tub of hot water with **Rebirthing**; or by learning to emit the Primal Scream in **Primal Therapy**.

The range of spiritual and mystical meanings that such therapies may have for their practitioners has led to many of the groups being attacked as quasi-religious and/or harmful by the **anti-cult movement.** On the other hand many of the techniques, especially those developed in some encounter groups, are used by the clergy in prisons and hospitals and for training in a number of socially respectable institutions. (E.B.)

Ellwood, 1973; Oden, 1972; Rosen, 1978

INDEPENDENT CHRISTIAN CHURCHES

See **Campbellites**

INTERNATIONAL SOCIETY FOR KRISHNA CONSCIOUS (ISKCON)

See **Hare Krishna**

IRVINGITES (CATHOLIC APOSTOLIC CHURCH)

See **Adventism** or **New Apostolic Church**

JEHOVAH'S WITNESSES

Jehovah's Witnesses, originally known as Russellites, were founded c. 1870 in Pittsburgh, Pennsylvania by Charles Taze Russell (1852-1916) as the International Bible Students' Association. Russell's work was consolidated by his successor, Judge Rutherford (1869-1942). As a result of its in-intense missionary zeal, the group has established branches worldwide and continues to grow—notably in Latin America and Japan. Membership is now well over one million.

Converts have traditionally come from amongst the socially and economically deprived and from all age groups. Education and worldly achievement is despised for the concern of members is with "God's Kingdom", shortly to be established on earth, rather than "the world" which they be-believe to be under the sway of Satan. Wars and the political and social troubles of the twentieth century are seen as signs heralding the end which will be inaugurated at the battle of Armageddon when Satan and his world system will be destroyed. As members of God's Kingdom, Witnesses consider themselves politically neutral in earthly politics and, whilst honest and generally law-abiding, will not bear arms or swear allegiance to the state. Both in democratic and totalitarian countries they have suffered for this behavior. They are currently experiencing intense persecution in Argentina and in Communist countries.

The movement is organized on authoritarian lines and teaching is interpreted by the central government. All members undertake door-to-door missionary work and the sale of literature including the famous Watchtower. They are unorthodox in many areas of theology such as Christology and the Trinity, and are seen by most mainstream Christians as heretics. Witnesses are known for their strict moral code, their refusal of blood transfusions, and their predictions of the date of the end of the world. (C.K.)

Beckford, 1975; Harrison, 1978; Penton, 1976

JESUS PEOPLE

The Jesus Movement or Jesus Revolution is an umbrella term used to describe the large number of conservative evangelical Christian groups that emerged in the late 1960s and spread throughout North America and Europe during the 1970s. The terms "Jesus People" or "Jesus Freaks" were used to describe the members of these groups who, partly in reaction to the counterculture of the 1960s, publically displayed their "rediscovery" of Jesus with Jesus posters, Jesus bumper stickers, and Jesus Loves Me sweatshirts. Much of the movement was contained within the **Evangelical** or Pentecostal branches of traditional Christianity, but several new groups and communities were formed some of these being viewed with utmost suspicion as dangerous heresies by more orthodox Christians and the **anti-cult movement** (e.g., the **Children of God**). One of the original movements which was militantly active in California was the Christian World Liberation Front (CWLF). Associated by some with the general trend were other movements such as the Catholic Charismatic Renewal and the Jews for Jesus, a movement which, through the Christianization of Jewish youth, has caused some concern among orthodox Jewry. (E.B.)

Richardson, J., 1979

JONESTOWN

See **People's Temple**

KERISTA

Founded in 1971, Brother Jud (now in his early sixties) and Even Eve are two of the movement's longstanding main figures. The movement is rather small, with only between twenty and thirty members, and is typical of many in the San Francisco bay area, although it has wider international impact through a number of publications. It is difficult to characterize their open-ended outlook and life-style for as Eve writes, "we have a tendency to delve into whichever subject is hot, very throughly, immersing ourselves in it for days and weeks on end; then at some point we feel it is used up and we wait for the next important issue to present itself". At various times exploration has been into religion (Kerista Consciousness Church and the Monastic Order of Kerista), sexuality (polyfidelious families), psychology (Gestalt-O-Rama, to eliminate Inner Uglies, and Wholism), and, pervasively, communal living ("autonomous self-containment and positive, nonalienated involvement with the rest of the world"). Their marked self-consciousness, which strives for "intentional community", has resulted in a proliferation of advice; but at the same time the basic orientation and core activies (in particular Gestalt-O-Rama) have remained relatively constant. (P.H.)

KONKOKYO

Konkokyo began in 1859 when Kawate Bunjiro, a farmer in Okayama prefecture, had revelations about the Parent-God of the Universe, whose purpose, he discovered, was the prosperity of all mankind. This large shinto sect has about half a million adherents in Japan. Piety in daily life is a central concern, and although doctrine (based on the sayings of the founder, who left no written records) is by western standards somewhat fragmentary, Konko is free from magical preoccupations. Man's sins and problems are carried to God through the mediation of the Patriarch who, to fulfill this task (toritsugi), remains in meditation all day and every day in the temple at Konko. (B.W.)

KRISHNA CONSCIOUSNESS

See Hare Krishna

MILLERITES

See Adventism and Seventh-Day Adventists

MEHER BABA

A relatively loose-knit movement consisting of "Baba-lovers" who try to follow the teachings of their mentor, Meher Baba. Western devotees are mainly, though not exclusively, to be found in the United States. They accept that Baba, who died in 1969, was incarnated God (the Avatar) and that the most direct path to self-realization is love and complete surrender to Baba. (E.B.)

Needleman, 1977

"MOONIES"

See Unification Church

MORMONS

Joseph Smith (1805-1844) was the prophet, seer, and founder of the Church of Jesus Christ of Latter-Day Saints (the Mormons). Smith received the revelation of hidden plates, now transcribed as the Book of Mormon, upon which was inscribed the history of salvation on the American continent before the time of the Indians. In founding the Mormon Church, he restored the ancient gospel and prepared the way of the heavenly Zion on earth. Persecuted for a number of reasons, especially their former practice of polygamy, the Mormons were driven from the East and Midwest into the western desert under the leadership of Brigham Young, who took over command after Smith's lynching at the hands of a mob, and, in spite of internal divisions, they civilized and virtually control what is today the state of Utah.

The now wealthy and influential church has three million members, two-thirds of whom are in the U.S.A. Family life, dietary rules and tithing are important. Nearly all male Mormons are ordained, and teaching includes baptism for dead ancestors, celestial marriage, and the doctrine of pre-existence. Missionary work is undertaken on a two-year, self-financed basis by most male Mormons and the church is known for its cultural and sporting activities. (W.L.; C.K.)

Allen and Cowan, 1964; Anderson, 1942; Eggenberger, 1978; McConkie, 1966; O'Dea, 1957

NEW APOSTOLIC CHURCH

A schism from the Catholic Apostolic Movement founded in London in 1832, this group was founded by Heinrich Geyer in 1863, with its headquarters in Frankfurt am Main.

It is adventist in expectation and appoints apostles, believed to be in the true apostolic succession under a chief apostle, who has quasi-papal powers. These apostles preach the return of Christ. In many areas of belief the group is orthodox, for example, on the Trinity, Christology, and Eschatology. It is an urban middle-class church, wealthy, respected, and conservative in outlook.

In spite of dubious relations with the Nazis the church has witnessed post-war growth, particularly in West Germany. There are branches in Holland, South Africa, Switzerland, France, Latin and North America. (C.K.)

Eggenberger, 1953, 1978; Gründler, 1961; Hutten, 1950

ONEIDA COMMUNITY

John Humphrey Noyes (1811-1886) was the main founder and
central figure of the Putney, Vermont, and, later, Oneida,
New York, Perfectionists. These communitarians became famous on the frontier for their production of steel traps and
other useful products. Oneida is still a well-known name
in silver plate, though the factories are now owned by a
joint stock company, not by a church. Noyes taught that
the Second Coming had already been fully realized and
that earthly life was now perfectible for those who would
earnestly engage in "mutual criticism". Most notorious of
his teachings was "complex marriage", a form of nonmono-
gamous, communal sexual experimentation, and eugenics,
premised on a rigorous use of coitus interruptus and a definition of sexuality as friendship and communication. (W.L.)

DeMaria, 1978; Robertson, 1970; 1977; Whitworth, 1975

ÖREBRO MISSION

Örebro Mission was founded by Reverend John Ongman in
1892 with its main center in Örebro, Sweden. Ongman was
influenced by the American religious groups he visited from
1868 to 1869. Although associated with the Baptists, by 1889
he was holding large evangelical meetings, Bible classes,
and organizing Sunday schools.

Since its establishment in 1892, the Örebro Mission has remained an independent religious body which today has approximately twenty thousand members of all ages.

The organization is open and informal. The services have
a strong evangelical character and stress is placed upon
individual religious commitment to Jesus Christ. (T.N.)

PEOPLE'S TEMPLE

The Reverend Jim Jones founded the People's Temple in the
early 1950s in his hometown of Indianapolis, Indiana. He
moved west in 1965 to the Redwood Valley near Ukiah,
California, where he hoped to escape what he perceived to
be racism in the Midwest. In 1971, Jones took his congregation to San Francisco, where he became heavily involved
in city politics.

While the majority of members came from a lower-class black
background, Jones also enlisted the support of liberal
whites and secured the praise of several well-known

persons for his radical politics and good works. By 1977, however, various questions were being raised about the practices of the Temple and the treatment of its members. Jones moved most of his followers to Jonestown, Guyana, shortly after the publication in 1977 of an article in <u>New West</u> which was highly critical of the Temple.

Pursuing allegations that some members were being held against their will, Congressman Leo Ryan, (D-San Mateo, Calif.) went in November 1978 with some journalists to Jonestown. Ryan and four others were killed in a fusillade of gunfire at Port Kaituma airstrip as they were leaving the jungle. Others were wounded in the attack at the airstrip. Hours later, 914 persons died in a death ritual in which Jones forced them to drink a fruit punch laced with cyanide. Bullet wounds were found in some of the bodies, including Jones'.

The Jonestown tragedy has had repercussions affecting more than those who were most directly concerned. The **anti-cult movement** was given a new impetus by the event and much anxiety has been inflamed concerning the possible consequences of membership of all new religious movements—especially those with a charismatic leader who expects total commitment from his followers. (E.B.; G.B.)

Kilduff and Javers, 1978; Krause, 1978; Mills, 1979

P L KYODAN

P L Kyodan (Perfect Liberty Kyodan), though it has some pre-war precursors, is essentially a post-war Japanese religion, deriving much from the Shinto tradition. Because its central teaching proclaims that the purpose of life is art, members dedicate themselves to leading an artistic life. God is said to have revealed a number of precepts which together amount to an artistic creed (e.g., "The individual is a manifestation of God" and "We suffer if we do not manifest ourselves"). The movement maintains its own hospital, laboratories, and horticultural experiment stations, in which religious teachings are employed in association with conventional therapeutic and scientific techniques. The headquarters of the sect are near Osaka, and the movement claims several hundred thousand followers, mainly in Japan. (B.W.)

PERFECTIONISTS

See **Oneida Community**

PLYMOUTH BRETHREN

See Adventism

PRIMAL THERAPY

Primal Therapy was popularized and formulated by Janov's
The Primal Scream (1970). Although rooted in the psycho-
therapeutic tradition that adult neuroses are the result of
the suppression of childhood mental discomforts, Janov went
back to early Freud (not to pure analysis) to emphasize
emotional re-education through action -- the re-experiencing
and catharsis of unpleasant history. Post-Primal man is
thereby freed from tension and defense. The movement is
widespread amongst younger middle-class American adults.
As of 1979 there were no Janov-certificated therapists in
the United Kingdom. However, the Clinical Theology Association uses the process, thus indicating its religious application along the theme of perfecting the self. Generally,
speaking, Primal Therapy is a short-term activity, not
providing a comprehensive life-style. (P.H.)

Janov, 1974

RAMAKRISHNA VEDANTA SOCIETY

See Vedanta

REBIRTHING

Rebirthing, rather literally, from a deep tub of hot water
is the central activity of a multiservice, psychospiritual
movement, called Theta, which was founded by Leonard Orr
in the U.S.A. at the end of the 1960s. Similar to Primal
Therapy, but more spectacular in its ritual, and quicker,
it is believed, developing the ideas of Leboyer, that one
only needs to re-experience one's birth to "let go of the
Big Feeling". The religious aspect of Rebirthing is revealed
in concepts such as Infinite Intelligence, Divine Mind, and
Divine Energy. These concepts explain how it is possible
to have memories of birth and to exercise powers of the
self (mind) to create suitable realities. (P.H.)

Orr and Ray, 1977; Rosen, 1978: 118-135

RESTORATION MOVEMENT

See Campbellites

REVIVALISM, AMERICAN

Charles Grandison Finney (1792-1875) was the outstanding preacher of the Second Great Awakening and the codifier of American Revivalism. An emotional form of evangelical conversion strategy, Revivalism sought to reduce sinners to tears of repentance and free-will renewal of the spiritual life at the "anxious seat" and in other ways to experience an affective moment of grace. Revivalism has continued to be the most vital single element in American religious life, it being the style of famous revivalists, such as Billy Sunday, Billy Graham, and Oral Roberts, and its supporters providing the interdenominational base for the new empires of the radio and television religion hucksters as well as the politically and economically powerful Neo-**Evangelicals**. (W.L.)

Carwardine, 1978; Cross, 1950; McLoughlin, 1978; Smith, 1957

RISSHO KOSEI KAI

Rissho Kosei Kai (the Society for the Establishment of Righteousness and Friendly Intercourse) began when Mrs. Naganuma Myoko and Niwano Nikkyo broke away from another Nichiren Buddhist sect, Reiyukai, in 1938. The movement regards itself as reviving the original teachings of Sakyamuni Buddha as transmitted through the monk Nichiren. Its teachings are based on the Muryogi Sutra, the Lotus Sutra, and the Kanfugen Sutra. The mandala, drawn by Niwano, is revered and Nichiren precepts are followed, but worship is for Sakyamuni Buddha, who is the eternal truth. The invocation (Daimoku) of the mandala is an important part of worship, but it is not regarded as possessing in itself the power to break the law of causality, which can be attained only by true repentance. Group counseling is an important function, and proper devotion to ancestors is exhorted. Rissho Kosei Kai has about five million members principally in Japan. (B.W.)

RUSSELLITES

See **Jehovah's Witnesses**

SCIENCE OF CREATIVE INTELLIGENCE

See **Transcendental Meditation**

SCIENTOLOGY

Scientology first emerged in 1950 as a lay psychotherapy, Dianetics, which became a short-lived fad in America. As interest waned and internal dissension began to appear, L. Ron Hubbard, its founder, transformed the movement into a religious philosophy and subsequently incorporated the Church of Scientology.

The movement views man as an essentially spiritual entity weighed down by the guilt and beliefs acquired over innumerable rebirths. Its practices are oriented to releasing the spiritual being, the Thetan, and rehabilitating its supernatural powers.

The movement has been financially successful as a result of aggressively marketing its services ("auditing" and "training") and the focus of considerable hostility because of its aggressive response to investigation. Some of its leaders were convicted in 1979 on charges related to the theft of documents from U.S. government offices. (R.W.)

Wallis, 1976

SEVENTH-DAY ADVENTIST CHURCH

Following the teachings of the **Adventist** William Miller (1782-1849), Mrs. Ellen G. White (1827-1915) founded the Seventh-Day Adventist church in America in 1863. The movement is intensely missionary and has over one million members worldwide. Its missionary work is often undertaken in underdeveloped areas.

Part of the appeal of the movement is in its educational and health organizations. Members come largely from the socially and economically underprivileged but because of a system of tithing, the church is quite wealthy.

Millennial in expectation, they believe the end will come when the Adventist message is proclaimed all over the world. An important part of that message is the celebration of the Sabbath from Friday sunset to Saturday sunset, and obedience to strict Old Testament-based health and dietary laws. They are best known to the public through their welfare work. (C.K.)
See **Adventism;** Eggenberger,1978; Gründler,1961; Hutten,1950

THE SHAKERS

Ann Lee (1736-1784), born in Manchester, England, migrated to America with her small group of Shaking Quakers and thereby "opened the Gospel in the West". Convinced by revelation and her own disastrous experience with marriage and childbirth that exercise of sexuality per se is the original sin, she required strict celibacy on the part of all her followers. The Shakers settled near Albany, New York, and commenced their communal life and preaching. They were severely persecuted for their conscientious objection to participating in the American Revolution and were suspected of being British agents. There was also considerable suspicion raised at their being led by a woman and at their eschewal of sexual relations. Mother Ann was revered by her followers as "the second coming of Christ according to the female line", particularly after the charismatic awakening during the nineteenth century which was interpreted by Shakers as "Mother's Second Work". Shaker-inspired crafts, particularly simple furniture, are still beloved by many Americans. The Shakers were the first to package and sell garden seeds, and they invented the flat broom and the automatic clothes washing machine. Mother Ann's motto was: "Hands to work and hearts to God". (W.L.)

Andrews, 1953; Campion, 1976; Whitworth, 1975

SIDDHA YOGA DHAM

Siddha Yoga Dham (also the Siddha Yoga Meditation Center) is headed by Swami Muktananda (born in Mangalore, India, 1908). When Swami Muktananda's guru, Bhagavan Nityananda died in 1961, Muktananda became the leader of of a form of Kashmir Sivaism. Sivaism traces its history through a lineage of Siddhas (realized Yogis) who practice a yoga which aims at awakening Kundalini (mystical energy within the central nervous system) through a direct transmission of an activating force called Skaktipat (also metaphysical but capable of being experienced).

In 1976 Werner Erhard (founder of est) brought Muktananda to the United States where a center was established in the Catskill mountains. Today there are over a hundred centers in fifty-two countries with approximately thirty thousand devotees. His Ashram in India, Gurudev Siddha Peeth outside Bombay, has in recent years become a place of pilgrimage for his followers.

Organization is informal. The main purpose of the centers is to spread the teachings of Baba (meaning father) and to hold "intensives" for the transmission of Skaktipat, accompanied by chanting, meditation, videotapes of Baba and lectures. The new devotee is expected to meditate daily,

guided by his or her spontaneous inner experiences (usually accompanied by pictures and literature of Baba).

Although there are no strict rules, most devotees are veg-
etarians and attempt to lead a disciplined life conducive
to their practice of meditation. (T.N.)

SOKA GAKKAI

Soka Gakkai (Value Creation Society) is a lay Buddhist organization attached to Nichiren Shoshu, a Buddhist sect devoted to the Lotus Sutra as expounded by the thirteenth-
century monk, Nichiren. After its foundation by Makiguchi
Tsuneseburo in 1930, it began to expand under its second
president, Toda Josei in the 1950s, to become a huge national movement of perhaps fifteen million under its third
president, Daisaku Ikeda. The Gohonzon, the mandala inscribed by Nichiren, is the object of worship, and its name
is invoked (Daimoku) in worship as a prayer of unlimited
power. The mandala is housed at Taisekiji temple near Mt.
Fuji. Members are committed to the universal dissemination
of their faith (kosen rufu) by vigorous techniques of conversion (shakubuku). (B.W.)

SPIRITUAL REGENERATION MOVEMENT

See **Transcendental Meditation**

SRI CHINMOY CENTER

The center was founded by Sri Chinmoy who was born in
East Bengal, India in 1931 to the family of Shashi Kumar
Ghose. The main Sri Chinmoy Center became accredited as
a Non-Governmental Organization in New York in 1975.

At the age of thirty-two Sri Chinmoy went to New York
where after a few years he began teaching and lecturing.
In 1970 he became Director of the United Nations' Meditation Group and in 1972 embarked on the first of many world
tours. He has lectured at major universities and met with
government leaders while also publishing more than 250
books of spiritual poems, aphorisms, essays, stories, and
plays. His devotees believe that he has attained nirvikalpa
samadhi, a high state of consciousness where the individual is said to have united with the Vedic concept of God.

Membership and organization is informal. All activities of
the more than 60 centers worldwide revolve around Sri
Chinmoy and his teachings. The typical devotee visits Sri

Chinmoy at least once a year and the relationship is one
of Guru-disciple, where Sri Chinmoy is said to lead the
seeker to higher states of consciousness. Daily meditation,
vegetarian diet, and a moral life characterize most devotees. Men and women are in their late twenties and thirties and about equal in number.

The centers survive on donations and voluntary help along
with the sales of books. Although they seek to spread the
teachings of Sri Chinmoy, outright proselytism is rare.
(T.N.)

TAIPING MOVEMENT

The Taiping movement was founded by Hung Hsiu Ch'uan
(1814-1864), who came from near Canton of Hakka stock.
Contact with missionaries and shamanistic experience led
him to evolve a faith with Christian aspects, in which he,
Hung, was prophet and younger brother of Christ. Puritanical, the creed enjoined the smashing of pagan idols, the
pure worship of God, and various radical social reforms.
A vast part of central China came under Taiping revolutionary control, after an uprising commencing in 1850. The
southern capital Nanking became the new Taiping center.
The hope was to realize a new kingdom of heavenly peace
(t'ai p'ing t'ien kuo). Corruption of the ideals and the
hostility of foreign governments were factors in the collapse
during an upheaval in which about thirty million lost their
lives. But Taiping ideals seem to have gone underground
and nourished rebellion in south-central China till the Communist era. (N.S.)

TENRIKYO

The Tenrikyo movement began in the 1830s, when Nakayama
Miki, the wife of a farmer, had revelations which led her
to develop special teachings, to practice a rigorous ascet-
icism, and to undertake a healing ministry in the name of
God the Parent, Lord of Divine Wisdom, who had inhabited
her body. Tenri teaches that, despite all the suffering in
the world, God means that men should have joy. Man must
realize that he borrows his body, even though his soul is
his own. If a man uses his body as if it were his own,
then evil--symbolized as dust (hokori)--accumulates and
man suffers. Man must shake himself free of this dust,
realizing that there is no evil. He is enjoined to undertake good works (hinokishin). Tenrikyo claims about two
million members, mainly in Japan, but also among Japanese
in the United States, Brazil, and other Latin American
countries. (B.W.)

THEOSOPHICAL SOCIETY

The Theosophical Society was founded in New York by Helena P. Blavatsky (1831-1891) and Henry S. Olcott (1832-1907) in 1875 to: build a center for the brotherhood of man without consideration of race, color, sex, religious belief, or social position; to support comparative studies of religion, philosophy, and science; and to study unexplained natural laws and latent powers of man.

Its central tenet of spiritual evolution through the self-realization of cosmic life through multiple incarnations, perfecting humans and all beings naturally, was a novelty in the West in the nineteenth century. Human being, said Mme. Blavatsky, exists at seven levels, corresponding to the yogi chakras, and provides a reflection of the hierarchic constitution of the universe and the focal plane for conscious crystallizations of spirit into matter, the descent of intelligence into matter, and the ascent of matter into spirit. Evolutionary reincarnation according to one's karma leads ultimately to nirvana.

The movement was ridden with numerous divisions, being led subsequently by Annie Wood Besant in London. Its course led it into association with the Old Catholic Church; one group within it proclaimed Krishnamurti the reincarnated Messiah (which he renounced); one of the original founders, William O. Judge, founded another breakaway group in 1891 in Pasadena, California; and Rudolph Steiner broke away from Theosophy in 1921 to found the **Anthroposophical Society**. Presently there are centers in fifty-nine countries with over thirty-three thousand members, the majority being over forty years of age, and often from the upper middle classes. (W.L. & T.N.)

Braden, 1970; Farquhar, 1951; Judah, 1967

THETA

See **Rebirthing**

3HO

See **Healthy-Happy-Holy Organization**

TRANSCENDENTAL MEDITATION

Transcendental Meditation (TM) has the following divisions:

Spiritual Regeneration Movement (SRM); Students International Meditation Society (SIMS); Maharishi International University (MIU); International Meditation Society (IMS); and Maharishi European Research University (MERU). TM was founded by Maharishi Mahesh Yogi in 1959 as the Spiritual Regeneration Movement, a deliberately popularized version of <u>Vedanta</u> influenced by Maharishi's college education in physics and inspired by 14 years as a close disciple of Swami Brahmananda Saraswati (or Guru Dev as he is often called by the Shankara school of yoga philosophy).

The Maharishi became known through his association with the Beatles in the 1960s. Today TM claims over one million initiates in over 90 countries. The TM method centers around a "personal mantra" and a scientific technique for meditation, usually referred to as the Science of Creative Intelligence, for developing the latent potentialities of the individual.

The TM organization is hierarchial with many divisions. Initiates are usually left to meditate on their own (15-20 minutes each day is recommended) with little formal instruction or ritual. Those who advance to become TM teachers receive additional training and exposure to Vedantic philosophy and ceremony. A "siddha" program for advanced TM meditators (marked by the said ability to levitate) and a plan for a New Age World Government has recently been added to the organization.

Fixed fees for services rendered, returns on investments, and some private donations have made TM a liquid and growing business. (T.N.)

TRANSCENDENTALISM

New England Transcendentalism centered upon Ralph Waldo Emerson (1803-1882), spokesman for American Frontier Romanticism, self-reliance, and nature. Influenced by Coleridge, Wordsworth, and Carlyle, and as well by Oriental thought, Emerson combined the Puritan tradition of Jonathan Edwards with the progressive optimism of the nineteenth century and broke with Harvard Unitarian organized religion in preference for a looser association of like-minded friends. He taught a naturalism of "the aboriginal Self" under the "over-soul", a feeling of organic unity of the psyche with the rest of the world (which enables the human person to transcend him or her self), and a sense of individualism predicated on the uniqueness of each person in confrontation with the pantheistic, living universe (which he saw as a descending manifestation of spirit). Emersonian thought, like its contemporaries, **Theosophy** and

Christian Science, is part of the liberal, not traditionally Christian, foundation of twentieth century psychologism and neo-hinduism within the new religions. (W.L.)

Hutchinson, 1959; Miller, 1950

UNIFICATION CHURCH

The Unification Church is also known as the Holy Spirit Association for the Unification of World Christianity, the Unified Family, and Tong Il and is the parent organization of groups such as C.A.R.P. (Collegiate Association for the Research of Principles), I.C.F. (International Cultural Foundation), and Creative Community Project. The movement was founded in Korea in 1954 by the Reverend Sun Myung Moon. It spread to Japan but did not have much success in the West until the late 1960s. By 1980 membership in the U.S.A. numbered around three thousand full time members with most European countries having several centres though none having more than a few hundred members. The world-wide full time membership is unlikely to be many more than a quarter million. The international headquarters are now in New York and the main recruitment center in the West has been in California.

Unification theology, one of the most comprehensive to be found among the contemporary new religious movements, is millenial and messianic. It is to be found in The Divine Principle, which offers a special interpretation of the Bible with additional revelations, which, it is claimed, Rev.Moon received from God. The Fall is said to be the result of a (spiritual) sexual relationship between Eve and the Arch-angel Lucifer, followed by Adam and Eve having a sexual relationship before marriage. History is interpreted as the struggle to restore the world to the state originally intend-ed by God. As part of this process Jesus should have mar-ried, but his mission failed and he was able to offer only spiritual, not physical, salvation to the world. Unification reading of history since the time of Jesus suggests that now is the time when the Lord of the Second Advent is upon the earth. (Messiahship is seen as an office, held by a sinless man, born of human parents.) Most members believe Moon to be the Messiah although he himself has made no public statement to this effect.

Members, popularly known as "Moonies", typically join in their early twenties, are well educated, and from the mid-dle classes. Twice as many men as women join in the U.S. and Britain and in the West members usually live in com-munity centers. The life-style is one of hardworking, "sa-crificial" concentration on restoring the world. Frequently long hours are spent fund-raising in the streets or wit-nessing to potential converts. Celibacy outside of mar-

riage is taught. Rev. Moon matches marriage partners and mass wedding ceremonies (Blessings) are held at
intervals (1800 coupes were Blessed in S. Korea in 1975).
The Blessing is the most important Unification rite, the
movement having relatively little else in the way of formal
ritual apart from a weekly "Pledge".

The Unification Church owns several valuable properties and
businesses. It publishes a daily newspaper, Newsworld, in
New York, Washington and Tokyo. It has a theological
seminary in Barrytown, New York. The Church has received
considerable hostility from parents, the media, and the
anti-cult movement, their main accusations including: brainwashing, connection with the Korean C.I.A., splitting up
families, using "Heavenly Deception", amassing great wealth
for the leadership by exploiting the followers, tax evasion,
and the manufacture of armaments. The Church itself claims
victimization, particularly when its members are illegally
kidnapped and "deprogrammed". (E.B.)

Bromley and Shupe, 1979; Lofland, 1977; Moon, 1973;
Moon, 1973; Sontag, 1977; Barker, 1983

VEDANTA

The Ramakrishna Vedanta Society, the western branch of
the India-based Ramakrishna Math (Monastery) and Mission
Society, was perhaps the first organized, authentic Hindu
movement to proselytize systematically in North America.
It originated when delegates to the "Parliment of Religions"
which formed part of the World's Columbian Exposition held
in Chicago in 1893 were introduced to the Vedanta teachings and world view by Swami Vivekananda, an uninvited
'delegate' who was lionized by many of the more intellectually inclined members of Chicago society.

Vivekananda was born in 1863, received both a classical
Hindu and a western education and in 1880 met Ramakrishna, a semi-literate villager who was not yet renowned as
a teacher and mystic. Vivekananda succeeded Ramakrishna
after the latter's death in 1886 and came to believe that
it was his task to offer the treasures of India's spirituality to the West in return for the benefits of western
science, finance, and industry. The first Vedanta society,
established in New York in 1896 was proto-typical of those
which were to follow. It drew on the West for its organizational forms and financial support, looked to the East for
its teachings and spiritual leaders, and combined the lecture and class instruction style of western educational institutions with the individual spiritual instruction of the

Hindu guru-chela relationship.

The religious beliefs of the Vedantists rest on the loftiest
and most universalistic interpretations of the Hindu scriptures.   However,   Advaitist   Vedanta   (impersonal   monist)
teachings were introduced to the West by Vivekananda in
a   form   which   he   believed   was   especially   suited   to   its
needs   and   state   of   spiritual   advancement.   Strictly,   Vedantists   who   seek   full   salvation   should   have   nothing   to   do
with   the   world   of   mundane   reality;   but   Vivekanada   also
taught   that   the   individual   should   work   in   the   world   to   alleviate   the   material   plight   and   spiritual   desolation   of   the
mass   of   mankind.   Given   that   the   life   of   the   sanyasi—the
life   of   total   renunciation—is   not   for   everyone,   the   task   of
the   lay   Vedantist   is   to   work   for   the   good   of   others   in   a
selfless,   motiveless   way   without   emotional   involvement   in,
or   self-congratulation   for,   the   results   of   such   action.   (W&S)

See   Whitworth   and   Shiels'   paper   in   this   book   for   further
ethnographic   detail.

BIBLIOGRAPHY

Adams, Robert and 1972 "Mainlining Jesus: The New Trip" So-
Fox, Robert ciety, No. 9, (Feb.):50-56.

Adorno,T.W., Frenkel- 1950 The Authoritarian Personality, Harper
Brunswik et al & Brothers, New York.

Ahlqvist, Eva-Lena 1979 "Youth Unemployment in Sweden", "Current Sweden, Stockholm: Svenska Insti-
tutet No. 216 (4).

Akishige, Y. (ed.) 1968 Kyushu Psychological Studies, Bulletin
of the Faculty of Literature of Kyushu
University, No. 11, Fukuoka (Japan).

Allen, J.B. and 1964 Mormonism in the Twentieth Century,
Cowan, R.O. Extension Publication, Brigham Young
University, Utah.

Almond, G.A. and 1963 The Civic Culture, Princeton Univer-
Verba, S. sity Press, Princeton, N.J.

Althaus, Paul 1959 "Die Bekehrung in reformatorischer und
pietistischer Sicht¨ Neue Zeitschrift
für systematische Theologie,Vol.1:3-25.

Anderson, Nels 1942 Desert Saints: The Mormon Frontier
in Utah, Chicago University Press,
Chicago; also 1966.

Andrews E.D. 1953 The People Called the Shakers, Oxford;
Dover, 1963.

Ansbacher, H.L. 1951 "The History of the Leaderless Group
Discussion Technique", Psychological
Bulletin Vol. 48:383-391.

Anthony, D., 1977 "Patients and Pilgrims: Changing
Robbins, T., Attitudes Toward Psychotherapy of
Curtis, T., and Converts to Eastern Mysticism" Amer-
Doucas, M. ican Behavioral Scientist, 20, 6:861-
886.

Anthony, D. and 1978 "The Effect of Detente on the Rise
Robbins, T. of New Religions" Understanding New
Religions, Needleman & Baker (eds).
New York: Seabury.

	1974	"The Meher Baba Movement: Its Effect on Post-Adolescent Youthful Alienation" Religious Movements in Contemporary America, Irving Zaretsky & Mark Leone (eds)., Princeton University Press.
Arndt, John	1869	True Christianity tr. and ed. by Boehm, A.W. and Schaeffer, Lutheran Bookstore Philadelphia.
Asbury, Francis	1852	Journals, 3 vols., Lane and Scott,N.Y.
Atkins, Gaius Glenn	1971	Modern Religious Cults and Movements, AMS Press, New York (reprint of original edition, 1923).
Atkinson, John	1875	The Class Leader, Nelson and Phillips
Bach, George R.	1966	"The Marathon Group, Intensive Practice of Intimate Interaction" Psychological Report Vol. 18: 995-1002.
	1967	"Marathon Group Dynamics III - Disjunctive Contacts" Psychological Report Vol. 20: 1163-1172.
Back, Kurt	1972	Beyond Words:The Story of Sensitivity Training and the Encounter Movement, Russell Sage Foundation, New York.
Bakan, David	1965	Sigmund Freud and the Jewish Mystical Tradition, Schocken Books, Inc., New York.
Baker, George (ed.)	1979	New Religious Movements in America. Working Papers, The Rockefeller Foundation, New York.
Balch, Robert W. & Taylor, David	1977	"Seekers and Saucers: The Role of the Cultic Milieu in joining a UFO cult", American Behavioural Scientist 20, 6: 839-860.
Balswick, Jack	1974	"The Jesus People Movement: A Generational Interpretation" Journal of Social Issues, 30 (3): 23-42.

Balswick, J.   1974   "The Jesus People Movement: A So-
                                    ciological Analysis" Religion Ameri-
                                    can Style, P. McNamara (ed.) New
                                    York, Harper and Row.   pp. 359-
                                    356.

Barker, Eileen   1978   "Living the Divine Principle: Inside
                                    the Reverend Sun Myung Moon's Church
                                    in Britain" Archives de Sciences So-
                                    ciales des Religions, 45, 1: 75-93.

                            1980   "Free to Choose? Some Thoughts on
                                    the Unification Church and Other New
                                    Religious Movements" Clergy Review,
                                    Part I October, Part II November.

                            1981   "Who Draws the Lines Where?" Interme-
                                    dia Vol. 9 No. 2 March.

                            1983   Moonies: A Study of the Unification
                                    Church, Blackwell, Oxford.

Bavarian State Archives   in the Bayerisches Hauptstaatsarchiv,
                                    Munich.

Beazley, George C. Jr.   1973   The Christian Church (Disciples of
                                    Christ): An Interpretive Examination
                                    in the Cultural Context, Bethany.

Becker, Carl   1950   The Heavenly City of the Eighteenth
                                    Century Philosophers, Yale University
                                    Press.

Beckford, James A.   1975   The Trumpet of Prophecy: A sociologi-
                                    cal Study of Jehovah's Witnesses,
                                    Blackwell, Oxford and Halsted Press,
                                    New York.

Beckford, James A.   1979   "Politics and the Anti-cult Movement"
                                    Annual Review of the Social Sciences
                                    of Religion Vol. 3: 169-190.

Bell, Daniel   1971   "Religion in the Sixties" Social Re-
                                    search, Vol. 38, 3:447-497.

                            1976   The Cultural Contradictions of Capi-
                                    talism, Heinemann, London.

Bellah, Robert	1975	The Broken Covenant: American Civil Religion in a Time of Trial, Seabury, New York.
	1976	New Religious Consciousness and the Crisis of Modernity" The New Religious Consciousness, R. Bellah & C. Glock (eds.) Seabury.
	1978	"Religion and Legitimation of the American Republic" Society 15, 4:16-23.
Bennis, Warren G. and Slater, Philip E.	1968	The Temporary Society, Harper and Row, New York.
Berger, Peter	1964	"Social Mobility and Personal Identity", European Journal of Sociology, 5: 331-343.
	1965	"Towards a Sociological Understanding of Psychoanalysis", Social Research, 32, March: 22-41.
Berger, Peter and Berger, Brigitte	1976	Sociology: A Biographical Approach, Penguin, London.
Berger, Peter, Berger, Brigitte, and Kellner, Hansfried	1974	The Homeless Mind, Penguin, Harmondsworth.
Bibby, R.W., and BRinkerhoff, M.B.	1973	"The Circulation of Saints: A Study of People who Join Conservative Churches" Journal of the Scientific Study of Religion 12 (Sept.): 273-284.
Bible Society	1978	National Survey on Religious Attitudes of Young People, Bible Society, London.
Bird, F.	1975	"A Comparative Analysis of the Rituals used by Contemporary New Religions and Para-religious Movements" Paper delivered at the annual meeting of Society for the Scientific Study of Religion, Oct.
Blacker, C.	1971	"Millenarian Aspects of the New Religions in Japan" in D. Shively (ed.) Tradition and Modernity in Japanese Culture, Princeton, Princeton University Press, pp. 563-600.

Block, Fred L. 1977 The Origins of International Economic Disorder: A Study of United States International Monetary Policy from World War II to the Present, University of California Press, Berkeley and Los Angeles.

Boberach, H. 1971 Berichte des S.D. und der Gestapo über Kirchen und Kirchenvolk in Deutschland 1933-45 Veröffentlichungen der Kommission für Zeitgeschichte bei der Katholischen Akademie in Bayern, Mainz.

Bodamer, W.G. 1961 "Some Features of Pietistic Biography" Theologische Zeitschrift, Vol. 17 Nov.-Dec.: 435-437.

Bonner, Hubert 1959 Group Dynamics, The Ronald Press Co. New York.

Borhek, J.T. and Curtis, R.F. 1975 A Sociology of Belief, John Wiley, New York.

Bracher, K.D. 1970 The German Dictatorship, Penguin, Harmondsworth.

Braden, C.S. 1958 Christian Science Today: Power, Policy, Practice, Southern Methodist University.

Braden, C.W. 1970 These Also Believe: A Study of Modern American Cults and Minority Relgious Movements, Macmillan, London, New York

Braden, W. 1967 The Private Sea: LSD and the Search for God. Chicago, Quadrangle Books.

Bradford Leland Powers et al (eds) 1964 T-Group Theory and Laboratory Method, John Wiley and Sons, Inc., New York

Bromley, David and Shupe, Anson Jr. 1979 "Moonies" in America: Cult, Church, and Crusade, Sage, Beverly Hills.

Bryant, M. Darrol and Hodges, Susan (eds.) 1978 Exploring Unification Theology, The Edwin Mellen Press, New York.

Bryant, M. Darrol and   1978   A Time for Consideration: A Scholarly
Richardson, Herbert   Appraisal of the Unification Church,
(eds.)   The Edwin Mellen Press, New York.

Buber, Margaret   1949   Under Two Dictators, Victor Gollancz,
                                  London.

Buber, Martin   1948a Hasidism, Philosophical Library,
                                  New York.

                           1948b Tales of the Hassidim, 2 Vols.
                                  Schocken Books, Inc. New York.

                           1958   Paths in Utopia, Beacon Press, Boston.

Buber, Martin (ed.)   1947   Ten Rungs, Hasidic Sayings, Schocken
                                  Books. Inc.

Bundesregierung an den   1980   Jugendreligionen in der Bundesrepub-
Petitionsausschuss des   lik Deutschland (Youth religions in
Deutschen Bundestages   the Federal German Republic), The
                                  Federal Ministry for Youth, Family,
                                  and Health, Bonn.

Burke, R. and   1961   "Changes in Perception of Self and
Bennis, W.   Others During Human Relations Train-
                                  ing" Human Relations, Vol.II,165-182.

Burridge, Kenelm   1969   New Heaven, New Earth: A Study of
                                  Millenarian Activities, Blackwell,
                                  Oxford; and Copp Clark, Toronto.

Campbell, Colin   1971   Towards a Sociology of Irreligion,
                                  Macmillan, London.

                           1977   "Clarifying the Cult" British Journal
                                  of Sociology 28, 3.

                           1978   "The Secret Religion of the Educated
                                  Classes", Sociological Analysis, 39,
                                  2: 146-156.

Campion, Nardi Reeder   1976   Ann the Word: The Life of Mother Ann
                                  Lee, Founder of the Shakers, Little,
                                  Brown and Co., Boston-Toronto.

Canham, Erwin Dain   1958   Commitment to Freedom: The Story of
                                  the Christian Science Monitor,
                                  Houghton Mifflin Co., Boston.

Carden, M.   1969   Oneida: Utopian Community to Modern
                                    Corporation, Harper, New York.

Caroll, John   1977   Puritan, Paranoid, Remissive: A Soc-
                                    iology of Modern Culture, Routledge
                                    and Kegan Paul, London.

Cartwright, Dorwin and 1960   "Origins of Group Dynamics", Group
    Zander, A.F.   Dynamics: Research and Theory 2nd
                                    ed., Row, Peterson & Company,New York

Carwardine, R.   1978   Transatlantic Revivalism: Popular
                                    Evangelicalism in Britain and America
                                    1790-1865, Greenwood, West Port,Conn.

CEFM   1976   "The Unification Church: Its Activi-
                                    ties and Practices" A Special Report,
                                    2 Vols. National Ad Hoc Committee
                                    Engaged in Freeing Minds, A Day of
                                    Affirmation and Protest, Arlington,
                                    Texas.

Chirot, Daniel   1977   Social Change in the Twentieth Cen-
                                    tury, Harcourt Brace Jovanovich,New
                                    York.

Christophers, S.W.   1820   Class Meetings in relation to the
                                    design and success of Methodism,
                                    Wesleyan Conference Office, London.

Clark, John G. Jr.   1979   "Cults", Journal of the American Med-
                                    ical Association, 242 (July 20): 279-
                                    281.

Collingwood, R.G.   1944   An Autobiography, Penguin, London.

Common Ground   1979   No. 18 ("A directory of growth, heal-
                                    ing and spiritual experiences in the
                                    greater Bay Area").

Conference Episcopale   1975   "L'Eglise de l'Unification", Bulletin
                                    due Secrétariat de la Conference
                                    Episcopale Francaise, 7.

Conway, Flo and   1978   Snapping, J.B. Lippincott, Philadel-
    Siegleman, Jim   phia.

Cordeux, T.   1820   Class Book Containing Directions to
                                    Class Leaders,Methodist Press,London.

Corsini, R.J. and   1957   "Bibliography of Group Psychotherapy
  Putzey, L.J.   1906-1956" Psychodrama Group Psycho-
                                    therapy No. 29.

Cox, H.   1977   Turning East. New York: Simon and
                                    Schuster.

Cross, W.   1950   The Burned-Over District: The Social
                                    and Intellectual History of Enthusi-
                                    astic Religion in Western New York,
                                    1800-1850, Harper Torchbooks, New
                                    York.

Culberg, Samuel A.   1968   The Interpersonal Process of Self-
                                    Disclosure: It takes Two to see One,
                                    National Training Laboratories,
                                    Bethel, Maine.

Currie, Robert   1977   Churches and Churchgoers: Patterns
  Gilbert, A., and   of Church Growth in the British Isles
  Horsley, L.   since 1700, Clarendon Press, Oxford.

Dabney, D.   1980   God's Own Network. Harpers, 261,
                                    1563: 33-52.

Damrell, Joseph   1977   Seeking Spiritual Meaning: The World
                                    of Vedanta, Sage, Beverly Hills.

Daner, Francine   1974   The American Children of Krsna, Holt,
                                    Rinehart and Winston, New York.

Danto, A.C.   1972   Mysticism and Morality: Oriental
                                    Thought and Moral Philosophy   New
                                    York: Harper and Row.

Davidson, J.W.   1977   The Logic of Millennial Thought,
                                    Eighteenth Century New England, Yale
                                    University Press, New Haven, CT.

Davis, David Brion   1971   The Fear of Conspiracy. Images of
                                    Un-American Subversion from the Revo-
                                    lution to the Present,Cornell,Ithica.

Davis, Winston   1980   Dojo: Magic and Exorcism in Modern
                                    Japan, Stanford University Press,
                                    Stanford.

Decter, Midge   1979   "The Politics of Jonestown", Comment-
                                    ary, May.

Deeter, A.C. 1964 "Membership in the Body of Christ as Interpreted by Classical Pietism" Brethren Life and Thought, Vol. 9, Autumn: 18-49.

DeMaria, Richard 1978 Communal Love at Oneida: A Perfectionist Vision of Authority, Property and Sexual Order, Edwin Mellen, N.Y.

Dimond, S.G. 1926 The Psychology of Methodist Revival, Oxford.

Dole, Senator Robert 1979 Transcript of Proceedings. Information on the Cult Phenomenon in the United States, Washington, D.C.

Douglas, J.D. 1970A "Deviance and Respectability: The Social Construction of Moral Meanings Deviance and Respectability, J.D. Douglas (ed.) New York: Basic Books.

1970B Deviance and Order in a Pluralistic Society, McKinney & Tiryakian (eds.), New York: Appleton-Century-Crofts.

1971 American Social Order. New York: Free Press.

Douglas, Mary 1966 Purity and Danger: an analysis of concepts of pollution and taboo, Routledge and Kegan Paul, London.

1970 Natural Symbols, Barrie and Rockliff, London.

Douglas, P.F. 1935 God Among the Germans, University of Pennsylvania Press, Philadelphia.

Downton, James V., Jr. 1979 Sacred Journeys: The Conversion of Young Americans to Divine Light Mission, Columbia University Press, N.Y.

Drakeford, John W. 1967 Integrity Therapy, Broadman Press, Nashville.

Dreidger, L.   1974   "Doctrinal Belief: A Major Factor
                                    in the Differential Perception of So-
                                    cial Issues" Sociological Quarterly
                                    15 (Winter): 66-80.

Dreikurs, Rudolph   1959   "Early Experiments with Group Psycho-
                                    therapy" American Journal of Psycho-
                                    therapy Vol. 13: 219-55.

Dubnow, S.M.   1916   History of the Jews in Russia and
                                    Poland tr. by Friendlander, I. Vol.1,
                                    Philadelphia.

Durkheim, Emile   1957   Professional Ethics and Civic Morals,
                                    Routledge and Kegan Paul. London.

Dymally, M.M.   1974   Impact of Cults on Today's Youth.
                                    Hearing of California Senate Sub-
                                    Committee on Children and Youth.

Earhart, Harry Bryon   1970   The New Religions of Japan: A Biblio-
                                    graphy of Western-Language Materials,
                                    Sophia University, Tokyo.

Edwards, Christopher   1979   Crazy for God: The Nightmare of Cult
                                    Life, Prentice-Hall, Englewood Cliffs
                                    N.J.

Edwards, Jonathan   1742   Some Thoughts Concerning the Present
                                    Revival of Religion in New England,
                                    Boston; The Works of President Ed-
                                    wards, S. Converse,N.Y.,1980 iv 128 -
                                    133.

Eggenberger, O.   1953   Die Neuapostolische Gemeinde, Chr.
                                    Kaiser Verlag, Munich.

                            1978   Die Kirche, Sondergruppen und Relig-
                                    iose Vereinigungen, Theolog. Verlag,
                                    Zürich.

Eister, A.W.   1972   "An Outline of a Structural Theory
                                    of Cults" Journal for the Scientific
                                    Study of Religion 11 (December):
                                    319-334.

                            1974   "Culture Crises and New Religious
                                    Movements: A Paradigmatic Statement
                                    of a Theory of Cults" in Zaretsky,
                                    I. and Leone, M. (eds.) Religious
                                    Movements in Contemporary America,
                                    Princeton University, Princeton, N.J.

Bibliography   369

Ellenberger, H.   1970   The Discovery of the Unconscious, Allen Lane, London.

Ellwood, Robert S. Jr.   1973a One Way: The Jesus Movement and its Meaning, Prentice-Hall, Englewood Cliffs.

Ellwood, Robert S. Jr.   1973b Religious and Spiritual Groups in Modern America, Prentice-Hall, N.J.

                         1979   Alternative Altars: Unconventional and Eastern Spirituality in America, University of Chicago Press, Chicago.

Emerick, S.   1958   Spiritual Renewal for Methodism, Methodist Evangelistic Materials.

Emory, John (ed.)   1850   The Works of the Rev. John Wesley, 7 vols. Lane and Scott, New York.

Enroth, R.   1972   The Jesus People   Grand Rapids, Michigan: Erdmans.
  Erickson, E., and
  Peters, C.B.

Ensign, C.D.   1955   Radical German Pietism,Thesis,Boston University, University Microfilms, Ann Arbor, Michigan.

Erickson, K.T.   1966   Wayward Puritans New York: John Wiley.

Evans, Christopher   1974   Cults of Unreason, Farrar, Strauss and Giroux, New York.

Farquhar, J.N.   1919   Modern Religious Movement in India, Macmillan, London.

                        1951   The Theosophical Movement, 1875-1950.

Fenn, Richard K.   1972   "Toward a New Sociology of Religion" Journal for the Scientific Study of Religion 11 (1): 16-32.

Festinger, L.   1956   When Prophecy Fails, University of Minnesota Press, Minneapolis
  Riecken, H., and
  Schachter, S.

Fieldhouse, D.K.   1966   The Colonial Empires from the Eighteenth Century, Delta, New York.

Finney, Charles G.   1960   "What a Revival of Religion Is" Lec-
                                    tures on Revivals of Religion ed.
                                    McLoughlin, William G., Harvard
                                    University Press, Cambridge, Mass.

Fitzgerald, P.D.   1880   The Class Meeting, Southern Methodist
                                    Publishing House.

Fogarty, Robert   1973   "Communal History in America" Choice
                                    10 (4).

Freedom Leadership   1973   Communism: A Critique and Counter-
    Foundation   proposal, Freedom Leadership Founda-
                                    tion, Washington.

Freedom Leadership   1975   Korea: Vortex of Global Confronta-
    Foundation   tion, Freedom Leadership Foundation,
                                    Washington.

Gager, John G.   1975   Kingdom and Community: The Social
                                    World of Early Christianity,Prentice-
                                    Hall, Englewood Cliffs, N.J.

Galanter, M.,   1979   "The 'Moonies': A Psychological Study
    Rabkin, R.,   of Conversion and Membership in a
    Rabkin, J., and   Contemporary Religious Sect",American
    Deutsch, A.   Journal of Psychiatry,136,2:165-169.

Gallup, George   1976   The Gallup International Public Opin-
                                    ion Polls 1937-1975, 2 Vols. Random
                                    House, New York.

Gerdes, Egon H.   1968   "Pietism,Classical and Modern, A Com-
                                    parison of Two Representative De-
                                    scriptions" Concordia Theological
                                    Monthly, Vol. 39, April: 257-268.

Gerzon, M.   1977   "Counter-Culture Capitalists", New
                                    York Times, June 5.

Geyl, Pieter   1932   The Revolt of the Netherlands, 1555-
                                    1609, Williams and Norgate, London.

Glock, Charles Y.   1972   "Images of 'God', Images of Man, and
                                    the Organization of Social Life",
                                    Journal for the Scientific Study
                                    of Religion 11(1):1-15.

| | 1976 | "Consciousness Among Contemporary Youth: An Interpretation" The New Religious Consciousness Glock and Bellah (eds.) Berkeley, California pp.353-366. |

Glock, C. and Piazza, T. 1978 "Exploring Reality Structures" Society 15: 60-65.

Glock, Charles Y. and Bellah, Robert 1976 The New Religious Consciousness, University of California Press, Berkeley.

Glock, Charles Y. and Stark, Rodney 1965 Religion and Society in Tension, Rand McNally, Chicago.

Gombrich, Richard F. 1971 Precept and Practice: Traditional Buddhism in the Rural Highlands of Ceylon, Clarendon Press, Oxford.

Gordon, R. 1974 "The Aboutness of Emotions", American Philosophical Quarterly, Vol.11, Jan. :27-36.

Gottschalk, S. 1973 The Emergence of Christian Science in American Religious Life, University of California Press. Berkeley.

Gray, Francine du Plessix 1969 Divine Disobedience: Profiles of Catholic Radicalism, Random House, Inc., New York.

1979 "The Heavenly Deception", New York Review of Books, Oct. 25.

Gross, L. (ed.) 1959 Symposium on Sociological Theory, Row, Peterson and Co., Evanston, Ill.

Gründler, J. 1961 Lexicon der Christlichen Kirchen und Sekten, Vol. 1, Herden Press, Vienna.

Grupp, F.W. Jr. and Newman, W. 1974 "Political Ideology and Religious Preference: The John Birch Society and the Americans for Democratic Action" Journal for the Scientific Study of Religion 12 (Winter):401-414.

Gusfield, J. 1963 Symbolic Crusade: Status Politics and the American Temperance Movement. Urbana: University of Illinois Press.

Gustafsson, Berndt   1972   Människa i Sverige: En frageundersok-ning i kristet perpektiv AB Informa-tionstjänst, Stockholm.

Gustaitis, Rasa   1969   Turning On, The New American Library, New York.

Hall, J.   1978   The Ways Out: Utopian Communal Groups in an Age of Babylon, Routledge & Kegan Paul, London.

Hammer, Raymond   1961   Japan's Religious Ferment: Christian Presence Amid Faiths Old and New, SCM Press, London.

Hampshire, Annette P.   1979a   "Thomas Sharp and Anti-Mormon Senti-ment in Illinois", Journal of the Illinois State Historical Society, May, 72:82-100.

   1979b   "Mormonism in Illinois 1839-1847: A Study of the Development of Socio-Religious Conflict, unpublished Ph.D. Thesis, University of Durham.

Harder, M.W. and Richardson, J.T.   1971   "The Jesus Movement: Some Prelimi-nary Empirical Evidence" presented at Annual Meeting of Society for the Scientific Study of Religion. Chicago.

Harder, M.W., Richardson,J.T., and Simmonds, R.B.   1972   "The Jesus People" Psychology Today 6 (Dec.):45-50, 110-113.

Hardy, Alister   1966   The Divine Flame, An Essay Towards a Natural History of Religion, Collins, London.

   1979   The Spiritual Nature of Man, O.U.P., Oxford.

Harenberg, W. (ed.)   1968   Was glauben die Deutschen?, Christ-ian Kaiser Verlag, Munich; and Matthias-Gruenewald-Verlag, Mainz.

Harrell, D.E. Jr.   1966   Quest for a Christian America: The Disciples of Christ and American So-ciety to 1866, Disciples of Christ Historical Society, Nashville.

Harrison, B.G.   1978   Visions of Glory: A History and a
                                 Memory of the Jehovah's Witnesses,
                                 Simon & Schuster, New York.

Harrison, M.   1974   "The Sources of Recruitment to Cath-
                                 olic Pentecostalism" Journal for the
                                 Scientific Study of Religion 13:1
                                 (March):49-64.

Hay, David and   1978   "Reports of Ecstatic, Paranormal and
Morisy, Ann   Religious Experience in Great Britain
                                 and the USA: A Comparison of Trends",
                                 Journal for the Scientific Study of
                                 Religion Vol. 17, 3.

Heelas, Paul   1982   "Religion, Violence and Catharsis"
                                 in Marsh, P. (ed.) Perspectives on
                                 Violence, Blackwells, Oxford.

Heelas, Paul and   1981   Indigenous Psychologies, Academic
Lock, Andrew (eds.)   Press, London and New York.

Hibell, Björn   1977   Om utvecklingen av den svenska ung-
                                 domens alkoholvanor fran 1947 till
                                 1976, Doxa, Lund.

Hild, H. (ed.)   1974   Wie stabil ist die Kirche? Burckhardt-
                                 haus-Verlag, Gelnhausen.

Hill, Michael (ed.)   1972   A Sociological Yearbook of Religion
                                 in Britain Vol. 5, SCM Press, London.

Hobsbawm, Eric J.   1962   The Age of Revolution, 1789-1848,
                                 New American Library, New York.

                          1969   Industry and Empire, Penguin, London.

Hollis, Martin (ed.)   1977   Models of Man: Philosophical Thoughts
                                 on Social Action, Cambridge Univer-
                                 sity Press, London.

Hopkins, Joseph   1974   The Armstrong Empire: A Look at the
                                 World-Church of God, Eerdmans, Grand
                                 Rapids, Michigan.

Hori Ichiro et al   1972   Japanese Religion: A Survey by the
(ed.s)   Agency for Cultural Affairs, Kodansha
                                 International, Tokyo and Palo Alto.

Horowitz, I.L. and   1968   "Social Deviance and Political Mar-
Liebowitz, M.   ginality" Social Problems 15 (Winter):
                                 280-296.

Howard, John R. 1974 The Cutting Edge: Social Movements and Social Change in America, JB Lippincott, Philadelphia.

Hutchinson, W.R. 1959 The Transcendentalist Ministers: Church Reform in the New England Renaissance, Yale U. Press, New Haven.

Hutten, K. 1950 Seher, Grübler, Enthusiasten, Quell Verlag Der Evang. Gesellschaft, Stuttgart.

Jackins, Harvey 1970 Fundamentals of Co-Counselling Manual Personal Counsellors, Seattle.

Jacobs, John 1981 "Murders of Peoples Temple Critics Still Unsolved" San Francisco Examiner, March 9, 1981.

Jacoby, Russell 1977 Social Amnesia: A Critique of Conformist Psychology from Adler to Laing, Harvester, Sussex; Beacon Press, Boston.

Janes, E.S. 1868 Address to Class Leaders, Carlton and Lanahan.

Janov, Arthur 1974 The Primal Revolution, Garbstone Press, London.

Johnson, Paul 1959 Psychology of Religion, Abingdon Press, Nashville.

Judah, J. Stillson 1967 The History and Philosophy of the Metaphysical Movements in America, Westminster, Philadelphia.

1974 Hare Krishna and the Counterculture, John Wiley, New York.

1978 "Attitudinal Changes Among Members of the Unification Churches" Paper presented to the American Association for the Advancement of Science, Denver.

Kammen, Michael 1970 Empire and Interests: The American Colonies and the Politics of Mercantilism, Lippincott, New York.

Kanter, Rosabeth M.   1972   Commitment and Community, Harvard
                                   University Press, Cambridge, Mass.

Kehrer, Günter (ed.)   1981   Das Entstehen einer neuen Religion:
                                   Das Beispiel der Vereinigungskirche,
                                   Kösel, Munich.

Kelley, Dean M.   1977   Why Conservative Churches are Growing
                                   2nd edition, Harper   Row, New York.

Kelley, K.   1973   "Blackjack Love" Sidebar "Blissing
                                   Out in Houston" New York Review of
                                   Books, 20,20 (Dec.30): 36-42.

King,W.L.   1970   "Eastern Religions: A New Interest
                                   and Influence" Annals of the Ameri-
                                   can Association of Political and So-
                                   cial Science 387: 66-76.

Kilduff, Marshall and   1978   The Suicide Cult: The Inside Story
  and Javers, Ron   of the People's Temple and the Massa-
                                   cre in Guyana, Bantam Books, Toronto,
                                   New York, London.

Knorr, Klaus E.   1944   British Colonial Theories, 1570-1850,
                                   The U. of Toronto Press, Toronto.

Koestler, Arthur and   1969   Beyond Reductionism, Hutchinson, Lon-
  Smythies, J.R. (eds.)   don; and Beacon Press, Boston.

Kogon, E.   1972   The Theory and Practice of Hell,
                                   Octagon, New York.

Krause, Charles, A.   1978   Guyana Massacre: The Eyewitness Ac-
                                   count, Berkley Books, New York.

Kriesberg, Louis (ed.)   1979   Research in Social Movements,Conflict
                                   and Change, JAI Press, Greenwich,
                                   Conn.

La Barre, Weston   1971   "Materials for History of Crisis
                                   Cults: A Bibliographic Essay",Current
                                   Anthropology, Vol. 12, pp 3ff.

Lamott, K.   1969   "Marathon Therapy is a Psychological
                                   Pressure Cooker" The New York Times
                                   Magazine July 13.

Lang, A.   1941   Puritanismus und Pietismus: Studien
                                    zu ihrer Entwicklung von M. Butzer
                                    bis Methodismus, K. Moers,Neukirchen.

Lee, D.   1959   Freedom and Culture,   Prentice-Hall,
                                    London.

Lee, Jesse   1810   A   Short   History of the Methodists
                                    in   the   United   States   of   America,
                                    Magill and Cline, Baltimore.

Lemert, Edwin M.   1962   "Paranoia and the Dynamics of Exclu-
                                    sion", Sociometry, 25 (March):2-20.

Lévi-Strauss, Claude   1968   Structural Anthropology, Allen Lane,
                                    London.

Levitsky,   un-   "The Rules and Games of Gestalt
                            dated   Therapy"

Lewis Howard and   1971   Growth Games, Harcourt Brace Jovano-
  Streitfield, Harold   vich, New York.

Lofland, John   1977   Doomsday Cult: A Study of Conversion,
                                    Proselytization,   and   Maintainance
                                    of Faith, (Enlarged Edition), Irving-
                                    ton Publiishers, New York (original
                                    edition 1966).

Lofland, John and   1965   "Becoming a World-Saver: A Theory
  Stark, Rodney   Conversion to a Deviant Perspective",
                                    American Sociological Review 30: 862-
                                    875.

Lorentzen, L.B.   1980   "The Evangelical Life Style Concerns
                                    Expressed in Political Action" Sociol-
                                    ogical Analysis 41, 2:144-154.

Luckmann, Thomas   1967   The   Invisible Religion, Collier-
                                    Macmillan, London.

Luckmann, Thomas and   1964   "Social Mobility and Personal Identi-
  Berger, Peter   ty, European Journal of Sociology,V.

McClelland, David C.   1975a   Power, The Inner Experience, Irving-
                                    ton Publishers, New York.

                            1975b   "Love and Power: The Psychological
                                    Signals of War", Psychology Today,
                                    Jan. pp 44-48.

McConkie, B.R.   1966 Mormon Doctrine, Bookcraft, Utah.

McFadden, Cyra   1977 The Serial, Picador, London.

                        1979 in "Where the Dreams Come True",
                              London, Observer Magazine, 13.5.

McFarland, H. Neill   1967 The Rush-Hour of the Gods, Macmillan,
                              New York.

McGuire, M.B.   1975 "Toward a Sociological Explanation
                              of the 'Catholic Pentecostal' Movement
                              Review of Religious Research 16:2
                              (Winter): 94–104.

                        1978 "Dualism and the Millenium: Legiti-
                              mations in Developing Religious Move-
                              ments" Unpublished paper.

                        1981 Control of Charisma: A Sociological
                              Interpretation of the Catholic Pente-
                              costal Movement Philadelphia:Temple.

McLoughlin, William G. 1965 "Pietism and the American Character",
                              American Quarterly Vol.17 No.2
                              Part 2: 163ff.

                        1968 The American Evangelicals, 1800–1900:
                              An Anthology, Harper and Row, New
                              York.

                        1978 Revivals, Awakenings, and Reform:
                              An Essay on Religion and Social
                              Change in America, 1607–1977, Univer-
                              sity of Chicago Press, Chicago.

McNeill, John T.   1954 Modern Christian Movements, Westmin-
                              ster Press, Philadelphia.

McPherson, W.   1975 "Ideology in the Jesus Movement," Pa-
                              per delivered at Annual Meeting of
                              Society for the Scientific Study of
                              Religion, October: Chicago.

Maharishi Mahesh, Yogi 1962 The Divine Plan: Enjoy Your Own Inner
                              Divine Nature, SRM Foundation, Los
                              Angeles.

| Mannheim, Karl | 1952 | Essays on the Sociology of Knowledge, Routledge and Kegan Paul, London. |

Mannheim, Karl — 1960 — Ideology and Utopia, Routledge and Kegan Paul, London.

Marin, P. — 1975 — The New Narcissism: The Trouble with the Human Potential Movement Harpers, 251-1505:45-56.

Marsh, L. Cody — 1931 — "Group Treatment as the Psychological Equivalent of the Revival" Mental Hygiene Vol 15: 328-349.

Martin, Bernice and Pluck, Ronald — 1977 — Young Peoples' Beliefs, General Synod Board of Education, London.

Martin, David — 1965 — Pacifism: a Sociological and Historical Study, Routledge and Kegan Paul, London.

1969a — The Religious and the Secular, Routledge & Kegan Paul, London.

Martin, David (ed.) — 1969b — Anarchy and Culture, Routledge & Kegan Paul, London.

Maslow, Abraham — 1963 — "Notes on Unstructured Groups" Human Relations Training News, Fall.

1967 — "Synanon and Eupsychia" Journal of Humanistic Psychology, Spring.

Mauss, A.L. and Petersen, D.W. — 1973 — "Prodigals as Preachers: The 'Jesus Freaks' and the Return to Respectability" Social Compass, Vol. 21:3:283-301.

Meyer Baba — 1971 — Beams from Meher Baba on the Spiritual Path New York: Harper and Row.

Meyer, D.B. — 1956 — The Positive Thinkers: A Study of the American Quest for Health, Wealth and Personal Power from Mary Baker Eddy to Norman Vincent Peale, Doubleday, New York.

Melton, J. Gordon — 1977 — A Directory of Religious Bodies in the United States, Garland, New York.

| | 1978 | The Encyclopedia of American Religions, Consortium Books, Wilmington, N.C. |

Messer, J. 1976 "Who is Guru Maharaji-ji?" The New Religious Consciousness, Bellah and Glock (eds). Berkeley.

Miley, John 1866 Treatise on Class Meetings, Poe and Hitchcock, Cincinnati.

Miller, D. and Swanson, G.E. 1958 The Changing American Parent New York: Wiley.

Miller, Perry 1950 The Transcendentalists: An Anthology, Harvard University Press, Boston.

Mills, Jeannie 1979 Six Years with God: Life inside Reverend Jim Jones' Peoples Temple, A & W Publications.

Minister für Arbeit, Gesundheit und Soziales des Landes Nordhein-Westfalen 1979 Sachstandsbericht, Dusseldorf

Mintz, Elizabeth 1967 "Time-extended Marathon Groups" Psychotherapy May.

Mol, Hans (ed.) 1972 Western Religion, Mouton, The Hague, Paris.

Monod, Jacques 1972 Chance and Necessity: An Essay on the Natural Philosophy of Modern Biology, Collins.

Moon, Sun Myung 1967 Master Speaks, The Unified Family, Washington.

1973 Divine Principle, Holy Spirit Association for the Unification of World Chrstianity, Washington.

1976 America in God's Providence, Unification Church of America, New York.

1978 Reverend Sun Myung Moon Speaks 78--4-08, Holy Spirit Association for the Unification of World Christianity New York.

Moreno, Jacob L.   1911   Die Gottheit als Komödiant, Anzengru-
                                 ber Verlag, Vienna.

                          1914   Einladung zu einer Begegnung ("Invi-
                                 tation to an Encounter"), Anzengruber
                                 Verlag, Vienna.

                          1918   "Die Gottheit als Autor", Daimon,
                                 Anzengruber Verlag, Vienna.

                          1920   Das Testament des Vaters, Kiepenheu-
                                 er Verlag, Berlin-Potsdam.

                          1922   Rede über den Augenblick, Kiepenheuer
                                 Verlag, Potsdam.

                          1931   "Dramaturgy and Creaturgy" Impromptu
                                 Vol. 1, No. 1: 18-19.

                          1941   "The Philosophy of the Moment and
                                 Spontaneity Theatre" Sociometry Vol.4
                                 205-226.

                          1953   Who Shall Survive?, Beacon House Inc.
                                 Boston.

                          1969   "The Viennese Origins of the Encount-
                                 er Movement, Paving the Way for
                                 Existentialism, Group Psychotherapy
                                 and Psychodrama" Group Psychotherapy,
                                 Vol. XXII, 7-16.

Moreno, Jacob L. (ed.)   1960   Sociometry Reader, The Free Press
                                 of Glencoe, New York.

Mosse, G.L.   1970   "Changes in Religious Thought" in
                                 Cooper, J. (ed.) The New Cambridge
                                 Modern History, Vol. IV: The Decline
                                 of Spain and the Thirty Years War,
                                 1609-48/9 pp. 169-201, Cambridge Uni-
                                 versity Press, Cambridge.

Moustakas, Clark, E.   1968   Individuality and Encounter: A Brief
                                 Journey into Loneliness and Sensiti-
                                 vity, Howard A. Doyle, Inc.,New York.

Mowrer, O.   1961   The Crisis in Psychiatry and Religion
                                 Van Nostrand, London.

Muehlmann, W.E.   1961   Chiliasmus und Nativismus, Dietrich-
                                 Reimer, Berlin.

Muhlenberg, H.M.   1942– The Journals of Henry Melchior Muh-
                           1958   lenberg edited and translated by
                                  Tappert, T.G. and Doberstein, J.W.,
                                  3 vols. Muhlenberg Press.

Müller, Ernst   1946   History of Jewish Mysticism, Crown
                                  Publishers, New York.

Murray, Robert   1961   A Brief History of the Church of Swe-
                                  den, Verbum, Stockholm.

Myerhoff, B.   1975   "Organization and Ecstasy" in Moore,
                                  S. and Myerhoff, B. (ed.s) Symbols
                                  and Politics in Communal Ideology
                                  pp. 36–67, Cornell University Press,
                                  New York.

Nagler, A.W.   1918   Pietism and Methodism, Smith and La-
                                  mar, Nashville.

National Training   1968   "Objectives of Human Relations Train-
    Laboratories   ing" 92.

Needleman, Jacob   1970   The New Religions, Doubleday, New
                                  York (revised edition 1977).

                           1971   "Winds from the East: Youth and Coun-
                                  ter–Cults" Commonweal XCIV (April
                                  30).

                           1977   The New Religions, Dutton, New York,
                                  (original edition, 1970)

Needleman, Jacob and   1978   Understanding the New Religions, Sea-
    Baker, George (ed.s)   bury Press, New York.

Newman, Louis I.   1944   The Hasidic Anthology, Bloch Publish-
                                  ing Co. Inc., New York.

Newstead, R.   1843   Advice to One Who Meets in Class,
                                  Lane and Sandford, New York.

Newsweek   1979   "The Age of Cults", Newsweek (inter-
                                  national edition), 23 April: 23–4.

New York State Assembly   1979   Assembly Standing Committee on Child
                                  Care. Public Hearing on the Treatment
                                  of Children by Cults, 9–10 August.

Nordquist, Ted A.   1978   Ananda Cooperative Village: A Study
                                in the Beliefs, Values, and Attitudes
                                of a New Age Religious Community,
                                Monograph Series from the Religions-
                                historiska   Institutionen,   Uppsala
                                Universitet, 16.

Northrup, F.C.S.   1946   The Meeting of East and West, The
                                Macmillan   Company,   New   York   and
                                London.

Numbers, R.L.   1976   Prophetess of Health: Ellen G. White,
                                Harper, New York.

O'Dea, Thomas F.   1957   The Mormons,Chicago University Press,
                                Chicago.

                         1961   "Five Dilemmas in the Institutionali-
                                sation of Religion", Journal for the
                                Scientific Study of Religion,1:30-9.

Oden, Thomas, C.   1972   The Intensive Group Experience: The
                                New   Pietism,   Westminster   Press,
                                Philadelphia.

Offner, Clark and   1963   Modern Japanese Religions, with Spe-
Straelen, Henricus   cial Emphasis upon their doctrines
                                of Healing, Twayne, New York; Rupert
                                Endesle, Tokyo; E.S. Brill, Leiden.

Orr, L. and   1977   Rebirthing in the New Age, Celestial
Ray, S.   Arts, Millbrae.

Ortner, S.   1978   The Sherpas through their Rituals,
                                Cambridge University Press, Cambridge.

Outler, Albert C.   1967   John Wesley, Oxford University Press.

Patrick, Ted (with   1977   Let Our Children Go,Ballantine Books,
Dulack, Tom)   New York.

Peel, R.   1971   The Years of Trial, Holt, Rinehart
                                and Winston, New York.

                         1966   Mary Baker Eddy: The Years of Discov-
                                ery,   Holt,   Rinehart   and   Winston,
                                New York.

Penton, J.M.   1976   Jehovah's Witnesses in Canada: Cham-
                                pions of Freedom of Speech and Wor-
                                ship, Macmillan, London and New York.

Perls, Frederick, S.   1969   Gestalt Therapy Verbatim, Real People
                                   Press, Moab, Utah.

Perls Frederick, S.   1977   Gestalt Therapy, Bantam, New York.
   et al

Pico della Mirandola,   1956   Oration on the Dignity of Man, Henry
   Giovanni   Regnery Company, Chicago.

Polanyi, Karl   1944   The Great Transformation,   Beacon
                                   Press, Boston.

Prabhavanda, Swami   1965   The Spiritual Heritage of India. New
   with Manchester,   York: Doubleday.
   Frederick

Rabinowicz, Harry, M.   1960   A Guide to Hassidism, Thomas Yoseloff,
                                   Inc.

   Reasons, C.E.   1974   "The Politicizing of Crime, the Crimi-
                                   nal   and   the   Criminologist" Journal
                                   of   Criminal   Law   and   Criminology
                                   64:471-479.

Reed, C.   1978   "The Psychobabble Enigma", The Bedside
                                   Guardian, 27, London.

Richardson, Herbert   1977   Deprogramming: Documenting the Issue,
   (ed)   Report   prepared   for   the   American
                                   Civil Liberties Union, New York and
                                   the   Toronto   School   of   Theology,
                                   Toronto.

Richardson, James T.   1978a "An Oppositional and General Concept-
                                   ualization of Cult", Annual Review
                                   of the Social Sciences of Religion,
                                   2.

Richardson, James T.   1978b Conversion Careers: In and Out of
   (ed.)   the New Religions, Sage, Beverly Hills.

                           1982   The Deprogramming Controversy: Socio-
                                   logical,   Psychological,   Legal   and
                                   Historical Perspectives, Edwin Mellen
                                   Press, N.Y.

Richardson, James T.   1979   Organized Miracles: A Sociological
   Harder, M.H. and   Study of the Jesus Movement Organiza-
   Simmonds, R.   tion, Transaction Books, New Bruns-
                                   wick, N.J.

Richardson, J.T.,   1972   "Thought Reform and the Jesus Move-
    Harder, M. and   ment" Youth and Society (Dec.): 185-
    Simmonds, R.G.   202.

Richey, R.E. and   1974   American Civil Religion, Harper, New
    Jones, D.G.   York.

Rieff, Philip   1973   The Triumph of the Therapeutic, Pen-
                                 guin, London.

Ritschl, Albrecht   1880-   Geschichte des Pietismus, 3 Vols.,
                         1886   A. Marcus, Bonn.

Ritter, G.   1954   "Wunschträume Himmlers am 21 Juli
                                 1944", Geschichte in Wissenschaft
                                 und Unterricht, nr.3, pp. 162-68.

Robbins, T.   1973   "Contemporary 'Post-Drug' Cults: A
                                 Comparison of Two Groups" Doctoral
                                 Dissertation, U. of North Carolina.

Robbins, Thomas,   1976   "The Last Civil Religion: Reverend
    Anthony, Dick,   Moon and the Unification Church",
    Doucas, Madeline and   Sociological Analysis, 37, 2:111-125.
    Curtis, Thomas E.

Robbins, Thomas,   1978   "Theory and Research on Today's New
    Anthony, Dick, and   Religions", Sociological Analysis
    Richardson, James   Vol. 39, 2:95-122.

Robbins, T., and   1972   "Getting Straight with Meher Baba:
    Anthony, D.   A Study of Drug-Rehabilitation, Mys-
                                 ticism and Postadolescent Role-Con-
                                 flict" Journal for the Scientific Study
                                 of Religion 11 (June):122-140.

Robbins, Thomas and   1978   "New Religious Movements and the So-
    Anthony,Dick   cial System: Integration, Disintegra-
                                 tion, or Transformation" The Annual
                                 Review of the Social Sciences of Re-
                                 ligion, The Hague.

Robbins, Thomas and   1981   In Gods We Trust: Patterns in Ameri-
    Anthony, Dick (ed.s)   can Religious Pluralism, Transaction
                                 Books, New Brunswick, N.J.

Robbins, T.,   1973   "The Limits of Symbolic Realism: Pro-
    Anthony, D., and   blems of Empathic Participant Obser-
    Curtis, T.   vation in a Sectarian Context" Jour-
                                    nal for the Scientific Study of Reli-
                                    gion 12 (Sept.):259-273.

                            1974   "Youth Culture Religious Movements:
                                    Evaluating the Integrative Hypothes-
                                    is" Sociological Quarterly, Winter,
                                    1974.

Robertson, Constance   1970   Oneida Community, Syracuse Univer-
    Noyes   sity Press, Syracuse.

                            1977   Oneida Community Profiles, Syracuse
                                    University Press, Syracuse.

Robinson, Edward   1977   The Original Vision, The Religious
                                    Experience Research Unit, Manchest-
                                    er College of Oxford.

Rogers, Carl R.   1970   Carl Rogers on Encounter Groups,
                                    Harper and Row, New York.

Romarheim, Arild   1977   Moderne religiositet: en oversikt
                                    over ca. 30 nyere bevegelser og
                                    retninger som arbeider aktivt i
                                    dagens Skandinavia   H. Aschehoug
                                    & Co. Oslo.

                            1979   "Litteratur om nyreligiose beve-
                                    gelser", Tidskrift for Teologi og
                                    Kirke (50).

Roof, W.C.   1978   "Alienation and Apostasy" Society.
                                    15, 4: 41-45.

Rosen, R.D.   1978   Psychobabble,   Wildwood   House,
                                    London.

Rossel, R.D.   1970   "The Great Awakening: An Historical
                                    Analysis" American Journal of Sociol-
                                    ogy 75 (May):907-926.

Rosser, Leonidas   1855   Class Meetings, Richmond, Virginia
                                    (published by the author).

Roszak, Theodore   1976   Unfinished Animal: the Aquarian
                                    Frontier and the Evolution of Con-
                                    sciousness, Faber, London.

Royster, V.   1974   "The Public Morality: Afterthoughts on Watergate" American Scholar 43 (Spring):249-266.

Rubin, Jerry   1976   Growing (Up) at Thirty-Seven, M. Evans and Co., New York.

Ruitenbeek,   1970   The New Group Therapies, Avon
Hendrik M.   Books, New York.

Sarkar, P.R.   1973   Baba's Grace: Discourses of Shrii Shrii Anandamurti, Ananda Marga Publications, Los Altos Hills, Cal.

Schachter, S.   1971   Emotion, Obesity and Crime,Academic Press, New York.

Schechter, Solomon   1896   "Hasidim and Hasidism" Studies in Judaism Vol 1. Philadelphia

Scheff, T.   1977   "The Distancing of Emotion in Ritual" Current Anthropology Vol.18,3: 483-505.

Scheler, Max   1963   Schriften zur Soziologie und Weltanschauungslehre,A. Francke-Verlag, Munich.

Schmidt, Martin and 1965   Das Zeitalter des Pietismus, C.
Jannasch, Wilhelm(ed.s)   Schunemann, Bremen.

Schmoller, Gustav   1896   The Mercantile System and Its Historical Significance, Macmillan, New York.

Schneider, Louis and 1958   Popular Religion:Inspirational Books
Dornbusch, S.M. (eds)   in America, University of Chicago Press, Chicago.

Scholem,   1941   "Personality Takes the Place of Doc-
Gersholem, G.   trine", Major Trends in Jewish Mysticism, Schoken Books, New York.

                     1974   "Der Nihilismus als religiöses Phänomen", Eranos-Jahrbuch, Vol.43, Leiden, pp. 13ff.

Schur, E.M.   1976   The Awareness Trap: Self-Absorption Instead of Social Change. New York: McGraw-Hill.

Schurmann, Franz   1974   The Logic of World Power: An Inqui-
                             ry into the Origins, Currents, and
                             Contradictions of World Politics,
                             Pantheon, New York.

Schutz,   1971   Here Comes Everybody: Body-mind
   William Carl   and Encounter Culture, Harper and
                             Row, New York.

Schwartz, G.   1970   "Sect Ideologies and Social Status"
                             Chicago: University of Chicago Press.

Scott, Joseph W. and 1969   "Multiversity, University Size, Uni-
   El-Assal, Mohamed   versity Quality and Student Protest:
                             an Empirical Study", American So-
                             ciological Review, (Oct.) Vol.34,
                             5:702-709.

Seashore, Charles   1968   "What is Sensitivity Training?, In-
                             stitute News and Reports Vol.II No.2
                             April.

Shaffir, William and 1982   Identification and the Revival of
   Greenspan, Louis (ed.s)   Orthodoxy, Wilfred Laurier Press,
                             Canada.

Shepherd, A.P.   1954   A Scientist of the Invisible: An In-
                             troduction to the Life and Work of
                             Rudolph Steiner, Hodder and
                             Stoughton, London.

Shupe, Anson Jr. and 1980   The New Vigilantes: Anti-Cultists,
   Bromley, David   Deprogrammers, and the New Reli-
                             gions, Sage, Beverly Hills.

Shupe, Anson, D. Jr. 1977   "Deprogramming: the new exorcism",
   Spielmann, Roger   American Behavioral Scientist, 20,
   Stigall, Sam   6:941-956.

Sigelman, Lee   1977   "Multi-Nation Surveys of Religious
                             Beliefs" Journal for the Scientific
                             Study of Religion 16(3):289-294.

Simkin, James   un-   "Introduction to Gestalt Therapy"
                      dated   mimeographed paper.

Simon, John   1937   John Wesley and the Methodist Socie-
                             ties, 2nd ed. The Epworth Press,
                             London.

Sinz, K.   1933   "Der Retter", Der Christliche Haus-
                                   freund, Vol. 2, No.5.

Smart, Ninian   1974   Mao, Fontana, London.

Smelser, Neil J.   1962   Theory of Collective Behavior, Rout-
                                   ledge and Kegan Paul, London.

Smith, T.L.   1957   Revivalism and Social Reform in
                                   Mid-Nineteenth Century America,
                                   Abingdon, Nashville.

Snelling, C.H. and   1972   "Problem-solving Behavior in Reli-
    Whitely, O.R.   gious and Para-religious groups"
                                   Prepared for Annual Meeting of the
                                   Society for the Scientific Study of
                                   Religion. Boston.

Spangenberg, A.G.   1779   Idea fidei fratrem oder kurzer Be-
                                   griff der Christlichen Lehre in den
                                   evangelischen Brüdergemeinden,
                                   Barby.

Spear, Percival   1965   A History of India, Vol.2, Penguin,
                                   Harmondsworth, Middx.

Sontag, Frederick   1977   Sun Myung Moon and the Unification
                                   Church, Abingdon, Nashville.

Stachura, P.   1978   The Shaping of the Nazi State,Croom
                                   Helm, London.

Starr, Jerold M.   1978   "The Causes of Youth Protest: A Cri-
                                   tical Review of the Principal Theor-
                                   ies", Paper presented at the IX
                                   World Congress of Sociology,Uppsala.

Steiner, Rudolph   1969   Occult Science (first published in
                                   1908); translated by George and
                                   Mary Adams, Rudolph Steiner Press,
                                   London.

Stoeffler, F.E.   1965   The Rise of Evangelical Pietism,
                                   E.J. Brill, Leiden.

Stoller, Frederick   1967   "The Long Weekend" Psychology To-
                                   day, Dec. 28-33.

Streiker, L.D.   1971   The Jesus People. Nashville, Abing-
                               don Press.

Sundström, Erland   1979   Nyandliga vindar - varifran och
                               varthän? Gummessons, Stockholm.

Sweet, William W.   1933   Methodism   in   American   History,
                               Abingdon Press, Nashville.

Sykes,G.   1974   "The Rise of Critical Criminology"
                               Journal of Criminal Law and Crimi-
                               nology 65:2, pp. 206-213.

Taylor, David   1977   "Thought Reform and the Unification
                               Church" Paper presented to Society
                               for the Scientific Study of Religion,
                               Chicago, October 28-30.

Taylor,I.and   1973   Politics   and   Deviance.   Baltimore:
Taylor,L.(eds.)   Penguin.

Telford, John (ed.)   1931   The Letters of the Rev. John Wesley
                               8 vols. The Epworth Press, London.

Teng, Ssu-yu   1971   The Taiping Rebellion and the West-
                               ern Powers: A Comprehensive Survey
                               Oxford University Press, Oxford.

Tholuck, A.   1970   Geschichte des Rationalismus,Scienta
                               Verlag, Aalen, originally published
                               in 1865.

Tilly, Charles   1969   "Collective Violence in European
                               Perspective" in Graham, H. and
                               Gurr, T. (ed.s),Violence in America,
                               Bantam, New York.

Tiryakian, E.A.   1967   "A Model of Social Change and Its
                               Lead Indicators" The Study of Total
                               Societies. Klausner (ed.) New York:
                               Doubleday.

Tomasson, R.F.   1968   "The Religious Situation in Sweden",
                               Social Compass 15:491-498.

Treat, Robert J.   1967   "Pastoral Care: According to Wesley"
                               Christian Advocate, July 27:13ff.

Troeltsch, Ernst   1960   The Social Teachings of the Church-
                                  es, Harper & Row, New York. (Mac-
                                  millan, New York, 1931).

Turner, Victor   1969   The Ritual Process, Pelican, London.

                          1974   Drama, Fields and Metaphors, Cor-
                                  nell University Press, Cornell

Tuveson, E.L.   1968   Redeemer Nation: The Idea of Ameri-
                                  ca's Millenial Role, University of
                                  Chicago Press, Chicago.

Underleider,   1979   "Coercive Persuasion (brainwashing),
   J. Thomas and   religious cults, and deprogramming"
   Wellisch, David K.   American Journal of Psychiatry, 136,
                                  3 (March): 279-282.

Urban, G. (ed.)   1971   The   Miracles   of   Chairman   Mao,
                                  T. Stacey Ltd., London.

Usener, H.   1896   Götternämen: Versuch   einer   Lehre
                                  von der religiösen Begriffsbildung,
                                  Verlag Friedrich Cohen, Bonn.

Uttendörfer, O.   1935   Zinzendorfs religiöse Grundgedanken,
                                  Herrnhut.

Veysey, Laurence   1973   The Communal   Experience,   Harper
                                  & Row, New York.

Vidich, A.   1975   "Social Conflict in an Era of Detente"
                                  Social Research, 42, 1:64-87.

Wallace, Anthony F.C.   1956   "Revitalization movements", American
                                  Anthropologist 58:264-81.

Wallerstein, Immanuel 1974   The Modern   Wold-System,   Academic
                                  Press, New York.

Wallis, Roy   1976   The Road to Total Freedom: A Socio-
                                  logical   Analysis   of   Scientology,
                                  Heinemann, London.

                          1978   "The Rebirth of the Gods?" in New
                                  Lecture Series, No.   108,   Queen's
                                  University, Belfast.

                          1979   Salvation and Protest: Studies of
                                  Social   and   Religious   Movements,
                                  Frances Pinter, London.

Wallis, Roy (ed.)   1975   Sectarianism: Analyses of Religious
                             and Non-Religious Sects, Peter Owen,
                             London.

Watts, A.W.   1972   This Is It, Random House,New York.

                     1975   Psychotherapy East and West, Ran-
                             dom House, New York.

Weber, Max   1949   The Methodology of the Social Sci-
                             ences, (tr. by Shils, E. & Finch,
                             H.), Free Press, Glencoe, Illinois.

                     1965   The Sociology of Religion, New York:
                             Beacon Press.

Weigelt, Horst   1970   "Interpretation of Pietism in the
                             Research of Contemporary Church
                             Historians" Church History, Vol. 32
                             No. 2, June: 236-241.

Weinlick, J.R.   1956   Count Zinzendorf, Abingdon Press,
                             Nashville.

Wesley, J.   1974   Journal of John Wesley, P.L. Parker
                             (ed.) Moody Press, Evanston, Ill.

Westley, F.   1978   "The Cult of Man: Durkheim's Pre-
                             dictions and New Religious Move-
                             ments" Sociological Analysis 34, 2:
                             135-145.

Whitworth, J.M.   1975   God's Blueprints, Routledge & Kegan
                             Paul, London.

Wikström, Lester   1977   Nyandligt, Verbum, Haken Ohlssons,
                             Stockholm.

Williams, G.H.   1962   The Radical Reformation, Westminster
                             Press, Philadelphia.

Williams, R.M.   1970   American Society, New York: Alfred
                             Knopf.

Wilson, Bryan R.   1958   "An Analysis of Sect Development",
                             American Sociological Review, 24,
                             1: 3-15.

                     1963   "Typologie des sectes dans une per-
                             spective dynamique et comparative"
                             Archives de Sociologie des Religions,
                             8, 16: 49-63.

	1970a	Religious Sects: A Sociological Study Weidenfeld & Nicolson, London.
	1970b	Youth Culture and the Universities, Faber, London.
	1973	Magic and the Millenium, Heinemann, London.
	1976	Contemporary Transformations of Religion, Oxford University Press, London.
	1978	Sects and Society, The Greenwood Press, Westport, Conn. (reprint).
Wilson, Bryan R.(ed.)	1981	The Social Impact of New Religious Movements , Rose of Sharon Press, New York.
Wolf, Eric	1959	Sons of the Shaking Earth, University of Chicago Press, Chicago.
Wood, James	1809	Directions and Cautions Addressed to the Class Leaders, Wesleyan Conference Office, London.
Woodrum, Eric	1977	"The Development of the Transcendental Meditation Movement" The Zetetic 1,2, Spring/Summer: 38-48.
Worsley, Peter	1968	The Trumpet Shall Sound, Schocken Books, New York.
Wuthnow, Robert	1976a	The Consciousness Reformation, California University Press, Berkeley.
	1976b	"Recent Pattern of Seculariziation: A Problem of Generations?" American Sociological Review 41:850-867.
	1976c	"A Profile of the Religious Experimentor" The New Religious Conscioiusness Bellah & Glock (eds.). Berkeley.
	1977	"A Longitudinal, Cross-National Indicator of Societal Religious Commitment" Journal for the Scientific Study of Religion 16 (1): 87-99.

1978 Experimentation in American Religion: The New Mysticisms and their Implications for the Churches, University of California Press, Berkeley.

1981 "Political Aspects of the Quietistic Revival" In Gods We Trust, Robbins and Anthony, Transaction.

Wuthnow, Robert and Glock, Charles Y. 1974 "The Shifting Focus of Faith: A Survey Report", Psychology Today, Vol.8: 131-136.

Yinger, Milton J. 1957 Religion, Society, and the Individual, Macmillan, New York.

Yogananda, Paramahansa 1973 Autobiography of a Yogi. Los Angeles: Self-Realization Fellowship.

Young, Jock 1971 The Drugtakers, MacGibbon & Kee, London.

Zeretsky, Irving and Leone, M.P. (eds.) 1974 Religious Movements in Contemporary America, Princeton University Press, Princeton.

LIST OF CONTRIBUTORS

Dick Anthony is Research Director of the Centre for the Study of New Religions at the Graduate Theological Union, Berkeley, California. He is presently co-editing, with Thomas Robbins and Jacob Needleman, a volume on Coercion, Conversion and Commitment in New Religious Movements for Crossroads.

George Baker of Baker and Associates, San Francisco, has edited and contributed to several books in the interdisciplinary area of new religious studies, including New Religious Movements in America. His article on Buddhism in America appears in the Abingden Dictionary of Living Religions. He has been affiliated with the Program for the Study of New Religious Movements at the Graduate Theological Union, Berkeley, California, and has lectured at various American and foreign universities.

Eileen Barker is a member of the Department of Sociology at the London School of Economics. She carried out an intensive study of the Unification Church between 1976 and 1981, and has also investigated a number of other new religious movements in Britain and elsewhere. During the last decade, as part of her wider research interest into the relationship between images of science and contemporary expressions of belief, she has been studying various groups within which members of a new priesthood of scientists promote diverse religious or ideological positions from what they claim to be a scientific perspective.

James A. Beckford is Senior Lecturer in Sociology and Dean of the Faculty of Social Sciences at the University of Durham, England. He is particularly well known for his study of the Jehovah's Witnesses. Recently, Dr. Beckford has been studying the development of new religious movements in various parts of the world, the process of withdrawal from an authoritarian religious sect, and the growth of anti-cult sentiment in a cross-cultural perspective. He is currently writing a monograph based on his empirical study of social responses to new religious movements, and plans, in the future, to prepare a volume on the legal, moral and constitutional issues surrounding present-day changes in religious practice in various countries.

David G. Bromley is an associate professor and chairman of the Sociology Department at the University of Hartford, Connecticut. He is co-author, with Anson D. Shupe, of three related monographs: The Moonies in America, The New Vigilantes, and Strange Gods. He is currently writing a book on religious apostates.

395

Bruce C. Busching is an associate professor of sociology at James Madison University, Virginia. With David Bromley and Anson Shupe he has co-authored several papers on new religious movements. He is currently doing research on social exchange theory.

Colin Campbell is a senior lecturer in sociology at the University of York, England. His doctoral thesis was on the Humanist Movement in Britain (Campbell, 1971). His interests have embraced the study of the cult and the cultic milieu as well as the wider cultural context within which the new religious movements appear to flourish. This interest has included research on the counter-culture of the 1960s. At present, Dr. Campbell is engaged in research on the demography of belief.

Bert Hardin is a member of the Department of Sociology at the University of Tübingen. In 1978 he conducted the first research project concerning new religious movements for the German Ministry of Youth, Family and Health. His studies have concentrated mainly on the Unification Church, the Children of God and the Ananda Marga. His research interests also include the sociology of beliefs and the history of sociology in both America and West Germany.

Paul Heelas is a member of the Department of Religious Studies at the University of Lancaster. His area of study is focussed on the "true" psychology of religion, in particular the question of the impact of the religious upon the self. This study has prompted him to investigate and carry out participant observations of the new religious movements, especially such "self-religions" as Exegesis and EST. He is currently directing research into a community of Bhagwan Rajneesh's Sannyasins.

Günter Kehrer is Professor for the Sociology of Religion in the Department of Cultural Studies at the University of Tübingen. He has published many articles on organized religion, religion in modern society and the new religious movements, and has recently completed editing an anthology on the subject of the rise of the Unification Church.

Christine King is an Open University tutor and Senior Lecturer in the faculty of Social Studies and Humanities at Preston Polytechnic. She holds degrees in history and theology; her doctoral thesis was on the survival strategies of five minority Christian groups in the Third Reich. Her research interests have led her to study shrines and pilgrimage in medieval England, and, currently, the responses to the Christian Science Church in England since 1900.

Warren Lewis has studied theology and church history at Harvard Divinity School, the Pontifical Institute of Medieval Studies in Toronto and the University of Tübingen. From 1975 to 1981, he was Professor of Church History at the Unification Theological Seminary in Barrytown, N.Y., and is presently Secretary to the Trustees of the Global Congress of the World's Religions.

David Martin, a member of the Department of Sociology at the London School of Economics, is internationally known for his work in the sociology of religion in general, and secularization in particular. During the late 1960s he wrote and broadcast using the descriptive concepts of religion to comment upon the student movement. As a conscientious objector he passed his two years National Service in the Non-Combatant Corps. For the last two years he has been actively involved in organizing resistance to liturgical change in the Church of England.

Ted Nordquist holds a doctorate from the University of Uppsala, Sweden and is now with its Department of the History of Religions. He has worked in Asian philosophy and done a field study of the Ananda Cooperative Village in the foothills of the Sierra Nevada Mountains. He is presently engaged in a three year study of alternative world views in Sweden.

Thomas C. Oden is Professor of Theology and Ethics at the Theological and the Graduate Schools of Drew University, Madison, New Jersey. His Yale doctoral dissertation was directed by H. R. Niebuhr on the subject "The Idea of Obedience in Contemporary Protestant Ethics". He has written numerous books on a variety of subjects which cross the boundaries of traditional, cognitive theology with modern psychotherapy and encounter groups.

Thomas Robbins holds a Ph.D. from the University of North Carolina and has taught at Queen's College, Yale University, and the Center for the Study of New Religious Movements in Berkeley. Two major concerns have dominated his work: interpreting contemporary spiritual ferment in terms of a broad legitimation crisis in modern society, and exploring the legal, civil liberties and social policy issues involved in controversies over "cults". He has written a large number of articles on the new religions frequently in partnership with Dick Anthony, with whom he is also co-editor of In God We Trust.

Martin Shiels is currently enrolled as a graduate student at the London School of Economics. In the past, his areas of research have included studies of the Hare Krishna and the Ramakrishna Vedanta Society. His present research is into the Hindu roots of several movements represented in the west.

Anson D. Shupe, Jr. is an associate professor of sociology at the University of Texas at Arlington. He is the co-author, with David G. Bromley, of three related monographs: The Moonies in America, The New Vigilantes, and Strange Gods. He has recently written Six Perspectives on New Religions, published by The Edwin Mellen Press.

Ninian Smart has chairs in two Departments of Religious Studies, one at the University of Lancaster and the other at the University of California at Santa Barbara. His areas of interest include the philosophy, history, anthropology and sociology of the religions of five continents. He has written more than a dozen books, including The Yogi and the Devotee and Mao. He was the chief religious advisor for, and wrote the background book to, the BBC television series, The Long Search.

Roy Wallis is head of the Department of Social Studies at The Queen's University of Belfast. Areas of research have included Scientology, the Children of God, the Aetherius Society, and the Festival of Light. In recent years he has been working on general typological analyses of the contemporary phenomenon of new religious movements as a whole.

John Whitworth is a British sociologist in the Department of Sociology and Anthropology at Simon Fraser University, Vancouver. He has investigated and written on a range of new and established sectarian groups including the Hutterites, the Doukhobors, the Hare Krishnas and the Ramakrishna Vedanta Society. He is currently working on a book on the Social Theories of Thorstein Veblen.

Bryan Wilson, a Fellow of All Souls, is the Senior Sociologist at the University of Oxford. His work has included extensive field research into a variety of movements in Europe, America, Africa and the far East. He has written, edited and reviewed a large number of books, journals and articles on this subject.

Robert Wuthnow is a professor at the Department of Sociology at Princeton University. In 1971 he was involved in the Survey Research Center and served as Project Director for the survey phase of the Religious Consciousness Project in the San Francisco Bay Area (Glock & Bellah, 1976). He has researched new types of religiosity and their impact on American churches, and is presently studying religious movements in the widest social context possible -- that of world order.

R.J. Zwi Werblowsky is a professor in the Department of Comparative Religion at the Hebrew University in Jerusalem. His international roles include editor of Numen and secretary general of the International Association for the History of Religions. His research has encompassed a wide range of religious movements all over the world.